Advance Praise for *Website Optimization: An Hour a Day*

Attempting to achieve digital success without a robust experimentation and web analytics strategy is like trying to go to the moon on a bike. It will take a long time, might even be impossible. In nine exciting chapters Rich shows you, soup to nuts, exactly how to leverage usability, testing, and web analytics to transform your organization and achieve magnificent success!

—Avinash Kaushik, author of *Web Analytics 2.0* and
Digital Marketing Evangelist, Google

Rich Page has done the impossible with this book. Before reading it I'd have sworn no single book could explain conversion optimization and provide a road map for how to do it properly. I stand corrected. If you want to learn how to supercharge your website business performance, this is the book you've been waiting for. It's practical, actionable advice from a master practitioner. You could pay an optimization consultant $100K, or you could buy this book.

—Lance Loveday, CEO of Closed Loop Marketing and author of
Web Design for ROI

These days, there are thousands of guys who say they are "website optimization experts." Ninety-nine percent of them couldn't improve a web page—much less a site—if their lives depended on it. Rich Page is different. He's among the one percent, and this "optimization bible" proves it. Jam-packed with proven tips and tricks on how you can improve your website without breaking the bank, you'll find everything you need to know about how to set benchmarks, develop meaningful tests, design shopping carts and lead forms for maximum conversion, enhance your performance, and much more. This isn't a book from someone who did a bunch of research on Google; it's written by someone who has done the work and knows the answers.

—Amy Africa, CEO, EighyByEight

The value of site optimization is clear. It is an absolute must for all companies serious about the digital channel, but most companies struggle with how to make it core to their digital strategy. Rich does a great job of identifying the needed steps to build a successful optimization strategy. This book is a must-read for companies serious about site optimization whether you are new to the game or have tried it with limited success in the past. Follow his steps and avoid the common mistakes that will derail your efforts!

—Jason Burby, Chief Performance Marketing Officer,
ZAAZ/Possible Worldwide

Website Optimization: An Hour a Day *should become a bible for any individual or business wanting to get maximum value from their own or their clients' web properties. A focus on optimization is a no-brainer for companies at a time when competition for customers has never been greater. The an-hour-a-day approach is perfect for those who want to take a systematic and step-by-step approach to understanding how they can optimize their websites. The book is full of useful tips and insights, which will help you turn a sea of data into meaningful insights which will improve your business performance and bottom-line. The book will inform both the more experienced digital practitioner, as well as those who are new to the arts and science of conversion rate optimization.*

—Linus Gregoriadis, Research Director, Econsultancy

Optimization is a hot topic in our industry today, and many people don't know where to begin. Choosing the right tool for the job is tough enough, let alone having to come up with the appropriate tests and strategies for your business. Fortunately, Rich has provided a fantastic resource in Website Optimization: An Hour a Day. *This book has something for everyone, regardless of your level of familiarity with optimization. The amount of tips, action items for you to implement right away, and example tests will not only help you move forward but it will also help you build the business case internally for a successful testing program. If optimization is on your wish list this year in your organization, this is the book for you.*

—Bill Bruno, CEO, Stratigent

Rich Page provides a detailed road map for creating a powerful conversion improvement practice at your company. Get this book before your competition does!

—Tim Ash, Chair of Conversion Conference, CEO of SiteTuners, and author of *Landing Page Optimization*

Page has done an outstanding job of thoroughly covering the landscape of the many aspects of measuring and improving the performance of your website. This is a must-read both for novices who need to understand the process and experts who want to ensure they aren't missing anything. Solid and comprehensive!

—William Sears, Senior Manager, Search Engine Marketing, Walt Disney Interactive Media Group

Website Optimization: An Hour a Day *is great for any online business that wants to learn how to better test and improve their website, and lays out some great foundations that optimization novices and even experts will find useful. It's definitely worth a read if you are in online marketing—you'll find it hard to put down!*

—Kimen Field, Senior Product Manager, Adobe

Ecommerce is changing the global economy and it's amazing how few companies have deep insight into their web business. You can quickly identify the winners and losers based upon the emphasis they place on analytics. Rich carefully builds on this and creates a testing and optimization plan to help you take your business to the next level. With a combination of practical suggestions and current optimization theory, this book defines the basics that will help eliminate the guess work. The most important aspect that Rich clearly illustrates is that optimization is not a one-time activity, it's a change in your website culture and process. Success can be hard to achieve, but Rich will give you the confidence to define a strategy that keeps your web business achieving goals.

—Brian Rogers, Director of Global eCommerce, 5.11 Tactical

You've got a website and you haven't optimized yet? What are you waiting for?! Block off an hour a day and, for the next 27 weeks, follow Rich Page's detailed, step-by-step guide for getting started with website optimization. It could be the most profitable hour of your day.

—Chris Goward, President of WiderFunnel Marketing Optimization and author of *You Should Test That!*

About time! Optimization has been shrouded in a mist of ineffective tips and advice from people who think it's easy for way too long. Rich's book stands out by honestly stating that optimization is actually hard and that intent doesn't equate to success. He then breaks down the multiple required disciplines in a way that makes it accessible for any web/marketing practitioner to increase the ROI of their online business.

—Oli Gardner, Co-founder of Unbounce.com

Website Optimization

An Hour a Day

Website Optimization

An Hour a Day

Rich Page

John Wiley & Sons, Inc.

Senior Acquisitions Editor: Willem Knibbe
Development Editor: Kathi Duggan
Technical Editor: Lisa Bustos
Production Editor: Eric Charbonneau
Copy Editor: Adept Content Solutions
Editorial Manager: Pete Gaughan
Production Manager: Tim Tate
Vice President and Executive Group Publisher: Richard Swadley
Vice President and Publisher: Neil Edde
Book Designer: Franz Baumhackl
Compositor: Maureen Forys, Happenstance Type-O-Rama
Proofreader: Nancy Bell
Indexer: Jack Lewis
Project Coordinator, Cover: Katherine Crocker
Cover Designer: Ryan Sneed
Cover Image: © Lise Gagne/iStockPhoto

Published simultaneously in Canada

ISBN: 978-1-118-19651-9

ISBN: 978-1-118-22770-1 (ebk.)

ISBN: 978-1-118-24060-1 (ebk.)

ISBN: 978-1-118-26530-7 (ebk.)

For general information on our other products and services or to obtain technical support, please contact our Customer Care Department within the U.S. at (877) 762-2974, outside the U.S. at (317) 572-3993 or fax (317) 572-4002.

Wiley publishes in a variety of print and electronic formats and by print-on-demand. Some material included with standard print versions of this book may not be included in e-books or in print-on-demand. If this book refers to media such as a CD or DVD that is not included in the version you purchased, you may download this material at http://booksupport.wiley.com. For more information about Wiley products, visit www.wiley.com.

Library of Congress Control Number: 2012934988

10 9 8 7 6 5 4 3 2 1

Dear Reader,

Thank you for choosing *Website Optimization: An Hour a Day.* This book is part of a family of premium-quality Sybex books, all of which are written by outstanding authors who combine practical experience with a gift for teaching.

Sybex was founded in 1976. More than 30 years later, we're still committed to producing consistently exceptional books. With each of our titles, we're working hard to set a new standard for the industry. From the paper we print on to the authors we work with, our goal is to bring you the best books available.

I hope you see all that reflected in these pages. I'd be very interested to hear your comments and get your feedback on how we're doing. Feel free to let me know what you think about this or any other Sybex book by sending me an email at `nedde@wiley.com`. If you think you've found a technical error in this book, please visit `http://sybex.custhelp.com`. Customer feedback is critical to our efforts at Sybex.

Best regards,

Neil Edde
Vice President and Publisher
Sybex, an Imprint of Wiley

Acknowledgments

First of all, huge thanks go to my mentors and inspirations in the world of website optimization and web analytics. Without their words of wisdom and help, I would not be where I am now. First, a special "bow down" and big thanks to Tim Ash, who has been a great mentor to me and who also gave me the great privilege and honor of helping him write the 2nd Edition of *Landing Page Optimization: The Definitive Guide to Testing and Tuning for Conversions* (Sybex, 2012). Without first doing that, I don't think I could have written this book!

Huge thanks and respect then go to the authors who kickstarted my passion for website optimization and web analytics: Bryan and Jeffrey Eisenberg (their *Call to Action* [Thomas Nelson, 2006] was a real optimization eye opener to me), Avinash Kaushik (who "converted" me into a web analyst with his fantastic *Web Analytics: An Hour a Day* [Sybex, 2007] and his blog), Steve Krug (for his pioneering *Don't Make Me Think* [New Riders, 2005], and Jakob Nielsen (for his great books that began my love affair with website usability many years ago).

Thanks also to some of the genius website optimizers and bloggers whom I have learned a lot from: Linda Bustos (for her outstanding GetElastic blog and her fantastic tech editing on this book), Chris Goward at WiderFunnel, and Amy Africa at EightbyEight.

A big "cheers" also goes out to all the consultants, account managers, product specialists, and clients whom I have had the privilege of working with and learning from in my website optimization role at Adobe. Also a mention and thanks to my great boss at Disney Online, Erik Tarui, for the support and helpful knowledge of testing he gave me during my time there.

And last, I would like to express my great appreciation for the wonderful team at Sybex who helped me put this book together, including Willem Knibbe, Pete Gaughan, and Kathi Duggan. Without them, the words in this book would still only be in my head, itching to get out.

Oh, and I guess I should also give thanks to Starbucks for their free wireless Internet and also their good coffee keeping me awake during the countless hours I spent working there on this book!

About the Author

Rich Page has been analyzing and improving websites for over 10 years, and is currently a Conversion Solution Specialist at Adobe, where he helps major Fortune 500 clients improve their testing and optimization strategies. Before this, he worked for Disney Online in their web analytics and optimization team.

Rich comes from a background in online marketing, website usability, and web analytics, and has previously worked in roles like these for Z57 Internet Solutions, Gartner, and several startup web companies. He has considerable expertise with Adobe SiteCatalyst and Test&Target, in addition to Google Website Optimizer and Google Analytics.

Rich graduated with a master's degree in Information Technology from the University of San Diego, where he did a thesis on website usability. Rich also holds a bachelor's degree in Management from Royal Holloway University of London, where he did a pioneering thesis on e-commerce. For the last five years, he has been the author of a popular blog about web analytics and optimization topics at his website (`www.rich-page.com`) and is a regular speaker at the Conversion Conference and other industry conferences.

He has spent much of the last 10 years living and working in sunny Southern California and is currently living back in London, England, for a while. In his spare time, he is a passionate classic rock fan, loves to play tennis, and is a karaoke aficionado.

Contents

Foreword

When my brother Jeffrey and I first began evangelizing for conversion optimization in the late 1990s, most companies had dreams of the "new economy" and accompanying fantasies of "eyeballs" being the most important metric; we naively saw this as a C-suite responsibility. Today, most organizations have many people responsible for driving traffic but virtually no one responsible for converting that traffic into revenue. In the offline world's equivalent, there is an executive responsible for sales (conversions) and an executive responsible for marketing, but online marketers have no counterpart.

E-commerce managers may be responsible for revenue, merchandisers for the product selection and presentation, user experience and development teams for the experience, and analytics for measurement; but it's unclear who owns the crucial multi-disciplinary function of conversion.

I have seen a handful of companies with individuals who have conversion in their title, but they are quite rare. In those companies that do, their conversion people have access to tools and resources that demonstrate a very different corporate metabolism than those that don't have them. These companies are also passionate about being customer-focused and data-driven, testing continuously, understanding lifetime value, and are quick to act.

Most companies aren't structured to make conversions a core responsibility. They may assign "conversions" to the PPC manager or even the director of analytics, but they only look at it from their narrow vertical and they aren't given the resources needed to gather the insights, to create and modify landing pages, and to set up personalization and go beyond landing pages into complex testing of customer paths.

Increasing sales conversion rates offers a greater ROI than what you can get from optimizing your traffic; either from paid or earned media. The math is simple— even if many never do the calculations. Companies with higher conversion rates almost always have better marketing efficiency ratios (net contribution/marketing expenses). The upside is that these companies make more money, and that's a good thing. The downside is that it's hard work to accomplish better marketing efficiency ratios. These companies are led differently; they have higher levels of collaboration and higher standards of accountability.

The top performing companies consistently convert visitors to sales at rates in the double digits. They've been doing that for years, while the vast majority converts at low single-digit rates. The gap between the top performers and the middle of the pack continues to grow.

However, there is great news. Over the last few years there has been an explosion of tools to help companies identify opportunities to improve, as well as tools to create landing pages and to do testing. In your hands is another critical component; *Website Optimization: An Hour a Day* is the resource you need to learn how to optimize your site daily. The final piece of the puzzle is, will you dedicate your time and resources to getting it done?

Bryan Eisenberg
Marketing Speaker, Advisor, and best-selling Author

Introduction

Website optimization is a newer art that tests and improves websites to better engage and convert their visitors, by combining website testing, analytics, usability, and online marketing best practices. Unfortunately, it's not something that is quick or easy to do, and you need much more than just a testing tool. That's where this book comes in!

Website Optimization: An Hour a Day will help you test and improve your website (no matter what type) by navigating you through important steps and common pitfalls and ultimately help you build a long-term successful website optimization program. From learning how to measure success and picking the right tools to learning best practices and high-impact test ideas for many common types of pages, you will develop a much deeper understanding of website optimization every week.

By implementing the best practices and test ideas in this book, you will stand a much better chance of improving your website in several ways, by engaging your visitors so that they come back more often, improving your conversion rates and success metrics, and ultimately increasing the bottom line revenue for your online business. Everyone wins!

And remember that testing and optimizing your website is a journey, not a destination—this unique book will ultimately serve as a great companion and compass to check while you head down the long winding road of website optimization.

Who Should Read This Book

This book is intended for anyone that wants to optimize a website for an online business and generate more revenue from it. Website optimization and testing beginners will find it very useful, in addition to those with more experience who will find advanced techniques to get even more juice from their optimization efforts.

It will be particularly useful for many types of web professionals who want to expand their understanding of the subject and help improve a website, including online marketers, web designers, web project managers, website optimizers, web analysts, web information architects, and web strategists. It will also be useful for web developers to understand the reasons why testing tools need to be implemented on websites.

It's also beneficial for anyone who is considering moving into this newer website optimization field from a closely related online field like online marketing or web analytics (as I did). As you will read about in Chapter 1, previously there was little understanding of this field, let alone job titles relevant to it. But these days, there are many more opportunities for individuals who are skilled in website optimization and testing; for example, you can much more easily become a director of website optimization or a test manager. And it really is quite amazing to be able to influence what millions of visitors do and experience on websites.

Even "offline" business people will find it valuable to read this book and gain an understanding of optimizing online business, particularly as the line continues to blur between online and offline business worlds.

The best practices and test ideas found in this book are great for all kinds of businesses that are engaged in some kind of online business (or want to be), from individual startups to major Fortune 500 companies. It also doesn't matter if you have a small real estate agent website or a huge multi-national online store—there are specific sections that cover test ideas for key types of pages found on many types of websites.

What You Will Learn in This Book

You will learn literally hundreds of test ideas and best practices that are designed to optimize any type of website. You will also discover how to make use of many website tools and techniques to become even more effective at optimization. Ultimately, you will learn how to better engage and convert your visitors, improve your website success metrics and conversion rates, and by doing so, make a big impact on revenue and profits for your online business.

What You Will Not Learn in This Book

You won't learn perfect conversion rates, because there is no such thing—every online business is different and comparing is foolish. It's much more important to beat your own current success metrics.

For the same reason, you also won't discover a silver bullet test idea that will improve any website 100 percent of the time. While some tests have a higher chance of impact than others, there is no such thing as a perfect test—you will need to try running and iterating many of the tests found in this book before you find one that has greatest impact.

And although you won't learn about search engine optimization (SEO) best practices in this book, you will learn about the key differences between website optimization and SEO in Chapter 1.

How Long until I See Good Results?

It's possible to get some optimization results from using this book fairly quickly, and this can be as short as it takes for you to create and test different versions (plus a few weeks to gather some results). However, it may take much longer to get results (up to many months in the worst case), depending on how much effort is required to prioritize the test, create test variations for it, and implement.

Getting "good" results is another matter entirely. Just creating a test doesn't ensure you will get good results, and you will need to continually iterate and learn from your tests to gain really good results. You may get lucky and get good results from one of your first tests—or you may have to wait until many more before you get your first good result. The key is to always learn from test results and to not give up!

Also, it's not as simple as just setting up tests and waiting for results, either. As you will learn in this book, there are many internal processes you need to adopt and barriers to break down, and there are many testing best practices and fundamentals that you need to know before you can truly become effective with your website optimization efforts.

What You Need

Having an understanding of any of the major disciplines needed for effective website optimization is definitely very useful to increase the chances of success. These disciplines are web analytics, web usability, website marketing, and website testing. This book will definitely help plug some of those knowledge gaps that you might be lacking, though.

You will also need to use several tools, including web analytics tools, testing tools, usability tools, and survey tools. In order to use the more advanced tools that you will learn about in this book, you will need to obtain a budget for them (although there are some free options, which you will learn about in this book as well).

And last, you will need patience. Things won't improve overnight, and as mentioned previously, there is no silver bullet test that will improve every website. You will require a great deal of persistence, innovation, and ability to learn from your test efforts, and by doing this, you will be rewarded with a much greater chance of website optimization success.

What Is Covered in This Book

Chapter 1: Setting the Website Optimization Scene. In the first chapter, you will get an introduction to this art, learn about the history of website optimization, and then learn about key differences between other similar web testing fields.

Chapter 2: Set Up and Improve Usage of Key Web Analytics and Testing Tools. Here, you will learn the importance of analytics and testing tools and how to set them up. You will then learn key success metrics for your website and set targets.

Chapter 3: Lay the Foundations for Optimization Success. This critical chapter teaches you some key organizational and testing fundamentals that you need to learn before you can embark on an effective website optimization program.

Chapter 4: Understand Your Visitors and Their Needs—the Keys to Website Optimization. Learning more about your website visitors is essential to be able to meet their needs, engage them, and convert them better. This chapter covers creating use cases, personas, and a unique value proposition for them, and how to generate important insights from them.

Chapter 5: Build the Foundation of a Better Converting Website. This chapter helps you build a better foundation that will maximize your conversion and engagement rates and includes key website usability and design best practices.

Chapter 6: Learn the Power of Influence and Persuasion on Visitors and Conversions. Here, you will learn some great ways to influence your visitors so that they engage and convert more often on your website that involve building trust and social proof, and optimizing your use of calls-to-actions, images, and other influencers.

Chapter 7: Optimization Best Practices and Test Ideas for Different Page Types and Flows. In this chapter, you will start to learn ideas and best practices to optimize particular types of website pages and conversion flows, from home pages to checkout flows.

Chapter 8: Keep Them Coming Back—Optimize for Repeat Visits. It's critical to get your website visitors to come back, because repeat visitors are more engaged and convert at a higher rate. In this chapter, you will learn how to do this by optimizing key pages on your website and your email marketing campaigns.

Chapter 9: Review and Learn from Your Results, and Keep Testing and Optimizing. In this last chapter, you will revisit your recent optimization efforts to see how they have been faring, learn from them, set more targets, and continue optimizing.

Appendix A gathers together the many important website optimization tools that are discussed in this book.

Appendix B gives you a worksheet to list and prioritize your test ideas.

Appendix C gives you a worksheet to store your test results and help you learn from past results.

How to Contact the Author

You can contact Rich Page on his blog at `www.rich-page.com`, and you can also contact him via Twitter at `www.twitter.com/richpage`.

Legal Disclaimer

The website optimization best practices and test ideas that are discussed in this book represent the views of Rich Page and his experience and knowledge, and not the views of any of the companies that he works for or has worked for, including Adobe Systems and Disney Online.

1

Setting the Website Optimization Scene

Before diving into the many website optimization best practices and test ideas in this book, it's important to first give you some background and history on this subject and also some key differences between this and other types of optimization relating to websites and search engines.

Chapter Contents

Introduction to Website Optimization

The online business world continues to change and evolve at a frenetic pace. No longer are online businesses just throwing money at creating and marketing their websites and hoping for success; many are now getting increasingly savvy when analyzing and improving their websites.

Unfortunately too much emphasis is still placed on two things: the aesthetics of the website and how to best drive traffic to it. Very little emphasis is placed on the actual visitors to the website and how well it engages and converts them for key goals like purchase or signup—in a nutshell, how well optimized the website is. To illustrate just how little attention is usually placed on conversion, recent studies by Forrester and eMarketer found that for every $80 spent online to acquire traffic to websites, just $1 is spent to proactively convert this traffic once it has arrived.

Remember, you could have the best-looking website in the world, but if your visitors find it hard to use or it doesn't fulfill their needs , they often won't come back (and will likely go to a competitor that's only a few clicks away on Google). And you could spend hundreds of thousands on paid search and Facebook ads driving visitors to your website, but if your website isn't optimized to engage and convert them for your key goals and doesn't influence them to come back, much of this money will be wasted down the drain.

This is why it is so critical to build and run an effective website optimization program for your online business so that it does indeed engage and convert your website visitors much better. More important, as a result of having a website like this, your online business is far more likely to generate greater revenue and profits in the future.

Unfortunately though, this optimization and improvement of websites isn't as easy as you might expect, and you need much more than just a website testing tool. In addition to this, there are many disparate online disciplines you need to learn and apply before you can become truly great at optimizing websites. Web analytics fundamentals are vital for analyzing success metrics and key reports, and to generate better test idea insights from them. Web usability best practices are essential to make your visitors happier when they interact with your website. A great grasp of online marketing best practices (in particular copy writing) is a must if you are to be able to truly influence your visitors with your headlines, images, and calls-to-action. Finally, website testing skills are essential to create high-impact tests needed to optimize your website. See Figure 1.1 for a visual representation of how these disciplines overlap to form website optimization.

Rather than have people need to rely on reading multiple separate books in all of these disciplines, I decided to make website optimization easier to learn by pulling all these skills together and presenting them in the format of Wiley's Hour-a-Day popular book series.

Figure 1.1 Interlocking disciplines needed for website optimization

In particular, one of the most important skills you need to help power your website optimization and testing efforts is a sound understanding of how to use web analytics. This is because web analytics data not only helps you measure the success of your optimization efforts, but they can also provide you with some excellent insights to help form your test ideas. Web analysis techniques will be put to great use throughout this book, from learning and measuring the success metrics for your type of website to learning advanced analysis techniques to find high potential conversion pages.

However, even before starting your website optimization and testing efforts, you will likely be met with several challenges in your organization preventing you from doing so with speed and efficiency. Therefore, you will also become versed in fundamentals to help overcome these, improve your internal processes, and ultimately help build an optimization organization that will ensure you get the most out of your optimization efforts.

To help you make changes to optimize your website, you will then learn important website testing strategies and fundamentals, including how to target and personalize your content to better meet the needs of your all-important visitors. These strategies and fundamentals will ensure your A/B and multivariate tests are set up, run, and analyzed optimally for the most impact on your conversion rates and success metrics.

You will also learn to focus on your visitors and their common journeys through your website so that you can better meet their needs, engage them, and convert them. You will learn how to build personas and use cases to help you do this, in addition to gaining the voice of your visitors by using survey, feedback, and task completion rate analysis tools. Remember that your website would be nothing without your visitors!

Over the remainder of the book, you will then learn many advanced best practices, tools, and tips that will help increase your conversion rates and keep your website visitors coming back for more—no matter what type of website you have. You will also learn some "out of the box" optimization best practices that involve more than just your regular website—for example, emerging mobile website best practices and vital email marketing best practices.

Understanding and adopting these optimization best practices and test ideas will also help give you a competitive edge over your rivals. This is because they more than likely aren't doing a very good job of testing and optimizing their websites, and it will have them wondering exactly how your website is doing so well.

In order to get the most out of this book, I suggest that you spend one day reading each week, and try not to be too tempted to skip through the weeks and read it all in one sitting. I also recommend that you take notes while reading the book and mark down any particularly relevant tips you notice for your website. Don't forget to use the test idea tracker in Appendix B to list any tests in this book you want to try on your website, and then use the test results tracker in Appendix C to document and help you learn from your results.

The final chapter is also very important to pay attention to, because this is when you will revisit your key success metrics and conversion goals to see just how much you have optimized them and, therefore, your website.

The Rise of Website Optimization: The Aftermath of the Dot-com Bubble Bursting

What started off as just a way of exchanging research between institutes in the early 1990s, the World Wide Web quickly came to mainstream prominence in the mid-1990s. This was due to the increasing ease of online access and the rise of websites like Yahoo .com and Amazon.com, with millions of people coming online to experience new exciting ways to find information and shop. And with this huge demand for these new websites quickly came huge revenues from advertising and product sales for many online businesses.

Traditional businesses and new business ventures began to invest millions in getting their own online business to get their slice of the pie, with these online businesses quickly and affectionately become known as dot-coms.

The growth in revenues for many of these dot-coms increased with amazing velocity, and with that came crazy high market valuations. As a result of this, major investments were made by venture capitalists into these hot dot-coms and new dot-com startups, eager to also earn their slice of the pie. Unfortunately though, in this new gold rush, very few checks and balances were put in place to make sure these dot-coms' long-term strategies and business plans were sound.

As a result of this, money was usually spent very fast to grow most dot-coms and their market share as quickly as possible, often by expensive lavish marketing campaigns aimed at attracting as many new visitors as possible. The 2000 Super Bowl ads were the pinnacle of this frenzied spending, with 19 dot-coms like Pets.com spending millions on advertising that looked and seemed cool but yielded extremely low return on investment (ROI). Eight of those no longer exist.

All this investment in marketing meant very little money was spent on understanding the visitors to these websites and improving the usability of them so they better engaged and converted their visitors. Consequently, many of the visitors to these dot-com websites either rarely came back or purchased very few times in the future. Certainly not enough to warrant the huge marketing investments made.

Soon after this, the stock market valuations of these dot-coms became untenable, with many dot-coms still leaking money like a sieve, constantly looking for the next round of funding to stay alive. In March 2000, the stock market came crashing down with the emerging realization of this, and the dot-com bubble had burst. Many dot-coms folded soon after this, and it was only then that surviving and new online businesses began to become more prudent with their spending and analysis of online business.

This overdue rise in web analysis in 2000 was helped by the growing demand for new advanced log-file website analysis tools like WebTrends (which was a pioneer in this at the time). However, most of the analysis being done was concerned with measuring website hits (as they often were referred to) and revenue. Very little emphasis was placed on understanding visitor interaction and ways to improve websites, and what was done often relied on obtaining this from expensive usability labs.

Along with this rise in web analysis was a long-overdue emphasis on website visitors and the usability of websites. Usability experts like Jakob Nielsen released books that exposed the huge number of issues that many websites had at the time and detailed how to resolve them. Steve Krug's groundbreaking book *Don't Make Me Think* (New Riders, 2001) helped put usability and user focus further into the spotlight, using a very simple format that was very easy for anyone to understand (including examples of how to email your boss to start cheap usability testing!). I strongly suggest you read this if you haven't done so already.

However, at this time there weren't many tools available that could easily test these recommended usability improvements, and there was a lack of understanding of the ROI from doing so. This meant that online businesses were doing very little website testing when building or launching new content, merely hoping their efforts would perform better.

The testing that was done was usually handled informally with no tool, by putting up a new version for a while to see which version seemed to do better. This often resulted in bad consequences for website stability and user experience. And it wasn't until years later when some online businesses started showing great results and ROI from improved testing rigor and process that other online businesses started to notice and slowly follow suit.

Unfortunately, creating and optimizing websites then took a further step back with the rise of tools that made it very easy to create and launch websites with no programming knowledge. This meant that anyone could create an online presence with very little expertise, which unfortunately meant a deluge of quickly built but bad websites with poor user experiences, with little understanding about how to engage and convert visitors (none more so than the rush of slow-loading intro splash pages).

All of this meant that testing and optimization continued to take a back seat to marketing websites for the first half of the 2000s. This didn't really change much until 2004, when website testing tools like Offermatica and Optimost started to appear that made it much easier and less risky to test making improvements to websites and understand the benefits and ROI from doing so.

Then in 2007, testing became accessible to a much wider market with the launch of Google's free Website Optimizer tool. Although much more primitive than paid testing tool solutions, it allowed online marketers to finally start to dip their feet in the testing waters with little cost or technical knowledge.

Now five years later, there is a much better understanding of the need to optimize and test websites and the ROI and benefit from doing so. This has resulted in the appearance of many new testing tools offering greater functionality but at a fraction of the cost of expensive tools. For example, testing tools like Visual Website Optimizer have allowed businesses to test with better functionality than Google Website Optimizer but at a far lower cost than Offermatica (now called Adobe Test&Target). This has helped begin a long overdue shift away from just visitor acquisition, with much greater focus on and understanding of the need to improve and optimize websites.

However, even with these newer and better testing tools and increased focus on testing, you should realize that website optimization is still in its infancy and that few online businesses are doing a great job of this (particularly in regions outside of the U.S.). This means that you have a huge opportunity to capitalize on this and beat your competitors in the online world by testing and optimizing your website to a better extent.

Indeed, had many of the dot-com companies devoted more money to understanding the needs of their visitors better, made better use of analytics to make more informed decisions on their website, and adopted more focus and rigor in their testing initiatives, many of them would have made greater profits and survived much longer.

The Differences between Landing Page Optimization, Conversion Rate Optimization, Website Testing, and Website Optimization

Before you discover and learn how to optimize your website, it's important to actually know what website optimization actually *is*, and how it differs from other similar web improvement fields. And there are many of them: landing page optimization, conversion rate optimization, website testing, and A/B testing.

All of these terms are bandied about, often with little understanding of the differences between them, and this can often confuse people. They all mean very similar things in that they all help improve aspects of websites, but let's review these to help clear up any confusion. This will also help you articulate this to others in your organization, which will be a key part of building a website optimization culture there. Here are the main different common fields associated with website optimization:

Landing Page Optimization Many people consider this the same as website optimization, but it is often considered as the art of optimizing pages that visitors directly land on after clicking on a search engine or other advertising link. The problem with this though is that the page doesn't have to be landed on directly to have an impact on your conversion rates—any page on your website can have potential impact on your conversion rate, regardless of whether visitors arrive on it from Google or a newsletter, or arrive from another page on your website. You also need to optimize a visitor's whole journey through your website and common conversion-related page flows, not just their landing page.

Conversion Rate Optimization Conversion rate optimization is quite similar to website optimization, but it places too much emphasis on solely increasing conversion rates. While it is very important to increase your conversion rates, this is somewhat shortsighted because you can increase your conversion rate in many ways, but it doesn't always mean that your website visitors will be happier or more engaged. And for certain types of pages and websites like media ones, there is no major conversion goal due to them not really selling anything or capturing leads. Therefore, these websites are generally left ignored when discussing conversion rate optimization, to the detriment of these and their visitors.

Website Optimization The art that you are learning about in this book covers much more than the previous two disciplines and places greater emphasis on testing and improving websites from a usability and visitor perspective, in addition to testing and improving conversion rates and success metrics. It also involves optimizing any kind of page, whether it's landed on from offsite or not, and whether there is even a major conversion goal for it or not.

Website Testing (or A/B Testing) Last, website testing is actually the act of testing changes on your website in order to optimize it for one of your goals, whether this involves doing simple A/B testing (a popular euphemism for website testing) or advanced multivariate testing. This is done with a testing tool and is a very important process of any of the fields mentioned previously.

The Difference between Website Optimization and Search Engine Optimization (SEO)

It's also really important to clear up another common misinterpretation. Many people not very familiar with the term website optimization often confuse it with search engine optimization (SEO). SEO companies even still continue to bid on the phrase "website optimization" in Google, which only serves to confuse people even more. To help clear this up, first here are definitions of the two:

Website Optimization Website optimization is an art that tests and improves websites to better engage and convert their visitors, by combining website testing, analytics, usability, and online marketing best practices (Source: Rich Page).

Search Engine Optimization Search engine optimization (SEO) is the process of improving the volume and quality of traffic to a website from search engines via "natural" (or "organic") search results (Source: Wikipedia).

Next, here are some other reasons why website optimization is different from SEO and why it's important:

- Website optimization affects your visitors when they arrive on your website and how they engage and convert for your goals. SEO has an effect on the visitor *before* they get to your website, in the actual search engine results pages (SERPs).
- It doesn't matter how much you optimize your website rankings in Google if your website isn't fully optimized to meet your visitors' needs and convert them. You are simply pouring money down the drain if you don't optimize your website—many visitors from search engines will simply leave if their needs aren't met.
- Website optimization initiatives are often much cheaper to execute than running expensive SEO campaigns. In fact, leading web analysts like Avinash Kaushik firmly believe that in order to start optimizing your website, you need just 10 percent of your SEO budget.
- Once you optimize your website so that it engages and converts your current traffic better, you should then engage in SEO to drive further traffic, and then optimize how well this SEO traffic converts on your website.

I'm not saying that you should ignore SEO—in fact you should start to think of onsite factors that influence SEO while doing website optimization (URL structure, page names, page interlinking, and keyword usage). Indeed, any website owner who wants the best chance of generating significant revenues and profits in the long run should engage in SEO, but just make sure you optimize your website to engage and convert your visitors before heavily focusing on it.

Set Up and Improve Usage of Key Web Analytics and Testing Tools

Before you can begin to optimize your website, you first need to arm yourself with and make better use of web analytics and website testing tools. These will help you measure and analyze the performance of your website and then test new versions to help improve it. Without making effective use of these tools, your optimization efforts will be blinded, inefficient and usually end with disappointing results.

2

Chapter Contents

Week 1: Learn the Importance of and Set Up an Analytics Tool

For the first week in this book, you will focus on the growing importance of web analytics tools, the website data they provide, and the key role they play in helping optimize websites. You will also learn about various web analytics tools available to you and how to set up goals and segments within these tools to maximize the insights you will gain from them.

Monday: Understand the Need for Web Analytics Data to Help Website Optimization Efforts

First you need to learn the importance of web analytics and their key relationship with website optimization efforts, as you are essentially blinded without having access to and usage of them.

In order to truly begin optimizing your website, you first need to understand your current website performance; for example, how visitors interact with it, the amount of sales or leads it generates, and the trends that are occurring on it. The best and easiest way to gather this important information about your website is to set up a web analytics tool on it to collect web analytics data about the usage of it. In other words, you are using this analytics tool to gather visitor click stream data that reveals such things as where your visitors come from, where they arrive on your website, what they look at and click on, and where they leave.

Having this website analytics data and insight is essential for your website optimization efforts for the following four key reasons:

1. They Help You Discover and Monitor Key Success Metrics for Your Online Business The first and most important use of web analytics data is that it helps you discover and monitor key success metrics for your online business, such as a signup form completion rate or products ordered per visitor. These success metrics are essential for measuring the performance of your online business, as well as the impact of your optimization efforts (which you'll learn about throughout this book). Without knowing and monitoring these things, you would have no real way of knowing how successful your optimization and testing efforts are.

2. They Help You Understand and Prioritize What Needs Optimizing the Most on your Website Second, web analytics are essential to help you understand and prioritize what needs optimizing the most on your website. For example, insights from them will help you understand whether you need to optimize your homepage or your product pages first. By having this insight into what is happening on your website, you don't have to guess at what to improve first or risk wasting time and money on something that doesn't need fixing, or even worse, change something and damage your website in terms of conversions or visitor engagement.

3. They Help Arm You with Key Information to Challenge and Improve Web Decision Making Having this website analytics insight also helps you gather and arm yourself with key information to challenge and improve existing website decision making. This is particularly good for addressing wrongly conceived assumptions and decisions made by senior executives, often referred to by the acronym HiPPOs (Highest Paid Person's Opinion), who believe they know what is best for the website and visitors (which often is the polar opposite of what your website visitors actually want) and often may feel that testing isn't necessary.

4. They Help Provide You with Better Insights and Ideas for Testing and Optimizing Your Website Last, and most important for the context of this book, insights from your web analytics data are essential to help you create better test ideas for optimizing your website. Tests created this way also often result in higher conversion lifts than those created from just guesswork or someone's opinion.

Even with the rise in the understanding of and need for web analytics over the last five years, web analytics are often still neglected, with far too many online marketers thinking that just having a web analytics tool in place is good enough and as a result don't make much use of these tools.

There have also been several great new tracking technologies appearing in recent analytics tools, but unfortunately, many companies don't know about these or how to best implement them.

As a result of these factors, many online businesses' web analytics tools gather only basic, inaccurate, or incomplete web analytics data. This leads to decisions being made from inaccurate and misleading data, which then leads to sub-par or even negative website optimization efforts.

Even if you know you have a good web analytics implementation, your web analytics reporting and analysis may not actually be providing good insights for two common reasons. You may just be grinding out very basic high-level reports that don't offer much insight, and/or you may be overanalyzing your website data and therefore making it very hard to form actionable insights about it. Therefore, next week you'll learn about best practices for the key metrics and reports that you need to focus on.

Tuesday: Select a Web Analytics Tool for Your Website

Next, you need to evaluate the different web analytics tools and vendors that are currently available and select one to use on your website. With the recent popularity and importance in web analytics over the last five years, you probably already have a web analytics tool installed on your website, but you need to make sure that it uses newer analytics technologies and that it provides the depth of data you need. Therefore, it's important to quickly review the most common web analytics tools available, and hopefully discover some better ones that will help you gain greater level of insight into your website.

First of all though, you need to make sure you are using a modern onsite JavaScript-based analytics tool like Google Analytics that tags all of your pages to gather web analytics data. Surprisingly, some traditional companies still rely on older log file–based web analytics tools that track every file and image server call (like Webalizer or AWstats) instead of just tracking page- and visitor-based events. These have proven to be a very ineffective and misleading way of measuring web analytics in comparison to the newer JavaScript-based tools.

You should also avoid relying on a panel-based analytics tool like the one offered by comScore (`www.comScore.com`) to measure your website performance. This is because panel-based tools only provide you high-level metrics and don't enable you to analyze more in-depth visitor behavior patterns and obtain visitor insight. They also are based on sample data, much like how TV ratings work, so they aren't as accurate as JavaScript-based tools like Google Analytics.

Free and Budget Web Analytics Tools

Google Analytics (`www.google.com/analytics`) This free web analytics tool from Google is now one of the most widespread and popular web analytics tools in the industry. It has a fairly good feature set considering that it is free, but lacks ability to customize it to fully meet your needs, for example the ability to track multiple or advanced custom conversion goals. One of the other big positives of Google Analytics though is the very easy-to-use interfacefor it, and a steady stream of improvements to it, such as recent "Real Time" and "Intelligence Events" reports.

Because this tool is free, it comes with no official support or consulting, although there are many companies that Google partners with for you to obtain this product support (however, there is now a new paid service version of this tool, which includes this). This tool also integrates fairly well with Google's other free important web tool called Google Website Optimizer (which is covered in week 3 in more detail) but doesn't integrate very easily with other third-party tools like CRM systems or sales databases to help integrate sales or offline data. Figure 2.1 shows a screenshot of Google Analytics.

KISSmetrics (`www.kissmetrics.com`) For those of you interested in a slightly different web analytics approach to Google Analytics and a slightly better feature set, you could try using KISSmetrics. Their main differentiator is their focus on conversion-related reports (which is great for the optimization context of this book) and increased focus on tracking people rather than just page views and visitors. With very reasonable monthly plans (from $29 per month), they are great for dipping your feet into the world of enterprise analytics tools without a high cost.

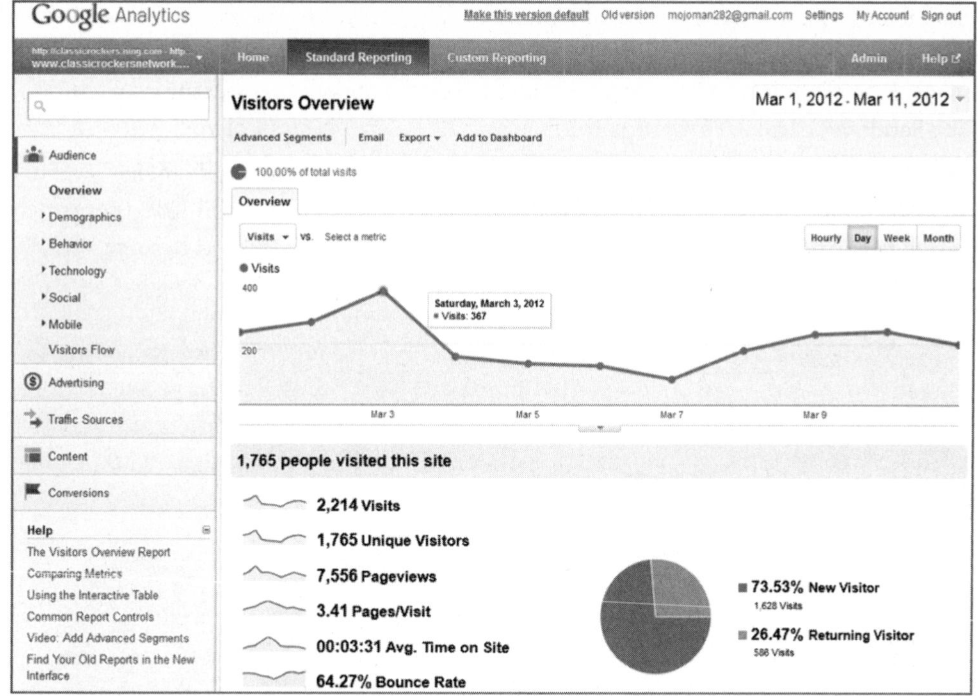

Figure 2.1 Screenshot of Google Analytics

Clicky (www.getclicky.com) Another great web analytics tool to consider, this offers some great unique tracking capabilities. For example, its Twitter tracking is better than most tools, and it offers some great video tracking that is not available even in many enterprise-level analytics tools. Although it doesn't compete with the enterprise-level tools in terms of flexibility and feature set, another added benefit of this tool is that basic support and help are included, which is a key differentiator between this and other free or budget tools.

Other budget web analytics tools that you could also consider are Woopra (www.woopra.com) and Yahoo Analytics (web.analytics.yahoo.com).

Enterprise-Level Web Analytics Tools

Adobe SiteCatalyst (www.omniture.com/sitecatalyst) For those of you with more complex web analytics needs, or those looking for a more robust analytics feature set and much greater ability to customize your tracking, this market-leader tool would be a much better fit. For example, you can easily customize individual webpage and section tracking; segment and drill deep down into your data; set up custom event tracking (for example, tracking advanced conversion goals or interactive elements on your website); and set up powerful campaign tracking. This tool integrates well with other third-party tools (such as SalesForce.com) and enables you to import and analyze offline data from sources like sales or marketing databases. It also offers powerful new social analytics capabilities that help you measure the impact of social media websites like Facebook.com and Twitter.com.

As for all of the enterprise level analytics tools, unfortunately this much higher level of analytics functionality comes with a greater cost of running it. For this tool, the cost is based on traffic volume, so the more you have, the more costly this can become.

Figure 2.2 shows a screenshot of Adobe SiteCatalyst.

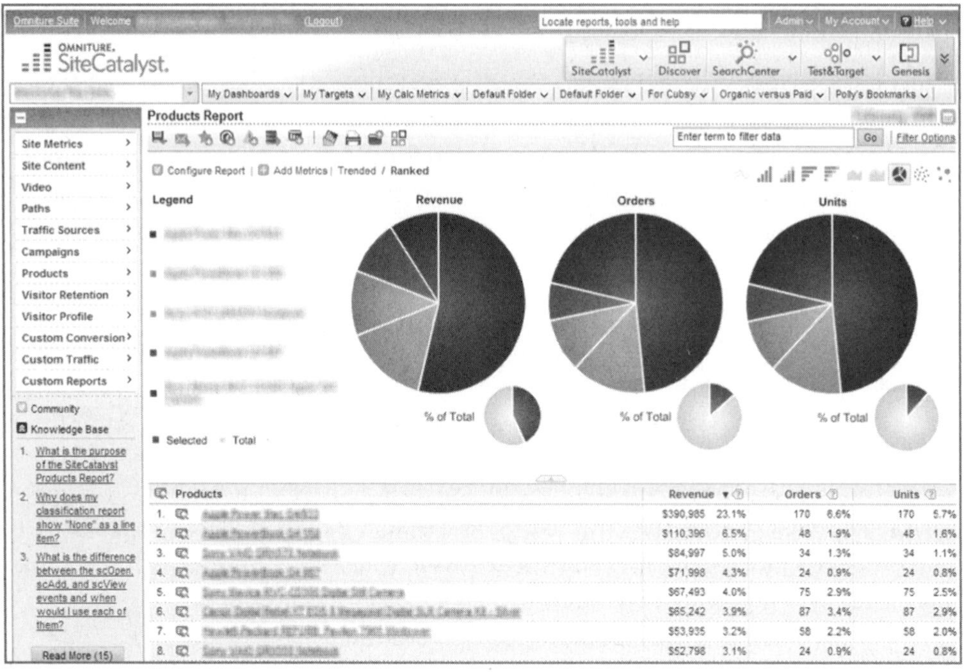

Figure 2.2 Screenshot of Adobe SiteCatalyst

CoreMetrics (`www.coremetrics.com`) This is a newer player in the enterprise-level web analytics tool field and has recently been acquired by IBM. They are quickly catching up with the industry leader SiteCatalyst in terms of its feature set and functionality.

The tool has some unique features, like the ability to easily benchmark traffic metrics within your industry to see how you might be comparing to your competitors (Google Analytics offers this too, but you have to opt in to be included), and the ability to do multi-channel sales analysis. They also offer pre-packaged industry-specific solutions that help give you a great kick start. Overall, this tool is definitely one to evaluate to see if it meets your needs better than the other enterprise tools and may work out slighter cheaper depending on your exact needs.

WebTrends (`www.webtrends.com`) This tool was one of the pioneering web analytics tools in the industry and has been around since the mid-1990s. Although they have lost ground over new smaller rivals recently and some cutting-edge features are lacking in comparison, they certainly still compete well with other enterprise tools and therefore should still be evaluated. For their recent version 10 of the tool, they have given it a great user interface and included new social analytics capabilities.

If you are currently using a web analytics tool that is not JavaScript tagging-based like these ones listed here, I definitely recommend you implement one of these and make it your main source of website metrics.

Other Things to Consider When Evaluating a Web Analytics Tool

While feature set and monthly cost are very important factors, there are a number of other things you should consider before choosing a web analytics vendor. First, you should understand the level of support and consulting that is included in the price of the tool, because this can vary hugely between the tool vendors. Having this official support can be particularly helpful when setting up the tool and customizing it on your website to make optimal use of its features and reach its full tracking potential.

Second, many of these vendors vary in terms of their implementation costs, so if you have a complicated website with particularly complex web analytics needs, I suggest you factor that into your decision and shop around in more detail.

Next, I suggest that you look at how well each tool integrates with the other web marketing tools or offline data sources you currently use or plan to use (like CRM or testing tools), because linking these together can help provide you even greater insight into your website performance. Tool integration can be costly if the web analytics tool doesn't link well with the tools you currently own, which is a good reason to use a vendor with several other web marketing tools like Adobe.

And last, but by no means less important, you should remember to not spend your entire analytics budget on the tool, because you will need to reserve a good part of this to invest in growing your web analytics team and their expertise. Without this expertise with the tool, it will be very hard for you to create insight for use in your optimization and testing plans. In fact, the analytics guru Avinash Kaushik, author of *Web Analytics: An Hour a Day* (Sybex, 2007), goes so far as to state that there should be a 90/10 split in analytics funding, with 10 percent spent on the tools and 90 percent spent on web analytics personnel to help interpret and build insights from the data.

Wednesday: Implement Your Web Analytics Tool and Test to Make Sure It's Working Correctly

Once you have selected the web analytics tool you want to use, you need to implement it on your website. Today you will learn more about this.

First of all, if you don't consider yourself a web analytics expert, you are going to need help from a web analyst to implement it. If you don't have a web analyst available in your company, you should try and hire one to help with this implementation, or get consulting help from your web analytics tool vendor or third-party vendor. You will also need to get help from your IT department to actually implement the tags on your website.

Obtaining this help with the analytics tool implementation is particularly important, because there is a much greater chance of mistakes being made if you try and implement it with limited web analytics knowledge or help. Not getting this help usually results in a negative knock-on effect on your ability to gain insights for improving your website optimization efforts.

Once you have implemented your web analytics tool, you need to perform quality assurance (QA) on it to see if the data is accurate and coming in as expected. If you had assistance implementing the tool, you would ideally use the same person to help perform QA on the data. Think of this as a means to prevent the garbage-in, garbage-out (GIGO) syndrome, meaning that if you don't have very good data coming in, you are not going to get very good data coming out of the tool to make good insights.

If you don't do a good job of QA on your web analytics data, you may end up gathering inaccurate data about your website and therefore unwittingly be making bad website decisions or damaging your ability to form reliable insights needed for your website optimization efforts.

Luckily, there are a number of tools that automate the checking of analytics code on each of your pages for web analytics tags, including a great one called WASP(`www.wasp.com`). In particular, you need to check that the analytics data is coming in correctly on the key pages of your website; for example, the shopping cart and checkout flow if you have an e-commerce website, or the lead capture pages if you have a lead generation website.

One of the key things you need to check for and improve is the names of your pages coming into your web analytics tool and ensure that each of your pages uses a good naming convention. Having this better page naming convention in place makes it much easier for you to interpret and understand your analytics data in the long run and leaves less room for error. The key for this good naming convention is to always make sure your page names have clarity and context. For example, instead of just using your product name for pages, you should also include the section that the page belongs in (for example, Electronics). You should also make sure that the name of the page is understandable without needing to look it up first.

Here are examples of good and bad page names:

Bad Product Page Name: cxnb37213n.asp

Good Product Page Name: Electronics:CanonPowerShotS95

Other important things to check in your tool are that your traffic sources are coming in to it correctly, including your search engine keywords being driven to your website. To do this, consult your web analytics tool help to find these reports and make sure that you are seeing data that you would expect.

Thursday: Know How to Set Up Your Website Conversion Goals

Setting up website conversion goals in your web analytics tool helps you understand what constitutes success for your online business and enables you to track the success of your website optimization efforts. If you don't set up any goals, you will be left in the dark regarding the impact of your efforts. Although you won't actually be setting these conversion goals until next week, it's important to first realize the importance of them and how to set them up in your analytics tool.

Before you set up your conversion goals, it's important that you fully understand what your key conversion goals are and what constitutes success for your website. Surprisingly, many online businesses don't have a firm understanding of their high-level conversion goals or don't know how to measure or track them. Some web analytics tools (such as Adobe SiteCatalyst) use the term conversion *events* instead of conversion *goals*. However, both of these terms mean essentially the same thing: a method that enables you to measure your website goals by how many visitors convert for them.

Types of Website Conversion Goals and Success Metrics

To help you understand what your high-level conversion goals are likely going to be for your website, Table 2.1 lists some basic examples of conversion goals for five major website types. This table also gives you an indicator of how you set up each goal in an analytics tool.

▶ **Table 2.1** Website goals

Website Type	Conversion Goal	Goal to Set Up in Your Tool
E-commerce	Product order	Order completion page
Lead generation	Generation of a lead	Form completion/thanks page
Media/brand websites	More ads seen/more ad revenue	Page views per visit is at least 5
Blog	Newsletter signup	Newsletter signup thanks page
Community	Member signup	New member confirmation page

However, please note that these conversion goals will vary depending on what your website offers and its unique value proposition, and you may also have multiples of them. Therefore you need to evaluate what constitutes conversion success for your website (usually these will be tied to your main business objectives) before selecting your high-level conversion goals.

Setting Up Conversion Goals in Basic Web Analytics Tools

Setting up these important conversion goals varies between web analytics tools. In basic tools like Google Analytics (and other tools should have a similar process), you simply need to go to the analytics settings for your website and add in a conversion goal. To do this in Google Analytics, click Add Goal, name your conversion goal, and enter the URL of the corresponding page that defines success (the goal URL). For example, if you are selling products, the page that defines success is your order completion page.

You should also include the page URLs for intermediary steps of the conversion flow (called Goal Funnel in Google Analytics), because this will help you measure when and how often your visitors abandon within key series of your pages like a shopping cart or registration process. Figure 2.3 shows an example of an e-commerce goal setup, including intermediary steps.

Enter Goal Information

Goal Name: Order Complete
Goal name will appear in conversion reports.

Active Goal: On Off

Goal Position: Set 1, Goal 2
Changing goal position will not move historical data for this goal

Please select a goal type

Goal Type: URL Destination
Time on Site
Pages/Visit

Goal Details

Match Type: Head Match

Goal URL: /orderthankyou.php (e.g. For the goal page "http://www.mysite.com/thankyou.html"enter "/thankyou.html")
To help you verify that your goal URL is set up correctly, please see the tips here .

Case Sensitive: URLs entered above must exactly match the capitalization of visited URLs.

Goal Value 0.0 optional

Goal Funnel optional

A funnel is a series of pages leading up to the goal URL. For example, the funnel may include steps in your checkout process that lead you to the thank you page (goal).

Please note that the funnels that you've defined here only apply to the Funnel Visualization Report.

Note: URL should not contain the domain (e.g. For a step page "http://www.mysite.com/step1.html" enter **"/step1.html"**

	URL(e.g. "/step1.html")	Name	
Step 1	/shopping cart.php	Cart - Checkout	Required step
Step 2	/address.php	Cart - Address	
Step 3	/payment.php	Cart - Payment	
Step 4	/confirmation.php	Cart - Confirmation	
Step 5			

+ Add Goal Funnel Step

Save Goal Cancel

Figure 2.3 Setting up a goal in Google Analytics

If you have the type of website that doesn't have specific page-based conversion goals, such as media websites, there is also an option to choose one of a few other goal measurements like Time On Site or Pages/Visit (shown in Figure 2.3 under Goal Type).

However, one of the disadvantages of using this type of basic tool is that it's hard to track complex conversion goals that are not page-based, such as button clicks or interactions with dynamic and interactive page elements. You may be required to do some custom technical work in order to implement these correctly.

One of the advantages of using basic analytics tools like these to track conversion goals though is that you don't usually need to tag your pages with code for the success goal, because the tool simply tracks it by load of the page that defines success. This can often ease the testing implementation burden on your IT department as well.

Setting Up Conversion Goals or Events in Enterprise Tools

To set up these conversion goals in enterprise tools like Adobe SiteCatalyst, although you get more flexibility in what conversion goals you can track, unfortunately much more of a technical effort is needed to set them up.

First, for every conversion goal that you want to track on your website, you need to create a new goal (or event) variable in your tool, with the name of the corresponding conversion goal (for example, registration). Then you need to tag the code for this variable onto the page that defines success (for example, your registration confirmation page). Most good enterprise web analytics tool vendors will help you set these up correctly.

After you have set up and tagged your conversion goals or events on your website, you need to make sure they are coming in correctly to your web analytics tool. To do this, complete a conversion goal on your website and see if it shows up by checking your goals report or pulling in the conversion event metric into a traffic report.

As mentioned at the beginning of this section, you don't have to actually decide on, set up, or test your specific website conversion goals yet—these things will be covered in detail for each type of major website next week. However, at this point, you should hopefully understand the importance of establishing conversion goals for your website, and how to set them up in your web analytics tool.

Friday: Set Up Key Segments of Visitors to Monitor and Target

It's important to understand that website traffic patterns and conversion rates can often vary significantly, depending on key characteristics of different groups of your visitors. This can vary depending on the quality and type of your visitors (for example, their intent or demographics), and where they have arrived from. For example, your newsletter visitors may behave very differently than first-time visitors arriving from a search engine keyword. If you don't set up these groups of visitors, you won't be able to gather insights that may be influencing your conversion rate and optimize them. An example of this insight might be that your overall site conversion rate is 4 percent, but your paid search visitors group might only convert at 1 percent, bringing down your average for the website, thus meaning that group needs more immediate optimization attention.

Not only is it important to understand and monitor these differences, but you can also leverage these different groups of traffic in your testing tools by targeting different content to each of them, helping provide more relevant content to them. This increased content relevancy for your visitors will then improve the chances of them converting. Doing this targeting also really helps to personalize what your groups of visitors see on your website, rather than having a "one-size-fits-all" approach. This visitor targeting will be covered in more detail in Chapter 3 to help you get much more juice from your optimization efforts.

In order to monitor and optimize these important groups of visitors and the effects they have on your conversion rates, you need to set up several segments of visitors in your analytics tool. Think of these segments as visitors that share common characteristics: for example, how they got to the site, how many times they have been here before, or if they have purchased anything from the site before.

Most web analytics tools (including Google Analytics) feature the ability to create and analyze visitor segments on the fly, which is extremely powerful for monitoring key segments in real time. (Adobe SiteCatalyst users will have to upgrade to version 15 to get this real-time feature.)

Table 2.2 lists some of the key visitor traffic segments that you should set up in your web analytics tool (depending on what type of website you have).

Table 2.2 Basic visitor traffic segments

Visitor Traffic Segment	Definition
Repeat Visitors	A visitor who has come to your website more than once
Loyal Visitors	A visitor who has come to your website at least three times a month
Registered Visitors	A visitor who has previously registered on your website
Repeat Purchase Visitors	A visitor who has previously bought from your website more than once
Loyal Purchase Visitors	A visitor who has previously bought more than three times from your website
Newsletter Visitors	A visitor who has arrived at your website from one of your newsletters
Google Search Visitors	A visitor who has arrived from a Google organic search
Bing Search Visitors	A visitor who has arrived from a Bing organic search
Paid Search Visitors	A visitor who has arrived from clicking on a paid search listing
Facebook Visitors	A visitor who has arrived from Facebook
Twitter Visitors	A visitor who has arrived from Twitter
Affiliate or Partner Visitors	A visitor who has arrived from one of your affiliate or partner sites
Multiple Purchase Visitor	A visitor who has purchased more than two times before

Table 2.3 lists some more-advanced examples of traffic segments that you should set up, monitor, and target (again depending on your website type) and the purpose for setting them up. These will often require some extra code to set up, particularly when setting up segments that involve detailed information from visitors (like knowing exactly what they have purchased previously). Please see the help section of your analytics tool to set up advanced visitor traffic segments like these.

▶ **Table 2.3** Examples of advanced visitor traffic segments

Visitor Traffic Segment	Description and Purpose
Goal Conversion Visitors	Depending on whether your visitors convert for your goals or not, they will often act a lot differently. This segment enables you to track these types of visitors and is great for understanding what causes them to sign up as well as to target them.
Visitors by Work/Non-work Hours	Your website may attract different types of visitors at different times of the day. This traffic segment enables you to target visitors based on what time they typically come to your website.
Visitors by Day of Week	Your website may attract different types of visitors on different days of the week. This traffic segment enables you to target visitors based on what day they typically come to your website.
Visitors by Geographic Region	Your website may attract visitors from different countries or regions. This traffic segment enables you to target content to visitors based on which region they are coming from to increase engagement and conversions.
Visitors at Different Phases of Signup or Purchase Process	If your visitors don't complete a signup or purchase process (for example, a shopping cart checkout, or a quote for something), you can target these visitors and show them content that persuades them to finish the process.
Registered Visitors Who Have Specific Demographics	You can segment and target registered visitors who represent demographics that are of particular interest to you, for example by different age group or income level. As long as you can pull this information from their account, you can segment these visitors to show them different content to increase engagement and conversions. This is a very advanced visitor segment to set up and target.
Visitors Who Have Purchased Specific Things	Depending on what your visitors have previously purchased, you can target different content to them to increase engagement and conversions—for example, to make sure they don't see promotions for products already purchased, and to show related or upsell items to what they have purchased previously. This is often the most advanced type of visitor segment to target.

Don't Worry about Creating Visitor Traffic Segments with Low Value

There are hundreds of visitor traffic segments that you can create in your web analytics tool, because you can usually create a segment out of any metric or reporting dimension. However, don't go over the top in your segments. In particular, you should not worry about creating the following traffic segments, because they often won't really reveal very actionable insights and have a low targeting value:

- Operating System (for example, Windows versus Mac)
- Browser (for example, Firefox versus Internet Explorer)
- Screen Resolution (for example, 1024×768 versus 800×600)

Setting these visitor traffic segments up varies depending on which analytics tool you have. Some of these tools (such as Google Analytics) allow you to set up segments based on rules that you create (for example, by particular search engines or which sections they visit), and other tools already have the most common visitor segments set up for you (such as the basic traffic segments listed in Table 2.2). Setting up segments related to your specific website goals requires that you have adequate conversion goal tracking set up, as you learned yesterday. As an example, Figure 2.4 shows the steps needed to set up a Facebook visitors segment in Google Analytics.

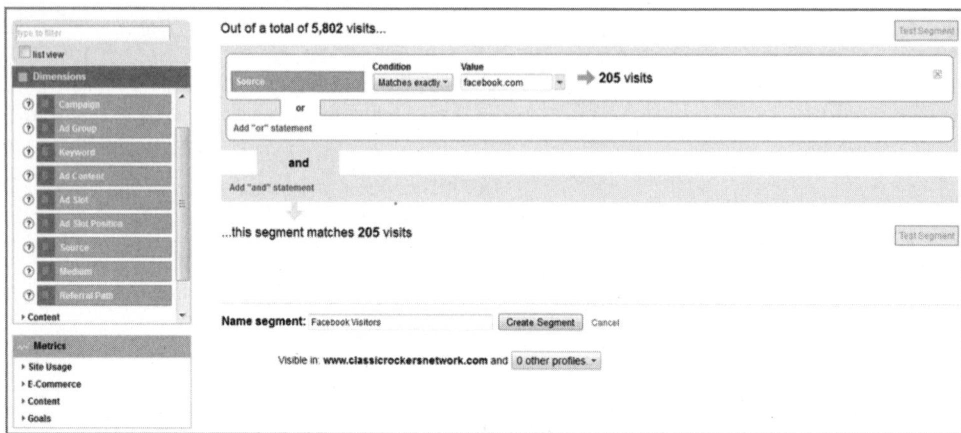

Figure 2.4 Example of setting up a visitor traffic segment in Google Analytics.

If you have a web analyst or analytics consultant available to you, I suggest that you get help from them to set these up. If you don't have this type of help available and want to get more details on setting these visitor segments up for your particular web analytics tool, please review the help section in your analytics tool.

The next thing you need to do is to check that these visitor segments appear to be working correctly. To do this, simply navigate to your newly created segment (often by using a drop-down navigation menu at the top of your reports) and check some reports to see if your newly filtered segment makes sense. For example, in your Google search visitor segment, you can check your search engine reports to make sure that only traffic is arriving from this search engine and no others.

Figure 2.5 shows an example of a traffic report with two different visitor traffic segments in relation to all visits (returning visitors and Facebook visitors).

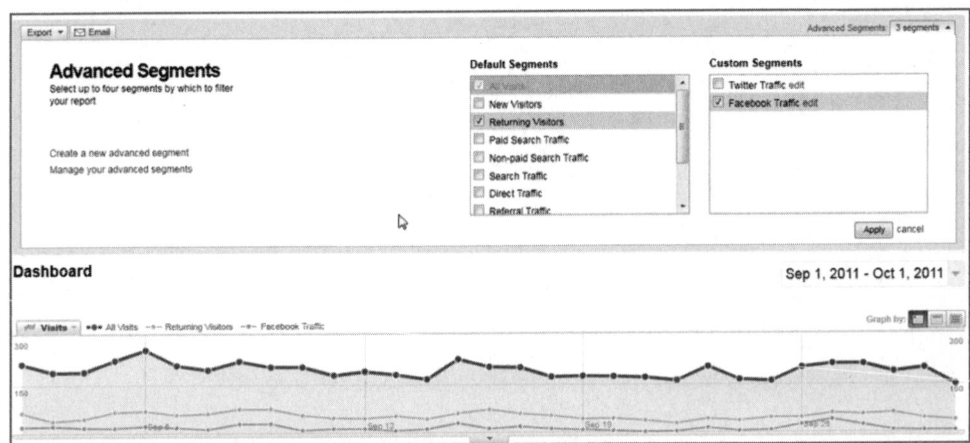

Figure 2.5 Example of a report containing visitor traffic segments in Google Analytics

After you have ensured that your visitor traffic segments are showing up correctly, you can focus on improving the performance and targeting of these segments (which you'll learn about later in this book).

Week 2: Find Your Website Conversion Rate, Success Metrics, Benchmark, and Set Targets

This week, you're going to focus on gauging how your website is currently performing in terms of conversion rates and success metrics. This is very important to do because it helps reveal what metrics and areas of your website need the most improvement and helps you set benchmarks and then targets to try and achieve.

Rather than only relying on your website's overall conversion rate metric as a barometer of your website's performance, you also need to use other success metrics to understand the root cause of your website's performance and better diagnose issues. It's much easier to optimize the performance of success metrics than it is to try and find and fix problems with your overall website conversion rate.

These success metrics usually have a direct correlated impact on your overall website conversion rate, and improving these metrics will usually raise that rate. For example, by reducing your shopping cart abandonment rate (which is a key success metric for e-commerce websites), you will also increase your website's overall conversion rate.

Let's start by discussing a few basic success metrics that can indicate how well your website is faring, no matter what type of website you have.

Monday: Check Your Current Traffic Levels and Set Targets

Today, you will check your most basic success metric, and that is your current website traffic levels. This is good to monitor because a well-optimized website is likely going to result in more repeat visitors (often equating to a greater amount of monthly unique visitors), and also increased usage when visitors are on your website (increasing your page views).

To check your current traffic levels, simply log on to your web analytics tool and run some simple reports to find the following high-level traffic metrics:

Page views: Average of your last six months
Monthly unique visitors: Average of your last six months

Next, you need to set a target to grow your traffic, and ideally you should set a target to grow your traffic by 20 percent over the next six months.

Tuesday: Check Your Website's Overall Conversion Rate and Set Targets

Next you will learn about the simplest yet most important metric to help you understand the performance of your website and how well optimized it is. This is your website's overall conversion rate. This is a great basic indicator of how many visitors are converting for any of your website goals out of the total that visit your website. This is usually also directly tied to the profitability of your online business.

In order to calculate your website's overall conversion rate, use the following formula to find the relevant metrics in your web analytics tool:

Your Website's Overall Conversion Rate =
(Number of website conversions ÷ number of website visitors) × 100

The other reason why it's so important to monitor and track this high-level conversion metric is because through your optimization efforts, you might end up optimizing a key success metric such as registration rate. That's great, but at the same time, you might unknowingly reduce your total website conversion rate. And at the end of the day, you really should be aiming to improve all your success metrics as well as the overall conversion rate of your website, not just focus on improving one stand-alone success metric.

To help you apply this calculation to your website, a unique website conversion can be in the form of orders or leads generated for example. You should also add together the values for multiple types of conversion goals if your website has more than one—for example, leads generated plus registrations generated—because both of them may be conversion goals for your website.

Unfortunately, many web analytics tools don't make it very easy to find this overall conversion rate, but many allow you to create a custom metric that you can pull into reports. For example, in fully customizable tools like Adobe SiteCatalyst, you can easily create a calculated metric and pull it into any report, but unfortunately, it's much harder to do in basic tools.

Don't Cheat Your Conversion Rate

One way to improve your conversion rate very quickly and easily without even changing your website is to reduce your traffic to only the highest converting sources by eliminating poorly converting traffic sources. The problem with cheating at optimization like this is that your overall number of conversions will also drop, meaning you get less revenue. Remember, optimizing your website is all about improving your website for all sources of your traffic, so don't be tempted to cheat your conversion rate like this.

Next you need to set a target for this metric. However, first it's very important to realize that this overall website conversion rate will be unique to your website. It's often useless and problematic to compare it to other industry conversion rates and can set unrealistic goals (as you'll see in more detail toward the end of the week). Instead, just set a target to beat your current overall website conversion rate. Realistically, you should be able to beat your current rate by more than 2 or 3 percent over the next few months if you start to implement and test the best practices found through the rest of this book. While that may not sound a lot, that small increase can have a huge impact on increasing revenue for your online business.

And as discussed in the introduction to this week, while this is a very simple general barometer website performance metric, there are more revealing and more specific success metrics to help you optimize your overall website conversion rate. You'll learn how to use these success metrics during the rest of this week.

Wednesday: Check Your Repeat Visit Rate and Set a Target

Another basic and very important success metric to check is your website's repeat visit percentage rate. This identifies the number of your visitors that come back more than once in relation to the total number of visitors to your website.

The reason why this metric is so important to understand, monitor, and optimize is because the more your visitors come back to your website the better. This is because they are usually more engaged if they return, and as a result, they're usually more likely to convert for your conversion goals in the future, and usually convert quicker than first-time visitors do. Therefore, overall a high repeat visit is a great sign of an engaging, well-converting website.

It's also much cheaper to get visitors to come back to your website rather than generating new visitors for it. If you have a basic tool like Google Analytics, the best way to check your repeat visit rate on your website is to pull up the New vs. Returning Report, and simply look for the percentage of returning visitors metric. If you need to work this out manually in other tools that don't have this built-in report, you just need to find the number of repeat visitors to your website, divide that by the number of total visitors to your site in the same timeframe, and then multiply by 100 to get a percentage. Once you understand how to find your repeat visit percentage rate, log on to your analytics tool and find the last 90 days' average for your repeat visit rate. Jot this number down somewhere so you can refer to it later.

Next, you need to set a target of what you would like your repeat visit percentage to be. A realistic goal would be at least 20 percent, because most websites that don't do a good job of attracting repeat visitors would have less than 10 percent repeat visit rate. Remember though, just as with your overall website conversion rate, there is no perfect repeat visit rate—this will vary by your website type and what your unique value proposition is. The main thing is to increase your current repeat visitor rate, hopefully by at least 5–10 percentage points.

In Chapter 8 you will revisit this topic in much more detail and learn best practices to specifically help increase your repeat visit rate.

Thursday: Find Specific Success Metrics for Your Website Type and Benchmark

Rather than just relying on and focusing on improving your overall website conversion rate, today we are going to focus on finding multiple micro-level success metrics for your website. These much more granular metrics help you diagnose and measure your optimization efforts better.

This is crucial because if you only focus on one single conversion indicator, you are likely to be missing out on crucial insights that would help you optimize your website even further. For example, you may have a really high checkout completion rate, but this doesn't mean as much if your top entry pages have a really high bounce and you aren't managing to get very many people to your shopping cart, let alone try and convert them.

These success metrics are also very important to use when you start running tests to optimize your website. This is because in testing tools they are used as the main way to define and determine testing success for each test you run.

You should also realize that while there are many types of website success metrics, they also vary depending on the type of website that you have. For example, e-commerce websites are going to have much different success metrics than a community website. Therefore, you need to understand the key success metrics specific to the type of website you have, and begin monitoring them to understand the success of your optimization efforts.

These success metrics can be broken down into primary success metrics and secondary success metrics, depending on the importance of them to your website's primary business purpose, and you should ideally be working to improve your primary ones first.

In the following success metrics tables, find the website type that best matches yours, and note the key primary and secondary success metrics that you will need to benchmark and monitor. This will give you a great head start for understanding which success metrics you need to monitor and improve. Ideally, you want to try and improve each of the success metrics for your type of website, not just one or two of them (for reasons mentioned earlier).

E-commerce Website Success Metrics

These types of websites are ones that focus on selling single or multiple products (for example, Staples.com and Amazon.com).

Success Metric	Definition	Importance
Shopping Cart Abandonment Rate	Percentage of visitors who start but don't complete your shopping cart flow	Primary
Product Visits to Cart Additions	Percentage of visitors to product pages who add an item to their shopping cart	Primary
Products Per Order	Average number of products per order	Primary
Total Site Order Conversion Rate	Total number of orders ÷ total website visitors × 100	Primary
Profit Per Order	Average revenue per order – operating cost per order	Primary
Average Order Value	The average monetary value of an order	Secondary
Average Number of Visits until Purchase	The average number of visits it takes before someone orders a product	Secondary

Lead-Generation Website Success Metrics

These types of websites are ones that focus on generating leads like sales leads signups (for example, Cars.com and BankofAmerica.com).

Success Metric	Definition	Importance
Signup Form Completion Rate	Number of visitors who visit the signup form page and complete it	Primary
Total Site Lead Conversion Rate	Total number of leads ÷ total site visitors × 100	Primary
More Info Request Rate	Average number of visitors requesting more information (e.g., white papers, demos, guides, etc.) ÷ total visits × 100	Primary
Average Number of Leads Per Day	The average number of leads generated on your site per day	Secondary
Average Number of Visits until Lead Generated	The average number of visits it takes someone to sign up to your lead generation form	Secondary

Service Website Success Metrics

These types of websites are similar to an e-commerce website, but they focus on selling services instead of products and have different success metrics. Examples include Monster.com and ConstantContact.com.

Success Metric	Definition	Importance
Service Signup Flow Completion Rate	Percentage of users who start and complete your service order flow pages	Primary
Exit Rate for Your Service Signup Page	Visitors who leave your signup page without starting the signup process (exits ÷ visits × 100)	Primary
Total Site Service Signup Conversion Rate	Total number of signups ÷ total site visitors × 100	Primary
More Info Request Rate	Average number of visitors requesting more information (e.g., white papers, demos, guides, etc.) ÷ total visits × 100	Primary
Service Demo Video Interaction	Average number of visitors who complete watching your service demo video ÷ total visits × 100	Secondary
Average Number of Signups Per Day	The average number of signups on your site per day	Secondary
Average Number of Visits until Service Ordered	The average number of visits it takes someone to sign up to purchase your service	Secondary
Self-Service Support Completion Rate	The number of visitors who visit and successfully use the self-service FAQ and online help section.	Secondary

Media and Brand Website Success Metrics

These types of websites usually rely on advertising for revenue and often do not have any major success metrics; instead, they have many secondary success metrics that all combine to determine overall website success. Many of these success metrics are related to improving visitor engagement. Examples include Coke.com and ESPN.com.

Success Metric	Definition	Importance
Page Views Per Visit for Site or Site Sections	The average number of pages seen per visitor each time they visit	Secondary
Average Time Spent	The average time a visitor spends on your website	Secondary
Newsletter or RSS Feed Signup Rate	Newsletter or RSS signups ÷ total site visitors × 100	Secondary
Average Ad Revenue Per Page	The average amount of advertising revenue generated per page	Secondary
Average Ad Revenue Per Visitor	The average amount of advertising revenue generated per visitor	Secondary
Subscription Signup Rate	Total number of subscribers ÷ total site visitors × 100 (this could be for a magazine or premium content)	Secondary
Average Time Spent Watching Video	The average time that visitors spend watching videos on your website (good sign of engagement)	Secondary
Average Number of Comments Per Item	The average number of comments per article, photo, or video on your website (good sign of engagement)	Secondary
Average Usage of Refer-a-Friend and Social Tools	The average number of usages of refer-a-friend and social tools like Facebook and Twitter	Secondary

Community and Social Networking Website Success Metrics

These types of websites are ones that are heavily reliant on member signup and engagement (for example, LinkedIn.com and Facebook.com).

Success Metric	Definition	Importance
Average Number of New Registered Users Per Day	The number of new registered users per day on your website	Primary
Registration Form Completion Rate	Number of visitors who visit the registration form page and complete it (completions ÷ visits × 100)	Primary
Page Views Per Visit	The average number of pages seen per visitor each time they visit	Secondary
Average Time Spent	The average time a visitor spends on your website	Secondary
Average Number of Site Contributions Per User	The average number of contributions a visitor makes on your website (like comment or rate something)	Secondary
Average Usage of Refer-a-Friend and Social Tools	The average number of usages of refer-a-friend and social tools like Facebook and Twitter	Secondary

Blog Website Success Metrics

These types of websites usually rely on advertising for revenue and often do not have any major success metrics; instead, they have many secondary success metrics that all combine to determine overall website success. Examples of these are TechCrunch.com and ProBlogger.com.

Success Metric	Definition	Importance
Page Views Per Visit	The average number of pages seen per visitor each time they visit	Secondary
Average Time Spent	The average time a visitor spends on your website	Secondary
Newsletter or RSS Feed Signup Rate	Newsletter or RSS signups ÷ total site visitors × 100	Secondary
Average Ad Revenue Per Page	The average amount of advertising revenue generated per page	Secondary
Average Ad Revenue Per Visitor	The average amount of advertising revenue generated per visitor	Secondary
Average Number of Comments Per Article	The average number of comments per article, photo or video on your website (good sign of engagement)	Secondary
Average Usage of Refer-a-Friend and Social Tools	The average number of usages of refer-a-friend and social tools like Facebook and Twitter	Secondary

Additional Success Metrics to Monitor for Any Kind of Website

There are also several other good success metrics that you can use for any type of website. Here is a list of some that you can use:

- Bounce rate of your homepage (more on this in a later week)
- Task completion rate (more on this later in a later week)

- Exit rate of your top entry pages (more on this in a later week)
- Repeat visit rate (as discussed earlier this week)
- Lifetime value of visitors and conversions (for information on how to calculate this complex value, visit `http://blog.kissmetrics.com/how-to-calculate-lifetime-value`)

Friday: Set Targets for Your Success Metrics

After you have determined the success metrics for your type of website and benchmarked their current levels, you need to set targets for each of them. Realistic improvements of these should definitely be achievable after you have implemented the website optimization best practices and tests in this book.

However, you are probably looking for some guidance in what your conversion rate and success metrics should ideally be, and this is a common question in the website optimization world. Unfortunately, you won't find that in this book for one major reason.

This is because there is no "perfect" conversion rate or "perfect" number for your success metrics. These can vary hugely, not only by the type of website, but sometimes even for websites of the same type. It all depends on your website's business model and value proposition. For example, two websites may sell the same products, but one may place more value on getting registered users and marketing to them while the other may offer free shipping. Both of these value propositions can influence conversion rates and success metrics very differently.

And you shouldn't pay attention to or worry about what you read on optimization and analytics blogs that say you should have X percent or Y percent high conversion rate or specific success metric results. Such sweeping statements about what these should be are way too subjective and simplistic, and they can get you in trouble by influencing you to set unrealistic and unobtainable goals.

Instead, as mentioned earlier for other basic conversion metrics, the most important thing to focus on is to improve upon your current success metrics. Ideally, you should try and beat them by at least 10–20 percent, which should definitely be achievable after implementing and testing many of the best practices in this book. It's also very important to continually improve your conversion rates and success metrics even if you beat these initial targets. Another important thing to emphasize is that you should reward yourself and others involved for helping to achieve your success metric targets (and overall conversion rate targets). Even a simple gift certificate given to people who contributed to hitting targets can go a long way to building a better testing culture at your organization, which is a topic that will be discussed in more detail in week 4.

Week 3: Learn the Importance of and Set Up a Website Testing Tool

The next thing you need to do is to set up a website testing tool, because this is going to be one the most important tools to help you improve your website's conversion rates and success metrics. A testing tool will enable you to experiment with elements on your website and see what resonates with your visitors and converts them to your goals the most effectively. Without a testing tool, it will be hard to run effective, measurable tests on your website, and it will take you much longer to improve your conversion rates.

Monday: Understand the Importance of Having a Testing Tool

Today you will learn why it's so important to have a website testing tool in order to be successful with your optimization efforts.

Prior to the popularity of website testing tools, companies often did testing in an unofficial manner with no official tool. This was often done purely by just running one website version for a set period of time followed by running another version for another set period of time and then comparing the difference.

Unfortunately many website companies still do this and don't understand the many disadvantages of testing not using an official website testing tool. You will now learn the reasons why it's so important to use one.

First, there are several technical challenges if you try and test with no tool. For example, it is much harder to serve up the different versions of test content over the same time period without technical challenges or inconsistent visitor experiences. This gets significantly harder to do as soon as you start trying to segment and target your visitors with different content, which as you will learn about in Chapter 3, is an essential part of any successful optimization program. And if you just simply test two different variations one after the other, you will run into issues of potentially different sources and quality of traffic during those different test periods, affecting conversion rates and your ability to analyze the test effectively.

Second, without a testing tool it is very hard to run analysis on test results to discover a statistically significant winner, and determine the conversion lift over the default and other test versions. Without this statistical analysis of test version performance, often suboptimal winning tests get pushed live, and worse still can have a negative impact on conversion rates and the visitor experience. This functionality is built into all testing tools and enables you to make better and more accurate analysis of your test results and optimization efforts.

And last, without using a testing tool it is often going to be much riskier and costlier when developing and launching website changes, just in case it doesn't work as well as expected. Instead of doing this and hoping that the changes work well, testing using a tool helps mitigate these costs and risks. This is because using a testing tool gives you much more control over only testing specific elements of pages, lowering the percentage of traffic that you test, and makes it much easier and quicker to turn off a test if it is not doing very well.

Tuesday: Familiarize Yourself with the Available Website Testing Tools

With the recent rise in understanding the importance of website testing, there's been a huge growth in the number and diversity of website testing tools that are available, each with different costs and different benefits. This is great for online marketers and analysts who were previously stuck with only a few basic website testing tools, or had to rely on an in-house built tool.

There are three types of testing tools that you will now learn about, including the advantages and disadvantages of each.

Free Basic Testing Tools

Free testing tools have very limited functionality and very little support and consulting but are often very simple to use, so they are ideal for a company that is beginning down the website testing and optimization path. Currently there is only one major free website testing tool, Google Website Optimizer.

Google Website Optimizer (`www.google.com/websiteoptimizer`) This testing tool from Google has become very popular not only because it's free, but because it is simple to use and easy to set up, which is great for inexperienced testers. It is perfect for testing simple things like comparing the performance of two different page designs, or different images and buttons. The tool offers both A/B and multivariate test functionality, although it is somewhat limited (you will learn more about these types of tests later in the week).

This tool is also great because it requires little technical knowledge to use it, with just a few cut-and-paste scripts that you place on your website. The drawbacks of this tool are that it is limited in functionality and is better suited for websites that have specific conventional goals like product purchase or lead capture, because it is hard to test nonconventional goals or multiple goals simultaneously. Other limitations of the tool are that there are no segmentation or targeting capabilities, the reporting runs a day behind so you can't access latest test results in real time, and you can't import sales data into it to measure revenue lift inside the tool.

One of the biggest drawbacks is that there is no support or consulting to help with test implementation or test strategy, with most users having to use third-party providers to get this help. Overall though, this tool is certainly a great place to dip your toe in the optimization waters and hopefully build some good results and a case for a tool with more functionality.

Mid-level Testing Tools

These mid-grade testing tools are perfect for an online business that wants expanded features of its testing tool, without considerable expense. Most of the tools are aimed at marketing executives who value the ability to simply and visually create tests.

Optimizely (`www.optimizely.com`) This is a newer testing tool that is a step up from Google Website Optimizer in terms of its feature set. This tool is perfect for markets and designers who like tools with visual editors, because it has a great visual interface that allows you to easily design tests. Another benefit of this tool is that it allows you to easily implement tests on your website with minimal technical changes needed. You simply make the visual changes and then add some simple code on the pages that you want to test, and the tool takes care of everything else for you, including running the test and reporting on it.

Service plans are fairly low cost, and generally based on how much traffic your tests get, also offer extra functionality at the higher service levels. Plans start at $19 for the basic level and features, all the way up to $400 per month for sites with high traffic and users who want all the advanced features.

Visual Website Optimizer (`www.visualwebsiteoptimizer.com`) This is another great visual design tool that lets you actually design tests based on your current pages, by rearranging and making edits to your pages using a simple to use WYSIWYG editor. It then gives you simple tags to place on your website for the version you just visually created, and then it begins showing the test variations to your visitors and running the test. Figure 2.6 illustrates some of the visual design capabilities of this tool.

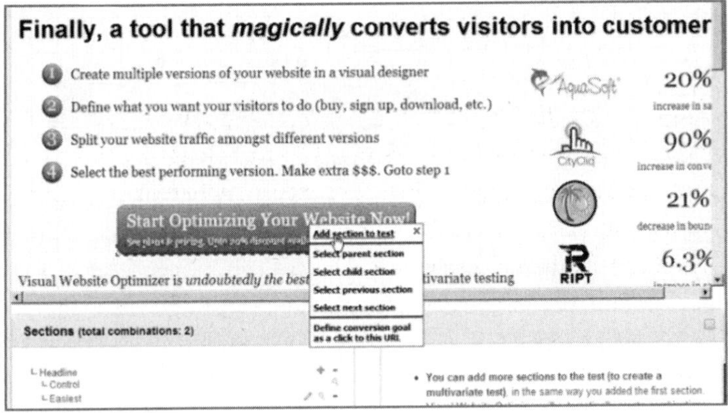

Figure 2.6 Screenshot of Visual Website Optimizer

It also offers click maps for when you want to see what your visitors are clicking on during your tests and basic visitor segmentation. This tool is very easy to use for someone who is new to testing and is relatively cheap with plans starting at $49 per month.

Overall, this tool is definitely worth checking out as a better alternative to Google Website Optimizer.

Unbounce (`www.unbounce.com`) This testing tool is particularly valuable and unique. Unbounce allows you to create and test new web pages, rather than test your existing pages like most other testing tools do. Unbounce lets you easily create your own pages (called landing pages) from a library of landing page templates that have built-in website optimization best practices (as shown in Figure 2.7). It then allows you to test different elements and even hosts them for you on their web servers. All you have to do is send traffic to these new pages to start testing and converting your visitors.

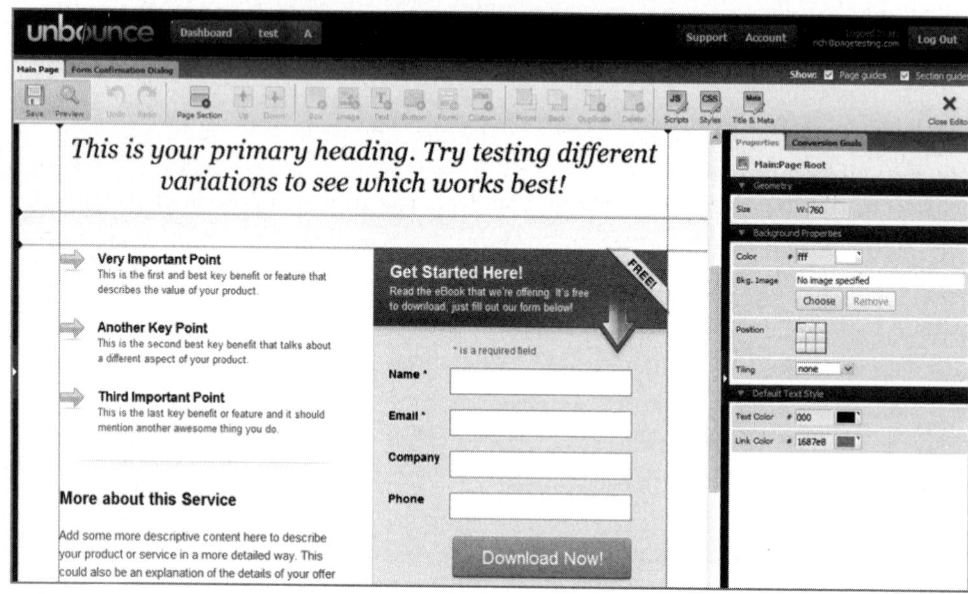

Figure 2.7 Screenshot of Unbounce

This tool is particularly ideal if you are selling single products or services that have a lead generation form and want to test and optimize them. It is also well-suited to creating and testing paid search landing pages. A great benefit of this tool is that it requires no knowledge of programming code to create the landing page and run the tests and is much quicker to set up than any other testing tool. It's also fairly cheap to use.

Enterprise Testing Tools

These testing tools offer advanced functionality and flexibility as well as full support and consulting to help with test implementation and test strategy. However, because of these advanced features, these tools can often be very expensive and many companies will need to build a case for needing these tools (more on this subject in Chapter 3).

Adobe Test&Target (`www.omniture.com/en/products/conversion/testandtarget`) This tool is considered by many to have the most functionality of all website testing tools. As the tool name suggests, in addition to offering testing functionality, this tool also offers great visitor targeting capabilities to target groups of your visitors and show them more relevant content. This usually increases the chance of them engaging and converting on your website. This tool also features the great ability to automate which best-performing content to show to your visitors, thus taking a lot of the manual work out of pushing winners live to various groups of your visitors.

This tool also integrates well with Adobe's SiteCatalyst web analytics tool. This enables you to perform more in-depth test analysis if needed in SiteCatalyst, and to use any advanced visitor segments from SiteCatalyst to better segment and target your tests.

You can also use the tool to help optimize and test your other online channels, including banner advertising on other websites and your email campaigns.

Support and consulting is great with this tool, and Adobe also offers a full-service testing agency that does everything for you, from test strategy to test implementation, called Adobe Digital (which is great for plugging any testing resource or experience gaps that you will learn about in Chapter 3).

Autonomy Optimost (`www.optimost.com`) This tool is considered the other major enterprise testing website tool and is gaining rapid market share. It offers very similar functionality to the Adobe Test&Target tool, although it doesn't offer as many targeting capabilities, and its integrated analytics offering doesn't compare to the functionality of integrating Test&Target with Adobe SiteCatalyst.

It does have some unique selling points, particularly its ability to easily create and test landing pages for paid search and email marketing purposes, and its strong banner ad testing capabilities. It also has a relatively simple implementation in comparison to other enterprise offerings, with an easy to set up single line of code able to test multiple pages elements.

Optimost also comes with great consulting services to help with test implementation and strategy, and it also offers a full-service approach to your testing that will do everything for you, including test strategy and test implementation.

SiteSpect (`www.sitespect.com`) This enterprise testing tool has a very unique website testing proposition that can often help remove technical barriers to implementing a testing tool (a common issue). This is because this tool actually runs behind the scenes and not directly on your website and requires no actual code on your website to test. This means that once you have set it up once, it is very easy to perform tests anywhere on your website. However, some organizations find it hard to work with their unique style of implementation, because it requires all your traffic to flow through their platform first in order to serve up the tests.

This tool has a strong and unique feature to help optimize your mobile website offerings and a great feature to help speed up your website performance, thus helping to increase engagement and conversions. However, this tool lacks some of the advanced testing functionality of Optimost and Test&Target. In particular, it lacks good targeting capabilities, and it doesn't offer any in-house website analytics features. Overall, this tool is worth considering though, particularly if you have complicated technical issues that limit your ability to add test code to your website.

Monetate (`www.monetate.com`) This enterprise testing tool is particularly great for e-commerce websites. It has a great built-in recommendations engine, advanced personalization and targeting services, and a built-in CRM system and merchandising feature that allows you to test and optimize product placement. All of those features are essential for fully optimizing e-commerce websites. However, because it has so many diverse features, the testing capabilities aren't as sophisticated as some of the other leading enterprise testing tools.

This tool also prides itself on its great easy-to-use interface, which is ideal for online marketers. Also, it requires very little technical work to make this tool work on your website, with just a simple code snippet needed for your website to use all their features. Overall, this testing tool is definitely worth considering if you have an e-commerce website.

Wednesday: Determine a Budget and Understand Possible Technical Barriers for Tool Selection

Today you are going to learn about two essential things that you need to do before you actually choose a website testing tool. First, you need to try and determine a testing budget so you know which of the testing tools you can afford, and then you need to understand potential technical issues and barriers that may influence your tool selection.

Build a Case for a Good Testing Tool Budget

The more testing budget you can obtain, the better testing tool you can start using, and the better results you will get from your testing and optimization efforts.

You will often need to build a case to senior management to obtain a higher amount of testing budget, and the best way to do this is to create a short presentation to review with them. In order to make this presentation most effective, it should highlight the anticipated return on investment from using the testing tool in the first year, the potential higher conversion rates, and most importantly for these senior level staff, the associated increase in revenue from these improved conversion rates (even presuming a basic 2-percent lift will usually get some great increases in revenue).

Your presentation should also highlight potential pages for testing on your website, particularly ones associated with key conversion flows such as your shopping cart or signup pages. Including screenshots of page issues and reports showing pages with high bounce rates will help too. Ideally though, you should wait until you read this whole book and gather test ideas from it to put in your presentation.

If you have trouble convincing senior management of this in your first attempt, then you could try getting help from an external consultant to analyze your website for potential tests and bring them in to make a presentation. Senior management are quite often more likely to trust and believe an expert from a testing and optimization company as opposed to someone within the company who has a vested interest in this project.

Use Case Studies to Help Build a Case for More Budget

One simple way to build a case for more testing budget is by looking for and presenting testing case studies from companies in the same industry as yours. You can find some good testing case studies at `www.ABtests.com`, `www.marketingsherpa.com`, and `www.marketingexperiments.com`. You can also obtain case studies from any of the testing tool vendors that you just learned about, and there are also examples that you can use from website optimization firms like WiderFunnel and ElasticPath.

Another strong case that you should make is to start with at least a mid-level testing tool. This is because even though Google Website Optimizer is great and free, you will soon outgrow that tool's limited functionality, which means you will have to implement and learn another tool, which can be costly.

Last, it's important to remember to allocate at least 50 percent of your testing budget toward obtaining testing personnel. Without trained power users who know how to make best use of the tool and what to test, you will be wasting money on the advanced functionality of enterprise level tools, because you won't know how to use them effectively.

Understand Technical Barriers for Tool Selection

Other than determining a good budget for your web analytics tool, the most important thing to consider is the potential technical barriers when trying to use your testing tool. This is because one of the biggest obstacles to an effective testing program is an internal one, and this is your information technology (IT) department. They often have the power to quash any plans that involve making extensive frequent changes to your website, which of course is needed for any long-term testing plan.

The best way to help reduce the potential negative impact of an uncooperative IT department is to involve them early on in your plan for testing, particularly when choosing and implementing a testing tool.

First, you should share with them the presentation that you gave to senior management, so they can understand the reasons why you are trying to run tests. You should then find someone in the IT department to help you evangelize your testing efforts to senior IT members; ideally someone who is well respected in that department and fairly senior.

Next, you need to work with them to understand how much effort is needed to technically deploy the testing tool programming code that is necessary to begin testing on your website. As previously mentioned, the technical requirements can vary between the tools, and some are easier to work with than others.

Another thing you should work on with your IT team is picking a testing tool that can integrate well with your website platform and CMS (content management system).

Technical Warning Signs and Barriers to Overcome

There are also numerous internal technical and IT warning signs that you need to address early. If left unresolved, these issues can severely hinder your ability to test quickly and effectively and may even hamper your ability to implement a testing tool and make it work.

- Long website release cycles that will prevent you from adding new code for test elements on pages in a frequent manner. Ideally, you should have at least a couple of website release versions per month, not a couple per year.
- Old legacy website and CRM platforms that are hard to integrate testing code into. I suggest you make a case for upgrading the platform, or try testing on pages that are not housed on old platforms (such as paid search landing pages that can be hosted on separate platforms).
- Areas of the website that IT claims are technically off-limits for testing. The IT department often has sacred grounds on the website where they don't let anyone test, and these should be overcome early on. Gaining buy-in and advocates from the IT department is a great way to try and overcome this.

Once you have armed yourself with the information and help you need to decide on a testing tool, pull the trigger and start the service with your chosen tool. Tomorrow, you're going to implement your tool and set up a test campaign.

Thursday: Implement Your Testing Tool, Setup, and QA Test Campaigns

The next thing you need to do is to actually work with your tech department to implement your testing tool and make sure it is set up correctly and working as expected. If you have chosen a more expensive and robust tool, you will also need to get consultant assistance from the testing tool vendor to help you set up the tool and first campaigns. As discussed yesterday, you may have to try and overcome some challenges when trying to add the code to your website.

The first thing you usually need to do is to log on to your testing tool and set up a dummy test campaign that involves changing something very simple, such as an image or some text. Don't forget to give your test a good name that describes your test, because a good naming convention is important when reviewing current and historical tests.

Most website testing tools have a fairly good intuitive user interface that actually steps you through this test creation process, including helping you specify the variations of the page elements that you want to test.

Once you have created this first test in the tool, the tool will usually inform you of the JavaScript code that you need to place on your website in order to run the test. This usually involves placing at least three different pieces of code on your web pages. The first is a small JavaScript snippet that references an external file for your overall test settings and acts as the main controller of the test. This code usually goes in the head section of your website pages. You can think of this code as a traffic cop who decides which traffic participates in the test and which doesn't, depending on whether it meets the test's requirements and rules or not.

The second type of code that you need to install are scripts that determine which elements of your web page content you want to test, such as headlines, buttons, or images. For example, in Google Website Optimizer, these code elements are called *sections*, and in Adobe Test&Target, they are called *mBoxes*.

The third and last code script that you need to add to your website is the conversion script on your web page that defines success for your test (for example, a "thank you for registering" page). This conversion script triggers whenever someone participating in the test sees this conversion goal page and is essential for determining which tests are performing the best. Therefore, it is critical that you add this last part of test code to your website.

Next you need to perform QA (quality assurance) on your dummy test campaign to see whether it is working as expected and not breaking anything. Performing this QA can be quite a long and laborious task, so you should get help from your IT department to do this.

QA efforts should include checking the test on all the major browsers (currently Internet Explorer, Firefox, and Chrome) as well as on mobile platforms.

You will also need to make your testing tool work on a QA server because this enables you to test and check your tests without the risk of your visitors seeing any issues that might arise. One of the more common issues to look for is called *flicker*, which is when a page loads first, and then the content changes seconds later to show the alternate test version.

Friday: Understand Web Testing Tool Terminology, Concepts, and Reports

After you have selected your tool and have it up and running successfully, there are some key terms, concepts, and reports that you will need to understand before embarking on your testing and optimization journey.

The Difference between A/B Testing and Multivariate Testing

The two most common website tests are A/B tests and multivariate tests. It is important that you understand the differences between these tests, their advantages and disadvantages, and when to use each type of test. The core difference between these testing approaches is that multivariate tests allow you to test multiple elements simultaneously with much greater ease and speed than using an A/B test.

A/B Testing

A/B tests are the simplest type of website test and are usually the easiest to set up. As a result of this, many people new to website testing will learn and use these first. This basic form of testing can be run in any testing tool, regardless of the level of the tool.

Here are the pros and cons of using A/B tests for your optimization efforts:

Pros These types of tests are ideal for people with little testing expertise and for simple tests when you want to test only thing per page at a time or for comparing performance of two different page variations. They are also ideal for running a basic follow-up test to see if the winning elements of a multivariate test actually beat the control version (more on this best practice in a later week). Due to these tests usually being less complicated, they require less traffic than a multivariate test to gain significant test results and determine a winner.

Cons If you test a completely new page that contains different elements (such as a different headline, image, and/or call-to-action) against the current version, you won't be able to determine which elements of the new page caused the most influence in conversion. This is because these tests only measure the whole page performance and not the individual parts of the page. By doing this, you also potentially risk pushing an element that actually has a slight negative impact on conversion. It also takes a lot longer to test many elements per page, because each page element ideally requires a separate A/B test to be set up for it.

Most online marketers start off using this more basic form of testing before evolving into needing more complex testing types like multivariate tests (which are described next). Figure 2.8 shows an example of two different styles of pages being tested against each other in an A/B test, with different layouts of modules, banners, and images.

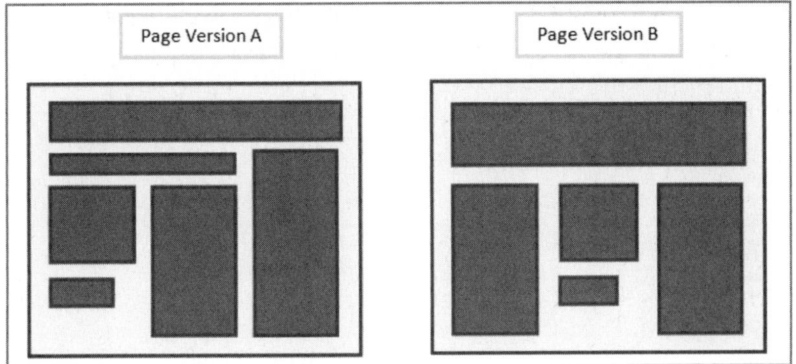

Figure 2.8 Example of two different A/B test pages

Multivariate Testing

Multivariate tests (MVT) are designed to allow you to test many page elements simultaneously with greater speed and ease.

To help you test potentially hundreds of different combinations of elements for multivariate tests more quickly, most testing tools use the Taguchi statistical method (also known as fractional factorial testing) to come up with a representative sample of test content combinations, rather than having to test each combination.

Some tools like Google Website Optimizer actually test all the different combinations of elements simultaneously (called full factorial testing), but this takes significantly higher amounts of traffic and longer periods to get significant test results. Some tools actually give you the option to test using both of these types of multivariate methodology.

Here are the pros and cons of using MVT for your optimization efforts:

Pros These tests are great for testing many elements at the same time on a page or over a series of pages. The other main advantage of these tests is that they can determine which elements contributed most to helping increase conversion, thus helping you understand what page elements to test in the future (called test iteration, which you'll learn more about in Chapter 3).

Cons Because of the many different test combinations needed, multivariate tests are usually based on sample (fractional factorial) combinations of test versions (recipes), which can lead to you potentially missing out on the best combination of elements winning. Some experts even doubt the validity of testing using fractional factorial methods, but luckily there are some ways to overcome this that you will learn about in Chapter 3. Another issue is that higher levels of traffic are often needed than A/B tests to get a result, particularly if you are testing more than four elements at once per page.

Figure 2.9 shows two different recipes of page elements (annotated with different letter versions for each module) on one page that can be tested simultaneously in a multivariate test to find the best-performing combination of elements.

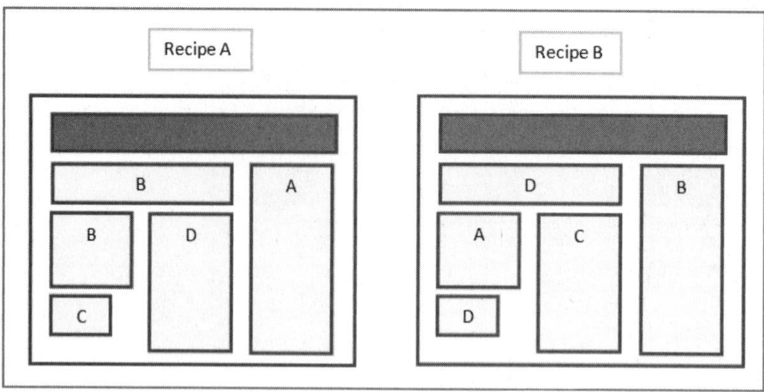

Figure 2.9 Examples of multivariate test recipes for one page

The Control or Default Content and Challenger Versions

Everything that you test on your website needs to be tested against what is currently being shown on your website. This original version of your content is called the *control* or *default* content, and this is pitted and tested against a *challenger* content variation of it to see which performs better for conversion. For example, if you are testing a signup button on your website, the version that is currently on your website is the control version, and the versions that you want to test against it are the challenger versions.

Don't Tweak Your Control Version before Testing against It

You always need to make sure you aren't modifying the original version before you test anything against it. Some testers make the mistake of jumping the gun by making small tweaks and improvements to the control version before actually testing it against other challenger versions. This can be problematic, because you may be making a bad tweak without realizing it and artificially skew the lift of the challengers higher, or if you do a very good tweak, you may limit the possible conversion lift from the test challengers and risk a sub-par test result.

Page Sections, Offers, mBoxes, and Similar Test Elements

These are the names for the actual elements and sections of your website that get tested. In your website testing tool, you create names for each of the elements on your page that you want to test—for example, a product image, a submit button, or a headline.

When setting up the names of these test elements on your pages, it's important that you use good naming conventions. This makes it much easier to analyze a test, particularly one that has many elements being tested at once (such as a complex multivariate test). It also helps you understand what was tested previously when you're looking back at historical tests.

A good naming convention to use for a test element would be `PageName_ElementName`, or `SiteName_PageName_ElementName` if you are testing multiple websites simultaneously. Using underscores between words as shown here helps make the names easier to read.

Here are a few examples of good naming conventions:

`Product_image`

`Product_banner`

`Homepage_slider`

`SiteX_Homepage_slider` (when you're testing multiple sites simultaneously)

Recipe or Experience

These testing terms are found in multivariate tests, and both basically mean the same thing. Each recipe or experience contains different variations of each of the elements you are testing, and your multivariate test will contain several of these (depending on how many elements and variations you are testing)

When you set up a multivariate test using the Taguchi method, the tool automatically creates a representative set of recipes (or experiences) and tells you which element variations you need to place in each recipe. Here is an example of two recipes:

```
Recipe 1 contains banner version B, with image C, with headline E
Recipe 2 contains banner version C, with image A, with headline B
```

Depending on how many elements you are testing per page, and how many variations of each element you are testing, this will result in a different number of recipes (or experiences) that the tool has to automatically create for testing. In Chapter 3 you will learn more about best practices for creating recipes that will get you results quicker.

Test Results Reporting Terms

To help you understand your website test results, this section defines a few of the most common terms and how to interpret them.

Conversion Lift or Observed Improvement

This is one of the key things you need to understand when analyzing the performance of your tests. The term *conversion lift* is usually found in most test results reports and is an indicator of which test versions (or recipes) gained lift over the original version you are testing against. In Google Website Optimizer, this is referred to as *observed improvement.*

This conversion lift is usually displayed in the form of a percentage to indicate the strength of the conversion lift over the original (or default) content.

In advanced testing tools, you can configure which success metric this conversion lift is based on. For example you can change it from "products ordered" to "average order value," and you will often get different results depending on what success metric you are using to define conversion lift.

You will learn how to interpret conversion lift results in much more detail in Chapter 3.

Confidence

Another key term you need to understand in your test results reports is *confidence.* As each test version (or recipe) gathers visits and conversions on your website, the tool begins to determine whether enough statistical significance data has been gathered to make the data valid; in other words, whether there is enough confidence that the result is valid. This is important because some test versions may get high conversion lift, but not enough supporting data has come through yet to determine statistical significance, and therefore, the confidence level regarding the accuracy of the test result is low.

This confidence level is visually shown in different ways depending on what testing tool you use. Usually, it is shown on a report as a color graphic (such as a bar chart), with green indicating confidence and red (or no color) indicating no confidence.

Ideally, you want to pick a winner that has high confidence (80 percent confidence in the least); otherwise, you may end up pushing something live that will actually lower your conversion rates in the long run. Figure 2.10 illustrates how confidence is shown in the Adobe Test&Target testing tool.

Experience	Visitors	Conversion Rate	Lift	Confidence	AOV	RPV	Sales	Engagement
Campaign	100.00% (22,861)	3.94% (900)	---	---	$0.00	$0.00	$0.00	0.00 (0.00)
Experience A [CONTROL]	11.06% (2,528)	3.36% (85)	---	---	$0.00	$0.00	$0.00	0.00 (0.00)
Experience B push winner	11.07% (2,530)	4.62% (117)	37.54%		$0.00	$0.00	$0.00	0.00 (0.00)
Experience C	11.25% (2,573)	3.69% (95)	9.81%		$0.00	$0.00	$0.00	0.00 (0.00)
Experience D	10.99% (2,513)	4.10% (103)	21.90%		$0.00	$0.00	$0.00	0.00 (0.00)
Experience E	11.17% (2,553)	3.49% (89)	3.68%		$0.00	$0.00	$0.00	0.00 (0.00)
Experience F	11.39% (2,603)	3.76% (98)	11.97%		$0.00	$0.00	$0.00	0.00 (0.00)
Experience G	11.05% (2,525)	4.32% (109)	28.39%		$0.00	$0.00	$0.00	0.00 (0.00)
Experience H	11.11% (2,540)	3.94% (100)	17.09%		$0.00	$0.00	$0.00	0.00 (0.00)
Experience I	10.92% (2,496)	4.17% (104)	23.92%		$0.00	$0.00	$0.00	0.00 (0.00)

Note: Report data may be delayed by up to 4 minutes.Audit data is only available for 4 weeks. We recommend using the auditreport API to automatically retrieve data on a weekly basis.

Figure 2.10 Confidence column in Test&Target

Element Contribution or Relevance Rating Reports

This is a common report for multivariate tests that you should look at to understand which elements of your test most impacted conversion rates. The Element Contribution or Relevance Rating Report helps in that it shows you all of the test elements broken down separately, thus enabling you to see which of your test elements had the greatest single impact on conversion rates. It also shows the confidence level of the influence for each element. Figure 2.11 shows an example of this element contribution report in Test&Target, which highlights the "predicted best experience" for each element being tested.

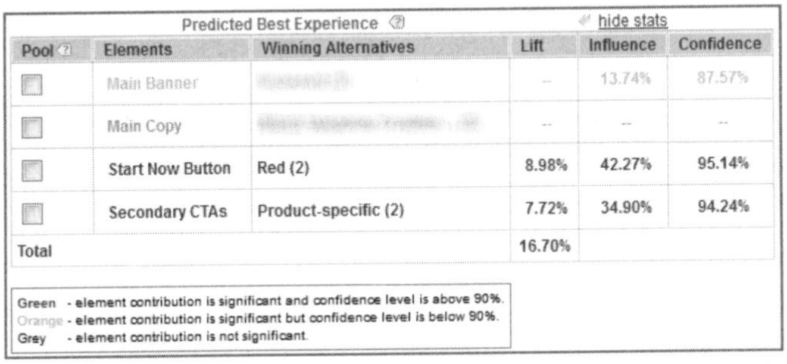

Predicted Best Experience				hide stats	
Pool	Elements	Winning Alternatives	Lift	Influence	Confidence
☐	Main Banner	[illegible]	--	13.74%	87.57%
☐	Main Copy	[illegible]	--	--	--
☐	Start Now Button	Red (2)	8.98%	42.27%	95.14%
☐	Secondary CTAs	Product-specific (2)	7.72%	34.90%	94.24%
Total			16.70%		

Green - element contribution is significant and confidence level is above 90%.
Orange - element contribution is significant but confidence level is below 90%.
Grey - element contribution is not significant.

Figure 2.11 Element Contribution Report in Test&Target

The main use of this report is to understand which of the page elements in your multivariate test would be good candidates for further testing to improve your conversion rates even further (iteration-based testing). You will learn more about this and all best practices for testing in Chapter 3.

Lay the Foundations for Optimization Success

Before you begin to optimize and test your website, first you should realize that it's not going to be as easy you might expect. You need much more than just tools—to help improve your chances of optimization success you need to understand and leverage website optimization and testing fundamentals. In this chapter you will learn these, in particular how to build an optimization organization and some great testing best practices.

3

Chapter Contents

Week 4: Learn Key Optimization Fundamentals to Help You Succeed

Now that you have set up analytics and testing tools, and checked success metrics and set targets, you may be eager to get started and apply the best practices you will find throughout the rest of this book. Unfortunately, when you begin to apply these, you are more than likely going to come up against some challenges and barriers within your company preventing you from quickly and easily running tests and making changes on your website to optimize it.

It's essential that you break down these barriers and foster a website optimization culture; otherwise, your website optimization efforts and ability to test are going to be severely compromised. This week you will learn some key fundamentals to help you do this, including how to build a great testing culture and strategy. At the end of the week, you will learn how to evaluate whether you should outsource some or all of your optimization efforts to a third-party vendor.

Monday: Identify Your Company's Current Website Optimization Performance

Before you go any further in this book, you first need to understand your company's current optimization and testing efforts, and then understand how they compare to companies using best practices. This will help you understand how much potential you have to improve your current testing and optimization efforts. Today you will evaluate this by using a website optimization checklist and a typical website optimization maturity lifecycle.

The Website Optimization Checklist

In order to start evaluating your current website optimization efforts, you first need to identify how your company currently performs. Begin by answering the checklist of questions in Table 3.1. The more questions you can answer "Yes" (and please be honest about your or your company's efforts), the more advanced your website current optimization efforts are.

▶ **Table 3.1** Website optimization checklist

	Question	Yes	No
1	Does your company currently run more than one test per month?		
2	Does your company use a better website testing tool than Google Website Optimizer?		
3	Does your company have more than two staff members dedicated to testing?		
4	Do you have a website optimization executive sponsor to help you gain budget and buy-in from key stakeholders?		
5	Does it take your company less than two weeks to get a test prioritized?		
6	Does it take your company less than two weeks to implement a test?		
7	Does your company act on test results and do follow-up tests to improve conversion lifts (iteration tests)?		
8	Does your company use your web analytics tool to generate insights for testing?		

▶ **Table 3.1** Website optimization checklist *(Continued)*

	Question	Yes	No
9	Does your company make use of any visual analysis tools to gain visitor insight, particularly for ideas for testing?		
10	Does your company use usability and feedback tools to gain visitor insight, particularly for task rate completion analysis?		
11	Has your company created key use cases for your website?		
12	Does your website make use of multiple social proof elements like reviews and testimonials?		
13	Does your company use targeting for your testing to improve your visitors' experience and conversion rates?		
14	Does your company have a test plan and strategy for at least the next six months?		
15	Has your company tried testing your key conversion flows such as checkout pages?		
16	Has your company tested your key entry pages?		
17	Has your company tested your call-to-action buttons?		
18	Has your company tested your headlines and other text?		
19	Has your company tested your email marketing campaigns?		
20	Has your company set up and tested a mobile version of your website?		

If you answered fewer than 5 questions with a yes, you have huge room for improvement in your optimization efforts. If you answered between 5 and 10 questions with a yes, you are well on your way to a good optimization start, but you still have plenty to learn. If you answered more than 15 questions with a yes, then your company is already in a great position to become a world-class website optimization organization. We will revisit this checklist in the last chapter to see how much your efforts have improved.

The Website Optimization Maturity Lifecycle

Now that you have used the checklist to understand your current optimization efforts, you need to evaluate how well your efforts compare to companies achieving an expert level of optimization.

To help you do this, Table 3.2 on the next page describes a typical website optimization maturity lifecycle that companies should evolve through to become expert at optimization. In this lifecycle, there are four main phases of optimization maturity listed as columns, with each phase consisting of nine rows of optimization elements and requirements (that you will learn all about in detail throughout the rest of this book). To reach the final expert optimization phase, you need to make sure you are fulfilling each requirement. This last stage is considered website optimization nirvana, because you are going to be armed with all the best practices, foundations, and tools necessary to continually optimize your website to its full potential.

Table 3.2 Website optimization maturity lifecycle

	Phase 1 – Rudimentary Optimization	Phase 2 – Basic Optimization	Phase 3 – Maturing Optimization	Phase 4 – Expert Optimization (Website Optimization Nirvana)
Level of Analytics Used for Optimization	Little use of analytics for optimization, with no segments or goals being used, and little analysis and poor performing pages. Little understanding of success metrics and which ones to use.	Better use of analytics to understand page performance of limited goals and segments set up. Limited success metrics being used, but mainly high level conversion rates.	Medium level use of analytics insights to form test and page optimization ideas, including multiple segments and goals set up and used. Multiple success metrics understood and tested against.	Maximum usage, with all test ideas driven by analytics insight. Full use of advanced analytics to look for conversion influencing and problematic pages and flows.
Type of Testing Tool Used for Optimization	No official tool used, or using in house or basic tool like Google Website Optimizer.	Testing done with at least a basic level tool like Google Website Optimizer and a targeting tool.	Testing and targeting with at least a mid-range tool (like Visual Website Optimizer), ideally an enterprise level tool.	Testing and targeting done with enterprise tool like Adobe Test&Target or Autonomy Optimost.
Types of Tests Run for Optimization, and Strategy	Few simple and random A/B tests with little impact. No testing strategy or understanding of the need for one.	Growing success with A/B tests and multivariate tests, but still with limited targeting or impact. Test ideas and optimization strategy begins to be created.	Better success with many concurrent multivariate and A/B tests and good use of targeting. Good short-term strategy developed with good test plans.	Sophisticated, high impact targeted tests based on insight and iteration. Long term testing strategy created. Nothing launches without gathering user feedback and being tested first.
Optimization and Testing Best Practices	Limited optimization best practices used or understood.	Using basic best practices on calls-to-action, images, and headlines. Use cases created, and unique value proposition is created or improved.	Strong understanding and usage of optimization and test best practices for many page types, and usability best practices well applied.	Advanced best practices used, including social proof, mobile, and email optimization.
Other Tools Used to Gain Insight & Lift Conversions	No other tools used, other than possibly limited visual analysis tools. Little understanding of need to use others or what should be used.	Good usage of visual tools and limited use of survey tools. Growing understanding of need to gather more visitor insights.	Several other tools now being used, now including usability tools (like Usertesting.com and Loop11.com). Learning best practices to use them.	All major tool types being used including retargeting tools, with advanced best practices used in all of them.
Internal Optimization Resources	Very limited, with no dedicated optimization resources, usually split across many people.	Limited but growing, now with at least one dedicated testing person. Limited help and resources though.	Strong, growing dedicated testing team (at least three members and executive sponsor) with improved level of resources available.	Dedicated full team (with all key roles) and full testing resources available in all departments needed.
Organization Buy-in for Optimization	Limited, with little understanding of benefit or ROI of optimization, with problematic HiPPOs and many barriers preventing effective testing.	Limited, but growing buy-in, mostly sporadic across departments, with several departmental barriers still existing.	Widespread across departments, with most big barriers broken down, but still lack of adequate senior management buy-in.	Full buy-in and support from all departments and senior management. All major barriers to optimization gone.
Company Process & Communication for Optimization	Testing not a part of company regular process, with limited attempts at communication and reviews.	Minimal integration into process, but basic communication and reviews about optimization efforts begin to occur.	Good integration into regular process occurring, with email updates and monthly meetings to discuss results, and using test tracking documents.	Full integration into company process, with good use of weekly and quarterly review meetings, brainstorming sessions, and shared space to store all testing documents.

Unfortunately, it isn't easy to get to the nirvana phase, and it can often take at least a year to arrive at this phase, depending on the scale and complexity of barriers and challenges within your online business. Indeed, with a lack of strategic help, many companies never even make it out of phase 2.

Many of you reading this book are likely to be in the beginning stages of website optimization, and therefore your company may only have elements of phases 1 and 2 at this point. Some companies may have many of the elements of phase 3, particularly ones relating to testing best practices, but many will be lacking the organizational and analytical elements, along with other essential tools to gain insight and improve conversion rates.

This lifecycle is also good to show your senior management and key stakeholders to make them understand what is need to be most successful when optimizing your website.

It's also important to understand how you will likely go about doing this optimization. If you have a small company, with less than 10 people, it's likely that you are going to be doing much of the optimization work yourself or hire outside help. But if you have a mid-size or large organization, you will need to help evolve it into and use an organization that lives and breathes website optimization, called the "optimization organization." Unfortunately, doing this is a huge uphill battle for many businesses—in fact, this is often where most companies fail in their website optimization efforts. To help you avoid this common pitfall, Week 5 is devoted entirely to creating an optimization organization and the benefits of doing so.

Tuesday: Evangelize and Create an Analytics and Optimization Culture

In order to increase the chances of your website optimization efforts being effective in the long run, the next thing you need to do is start building an analytics and testing culture into your organization. Most importantly, this will help you gain understanding and buy-in from key stakeholders, break down internal optimization barriers, and obtain the internal resources necessary to conduct your optimization efforts.

Report Regularly on Key Success Metrics and Goals

The first thing you need to do is make sure your analytics and success metrics are commonly available across your company and updated in the form of a one page report. Most importantly this should contain the performance of your website success metrics that you set up in Chapter 2.

Ideally, this report should be distributed via email on a weekly automated basis to all the members of your online company, and then stored in a shared online document storage place for anyone to access.

The goal of such reports is to provide insight and recommendations based on current overall website performance and to ensure that all the members of your company know what your success metrics are and the performance of them.

You should also include some commentary, recommendations, and insights each week at the top of the report. This helps readers interpret what your metrics are revealing, without them having to study the report and risk their jumping to incorrect conclusions.

At least every month, you also need to do a metrics and optimization review presentation for your company (or at least with your key stakeholders if the company is a large one). At this presentation, you should discuss your website's latest performance in comparison to the same period last year and last month, and then based on that, suggest recommendations and test ideas to help optimize it.

Run Regular Training Sessions

Web analytics and testing aren't easily understood by everyone, especially in departmental areas where members are more focused on the creative or technical aspects of the website. Unfortunately, if your company doesn't understand the importance of analytics and testing, it's going to be difficult for you to get them to buy-in to website optimization.

To help address these issues, you should provide regular website optimization training for all the departments across your company. This training should include the following:

- Monthly internal training sessions on success metrics and how they relate to website optimization efforts, with key ways to try and influence them. Ideally, this should be mandatory for all new employees.
- External training from industry specialists and experts on website optimization topics and new tools, given to all analytics and optimization team members.
- Brown bag training sessions over lunch to discuss specific analytics and optimization topics. This would be for a department-wide audience and should be more informal and not mandatory.
- Website optimization and analytics conferences and online training; for example, the conferences called eMetrics (`www.emetrics.org`) and Conversion Conference (`www.conversionconference.com`), and the training from MarketMotive (`www.MarketMotive.com`). These should be mandatory for all analytics and optimization team members to attend and complete.

Give Regular Company-wide Presentations

Another great way to build a testing and optimization culture is to give presentations about this topic and to help evangelize the importance of it. These presentations should be made to all departments in your company, and ideally should be done every month (or at least quarterly).

In the initial stages of your optimization efforts, you will need to discuss the performance of your website's current success metrics, your plans to test and optimize, and the potential impact on conversions and revenue. You should also present case studies from the industry that your website is in. These case studies should show the positive impact that website testing and optimization can have on your website.

Then as your optimization efforts grow, these meetings will need to focus on and communicate the results of recent tests and give updates on overall strategy and progress made.

Run Contests for Your Tests

Another great way to help build a testing and optimization culture and involve more people in testing is to run internal company-wide contests relating to your tests. Here are two ideas for contests:

- Ask people to submit their test ideas, and the person who submits a test that results in the highest improvement would win the contest.
- Show upcoming test versions and ask people to pick which version will win. The person who picks the most winning versions would win the contest.

You should even offer a small prize to the winners (such as an Amazon gift certificate), which can go a long way toward building a good testing culture.

Seek Out Company Influencers

Another great way to help evangelize and promote your website optimization efforts is to enlist influential members of your organization to help you do so. An ideal candidate for this would be someone fairly senior who is well-respected in your organization and has good communication skills.

After you have identified possible prospects, you should propose to meet each of them for lunch or after work so you can socialize and present your website optimization cause and plans to them. Offering free lunch or dinner to discuss this with them often works wonders.

Incentivize Your Team Based on Conversion Rate Improvements

Money is one of the biggest motivators to get someone to do anything. Therefore, to help drive the efforts of members of your optimization and testing team even further, you should consider changing your compensation model for these members so that they get bonuses based on reaching higher conversion levels. This could be in the form of tiered levels, meaning that they would get a higher bonus for each level of higher conversion rate reached—for example, a 10 percent bonus if they grow conversion by 10 percent.

Offering these monetary incentives is a great alternative way to drive your team even harder to improve your conversion rates. Therefore, if you manage an optimization and testing team you should try implementing this, or if you don't, work with your boss and human resources department to get this done for your testers and analysts.

Wednesday: Prepare a Better Initial Website Optimization Strategy

The next thing you need to do is understand how to prepare an initial optimization strategy for your website. Having this strategy is going to be critical, not only to help determine what to test and optimize, but also to help build the optimization organization in the following week. If you don't have a solid plan and strategy in place, it will be very hard to gain any buy-in from senior stakeholders and actually get much testing and optimization done.

Of course, you could do some ad hoc testing with no real strategy and get some limited results, but in order to really be effective at optimization in the long term, you need to prepare and stick to a long-term strategy.

Ultimately, to be more successful with your testing and optimization efforts you need to use a better initial optimization strategy. You will now learn several good approaches and best practices to help you form this.

Familiarize Yourself with the Test Idea and Test Results Tracking Documents

Rather than simply creating a long, unorganized list of test ideas for your website optimization strategy, you need to use a better approach. This involves using a test idea tracker document that allows you to state key details for each proposed test, including the hypothesis of your tests, a description, and location of the tests on your website. You also need to include ratings in terms of the difficulty of implementation and likely conversion lift value of each proposed test, using a rating system of 1–10 (with 1 being the lowest and 10 the highest). It is also best to organize your test ideas by area of your website—for example, tests for your top entry pages, product pages, and home page.

The test details and ratings in this tracker document will be essential for helping you and your senior executives and project management prioritize the order of your upcoming tests, and improve your optimization strategy.

This document is called the "Test Idea Tracker," and you can find it in Appendix B as well as on this book's companion website. I suggest that you download and print this out now so you can start filling it in as you go through the book. Here is the URL:

```
www.sybex.com/go/websiteoptimizationhour/test-idea-tracker.pdf
```

Next, you need to start tracking your test results by using another tracking document. In this document, for each test that you have run you need to include high-level test details, the impact on your relevant test success metric (percentage change) and what you have learned from running it, including insights gained from segmenting and targeting.

The details in this tracker will then help play a critical role in helping you iterate on your test results and improving your future test plan and optimization strategy.

This is called the "Test Results Tracker," and you can find this in Appendix C and also on this book's companion website. I suggest that you download and print this out now for when you start getting test results in. Here is the URL:

```
www.sybex.com/go/websiteoptimizationhour/test-results-tracker.pdf
```

Don't worry about trying to complete both of these templates yet, as you need to read through the rest of the book first to review the ideas and best practices for optimizing your website. This day is more about helping you kickstart your test strategy and helping you understand how to document and track ideas for helping optimize your website.

Look for "Low-Hanging Fruit" to Test First

While you are reviewing the ideas for tests in this book, there is a simple strategy to use that will help you build some good test results quicker. This effective strategy is to note the test ideas that are likely to be easier and quicker to implement that also have good potential for increasing conversion rates and success metrics. This is often known as looking for "low-hanging fruit," because you are in a sense expending the least amount of effort initially while still getting some good results. This is important because these quick testing wins will help you build a case for further budget and resources to improve your optimization plan.

Choosing these low-hanging fruit test ideas should require less technical, design, and marketing resources; therefore, they should be easier to implement. Some of the test ideas in this book, particularly simple text and call-to-action changes, may not even require any design help or resources at all, so they're particularly good candidates.

Often you can even go "under the radar" and unofficially run these low-hanging fruit tests and implement these tests yourself, or with the unofficial assistance of an empathetic web developer that you might be able to find. This can be risky if things go wrong and your efforts get discovered, because it may minimize your chances of gaining trust and buy-in from stakeholders (a topic that will be covered in more detail in Week 5).

Consider Initially Outsourcing to Gain Quick Wins

Another approach to consider is to initially outsource some of your testing efforts. This is a particularly good option if you are having trouble obtaining internal resources and expertise to help you test (often this can take time and be expensive to hire all at once). There are many website optimization companies that will help you fill in these gaps, before you eventually obtain the resources internally to do this testing in-house. You'll learn more about this outsourcing at the end of this week.

After Creating Your List of Test Ideas, Start Prioritizing the List and a Calendar of Tests

Earlier this week, you learned you need to create a list of ideas to test on your website. After you have gone through this book and created this list, you then need to return to this section and prioritize which tests you want to run first and start creating a test calendar. This will help form a big piece of your optimization strategy.

While you are prioritizing your test ideas, you should pay particular attention to the ratings you gave each test for difficulty of implementation and estimated conversion lift value. If possible, you should also consult with a project manager to get a more realistic idea of how difficult each test would be to implement. This is known as getting a *level of effort* (LOE), and your project manager can work with your IT department to gather this information for you.

Next, you need to come up with some potential launch dates for each of your proposed tests, and try to plan out at least three months' worth of tests in advance. Depending on how fast you can launch tests, this should be at least three tests per month. Companies that use an optimization organization can easily run 10–20 tests per month.

After you have done this you need to create a detailed test plan for each of your proposed tests. You will learn more about this tomorrow because these are going to be critical for you to gain test buy-in and prioritization from key stakeholders.

Once your tests have been prioritized by project management for launch, you should create a testing calendar that stores details of launch dates, and what part of the website they are on. This is important to keep tabs on which tests are going live and where, and it is critical to share this with other departments so they are aware (particularly so that the IT department doesn't make changes on a page when a test is on it and impact the running of it).

Thursday: Create Detailed Test Plans

To improve your website optimization efforts, it's extremely important that you create detailed test plans. These enable you to flesh out important details for each test and are key to enable you and stakeholders to approve and prioritize test launches.

Putting this extra detail into your test plans will mean you will run tests more efficiently and be able to learn more from the results of them. You should create one test plan per test, and it should be in the form of a PowerPoint, Word, or PDF document. During the remainder of this day, you'll learn what you need to put in an effective test plan.

Essential Elements for Better Test Plans

To make better test plans you first need to make sure your test plans contain essential elements, metrics, and details. Here are the most essential ones to include:

Hypothesis and Insight for the Test List the hypothesis and insight that led you to think of each test. This will help others understand your reasons and logic for each test. No test should be run without knowing and listing this, and you will learn more about this in Week 6.

The Web Page Locations of the Test List all pages on your website that the test will be initially run on.

The Test Audience: Percentage of Traffic to Be Tested and Sources State the percentage of traffic that will be involved in each test, and list the visitor segments that will see the test if it won't be shown to all visitors (more on this in Week 6).

How You Will Measure What Determines Test Success You should always state the success metrics that you will use to measure success for the test and try and limit this to two or three (always try to include revenue if relevant).

Likely Difficulty of Implementation You should include how hard it will likely be to implement the test (using a rating of 1–10, with 1 being the least difficult and 10 being the most difficult). This should come from your test idea tracker as discussed earlier.

Likely Degree of Positive Test Impact Include the estimated impact on your success metrics for each test (using a rating of 1–10, with 1 being the least likely positive impact and 10 being the most likely positive impact). This should also come from your test idea tracker as discussed earlier.

Visitor Segments and Target Content Needed for the Test List any visitor segments you want to analyze in your results, as well as the segments that you want to target different content to (more on this in Week 6).

List of Page Elements to Be Tested List all the page elements that would be involved in your test. Ideally, this should be in the form of a screenshot with annotations listing the elements to be tested.

List of Proposed Test Variations for Each Element List all the proposed test variations for each module you are testing. This should in the very least a verbal description of what they are, and ideally they should be visually mocked up (which will be discussed shortly).

The Results of the Test Your test plan should include a results page, with the conversion lifts and the key "learnings" to be filled in after the test has ended. This way, in the future you can reference older test results in more detail. This will also help you when you are creating future test plans, because you will be able to refer to these results to determine what worked well and what didn't.

Use Wireframing Tools to Create Better Mockups in Your Test Plans

To help convey your test ideas better in your test plans, and increase the chances of approval, you should also try and create a visual mockup of your pages, elements, and variations being tested. A great free wireframing tool that you can use to help with this is called MockFlow (`www.mockflow.com`). This tool allows you to quickly and easily create wireframes using a variety of existing page elements. Figure 3.1 shows a wireframe example of the YouTube.com website created using this tool.

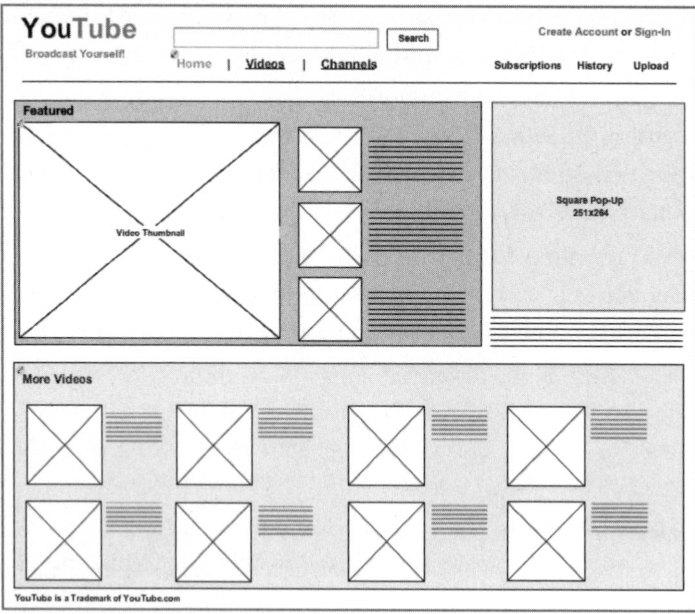

Figure 3.1 Example of a wireframe from the MockFlow tool

Friday: Consider Test Outsourcing—When and Why

The last important consideration you need to evaluate this week is whether you should outsource any or all of your testing and optimization efforts to a third-party vendor.

Because of the growing interest in website optimization, there are now several optimization companies that specialize in testing and optimizing websites. Many of these companies offer complete full-service solutions, including full-test creative services in addition to strategy and test implementation.

Although this is usually a more expensive way of doing testing, it can often bring some great expertise and fantastic results that you might not be able to achieve as easily by conducting in-house testing, particularly in the beginning when you may not have good testing resources or expertise available to your company yet. Indeed, many large companies completely outsource part or all off their website testing efforts, particularly companies that are savvy enough to dedicate considerable budget for testing and optimizing their website.

Major Reasons to Outsource

To help you determine whether to outsource some or all of your optimization efforts, here are the major reasons for doing so:

To overcome large bureaucratic company issues One of the most important reasons for considering outsourcing is if you work for a large bureaucratic company and are experiencing many ingrained barriers and obstacles for getting website optimization done effectively and efficiently. Outsourcing your efforts often removes many of these obstacles and helps you run much more frequent tests and achieve better long-term optimization success.

To overcome small company inefficiency issues Smaller companies that have very limited resources and personnel will often find it hard to allocate the necessary time and resources to effectively run a good website optimization program. In many small companies, employees already have varied and numerous job responsibilities and don't have much time to take on additional testing functions.

To learn from and collaborate with experts If you are completely new to website optimization and don't feel comfortable with using testing tools and implementing the best practices in this book by yourself, then you should consider outsourcing to learn from and collaborate with experts at optimization vendors. After you have built up some expertise and experience, you can consider bringing your efforts back in-house and creating an optimization organization (which you'll learn about in more detail next week).

To do effective testing in a much quicker timeframe Website testing and optimization can be a lengthy process, particularly if your company is small and would have to hire the necessary resources to conduct the tests. To ramp up to full-scale testing more quickly, many companies consider outsourcing initially until they can gain the necessary resources and budget to bring their website testing back in-house.

Pitfalls of Outsourcing

On the flip side, there are some distinct disadvantages of outsourcing your website optimization efforts. Here are three of the most common pitfalls:

Outsourcing is often very expensive. Depending on what optimization vendor you work with, outsourcing can be very expensive due to the many hours that the company's consultants will have to spend on your website.

You lose some or all control over your testing program. While you are often in great expert hands when outsourcing your optimization efforts, you should expect to lose some control and influence in your test program and strategy. However, if your own internal testing strategies do not seem to be working very well initially, this may be the best alternative.

Consultants are not as close to your business as you are. Another drawback of outsourcing is that third party consultants will find it harder to understand all the more complex and unique aspects of your online business. This will often take them a considerable amount of learning and mind share to obtain and use this knowledge to help improve optimization and test strategies and ideas for your website.

Examples of Website Optimization Companies to Outsource To

While website optimization companies aren't as common as web design or search engine optimization (SEO companies), they are now starting to gain in popularity. Over the last few years, several have appeared across the world, particularly in the U.S.

market where optimization is more mature. These companies vary in their offerings, with some focusing on testing strategies and others offering full-service capabilities such as test creation and implementation.

Here are some website testing and optimization companies for you to look up and evaluate that can help with your optimization efforts:

- Adobe Digital (United States)
- SiteTuners (United States)
- Wider Funnel (North America)
- Elastic Path (North America)
- Ion Interactive (United States)
- Future Now (United States)
- Closed Loop Marketing (United States)
- EightByEight (United States)
- Conversion Voodoo (United States)
- Conversion Works (United Kingdom)
- Conversion Rate Experts (United Kingdom)

In addition to these, the more robust and expensive testing tools like Adobe Test&Target or Autonomy Optimost also have their own consultants that specialize in assisting with the creation and implementation of test strategies that you can outsource some or all of your testing efforts to.

Another option for you to consider is finding a web agency that has a good optimization and testing division. There are many of these agencies, and some of them have very competitive pricing models. A few good ones to consider are ZAAZ and Razorfish.

Questions to Ask Potential Optimization Vendors

To make sure that you will get the best results from outsourcing your website optimization efforts, you should ask potential vendors the following questions:

What is your pricing model? Not only can costs vary, but the pricing model can also vary significantly by vendor. Some vendors charge by the number of tests run per month, some charge by the number of consulting hours required to implement your tests, and some charge based on a percentage of revenue generated from the tests. Depending on the complexity of your website, or the number of tests you think you can do per year, the pricing model can have a big impact on the cost of your testing efforts.

Do you have full-service or specialized offerings? Some vendors offer complete full-service test options that cover all elements of a testing program, including test strategy, design and implementation, whereas some optimization vendors don't actually help run the tests for you and are more focused on the strategy and test planning. Depending on what resources you have available internally, you should evaluate different options.

How involved do you get with our internal organization? Depending on which vendor you choose, the level of interaction and involvement with your company can vary. Some vendors have a more hands-on role and are usually present and contribute in key internal meetings, while other vendors take a more "back-seat" approach and have less frequent touch points. It is always good to know this upfront, because some companies prefer minimal contact and others prefer a much higher amount of hand-holding and interaction.

In general though, I strongly suggest you try running at least some initial testing efforts in-house first. This will at least give you some working knowledge and understanding of testing, and will allow for a more fruitful partnership with an optimization vendor if you later decide to go down that path.

Week 5: Understand and Create an Optimization Organization

In order to increase your chances of having an effective long-term website optimization program, much more is needed than just having a good website testing tool. Along with knowledge and usage of a good testing strategy and testing best practices, it is essential that you also help breed an *optimization organization* that increases your chance of success. This type of organization that lives and breathes testing and optimization and is often essential for the following three major reasons:

1. It reduces common internal barriers and obstacles to testing, thus enabling much greater testing efficiency.
2. It enables much higher frequency and concurrency of tests per month, instead of only being able to run just a few tests per month.
3. Ultimately, it leads to far greater positive impact on conversion rates and return on testing investment.

Sure, you can do some limited testing and optimization on your website without having a full optimization organization in place, and in fact, some small companies won't even need all aspects of this. But if you work for a medium- to large-sized company, this week will be one of the most critical to read, understand, and implement. This is because the larger the company, the more potential there is for website optimization efforts to fail, due to factors such as problematic bureaucracy and slow website change process. Therefore, through the rest of this week, you will learn the key factors that make up an optimization organization and how to begin building one.

Monday: Find an Executive Sponsor for Your Optimization Efforts

One of the most important things to help you build an optimization organization is to find an executive sponsor to help with your efforts in the future.

This isn't a full-time role; instead, it is more of a support function that someone in senior management takes on as part of their regular responsibilities. An executive sponsor doesn't actually do any of the actual optimization work or strategizing, and although their role is fairly small, they can have a huge positive influence on the overall effectiveness of a website.

An optimization executive sponsor will have several key tasks to perform. You must make sure that potential candidates for this role understand and will be able to carry out the following responsibilities:

- Be able to influence senior stakeholders such as CEOs, CTOs, and CMOs and have strong relationships with them.
- Help prioritize testing efforts at the senior level.
- Champion the benefits of testing and optimization to senior stakeholders.
- Help influence and determine budget and resources for optimization.
- Help break down internal silos and barriers to improve optimization efforts.
- Help evangelize the benefits of optimization across the whole company.

An ideal executive sponsor would be a senior executive from the marketing or the IT department. This is particularly beneficial because of the large role these departments will play in your optimization efforts, which will make it easier to gain buy-in from the key stakeholders in these departments (which will be discussed in more detail tomorrow).

In order to find an executive sponsor, you should do some networking to determine which senior staff members are familiar with the basics of testing and optimization and the potential benefits of it. Once you have found a potential candidate, take them out for lunch and explain what you are trying to do in terms of optimizing, and how they can help.

Last, depending on your seniority at your company, you may even be able to take on this role yourself. This would give you even greater ability to promote your website optimization efforts; however, you need to make sure you have strong relationships with senior stakeholders in order to do this job effectively.

Tuesday: Gain Buy-in from Key Stakeholders

After you have found your potential executive sponsor (or sponsors), you need to gain buy-in from key stakeholders in your organization in order to increase the chances of optimization success. This is because they usually hold the keys to decision making and prioritization and often control the budget and resources you need to effectively test and optimize your website. Without buy-in from them, it will make it that much harder to begin adequate website optimization efforts and severely hamper your ability to optimize your website conversion rates and success metrics in the long run.

Today, you will learn some best practices to help you gain this all important buy-in from key stakeholders.

Forge Optimization Relationships and Break Down Barriers with Key Departmental Stakeholders

It's important to realize that it's very hard to run effective website tests without gaining buy-in and resources from many different departments. Gaining this will make it much easier to gain approval for your tests from senior management who unfortunately often have the authority to end your testing program, sometimes even before it begins.

It is particularly important to gain buy-in from the IT department to help you, because without approval from them, you can't even implement and launch a website test or new testing tool, let alone be successful with it. Hopefully, by now you already have started to gain buy-in from the IT department using the methods outlined in Chapter 2.

You also need buy-in from the design and marketing departments to help you create the different versions of page elements in your tests. Often getting a "no" from just one of these departments can bring your testing efforts grinding to a halt.

The best way to forge these relationships is to reach out and explain your plans and goals to each of these departments and to make sure you involve them from the start. You should also always mention the potential high impact on revenue for the business. Once you have done that, you should look for testing advocates within each of these departments to help you gain buy-in from their corresponding department leaders.

If you work for a particularly large company, don't forget about forging positive relationships with the legal team too, because they can often have the highest authority to say "no" when reviewing proposed changes to your website and can turn your best call-to-action test plans into boring stale copy that loses the interest of your visitors and greatly limits your potential to convert them.

You should also forge relationships with brand guardians, because they are also notoriously hard to work with at large companies and often don't like to do any testing that involves changes to core brand messaging. An idea to help overcome resistance from them is to suggest running a test that relates to the brand, but only test a small percentage of the traffic. This way only relatively few people will see this test involving brand, and hopefully gain some good test results to prove brand guardians wrong.

If you continue to get little joy from the legal or branding team, you should communicate these issues higher up the command chain and get senior executives to try and influence them. This is why it is essential to have an executive sponsor help you when you run into issues like this that require senior management influence and power.

Always Mention the Potential Impact on Revenue and Profits from Testing

To help gain buy-in it's important to remember to inform your boss and senior management about the impact that your tests and optimization will have on revenue and profit. For example, you always need to mention that "If I test and optimize *X*, it will gain *Y* additional revenue and profit." Don't just mention that you will improve conversion rates either, because they may not fully understand what the true impact of that is. Mentioning a potential increase in revenue and profit will be music to their ears and help open the door to an effective website optimization program for your website.

You should also convey the overall impact on ROI and revenue that having an optimization organization in place will have. Generally, because of the increased ability to test more frequently with better results on ROI each time, it's definitely possible to achieve over 100 percent ROI in the long run, which if you invested $100,000 in optimization would equal an additional $100,000 ROI.

Table 3.3 highlights this by comparing results from a company that's in Phase 1 of the website maturity lifecycle to the results of a company that's in Phase 4 (the most advanced phase, as discussed in Week 4).

▶ **Table 3.3** Example of higher revenue

	Testing at Phase 1—Rudimentary Optimization *[With only one test expert, limited resources, and no testing best practices, org buy-in, or process]*	Testing at Phase 4—Expert Optimization *[With testing team, dedicated resources, best practices, full org buy-in, and integrated process]*
Number of tests per year	Less than 12 (one per month)	Over 50 (at least one per week)
Time taken for approval and to gain resources per test	One month	Less than one week
Length each test takes to implement	One month	Less than one week
Average ROI impact of each test	Low	High
Combined ROI of all tests on revenue	0–10%	50–100% or more
Monetary ROI impact on $100,000	10% ROI equals $10,000	100% ROI equals $100,000

Another good way to convey potential profit from testing is to show particular visitor segments that are not converting as high as the visitor average for your website, and work out the revenue that would be made if these poorly performing segments were optimized and matched the average on your website.

Show Evidence and Case Studies That Your Competitors Are Effectively Optimizing Their Websites

To help increase the chances of gaining buy-in, you should find which of your competitors are already doing testing and optimization. This way you can prove that your company may be losing competitive advantage by not doing optimization (by saying something like, "Our biggest competitors are doing it, so it must be a good thing, and we should do it too"). As discussed in the last chapter, there are several good places to find case studies in order to prove how well they are doing with their testing efforts. Many optimization vendors also have great case studies that are quick and free to use to help you highlight this.

To get more competitor evidence, you could also try networking with competing companies to see if they are testing and what their results have been so far (although some might be reluctant to divulge this).

Make a Formal Presentation to Key Stakeholders Outlining Your Strategy

Back in Chapter 2, while trying to determine a budget for your testing tool, you made a presentation to senior stakeholders. Now is a great time to revisit and update that with your next steps and plans and have another follow-up presentation. You should reiterate some of the great candidates for testing, and as just discussed, don't forget to mention the potential impact on revenue and profit.

You should also present the results from the 20-question optimization checklist from last week to make sure your senior stakeholders understand how the website is currently performing, in addition to showing them where your company currently stands in the website optimization lifecycle, and what needs to be in place to achieve expert website optimization (aka optimization nirvana).

Arm Yourself with Tips to Overcome Objections from Your HiPPOs

The HiPPOs (Highest Paid Person's Opinion) in your organization will likely be senior management like CEOs, CTOs, or senior marketing directors, and often create major barriers to successful website optimization efforts. Unfortunately, problematic ones often demand things tested that they want, or worse still, sometimes don't even allow testing on something if they have a strong opinion about it. Allowing HiPPOs to make website decisions regardless of any visitor insights or data that claim the opposite often has damaging implications to the conversion rates of your website.

To help overcome these issues and convince them to let you do more testing, you should always mention the following things to them:

- The potential impact of testing on revenue (as just discussed)
- That no-one is right 100% of the time, only your website visitors
- There isn't just one correct version of your website - it needs multiple variations to meet the varying needs of your visitors better.

You should also use web analytics data to support your reasoning for testing, and show them metrics highlighting problematic exit rates or poor conversion flows.

HiPPOs also often have website optimization objections based on the fear of negative potential impact of tests if they don't go well. If this is the case, you should assure them that you will test on low traffic pages first or test low percentages of your traffic.

To help you gain some broader ideas to influence them, I strongly suggest you read these two excellent books:

Influence: The Psychology of Persuasion [HarperCollins Publishers, 1998] by Robert Cialdiani

How to Win Friends and Influence People [Simon and Schuster, 1936] by Dale Carnegie

What to Do if Your Senior Stakeholders Are Not Seeing Value

Lastly, it's important to know what to do if your key stakeholders don't see value in your website optimization efforts or plans. In order to counteract this, the first thing you need to do is identify the true source of who is raising the objection and their real motivation. Often this may not be immediately clear, or shrouded by some hidden agenda. Often one resistor among senior stakeholders is enough to cause unrest and problems when trying to do long-term testing, so it's important to address their issues.

Once you have found the source and the reason, you can try and hone in on this. Set up a meeting with them (over lunch is a great way) and have a friendly discussion about why they aren't seeing value and try and counter their reasons.

Often they may not just see the true value, so reiterate some of the benefits of optimization and the potential impact on revenue. If that doesn't work, try and get them more involved with your testing so that they can take some of the credit when things go well.

If senior stakeholders are preventing you from running a first test, as a last resort you could go "under the radar" to run unofficially, using a developer's help. You could even exclude internal office IP addresses from your test so that stakeholders don't see it. Once you have got some good results, take them to stakeholders who aren't seeing value. This approach is risky though, and you have to be very sure that the test is going to have a great impact on revenue.

Wednesday: Assemble a Dedicated Optimization Team

Unfortunately, as noted in the introduction to this book, website optimization is often neglected and misunderstood by companies. As a result, testing and optimization efforts are usually an afterthought and are assigned as part-time responsibilities to just one or two people, usually in the marketing or analytics team. Even if the company is progressive in terms of its website optimization efforts, there is often just one full-time dedicated optimization expert.

This unfortunately has the effect of immediately hampering your potential website optimization efforts, because there is a lack of the time and knowledge that are needed for a good optimization program. Soon the limited number of employees dedicated to optimization will become bogged down with office politics and a lack of resources available, forever chasing and hounding other employees just to gain a few hours of assistance.

Indeed, even with the greatest of test plans and full support from key stakeholders, your website testing and optimization efforts are going to be limited at best if you don't have the correct team and skill set devoted to it. This lack of resources actually remains the biggest barrier to raising conversion rates, according to the "RedEye Conversion Rate Optimization Report 2011" by Econsultancy.

You also shouldn't try to be a hero and do website optimization on your own and in a silo, because at best, you will have mediocre results, and at worst, you will damage your long-term hopes of website optimization. While this may give you some initial quick wins, starting off the wrong way and getting bad results can have a long-term negative effect on senior management's opinion of website testing, damaging your chances of gaining optimization team members in the future.

Therefore, before you go any further with your testing and optimization efforts and strategy, you need to discuss building a great optimization and testing team with your boss and the necessary key stakeholders. Here are the ideal members of a successful website optimization team or department, ranked in order of importance:

1: Executive sponsor As discussed earlier, this is the person who plays a key role in helping obtain resources and communicating strategy and results at a senior level. They also will help get your tests prioritized and approved at a senior level. This person usually has a main job title in addition to this role.

2: Optimization manager This team member is a senior testing expert who helps to determine what to test, overall optimization strategy, and analysis of results. This role is often played by an online marketing manager, senior web analyst, or web project manager, and therefore these are good candidates for this position.

3: Testing power user This team member is a testing expert who helps execute the testing plan within the tool and the analysis of results. They report to the optimization manager and work closely with all other departments to ensure success. At smaller companies, this role is covered by the optimization manager. Many of these members often come from an analytics background.

4: Web developer This team member is a programmer in the IT department who is proficient with technical aspects of the testing tool and is dedicated to implementing website tests and to helping perform quality assurance (QA) on them. Ideally, this person should be dedicated to the optimization team and not be a shared resource and at least have a dotted line relationship to the optimization manager, if not directly report to them.

5: Marketing lead This team member is a marketing expert in the marketing team who focuses on creating different copy and calls-to-action for website tests. Ideally this person should be dedicated to the optimization team and not a shared resource and at least have a dotted line relationship to the optimization manager, if not directly report to them.

6: Web designer This team member is a web designer who focuses on the creation of the visual test variations needed to ensure a consistent look and feel on the website during test. Again, ideally this person should be also be dedicated to the optimization team and not a shared resource and at least have a dotted line relationship to the optimization manager, if not directly report to them.

There are actually a further two optional team members to help ensure even greater optimization and testing success:

7: User experience expert This person helps to improve visual test designs to ensure usability and, if used, can really help bring great incremental results.

8: QA expert This person helps to make sure website tests are implemented correctly, allowing the web developer to free up time to focus on the implementation aspects instead of also doing QA.

Ideally these website optimization team members should all be contained within one independent group or form part of a larger analytics and optimization group. To help illustrate this, the following figures show a couple of examples of where these teams would sit in a hierarchy. Figure 3.2 shows a centralized team that sits under a director of analytics and optimization, which often works very well. Figure 3.3 shows a decentralized dedicated team with key members continuing to report to their corresponding departments.

While it may sound expensive and daunting to build such a large optimization team, there are some things you can do to help build this team more efficiently.

First, you should try finding people who intially can handle more than one role. For example, try finding a web analytics expert who also knows the basics of website testing. The website optimization best practices that you will learn in this book may give you enough knowledge to effectively take on two roles yourself and kickstart your optimization efforts while you're looking for other dedicated website optimization team members.

Remember though, unless you have a very small company, in the long term you need at least one person in each role to ensure success. Don't try and cut corners by permanently assigning one person multiple roles of the testing team, because this may short circuit your long-term testing plans and foster a "good-enough" mentality in your company.

Finally, you shouldn't go in to meetings with your senior stakeholders with all guns firing and immediately request all these team members before you have even started your first website test or created a website strategy. You will have a far greater chance of succeeding if you wait to request these resources after you have gotten some good optimization results and built up a good case for them.

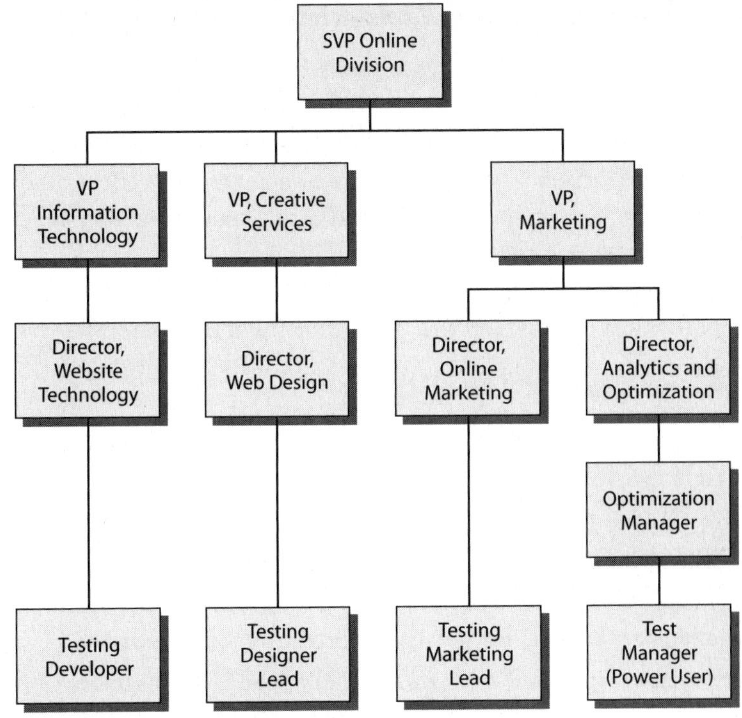

Figure 3.2 Centralized optimization team org structure

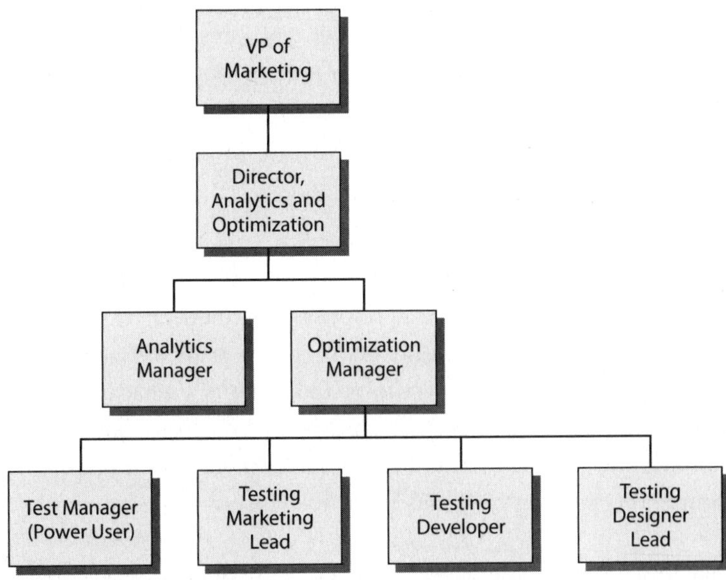

Figure 3.3 Decentralized optimization team org structure

Thursday: Integrate Testing and Optimization Web Processes into Your Company

One of the most important parts of trying to form a successful optimization organization is to integrate testing and optimization into your company's everyday functions. If your company doesn't have adequate processes or checklists to help embrace and push through website optimization efforts in a timely and efficient manner, your efforts and results are going to be limited at best, at worst negatively affecting your conversion rates.

Today, you will learn about this and begin doing it. While this may seem daunting, it will ensure that everyone in your company understands when website optimization strategy and efforts are most needed, and that your efforts will run smoothly.

Create an Optimization Checklist for New/Updated Website Content

All too often, an inconsistent method is used when a company launches new content or a new web design with a failure to adhere to a good process or checklist.

To help reduce the number of issues caused by this lack of process, here is an example of a website optimization and testing checklist you should run through when you are about to launch or update any content on your website:

1. Have objectives and goals been set for the new website content or update?
2. Have the website visitors' input and feedback been obtained (using usability studies and feedback tools)?
3. Are there test plans for the content as soon as it launches to improve conversions?
4. Has full QA been performed on the analytics and testing code?
5. Has the marketing team been fully involved with the test content creation?
6. Has the web design and user experience team been fully involved with the test content creation?

Understand and Use a Better Optimization and Testing Process

Next, you need to audit and improve your company's current process for website optimization. This is essential because an effective, continually used optimization and testing process is critical for long term optimization success. To get a better understanding of how this currently works at your company, I suggest you meet with all departments currently involved with your testing and optimization efforts and document what you find.

You will probably often find that the process is lacking in many areas, which causes lack of understanding and potential breakdown in communications and ultimately compromises your ability to effectively and efficiently run a testing and optimization program.

After you have determined your company's current process, you need to learn what steps are essential to help improve it and make it more efficient.

Here is an example of a process that will help ensure that your website optimization efforts are most likely to succeed in your company:

Step 1: Meet with key stakeholders to review proposed new content or updates.

Step 2: Define success metrics and goals of proposed new content.

Step 3: Conduct pre-launch usability and eye-tracking tests.

Step 4: Identify possible elements to test post-launch and document these in your test plans.

Step 5: Launch and gather insight from web analytics and feedback tools.

Step 6: Create and launch tests based on insights gained and previous test plans.

Step 7: Propose making changes (optimization) to content based on results of tests.

These steps form part of a continual circular process, with Step 8 leading back around to Step 1. This helps you to iterate and improve on your tests to better optimize your website. It also essentially means that you should continually be optimizing and testing your website and that your website should never be considered finished or perfect—there is always room for improvement.

Figure 3.4 is a graphical illustration of this important flow.

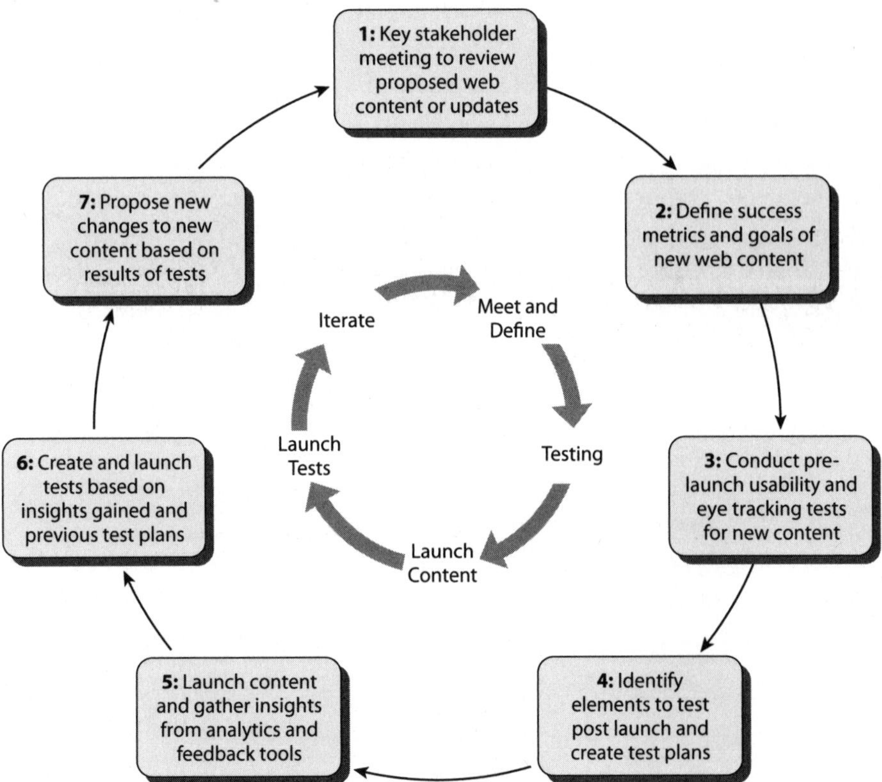

Figure 3.4 Website optimization and testing process flow

Once you have started to implement this process, you need to get continual feedback from all involved departments so you can iron out any kinks and make improvements to it. The best way to get this feedback is to run regular optimization meetings, which you will learn about tomorrow.

Improve Your Project Management Process to Help Optimization Efforts

Many companies still struggle with efficiently implementing new website projects in a timely manner, and instead find themselves dealing with frequent delays and having to readjust their initial priorities. This can become a major barrier to optimization efforts, because the key to building an effective website optimization program is being able to make quick and frequent changes to the website while testing and launching winning versions.

If this issue occurs frequently within your company and projects often get derailed or take much longer than predicted, you are going to have to influence the decision making and prioritization process to make sure it doesn't negatively impact your efforts.

One good way to try and do this is to get a project management expert within your company on your side and help them understand why you need to make quicker and more efficient changes to the website when running tests.

Ideally you should try getting the project manager to create a separate prioritization path that only contains projects and changes relating to optimization and tests. To increase the chances of this happening, you ideally need internal resources that are specific to just implementing these tests from a technical, marketing, and design aspect. This way, other major project plans that the company has won't derail and slow down website optimization efforts.

You should also identify your company's current project management process and work with a project manager to address any deficiencies. Ideally your company needs to be running what is known as an *Agile* (or *scrum*) process, which makes it easier to tackle much smaller and more frequently released projects as well as larger time-consuming projects that get released much less often. There are also tools that can help with running this, for example VersionOne (`www.VersionOne.com`).

Note: Agile is becoming a popular new project-management process. You can learn about it at `http://en.wikipedia.org/wiki/Agile_software_development`.

Friday: Communicate, Review, and Iterate

One of the most important steps to building an optimization organization is ensuring that your optimization efforts are communicated often, reviewed, and then iterated on.

Without these last steps, you will also find it hard to make any headway on a long-term testing strategy and to build upon your previous testing results to maximize your optimization efforts.

Perform Weekly and Quarterly Optimization Meetings

One of the simplest yet most effective means of communicating is to hold weekly optimization review meetings. These should be run by the optimization team, and a consistent set of cross-functional team members should be invited each week. The major goal of these meetings is to ensure that current testing efforts are understood across the company and to communicate upcoming test plans. A very high-level communication of recent findings should also be discussed in the meetings. Another benefit of these meetings is that they really help to embed an optimization culture in your company.

To build on the foundation of these weekly meetings, any long-term successful optimization program needs more in-depth quarterly meeting reviews. These are essential to review recent testing efforts and results and to plan and prioritize tests for the next quarter. This is best done by setting up a quarterly optimization meeting that all testing key stakeholders should attend. Ideally these meetings should be at least three hours in order to devote enough time to adequately review and prioritize new efforts.

All recent test efforts should be reviewed at this meeting, including the lessons learned from the tests that worked well and those that didn't work as well. This is vital to be able to iterate on your optimization efforts. In this quarterly meeting, it is also very important to review how your optimization process has been working and to identify and resolve any issues that still exist or have appeared.

Communicate Your Efforts via Regular Emails and Blogs

To ensure that testing efforts are consistently communicated and have high visibility across your company, another best practice is to set up a regular testing email communication schedule. These emails are sent every time a new optimization initiative or test is launched and should communicate details of page locations and timings of these tests or optimization initiatives, high-level results of previous tests and details on the winning versions that get pushed live on the website.

These email updates should be sent to all of the website optimization team members as well as senior management and key stakeholders. These emails should be short and to the point, and be formatted in bullet points to ensure that all recipients can read and digest the information quickly and easily.

Another great way to communicate your efforts is in an internal company blog that announces your latest optimization news and efforts. This blog can also serve as an education mechanism and include regular articles on optimization best practices and links to popular external blog articles.

Run Brainstorming Sessions

Another essential best practice to help communicate and iterate on your test results is to hold frequent brainstorming sessions. These should be run by the optimization team, and anyone from your company can come—the point of expanding the attendees of these is to promote that anyone from any department can get involved in testing and come up with test ideas.

These sessions should be held at least quarterly, and ideally a half day should be devoted to each session. The first half of the meeting should be an open forum where attendees put their ideas on sticky notes. The second half of the meeting is used to collate and prioritize these ideas based on their ease of implementation and likely impact on conversion.

To help improve this session and create better ideas for future tests, you should come prepared and bring a list of key pages to discuss that have high potential impact (top entry pages and ones relating to conversion key flows for example). Ideally you should also show visual click map data relating to these key pages, so attendees can understand what visitors are currently doing on them (you will learn more about this important visual analysis in Chapter 5).

Use Test Idea and Test Results Tracking Documents

As discussed earlier, it is essential to use tracker documents for storing your test ideas and results. These documents are essential to help communicate, review, and iterate on your efforts in your weekly and quarterly meetings. These templates are called "Test Idea Tracker" and "Test Results Tracker" and can be found in Appendix B and Appendix C, respectively, as well as on this book's companion website.

Use a Shared Space for Your Optimization Documentation

Your optimization documentation should be easily shared and communicated within your company to ensure your efforts are transparent and easily accessible by anyone.

This is best done by making use of a shared platform on your company's intranet to upload all of your optimization documentation. This should include uploading optimization meeting notes, test plans, test trackers, and they should be organized into categories that are easy to navigate and understand.

Ideally this shared space should be maintained by a single person in the optimization team to ensure the contents remain well organized and easy to use. If this doesn't occur, these shared space areas can often just become a disorganized dumping ground and not much better than having no central storage space.

There are a number of fairly cheap solutions to help you store your documentation on a shared platform, such as Microsoft SharePoint and eRooms.

Week 6: Learn Testing Best Practices to Improve Your Success

Throughout this book, you will learn some great ways to test your website to improve your website conversions and success metrics. However, if you aren't armed with website testing best practices, your testing may be inconclusive at best, and at worst, may actually hinder your conversion rates. To help you avoid this happening to your testing efforts, you need to understand and use a great testing approach, how to create good tests, and then learn some testing best practices. All of which you will learn about this long but very important week.

Monday: Use an Insightful, Hypothesis-Driven, and Iterative Testing Approach

It might seem easiest to just pick something to test on your website, come up with a few variations, and hope for good results. Although this may occasionally help improve elements of your website, you may often run tests that have very little impact on your website and your success metrics. Testing without using an adequate approach and process will also waste time on key resources and potentially damage the likelihood of being able to run more tests in the future.

Therefore, in order to gain the most success with your testing efforts, you need to first understand and follow an optimal approach and process to website testing. This five-step testing process flow is shown in Figure 3.5. As you can see, it starts with the creation of insights and a test hypothesis and ends with running test iterations to maximize the impact of your tests.

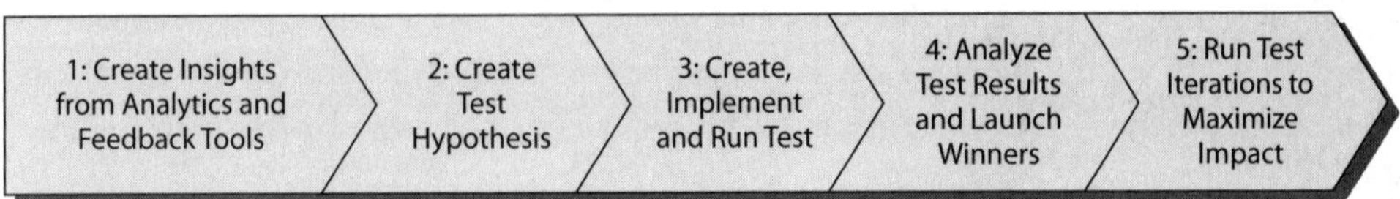
1: Create Insights from Analytics and Feedback Tools
2: Create Test Hypothesis
3: Create, Implement and Run Test
4: Analyze Test Results and Launch Winners
5: Run Test Iterations to Maximize Impact

Figure 3.5 Best practice testing approach

The following subsections describe the important parts of this optimization process flow that you need to understand and apply.

1: Create Insights from Analytics and Feedback Tools

The first step is to always try and look for insights to help formulate test ideas. Rather than just guessing at what to test, or listening to HiPPOs all the time, you should be using the analytics tool you set up in Chapter 2 and feedback you generate from your visitors (which you will learn about in Chapter 4) to create new insights into your visitor behavior. These insights should form the pillars of formulating your website test ideas and ensure that you are testing for a valid reason with your visitors in mind, rather than just doing random testing.

Examples of an insight generated would be something like "Our visitor feedback has revealed that our home page visitors seem to be confused by the number of options they can click on" or "Our analytics data reveals that our shopping cart has an unusually high drop off rate on the shipping details page."

Throughout the rest of the book, you will get some great ideas for tools and best practices to discover these critical visitor insights for your test ideas.

2: Create Your Test Hypothesis

You should always come up with a good reason to test something on your website; don't just test something for the sake of it. This reason should be in the form of creating a good hypothesis for each proposed test—in other words, your hunch of what is likely going to happen. A few examples of a hypothesis would be "Removing the phone number form field is likely to increase form completion rates" and "Adding in reviews for all products is likely to increase visitor social proof and as a result increase sales." The hypothesis you create should always relate to the initial insight you generated in Step 1 of the process flow.

Having a strong hypothesis will help ensure you don't encounter the GIGO (garbage in, garbage out) effect with your test. The better your hypotheses, the better the tests are likely to be. Doing this also makes it easier to persuade senior management why you want to run a particular test, and help you can gain approval, prioritization and the necessary resources to run the test.

3: Create, Implement, and Run Test

The third step is to actually get the test up and running on your website. This includes getting the variations created that are being tested, creating the actual test in your testing tool, implementing the test code on your website (include performing QA on it) and then pushing it live. All of the aspects of this will be covered in more detail throughout the rest of this week.

4: Analyze Test Results and Launch Winners

This next step is often where sub-par test results get pushed live without proper analysis. This subject will be covered in much more detail at the end of this week. To summarize though, when analyzing your results you should make sure you gather enough data (at least 2 weeks of results, and at least 100 conversions for each version being tested) and also make sure the predicted winner has enough statistical confidence from the tool to declare it a winner (at least 80 percent confidence). If you don't do this, you will risk pushing a version live that isn't actually the best version, thus reducing your potential conversion uplift.

You should also not just roll out and push live one winner to all your visitors; instead, you should segment your test results to find higher conversion lifts for different visitor segments (for example your paid search visitors may convert higher to a particular test version) and push a winning version to each of these visitor segments.

5: Run Test Iterations on Tests to Maximize Impact

Sadly, this last step is often neglected by many online marketers who are testing and optimizing their websites. Rather than simply moving on and testing something different, you should do further iterations on your test by learning from the results (even if the test didn't work well, you should be able to draw conclusions to learn from).

Doing this test iteration usually results in much higher conversion lifts than your initial tests generate. Many companies don't do a good job of this, so it will be a great source of competitive advantage if you do it well. This important subject of test iteration will be covered in more detail at several points throughout the rest of this week.

To ensure maximum impact from your optimization efforts, this approach then should continuously loop back around after the last part and back to the start again. This follows the same logic as a popular business theory called *Kaizen*, where improvement is a continuous process, not just a one-off thing.

Tuesday: Learn Strategies for Creating Effective Tests

One of the most critical parts of any effective long term optimization plan is the understanding and usage of strategies for creating tests that result in higher conversion lifts.

Today you will learn several different strategies that you can try, but remember there is no one specific test strategy that works every time. Depending on your website, your type of visitors, and your value proposition, some of these will work better in some situations than others. The first few of the test strategies described here usually work well initially though.

Go for Bigger, Radical Page Changes First (Innovation Tests)

One good initial approach to your testing plan is to run a basic A/B test between one of your influential conversion pages and an entirely new design and style of it. This should involve simultaneously changing, adding, removing, or moving many major design elements. For an example, a radically different version could be created by moving the location of your signup form, removing the sidebar, and reducing the header area size. The key here is to not just test a few small things per page—instead, go for many more radical changes.

This is effective because going for this more-radical approach is more likely to significantly influence your conversion rates, hopefully with a major positive improvement. This form of testing is often referred to as an *innovation test*.

When you find a radical new page design that drives great conversion lifts, don't just stop there and pat yourself on the back. It's essential that you do a follow-up multivariate test; otherwise, you are likely to be missing out on additional potential conversion rate increases. This follow-up test is often known as an *iteration test*. (You'll learn more about this type of test shortly.)

It's important to bear in mind that this style of innovation testing also has the potential to *lower* conversion rates just as radically as it might increase them (and don't be disheartened if not every innovation test that you run has good results). To limit any potential negative impact of this style of test, you should limit the percentage of your visitors who see this innovation test (although this can mean it takes much longer to get a significant test result if your page doesn't have much traffic).

You could try for another radical design or simply begin doing multivariate tests on more precise things that you know you are more likely to have higher increases (like testing calls-to-action, headlines, and images as discussed throughout this book).

In order to get this alternative page created, you will need to involve your design and marketing team and collaborate to create it. Ideally this new page should be based on at least some previous findings or ideas you may have and not an entirely random design. If you can get the resources, you could also try creating a third page version to test against, which may increase your chances of finding a more significant conversion lift.

Use Multivariate Tests to Look for Conversion Influence on Page Elements (Conversion Influence MVTs)

A simple initial approach to check for what is influencing conversions on any of your web pages is to set up an MVT for your key page elements and create just one alternative version for each element (either a variation, or turning it off).

This is known a *conversion influence MVT* and enables you to see which page elements are worth focusing on and doing further testing on to find the best variations. It also works well because it means you don't have to waste time creating and testing many different variations for a page element that might not even have much influence on your conversion rate.

To determine which versions have the biggest impact, you need to look for ones in your test results that have the greatest conversion influence. This can be done in most testing tools by examining conversion influencer reports—for example, the Element Contribution Report, as it's called in Adobe Test&Target, or the Relevance Rating Report in Google Website Optimizer. As mentioned in Chapter 2, this will indicate which of the elements being tested have the highest impact on conversion, and also which variation of the element causes this impact.

Once you find which page elements contribute the most to conversion, you should iterate by doing follow up A/B tests to hone those elements and improve conversion lift.

Note: The optimal number of page elements to use for a conversion influence MVT is seven, which is known as a 7 × 2 multivariate test design (seven elements tested using two variations).

Test Moving Key Elements on Your Pages to Check for Conversion Influencers (Real Estate Tests)

You may have elements on your pages that are performing poorly for conversion solely because their location may not be optimal. For example, if you have a highly converting module like "Latest Deals" but you are placing it too far down your page, you would generate more conversions if you gave it more prominence by placing it above the page fold. And never just presume your page elements are already in their best locations.

This conversion influence of key areas on your web page should be checked and tested to maximize your conversion rates. This can be done by setting up a test to move around key elements of your pages and is often known as performing a *real estate test.*

A few examples of this would be to test moving your benefits module to higher up in your sidebar and by moving your testimonials from your sidebar to high up in your main content page area. Generally though, you will find that areas above your page fold will have more influence on your conversion rates, so you should take that into account when setting up these tests.

You will often have to work with your web designers on this type of test because your page still needs to look good and flow well after you have moved elements and this may have an effect on your conversion rates.

Ideally you should do this type of testing in association with what you learn from analytics click map tools, because this will identify your most and least clicked page elements that you should consider moving.

Once you have found out which page areas and positions have the greatest conversion influence, you should iterate by doing follow-up tests on the elements found there to gain even higher conversion rates.

Turn Off Page Elements to Check for Conversion Influencers (Inclusion/Exclusion Tests)

A simple and often effective strategy is to test turning off elements on your pages to find conversion influencers. This is known as running an *inclusion/exclusion test.* For example, on your home page you could test removing a promo module, or remove a set of subnavigation links. This type of test works particularly well on pages with many elements on them, such as homepages or category pages. Running these tests results in less cluttered and more focused pages, which often increases engagement rates and conversion rates further.

To run this type of test you need to determine a few things to test removing from your pages. Once you have set up a test and gained some results, you need to look at how much each element influenced conversion. If the element removed had a negative impact on conversion, you know that it should be kept because it causes higher conversion by showing it (and you should then do follow up A/B tests to determine winning variations of these).

The elements removed that resulted in no reduction in conversion rates should be considered for removal from your page or moved to a less important page or location.

However, please be aware of removing elements, because you may actually end up removing a key one without realizing it. This is because the one being removed may be poorly designed, hard to understand or unusable for visitors and could actually be influential on conversions if you tested improving it first.

Therefore, you should always think before you remove elements from your pages, particularly ones you think may relate to use cases or conversion goals. If you are wary about removing it, consider creating a better variation and then retest it to see if it still has no influence on conversion. You could even consider surveying your visitors to see if they find the element useful. If they do, instead of removing it, you could de-emphasize it by moving to a less-visible area of your page or website.

Segment and Target Your Tests to Maximize Your Success and Conversion Lifts

To increase your conversion rates further and squeeze even more juice out of your test results, you need push live higher converting test variations to different segments of your visitors. This is known as segmenting and targeting your tests. This works because some of your test variations will satisfy the needs better for particular segments of your visitors, and as a result of this, they will convert much higher.

This also works because it results in your having a much more dynamic website that better meets the needs of many different types of visitors, rather than just trying to satisfy everyone with just one version of your website.

To do this, first of all, you need to create key visitor segments that you want to analyze and target your content to (for example, repeat visitors, and these should match the ones that you created in Chapter 2). Then you need to filter your test results and look for segments that converted much higher than your average conversion lift for the test. You then push live the winning version to each of your visitor groups that performed higher.

This can be done in most advanced testing tools like Adobe Test&Target or Autonomy Optimost, but unfortunately Google Website Optimizer doesn't currently offer this capability (and is a key reason to consider upgrading from it). These offer precreated visitor segments in addition to the ones you created in Chapter 2. To segment and target your tests, you need to filter your test results in your testing tool, review each of your segments and then push live any versions that you notice with particularly high conversion rate lifts. For an example of how to find these segments to review, in Figure 3.6 you can see how for Adobe Test&Target.

If you don't do this and only look at your test results holistically, you may be missing out on some good potential lifts. For example, your paid search visitors may convert much higher to a particular test variation, and if you pushed the overall test winner to them instead (and not the version they converted higher for), you would be getting a lower conversion rate from those visitors, thus reducing your potential conversion rate.

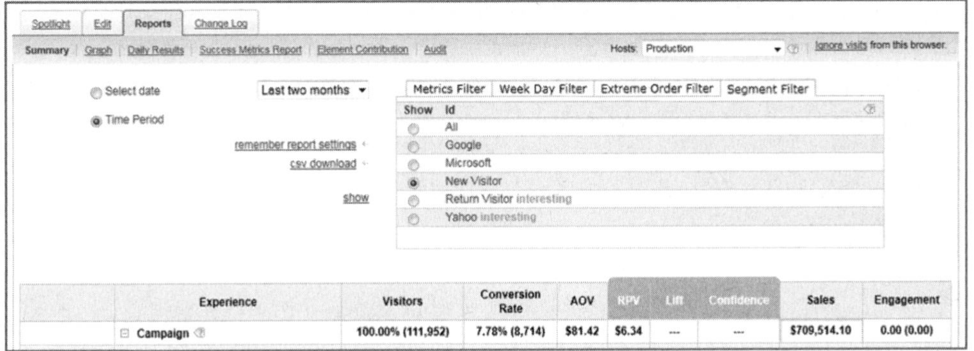

Figure 3.6 Segment filter list in Adobe Test&Target

You also need to understand that when you combine all the higher lifts you gain from pushing winners live to many visitor segments, this can be significantly higher than the conversion rate lift gained pushing live just one winning version to your whole website.

Note: Ideally there should not be just one single test winner to push live on your website—there should be a winner to push live for every key visitor segment, and doing this will result in much higher conversion rates.

You will learn advanced segmenting and targeting best practices and ideas tomorrow to increase your conversion rates even further.

Use Competitive Intelligence to Come Up with Test Ideas

Another good testing strategy is to analyze your competitors' websites to find great test ideas, just as you did to help improve your website's unique value proposition. Reviewing each of your main competitor's websites for their features, functionality, headlines, call-to-actions, and content offerings can be a goldmine for test ideas. Therefore, devote some time to check out what your competitors are doing and come up with some new test ideas. You should then repeat this every couple of months to see if they have launched anything new that you can create test ideas from. It's best to take screen captures of any test ideas you find because this will help your marketing and design team create similar versions to test.

This competitive analysis also helps you gain test buy-in by showing your senior executives that other competitor websites are already offering what you are proposing to test.

But do realize that just because your competition might be doing it on their website doesn't mean it will work on your website (or even work very well on their website).

Always Iterate Based on Your Test Results

This is one of the most important testing strategies that you should always use when testing and optimizing your website. You shouldn't just do random or ad hoc testing whenever you get an idea or whenever your boss wants you to test an idea that they have. Instead, you should always base your tests on previous "learnings" whenever possible or test an additional element relating to the initial test. This is known as *test iteration* and is vital for a long-term successful optimization strategy.

To help you understand this testing iteration principle a little better, Table 3.4 lists some examples of initial tests and iterations on them.

▶ **Table 3.4** Sample initial and related iteration tests

Initial Test	Iteration Test
1. Test the headlines on product pages.	1. Test the home page headline using learnings.
2. Test the wording of the "learn more" button.	2. Test the color of the "learn more" button.
3: Test the first page of the registration flow.	3. Test top previous pages to first registration page (known as testing higher up the conversion flow).
4: Test the location of the category page promo.	4. Test the wording of the category page promo.
5: Target the home page content to first-time visitors.	5. Target the home page content to repeat visitors.
6: Run a multivariate test to look for element conversion influence.	6. Run A/B tests on elements causing the highest conversion influence.

Example of a High-Impact Initial Testing Strategy

Now that you have learned some great test strategies, let's look at an example of an initial testing strategy that has high potential for success on a variety of website types. Here are the steps you would need to take:

Step 1: Using insights generated from your analytics and feedback tools and best practices from this book, pick a page to test that will likely have high potential impact on conversion.

Step 2: Identify your success metrics.

Step 3: Create an alternative page version to test against (an innovation test).

Step 4: Run a simple A/B test to see which version has higher lift.

Step 5: Identify the winner and push it live.

Step 6: Identify the elements that can be optimized on the winning page version.

Step 7: Set up a multivariate test that moves elements around the page to determine which locations have the highest influence on conversion (a real estate test).

Step 8: Based on results and learnings, move modules to areas where they will have the highest conversion lift.

Step 9: Test turning off page elements to see which ones have the highest influence on conversion (an inclusion/exclusion test).

Step 10: Based on learnings, consider removing elements that had very little impact on conversion rates.

Step 11: Based on learnings, set up a multivariate test for the elements that had the highest impact on conversion. Create two or three different versions of each element to test against the control versions, and set up some high value visitor traffic segments for your test.

Step 12: Push winning versions to each of your highly converting key visitor traffic segments (for example, push one version to new visitors and another version to newsletter visitors).

Can't Seem to Move the Testing Needle?

Don't give up. Here is a list of follow-up strategies if your tests don't seem to initially be moving the needle for increasing conversions:

- Try using visitor insight to understand what is potentially wrong with your current page (using the tools you'll learn about in Chapter 4).
- Try creating a radically different challenger version of your page to test against (using the innovation test that you just learned about).
- Segment your test results to look for micro-level wins (for example, perhaps one of your tests has better results for first-time visitors or visitors from paid search).

Wednesday: Learn the Power of Targeting and Personalization for Improving Conversions

Today you are going to learn about an emerging advanced optimization strategy that can have an extremely powerful effect on your website's conversion rates.

Historically, most websites offer the same version of their website to their visitors, no matter who they are or what their needs are. In a consumer-driven world that is increasingly customized, this "one size fits all" approach to websites is no longer good enough. At Starbucks you can have your drink made any way you like it, rather than them just having the same drink versions for everyone (such as a skinny soy mocha latte with light whip…), so why not have a website that can meet the needs of different types of visitors?

Smart website marketers are now beginning to realize the benefits of customizing their website to individual visitors based on their needs and previous behaviors—often with amazing impact on conversion rates. They are doing this by using tools that can target different segments of visitors with more relevant content that meets their needs better, and thus engage and convert them better. For example, they can detect whether the user is a new visitor and show them content designed to educate them about the benefits of the site or target offering special coupons for visitors who have purchased multiple times before.

Over the rest of the week, you will learn about tools and best practices for doing this to get even more out of your testing efforts.

Research Advanced Visitor Segmenting and Targeting Tools

This segment and targeting can be done fairly easily in most advanced testing tools like Adobe Test&Target and Autonomy Optimost. Some budget and free testing tools, such as Google Website Optimizer, don't offer this segment targeting ability though. However, there are now some free tools that you can use to run a basic level of segmentation and targeting, the major one being BT Buckets (`www.BTbuckets.com`). This tool actually works very well with Google Analytics, and you can pull in the visitor segments that you have created from that tool and target content to them.

For an advanced, hands-free way of doing this, you can use a tool like Adobe Test&Target 1:1, which is an additional feature you can purchase and add on to Test&Target. This is automated behavioral targeting at its best and it actually learns from visitor behavior to automatically predict what content individual visitors (rather than groups of visitors) are likely to engage with the most. Another good behavioral targeting tool that you can research is called Cognitive Match (`www.CognitiveMatch.com`); specifically, this tool does a great job of behavioral targeting in ads (which will be covered more in Chapter 8).

Next, you'll learn about several best practices for creating a more personalized and targeted website to help you push your conversion rates to the limits. Attempting some of these can often give your website optimization efforts a great boost.

Show New Visitors Content to Help Engage and Convert

As you will learn from several points throughout the rest of this book, visitors will often judge your website in a matter of seconds. Therefore it's important to recognize your first-time visitors when they arrive on your website, and show them targeted content that helps explain the value proposition of your website better (which you will create and improve in the next chapter).

One of the best ways to do this is to create a new visitor segment in your behavioral or advanced testing tool, and when they arrive, show them a "First-Time Visitor" module on your home page and possibly in the right-hand rail of your other pages. This module should be titled something like "First Time Visitor? See Our Quick Start Guide" and should contain your value proposition, with a link to a page that explains this in more detail.

You could also test showing cheaper products, or showing coupons or trial offers specifically to your first-time visitor segment to see if that helps increase conversion rates. You could also show them whitepapers or guides for them to download that help them understand better what your website offers.

In later chapters, you'll see examples of how to best engage your first-time visitors for different types of pages.

Target your repeat visitors with their most commonly browsed content or products

Wouldn't it be great if you walked into your local book store and saw your favorite types of books right at the entrance for your convenience? Well that would be pretty hard to do in the real world, but you can do things like this on your website by using targeting.

This process of showing favorite content or products to repeat visitors to engage them better is known as *content affinity targeting*. It represents a great way to improve the relevance of your web pages to better meet the needs of your visitors, and usually is a great way to increase conversions as a result of higher visitor engagement levels.

To do this, set up a targeted test that tracks visitor's favorite content (based on at least three views of a particular piece of content or product) that then shows them content relating to this in a module on one of your key pages. A pre-created option for doing this is available to you in advanced targeting tools like Adobe Test&Target. For example, you could use your hero or image slider on your homepage or category pages to show new or top links in that section that they browsed the most before. You shouldn't just show them content based on a single page they saw before though, because visitors often browse websites and see pages, but that doesn't mean that a visitor likes every page they see.

This is a particularly good targeting tactic to use on your home page, category pages, and top entry pages (as will be discussed in more detail in later chapters).

Create a Previous Purchaser Visitor Segment and Show These Visitors Recommendations and Coupons

It's also very important to segment visitors who have purchased from you before and show them targeted content that will encourage them to buy again. This is because it's often easier to generate orders from existing customers than from new visitors.

The best way to target these visitors is to create a segment that tracks visitors who have purchased before and include modules on your home page and your shopping cart page that show them product recommendations based on what they previously bought, and possibly offer them relevant coupons too. In later chapters, you'll see relevant examples for different types of pages.

Segment and Target Your Visitors Regionally

Another powerful way to segment and target your visitors is to capitalize on which geographic region your visitors are coming from. For example, you could target your home page visitors by showing them their nearest local store or showing them international-related content if they are arriving from a different country.

This is also particularly useful for targeting and showing products or services to regions that are weather and seasonality sensitive. For example, test promoting fans to visitors from regions that get particularly humid or hot in the summer.

Figure 3.7 shows a great example of this type of targeting by Macys.com. The content displayed on their homepage is specifically targeted to visitors who arrive at the Macys.com website from outside of the United States and helps provide greater value to these types of visitors.

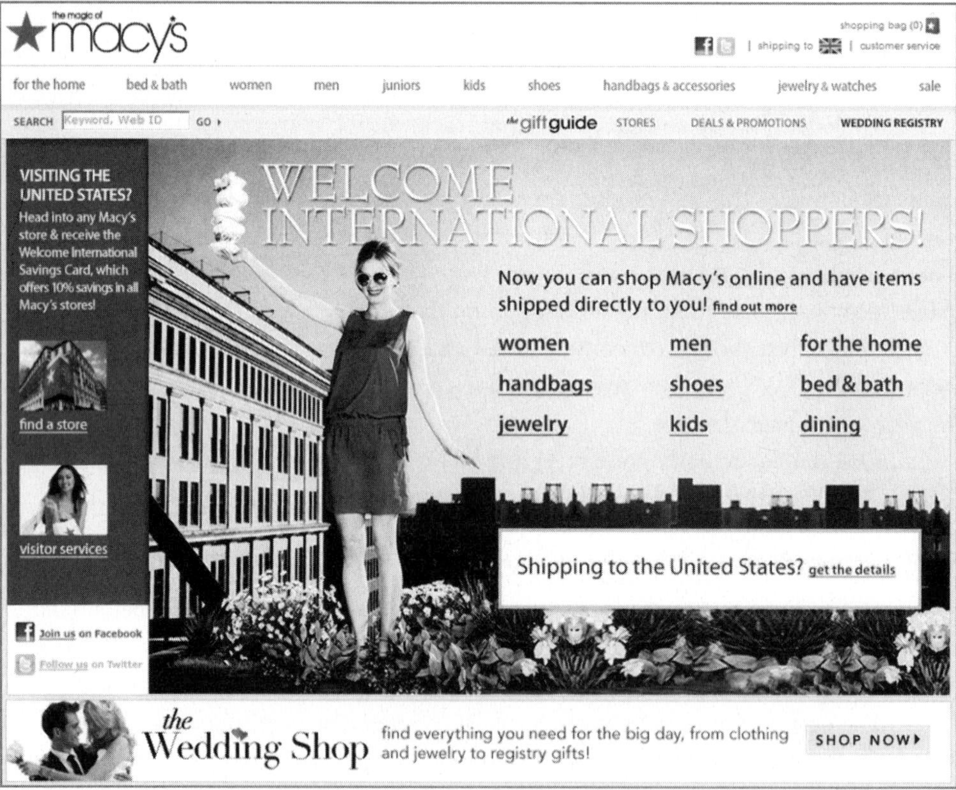

Figure 3.7 Example of international visitor targeting

Create an Abandoned Shopping Cart Segment for Retargeting

A visitor may abandon their shopping cart on your website before completing the purchase for any number of reasons, many of which are out of your control.

One great way of increasing the likelihood of a visitor returning to their cart and finishing purchasing is to create a segment of visitors who abandoned their shopping cart. When one of these visitors comes back to your website, you would target and show them a message that reminds them they still have items in their cart to try and influence them to complete the purchase. This could be in the form of offering a coupon for this purchase, mentioning that the price may go up in the future, or warning that an item may soon be unavailable.

You can also tie this segment of visitors into your email marketing efforts and target them by offering them a reason to finish their purchase (email marketing optimization like this is covered in more detail in Chapter 8).

Personalize Your Website Offerings Based on Peer Behaviors

Another great way to target your visitors and personalize what your visitors see is to use the social proof theory, which speculates that people are influenced by what their peers do. Using this theory that you will learn more about in Chapter 6, you would target visitors and show them content based on what purchasers with similar characteristics buy or look at.

Amazon.com has been doing this for years and has honed this to an exact science with some astounding results. The more you browse and buy on their website, the more intelligent it gets at predicting what you might like to see, as illustrated in Figure 3.8.

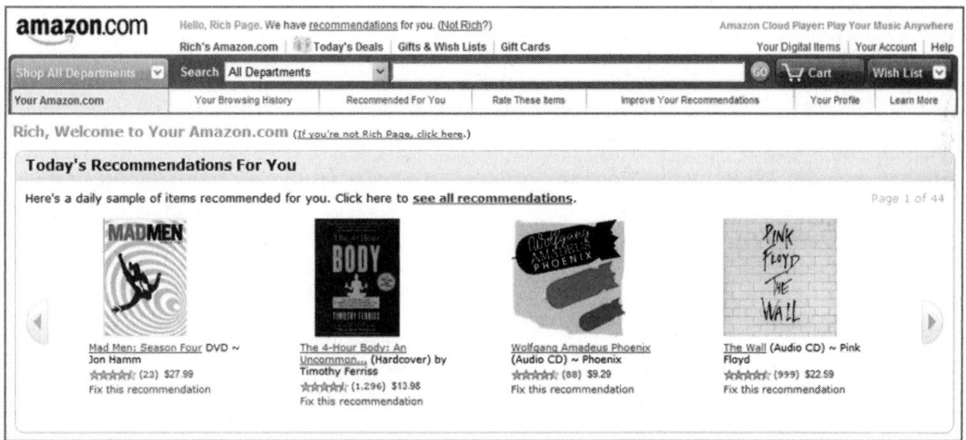

Figure 3.8 Example of personalized recommendations

Segment and Target Your Visitors Using Offline Data Sources

Wouldn't it be great if you could show different content on your website to someone who had never even been to your website but had previously talked to someone in your call center or had been contacted by your sales team via email?

Previously, it was pretty much impossible to bridge the gaps between web analytics, website optimization, and third-party offline data sources. This meant it was usually hard to determine if a visitor had purchased before or if they had been sent marketing materials.

With recent improvements in web technologies, if you are using an advanced website testing tool, it is now possible to do just this. Now you can target visitors based on a multitude of offline activities and provide a more contextual experience for the visitor, often resulting in much higher engagement and conversion rates.

The Adobe Test&Target tool even gives you the option to use offline traditional marketing segments from Alliant. These segments enable you to target certain visitor affinity groups and demographics. This is very valuable offline data that can help increase your conversion rates even further.

Segment and Target Your Mobile Phone Based Visitors

One of the most important visitor segments to target is the growing number of visitors who arrive on your website via mobile phones and devices. This is because a mobile visitor's needs are often a lot different due to the smaller screen size and slower connection speed, so they usually prefer seeing a different, easier-to-use version of your website. This will be covered in much more detail in Chapter 7.

Use Automated Predictive Learning to Improve Targeting

There are now advanced website testing tools that make these targeting best practices even simpler to use. These automate the process of continually showing the best content to individual and groups of visitors and often result in much higher conversions.

For example, Adobe Test&Target offers a great targeting add-on called Test&Target 1:1. This upgrade builds in-depth learnings from visitors' behavioral patterns to predict and automatically show individual visitors more relevant content resulting in higher conversion rates. All you have to do is create and load into the tool several variations of content, provide some rules and logic that determine conversion success, and then give the tool a week or so to learn about your visitors patterns, and it will automatically start showing the best content to them.

Unfortunately, these advanced automated predictive learning tools are currently not very cheap and require you to gain an additional testing budget to make use of them.

Thursday: Avoid Common Mistakes When Creating and Running Your Tests

Today you are going to learn about important principles to follow while you are creating and running tests on your websites. These will reduce the chances of you making errors when creating and running them and result in greater efficiency and impact from them.

Don't Go Crazy with the Number of Test Variations in Your Multivariate Tests

When setting up an MVT, don't try testing too many elements and variations per page. Testing over five different page elements with more than three different variations for each element will take much longer to get significant test results. This is because the tool will have to get enough traffic for each combination being tested before it can declare a significant winner, and if the page you are testing has low traffic, it can take many months to do this.

Not only does it take longer to gain significant results when testing a large number of test variations like this, but it will also take longer for you to create the many different test versions needed (particularly if you need significant help to create these versions). This can dramatically reduce the number of tests you can run per month and slow down your optimization strategy progress.

To avoid this issue when testing many page elements at once, ideally you should try to limit your test to seven elements with just two variations of each (this is a conversion influence test that we discussed earlier).

And if you want to test more than seven, I suggest that you run an innovation A/B test instead, where you create an entirely different page and test it against the current page. This will take much less time to get a significant test winner, and you could then do further follow up testing on the elements on the winning page.

Make Sure Your Test Challengers Are Sufficiently Different

One of the more common reasons for poorly performing tests is because the challenger versions are too similar to the control version and visitors barely notice the difference, let alone influence conversion rates. This is particularly problematic when you are testing graphical elements like banners or images that designers have creative control over. To help alleviate these issues, you should meet with the design team and ensure they know the reasons behind the testing motives and direction to give them some examples of what constitutes a big difference.

Ideally, you need to create one of the challenger versions to be significantly different. For example, don't just slightly change the color shade of a button; you should go for a bolder, more significant change, such as using very different imagery or wording. However, be aware that changing multiple things at once is not recommended without any iteration testing to find what elements of the change influenced conversion the greatest.

If your challenger versions require different text (for example, a new headline or call-to-action) you should always get assistance from your marketing team to help create your variations to increase the chances of it influencing your visitors better. Ideally you will have a marketing lead devoted to this function, and they would form part of the optimization team (as discussed earlier).

Don't Spend Too Much Time Making Your Test Challengers Perfect

One common reason for a lack of testing efficiency can be spending too much time designing perfect test variations for your challengers. You shouldn't spend hours on the design of them making them perfect, because most of the versions that are created won't even end up winning and staying on the website. Instead, you need to invest just enough time to convey the main point of the variation—spend 80 percent of the normal amount of time that you would use on it, and don't worry about spending the final harder, more time-consuming 20 percent on making it look perfect.

The key point to remember is that you can always tweak the winning version slightly if needed, such as exactly fulfilling brand requirements for example (as long as you don't change anything major about the winner version, otherwise that would invalidate the test results).

You should definitely emphasize this point with your design department and make sure they aren't spending too much time making each test design absolutely perfect. Doing this will mean fewer visual resources are needed to run tests, ultimately meaning you can run tests more often and more efficiently.

Plan Early for Your Test Resources

When you create tests, you will often need help from many different departments, including the IT department (to help implement your test), design department (to help design test variations), and marketing department (to help come up with marketing related improvements like calls-to-action or headlines).

Not planning early to obtain this help and resources will cause your tests to be created too slowly and inefficiently, ultimately reducing the frequency of tests (and you need to be able to test many things simultaneously for an effective long term testing program). The reason why this often happens is because last-minute test resource planning risks receiving pushback from other departments, and there are usually many last-minute questions that will need answering about the test, which will also delay the time of launch.

Therefore, you need to plan out and prioritize which resources you need as far in advance as possible and work closely with a project manager to increase your chances of success.

This planning is even more essential if you don't have the luxury of having your own dedicated team of testing resources to help with the technical, design, and marketing aspects of your tests.

Limit the Potential Negative Impact

While it's a good strategy to test and optimize pages that have the highest potential to increase conversion rates, you need to be cautious and make sure you limit any potential negative impact on your website if a test performs badly. Doing this will give key stakeholders less of a reason to question the value of optimization if your initial efforts go wrong.

There are two main ways that a test could have negative impact: first if you don't perform a high-level QA on your test, it may break your website or slow it down; and second, if your test doesn't do as well as anticipated, it actually lowers your conversion rate.

The best way to reduce this potential negative impact is to initially limit the number of visitors participating in your test to a small amount—for example, around 10 percent.

Then if the test shows no negative impact, gradually increase the amount of traffic seeing your test up to 100 percent. This option is available in most website testing tools and is fairly easy to set up (see your testing tool's help section to find out exactly how to do this).

Be Wary of Changes in Major Sources of Your Traffic During Tests

Another thing to be aware of is the impact of your traffic source patterns that might change during the period you are running your tests. As mentioned earlier, conversion rates can differ tremendously based on traffic source and therefore can play havoc with your test results.

For example, if you are testing on your website and you send out a large newsletter campaign to it, this is likely to increase conversion rates for a few days and make it look like your test is performing better than it actually is for a brief period. This is because newsletter traffic often converts higher because it's a higher quality source of traffic.

Another example would be if your marketing department started to run a paid search campaign to your website in the middle of one of your tests. This kind of traffic is also much more targeted and has a greater chance of converting, which will influence your results.

Most of the more advanced testing tools actually allow you to filter out segments of traffic to avoid situations like this. Therefore, before you launch a test, you should ask your marketing team whether they have any major traffic-driving campaigns planned during your test period that will likely change the quality of traffic on your website (thus affecting your test results), and then set up filters to remove these segments during the test.

Don't Remove Poorly Performing Test Versions in the Beginning

Quite often people running tests are tempted to remove and exclude test versions that don't seem to be working well, particularly if they or others are already convinced that these poorly performing versions aren't as good as the other test versions.

This is a bad thing to do, because sometimes test versions that start off doing the worst can often do much better over time and even end up winning the test. Therefore, you should keep all your test variations running until the test has finished.

Friday: Learn How to Analyze Results and Determine a Test Winner

Now that you understand best practices for running your website tests, there are several other testing best practices that you need to understand to be able to interpret your test results and determine test winners. Today you will learn about these.

Gather a Significant Number of Conversions before Declaring a Winner

First, when analyzing your results, it's important that you have enough conversions for each version being testing before deciding on a winning version. If you don't have enough conversions, the test results won't be statistically valid, and you will risk pushing live a version that actually isn't the optimal version. In the worst case scenario it could mean you end up pushing a version live that actually ends up lowering conversions.

A quick rule of thumb is that you need to have at the very least 100 conversions per element or recipe you are testing. The more results you can get, the better, because this increases the chances of finding a valid winner.

Always Check Your Confidence Level before Declaring a Winner

Having enough conversions is important, but you also need to check whether your testing tool has gathered enough confidence in the winner it is predicting. This is particularly important to pay attention to if many of your versions are showing a similar uplift in conversion. Most testing tools give you an idea of this testing significance level by showing a confidence level in the test reports, as you learned in Chapter 2 when reviewing key reports in testing tools.

Ideally, you want as high a confidence level as possible for a test version before declaring it a winner, and ideally at least 90 percent confidence should be your goal (which in Adobe Test&Target is represented by three full green bars). However, sometimes it may take too long to get to this point, so you might want to consider using slightly less confidence, like 80 percent.

Learn How to Interpret Your Conversion Rate Lifts

While testing tools show you the conversion rate lift for each version you are testing, it's important to understand what this is and what is considered a good conversion lift. This lift is calculated by comparing the conversion rate of each version being tested (test challengers) against the conversion rate for your test control (default) version.

Results for test challengers that show barely any conversion lifts like 1 or 2 percent, although positive, are not really considered to be very good and you might not want to consider pushing them live on your website.

Conversion rate lifts between 10 percent and 20 percent are considered relatively good and probably worth pushing live, while a good conversion rate lift is usually considered anything more than 25 percent.

If your test results manage to get above 50 percent lift, that is considered a very good conversion rate lift and not really that rare, particularly when you look for good results in your visitor segments (which will be discussed next). If you manage to reach over 100 percent conversion lift for any of your test results, that is really outstanding because you are essentially doubling the number of conversions on your website.

Anything below zero percent conversion lift obviously is going to be negative, but don't just discard your tests if none of your test challengers get above zero percent. You should learn from results that don't win, and use them to base further iteration tests on.

Always Segment Test Results to Find Higher Converting Versions

As discussed earlier, to achieve higher conversion rates you need to segment and target your visitors with more relevant content. Therefore, when you are analyzing your test results, you need to analyze each of your test visitor segments to look for higher conversion rates than the overall test result, and then push live those versions. For example, segments that quite often have a higher conversion rate lift are paid search visitors and newsletter visitors.

Don't Rush into Making Quick Decisions from Initial Test Results

Rushing into making test result decisions may lead to suboptimal or negative conversion rate improvements without your realizing it. Even if you see great initial spikes in conversion rates, it's essential that you wait for initial variances to level out; otherwise, you may pick a winning version that actually isn't the best. You need to get at least seven days' worth of nonfluctuating data before you can make a decision regarding the winners.

Many companies make this mistake of not waiting long enough and end up pushing live a test variation too early that isn't actually the best one, potentially even lowering conversion rates on their site.

Depending on your traffic levels to the pages being tested, you usually need to wait a couple of weeks to gather enough significant data. If you have a particularly low-traffic page, you may need to wait up to a month to get results; if you have to wait any longer, you should question the value of optimizing that page because it gets such little traffic.

Know When to End a TestThat Doesn't Beat the Original Version

Tests usually take at least a few weeks to provide significant data, particularly for a multivariate test or an A/B test that is being run on a page with lower traffic per day.

But it's important to know when to end a test if any of the challenger versions don't gain conversion lift over the control version. You shouldn't get bogged down by waiting months to get a result, because there will be times when you never actually get a winning version. If the results are still fluctuating quite a lot, then it may be worth waiting slightly longer than two weeks; but if the results have flat lined for over an extra week and still don't indicate a good winner, then you can consider ending the test.

If you end up with a result that doesn't beat the control version, as highlighted earlier, you should try iterating on your test and learn from possible reasons why it didn't work.

For MVT Tests, Do Follow-up Tests to Increase the Likelihood of the Best Version Being Found

Given the nature of how Taguchi multivariate tests determine a sample of sets of experiences it needs to show, multivariate tests aren't always perfect at predicting a winning test version. As a result, they can be occasionally prone to not revealing the best test variations, meaning that you might not always be pushing a test version live that has the highest lift on conversion rates.

The best way to make sure of the validity of your test results and that you are pushing live the best winning version possible is to do these follow-up tests:

Run a simple A/B test for the winning version against the control version. Doing this second follow-up test gives you extra assurance that the winning version that the testing tool determined is actually better than the control. This test is much purer and takes out the noise and potential impact of the rest of the versions that were being tested in your original test.

Use your element contribution report to create a follow-up A/B test. When you run an MVT, you should also check your element contribution report to see if it comes up with a different variation winner than your test results show. If this is the case, you should create a follow-up test that includes all the element variations found in your element contribution report and test it against your current winner to see if it improves conversion further. You need to do this because sometimes the best predicted version won't actually be a sample set that the multivariate test creates, and you may be missing out on the true winner if you didn't test your control against the best predicted versions.

Understand Your Visitors and Their Needs—the Keys to Website Optimization

Without happy, engaged and converting website visitors, your website will struggle to exist for a very long time. Therefore, in this chapter you will learn the importance of focusing on your visitors, including understanding their needs and how to help them better recognize the value of your website. You will also learn how to gather great insights from them to generate high impact ideas for testing and optimizing your website.

Chapter Contents

Week 7: Create Personas and Use Cases for Your Main Visitor Needs

Remember that your website visitors generate the income for your online business income, not your actual website by itself, and without pleasing them you would not remain in business very long. And even if you have good conversion rates on your website, this doesn't necessarily mean that it satisfies your visitors to a high degree. They could purchase or sign up for something, but that doesn't mean they found it easy to do, or that they will want to come back again. This then obviously has a major impact on your future conversion rates.

To make sure your website isn't guilty of not satisfying your visitors, you need to focus much more attention on recognizing them and their needs. To help you start doing this, this week you will learn about the benefits of creating personas and use cases for them. Analyzing and optimizing for these will help ensure that your website satisfies your visitors' needs, and better engages and converts them.

Monday: Put Yourself in Your Visitor's Shoes to Help Create Personas and Use Cases

Unfortunately, far too much focus is placed on marketing and creating websites without any great and consistent focus on the visitors' needs, so they largely get ignored or thought about using preconceived notions. Remember that your web analytics data, while consisting of very large numbers of page views and visits, are actually all caused by individuals like you and me, so it's important to think of your numbers as actual people.

To get an idea of how much attention you manage to devote to your visitors' perspective, ask yourself a few questions relating to some common tasks on your website such as these:

- When was the last time you tried purchasing or signing up for something on your own website?
- When was the last time you used the internal search tool on your website to find something?
- Have you tried recently to fully register on your website?
- Have you tried recently to find help on your website regarding your product return or refund policy?
- When was the last time you tried to comment on one of your articles or share it on social networks?

Surprisingly, a great number of people who work for online businesses never even consider trying out their own websites from a visitor's perspective, using the common "that's not my job" excuse.

To avoid this pitfall, you need to put yourself in your website visitor's shoes and use your website just as a new visitor would likely do—imagine that you have never been there before and spend some time reviewing it. In particular you need to re-create common tasks that visitors probably might want to do, such as using your navigation to find something or register on your website.

This understanding of what visitors do on your website is critical to be able to effectively build use cases and visitor personas for it, which is something that you will do during the rest of this week.

While you are doing this review of your website, you should take note of anything strange or tasks that are particularly difficult to achieve, or if anything is not working as expected or even broken. These issues that you find will be great candidates for testing and optimizing to improve visitor satisfaction and conversion rates.

Tuesday: Create Some Simple Personas for Your Visitors

Today you will learn how to get to know your visitors and their needs better by creating some simple personas for them. You may cringe when you see the word "personas" and think that the creation of these is only done by big marketing agencies that have money and time to burn. But in online business, one of the best ways for you to understand your website visitors' needs is to create personas for the major types of them.

As it is used in website optimization, the term *persona* simply means a fictional character that is created to represent a group of visitors who regularly come to your website.

Far too often, online marketers treat their website visitors as just numbers and metrics, not as real people. Creating personas for your visitors helps puts a personal human face on these large numbers and helps you understand your visitors better, including their main characteristics and the likely impact they will have on your conversion rates.

Let's get started and create a small set of personas for the major types of visitors that typically come to your website. You don't necessarily need to go into great detail when you are creating these (as more traditional marketing personas often do), but you should at least try and include some references to their online experience, as this can often play a large role in the likelihood of their conversion. You will now learn about some elements to use when creating your personas.

Elements of Personas You Should Consider Using

When you are creating your personas, you should use common elements and attributes to help define them, and note down the most commonly found characteristics of each. You will need enough answers to help form three to five personas.

Here are some elements you should consider using:

- The visitor's age bracket
- The visitor's gender
- How web savvy they are

- Their likely expectations
- Their goals
- Their motivations
- Their buying stage
- Their confidence
- How they interact with your website
- If they have used competitor websites

Examples of Visitor Personas

To help you understand and create personas better, here are some examples of visitor personas for a few different types of websites:

Simple Examples of Visitor Personas for a Dating Website

- A young lady who is new to online dating, and is fairly web savvy
- A middle-aged man who has old-fashioned dating standards and is not very web savvy
- A young lady who considers herself an expert online dater and has big expectations
- A middle-aged woman who wants to start online dating, but is skeptical and needs convincing
- A young man who is very visual and prefers seeing many photos instead of text when browsing

Simple Examples of Visitor Personas for an E-commerce Website

- A young man who is very tech savvy and is looking for the latest tech product offerings
- A middle-aged woman who usually shops in stores and is not very tech savvy
- An older man who uses the website purely to get reviews and prices before buying in a store
- A middle-aged woman who is traditionally a bargain shopper and only buys things on sale
- A young woman who usually uses a competitor's website but is considering trying yours
- A middle-aged man looking for customer support options to try and return something
- A young man who only uses internal site searches to find what he's looking for

Using these tips and examples, you should now go ahead and create some simple personas for your website visitors. Ideally, you should try to come up with at least three to five different personas. To make these even more realistic, relatable, and understandable across all departments of your company, you should try and give these key personas actual names and ideally even try to add a photo of what each type might look like.

Once you have created your visitor personas, this helps you not only understand your visitors better but will also make it easier to build some very important use cases for your website, which leads us into tomorrow's topic.

Wednesday: Create Use Cases for Your Website

Now that you have created some simple personas of your website visitors, you need to adapt them into use cases. These use cases will represent the most likely things that your visitors will want to do on your website and their most likely needs.

The reason why it's so important to create these is because it's essential that your visitors can complete your major use cases with ease; otherwise, they may often get frustrated and may leave your website prematurely. This therefore can have a major impact on your conversion rates and success metrics.

Determine the Most Common Tasks on Your Website

Next you need to determine the most common tasks that a visitor might want to do on your website. Understanding these will make it much easier to create your use cases. Here are some examples of tasks that your website visitors might want to achieve on your website:

- Watch a demo video of your service
- Get pricing information
- Find contact phone numbers
- Update their member profile
- Invite friends to join
- Find their closest physical store
- Register for a new webinar
- Compare product features
- Manage their online account
- Share a page on Facebook or Twitter
- Get product return information
- Comment on an article
- Purchase products
- Use an internal search tool to find a product
- Get help via web chat

- Schedule a call to learn more details
- Unsubscribe from a newsletter
- Get the latest investor and stock information
- Read company management bios

With the help of these examples and the personas you created yesterday, go ahead and create a list of all the tasks that a visitor might want to do specifically on your website, no matter how large or small it might be. Spend at least an hour or two trying to think of at least 20 of these tasks, and you should ideally set up a brainstorming session with others to help you create a more complete list.

Then after you have a good list, you need to rate and rank these tasks in order of how often each one is likely to occur on your website. This is because you will need to build your use cases out of the most common tasks on your website and pay less attention to the less common ones. For example, visitors to an e-commerce website are more likely to try and find product return information than to look for a job.

As a rating scheme for your tasks use a 1–10 scale, where 10 represents a task that occurs very often and 1 represents a task that does not occur very often. Using this scale, go ahead and rate your use tasks and re-rank them in order of highest score.

Doing this will help you understand what your pages need to focus on to help solve these most important tasks, and not risk confusing visitors by trying to solve hundreds of tasks at once that only a small percent might want to do.

Develop Your Most Important Tasks into Use Cases

Once you have come up with a ranked list of tasks, you need to take the top five or six most important tasks and create a *use case* for each one that explains it in more detail. For example, instead of just saying "purchase products," a use case would be "A first time visitor arrives looking for product X using the navigation menu."

To give some color to these use cases, try adding how the visitor arrived and navigated the website, if they have been here before, and what they are likely looking for or want to do. To help you understand the level of detail needed for your use cases, here are a few examples of major use cases for two different types of websites:

Example Use Cases for a Dating Website

- An existing member who comes back to search for other members in their area who don't have kids and who are younger than 35
- A repeat visitor who is trying to find the cancellation policy before signing up
- A first-time visitor who wants to compare pricing plans
- An existing member who wants to change their main profile photo and upload some more photos

Example Use Cases for a Website Selling Services

- A first-time visitor who wants to watch a demo of your service
- A customer who wants to upgrade their feature set
- A second-time visitor who is looking for a white paper to help convince his boss to use their services
- A customer who wants to find and use an FAQ (frequently asked questions) page to answer a technical question

Using these examples and tips, you now need to go ahead and create use cases for your top five visitor tasks on your website that you created yesterday. Tomorrow, you will put these major use cases to the test on your website and see how easy it is to complete them all, which is the key to ensuring that you have a highly optimized and converting website.

Thursday: Re-create the Use Cases on Your Website and Grade the Ease of Doing So

Now that you have created some good major use cases for your website, you need to put them to work and judge for yourself how easy it is to complete each of them on your website. This can provide some great insight into which pages and key conversion flows on your website need the most improvement.

The first step in testing your use cases is to list them in Table 4.1. Then go to your website and try to re-create each use case. As you are going through each use case, grade it according to how easy it is to complete. Use an A–F grading system to record these grades in Table 4.1. An A grade should be given if the use case is very easy to accomplish, a C grade if it was relatively hard to accomplish, and an F grade if you could not actually complete the use case.

And remember to be as honest as possible with your ratings, as the ultimate goal is to find weaknesses in your website that can be optimized and tested to improve your visitor engagement and conversion rates.

Table 4.1 Use case completion grade table

	Use Cases for Your Website	Your Website Completion Grade
1		
2		
3		
4		
5		

You may actually be surprised how hard or confusing it may be to achieve a fairly common use case on your website, particularly if your website has not been very customer-centric in the past.

After you have done the completion ratings for your top use cases, you need to note any of them you have particular trouble with and gave a D, E or F grade. The pages and flows that relate to your troublesome use cases are great candidates to perform testing and optimization on.

Over the rest of this book you will learn some great ways to make it easier for your visitors to complete your use cases, in particular from your homepage. In the last week of the book you will then revisit these and re-rate these use cases, because using the best practices in this book will likely make them easier to complete.

Friday: Learn How to Get Even Greater Value from Your Use Cases

You should not just create and test your use cases once and then forget about them. There are several other things you can be doing with them that you will learn about today.

Test Your Use Cases on Your Website Visitors

As discussed yesterday, it's important to make it as easy as possible for your visitors to complete your use cases. However, rather than just judging and rating using your own opinion, to get an even better and more realistic perspective, you need to involve your visitors and see how easy it is for them to complete them too. You will do this by revisiting them in Week 10 of this chapter and putting them to the ultimate test against your very own website visitors.

The use case completion rating results from your visitors will help form invaluable ideas to help optimize your website and to ensure you are keeping your visitors as happy and engaged as possible.

Create Your Use Cases as Visitor Segments in Your Analytics and Testing Tools

A great way to get even more from your use cases is to create visitor segments in your web analytics and testing tools that match the characteristics of your use cases. This allows you to analyze them to gain additional insights for your testing efforts, and then target them with even more relevant content. This will really help improve your conversion rates and success metrics. Therefore, next you should try to create these use cases as visitor segments in your analytics tool and testing tool. To do this you should refer back to Chapter 2 where this was discussed in more detail.

In advanced testing tools like Adobe Test&Target, these use cases can also be created as custom targets and profiles that you can segment and target. To do this, you would create a profile for each use case by defining the characteristics of your visitors using rules and definitions. For example, a profile could include which pages your visitors need to see (and how they get there) and which tasks they need to accomplish in order to complete the use case. To set these up, please refer to the help section regarding this in your testing tool.

Re-review Your Use Cases Every Few Months to Make Sure They Still Work Well

During your upcoming optimization efforts, you will likely be making many changes to improve and optimize your website. Ideally, every time you change something significant, you need to remember to make sure your visitors' use cases are still being met easily. This is because even if one of your success metrics increases based on a change that you make, your change might also unknowingly impact the ability of your visitors to complete one of your major use cases, and potentially negatively impact other success metrics.

Week 8: Create a Unique Value Proposition and Clearly Promote It

One of the common problems with many websites is that the creators/marketers of them often presume their visitors know why they should use the website, what they can do on it and what's in it for them, without actually directly informing them. This is particularly problematic because there are usually many websites that a visitor can choose from, and competitors are only a mouse click away. That means you have to work hard to make sure that your visitors quickly understand the benefit of using your website to ensure they stay and hopefully engage and convert.

A great way to ensure your visitors recognize the benefits of using your website is to have a good unique value proposition for it and clearly promote that. Therefore, this week you will learn how to create and promote a better one of these.

Even if you think you already have a good unique value proposition you should still try and improve it, and the best practices you will learn this week should help you do so. And while it is certainly possible to run a website with a value proposition that isn't unique, your website will be in a much stronger position if it is at least somewhat unique.

Monday: Understand Your Current Unique Value Proposition from Your Visitor's Perspective

The first step in terms of creating a great website value proposition is to understand the perspective of this from your visitors. This is important because while you or your company might think you know what your website's unique value proposition is, unfortunately your visitor's opinion of it may be very different, and you need to work to align these together better.

To help you do this, put yourself in your website visitor's shoes again and visit your homepage as if you were a first time visitor. Then ask yourself the following three questions and see if you come can up with answers very quickly (because your visitors will be judging your website very quickly too):

1. Which website am I on and where am I on it?
2. What can I do on this website?
3. Why should I do it on this website?

After your first attempt at answering these questions, you need to try pretending you landed on a few different common entry pages from a search engine, for example a product or service page, and see if you can still answer these three questions as easily.

Don't be surprised, though, if you can't answer these questions very well from the perspective of your visitor (particularly on your interior pages because it is harder to convey unique value proposition on non-home pages). This is because many online businesses don't realize the importance of showing their unique value proposition or find it difficult to create one.

Now try this exercise on some people who are likely to be unfamiliar with your website (like your mom) and see if they can answer the three questions listed previously. Try asking a few different types of people, including someone who is not very web savvy and someone who is. If they also can't answer these questions very easily, then you know you have a lot of potential room for improvement by creating and promoting a unique value proposition on your website.

Tuesday: Survey Your Visitors to Help Create Your Value Proposition

A great way to get further ideas to help with the creation or improvement of your unique value proposition is to survey your visitors to gain feedback on what they currently think it is. This can be done very simply by using a free survey tool like Survey Monkey (`www.SurveyMonkey.com`) to ask them a simple question regarding what they like most about your online business and website. Gaining this feedback is best achieved by using an open-ended text box survey question like "Please describe what you like the most about this site," or "What are some of the reasons why you like this website? In particular, do you prefer anything over any competitors' websites?" Don't worry about asking further questions in your survey at this point—you'll be learning more about that in Week 10.

Once you have gathered sufficient responses (at least 50), you need to analyze the results to look for patterns and common themes. This can easily be done by exporting the text of your responses into a text file and then importing into a word cloud tool like Wordle (`www.Wordle.net`). This helps you visualize which words are most commonly found in your responses—for example, "free shipping," "great customer service," "easy-to-use site." Pick the four or five most common phrases you see and make a note of them. You should also look for common phrases that don't match what you perceive your website's unique value proposition to be, and try to understand and address reasons why they might incorrectly think that way.

This survey response analysis will then be used to help create or improve your unique value proposition over the next few days.

Wednesday: Learn from Competitor Websites to Improve Your Value Proposition

Fairly often the dominant company in a website vertical isn't the one that started first but is the one that learned from other companies. Just look at the example of Google:

Yahoo was the giant in search engines first, but then Google came along, learned from them and did everything better and now completely dominates.

Therefore today you will learn from your competitors' websites to improve your value proposition (and also give you great ideas to test on your website).

Perform Competitive Intelligence to Gain Ideas

First you need to come up with a list of your major online competitors and then review each of them and look for things that you can try and improve or try using on your website. Here are some things that you should look for:

- New tools
- Marketing promotions
- Original content
- New products
- Personalized page elements

It might be worthwhile to see which of your competitors are doing the best in terms of traffic and pay special attention to gathering intelligence from their websites. To help you run competitive traffic analysis you can use free tools such as Compete (`www.Compete.com`).

When you are reviewing your competitor websites for ideas, you should aim to differentiate from them to make your value proposition more unique—don't just copy them. In addition to this, you should look for ideas to differentiate your website using ideas from other websites across your industry, as you will learn about next.

Look for Best Practices across Websites in Your Industry

Just because a website doesn't sell the same thing or offer the same services as you doesn't mean you won't be able to learn from them. Rather than just focusing on your direct competitor websites you should also think laterally.

First you should think of and learn from websites that are more niche than yours (that may only offer one particular product/content relating to your website). Then you should think of and learn from websites that match the same type of website as yours but sell different products or services—for example, if your website is for a lead-generation company, look around for other websites that focus on generating leads, regardless of what they are generating leads for.

Thursday: Create or Improve the Unique Value Proposition for Your Website

Now that you have got some ideas from your visitors and your online competitors, today you need to actually create or improve the unique value proposition for your website.

Using the best practices and criteria below, you need to create a couple of different unique value propositions for your website. You will then review and refine these into just one later on in this day.

Best Practices to Help You Create or Improve your Unique Value Proposition

Here are some other best practices to help you create or improve the unique value proposition of your website:

- Most important, you should always think if your visitors will be able to easily relate to your value proposition, understand it, and find it useful.
- Try and restrict your value proposition to less than 20 words. Any more and this will become too wordy for your visitors to quickly read and understand.
- Don't use words from your mission statement in your value proposition, because this is usually very sales-like and isn't very visitor-centric (for example "to be the biggest global provider of shoes online").
- Don't use words in your value proposition that are too sales- or marketing-like (such as "We are the best *X*"), because these also aren't very visitor-centric.
- Take out any fluff words that aren't really needed, as this will help keep your value proposition shorter and sweeter.
- Take out any jargon words from your unique value proposition that may confuse your visitor.

Meet the Following Criteria for an Effective Unique Value Proposition

Last and most important, to have an effective unique value proposition, it needs to meet the following three criteria for your visitors:

Appeal How good is the appeal of your unique value proposition, and is it engaging enough?

Credibility How credible is your unique value proposition? It has to be as believable and credible as possible because visitors won't stick around if it doesn't seem so.

Exclusivity How exclusive is your unique value proposition, and can you find other websites offering the same service or value?

If any of the two or three versions of your unique value proposition that you have come up with don't satisfy all of these criteria, try and refine them until they do.

Test Your Website Value Proposition Ideas Using Google Adwords

Testing your ideas for your unique value proposition helps you find out how engaging they are likely to be to your potential visitors. Using Google Adwords is a great way to do this. Create five different paid search ads to drive to your home page, with each ad title and text focusing on different elements of your value proposition ideas (you will have to condense your ideas a bit).

The ad with the highest click-through rate is going to be the one visitors like the most, so you should consider adopting most of the elements of this winning ad into your final chosen value proposition.

Now you need to decide on which version of your unique value proposition you want to use. To help you decide on the final one, you should review your two or three versions with your other colleagues to get their input, particularly ones from your marketing department, because they might be able to help you put a better spin on it and make it sound even better. You should then refine and combine them until you reach agreement on the best unique value proposition to use.

Tomorrow you will learn how to best promote your newly improved or created unique value proposition on your website.

Friday: Effectively Promote Your Unique Value Proposition on Your Site

Now that you have come up with your website's value proposition (or improved your existing one), the next thing you need to do is to clearly communicate this to your visitors in an effective way.

Promote on Your High-Traffic Webpages

The first and most important areas of your website to promote your unique value proposition are on your high traffic pages, for example your homepage and top entry pages. This is because you want as many people to see your unique value proposition as possible, and often your homepage not only gets considerable traffic, but is a page where you need to convince your visitors of the value of your website the most.

The best and most important way of doing this is to place a prominent module on the homepage that states your unique value proposition, ideally combined with a relevant, high impact image or video in it (more on the subject of image and video optimization in Chapter 6). This should be highly visible and should be viewable without the visitor having to scroll down to see it (above the page fold, as you will also learn more about in Chapter 5).

Mint.com is a great example of a website that has an effectively promoted good unique value proposition on their home page, as shown in Figure 4.1.

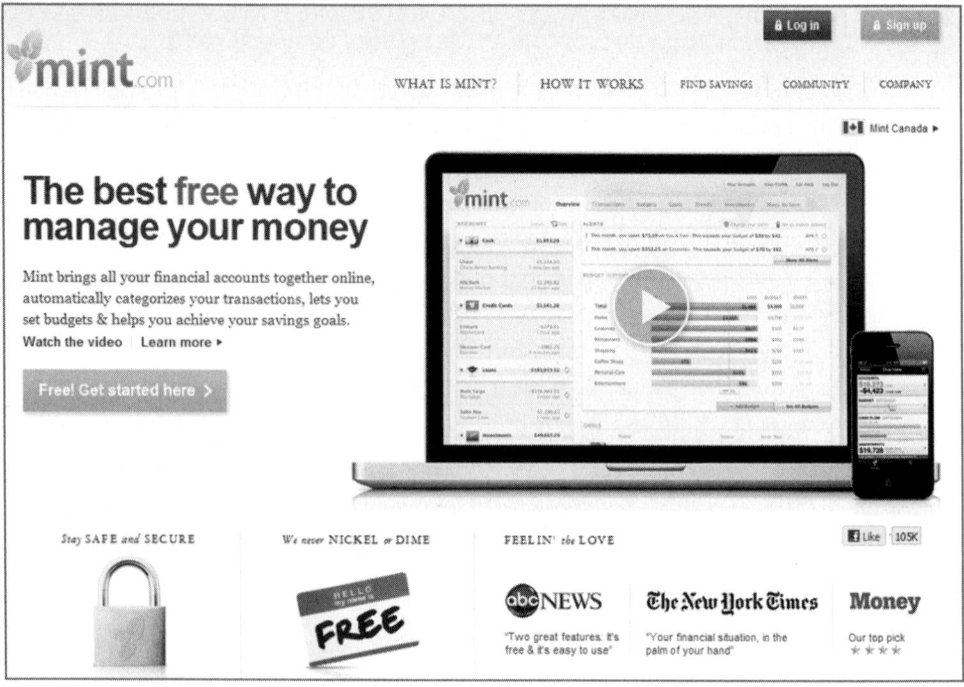

Figure 4.1 Example of a unique value proposition promoted well on a home page

Repeat Your Value Proposition in Your Checkout

Another essential area on your website that you need to re-emphasize your unique value proposition is on your checkout page or signup pages, because this is where visitors often need extra reassurance before they are willing to purchase or sign up. This will be covered in more detail in Chapter 7.

Create a First-Time Visitor Page

The next thing you should do is to try creating a "first-time visitor" page that focuses on giving more detail regarding your unique value proposition and the major benefits of using your website. This should be aimed at appealing to first time visitors and should contain tips explaining how to make effective use of your website (try creating and using a top five benefits list), and any top content or most popular products or services you offer. You should also show the reasons why your website is better than your competitors, and to do this you could try showing a grid that compares the features of your website to your competitors' websites.

Another thing you could offer on this page are coupons to first time purchasers, and this will hopefully have a great impact on your website conversion rates.

After you have created this page, you should then prominently link to it from your value proposition module on your homepage and in the footer of your website.

Use a Tagline on Your Logo

Another best practice to effectively communicate your unique value proposition is to create a shorter version in the form of a tagline and place this right by your logo (or even go so far as to make this part of your logo). The website logo is often one of the things that a visitor first looks at upon arriving on a website, and if elements of your unique value proposition are in the form of a tagline that is right next to it, then this is going to help your visitors understand the value of your website much more quickly. This is particularly helpful to use if you have a generic website name that is nondescriptive but not as important for websites with a strong brand already. To help you create some examples of this, Figure 4.2 shows a few examples of great tag lines that help reinforce a website's value proposition.

Figure 4.2 Example of taglines with a value proposition

Week 9: Understand Your Visitors' Intent by Visually Analyzing Them

This week you will learn about the benefits of visually analyzing your visitors' behavior on your website, and the great insights for testing and optimization that they form. You will then learn from several different types of visual analysis tools that you can use and the benefits of doing so.

Monday: Learn the Importance of Visually Analyzing Your Website Visitors

Traditional web analytics tools track visitor click stream data and are great at helping you determine insight into *what* your visitors are doing on your website. However, they don't tell you *why* your visitors are doing these things on your website, and you are left with guessing reasons for their behavior.

A great way of helping to bridge this analytical gap is to add additional tracking tools to your website that actually visually record what your visitors are doing. This helps you gain more clarity and context about your visitors' behavior on your web pages and possible reasons for why your visitors do what they do. For example, you can use these tools to determine what links they are clicking on the most and which page elements are least looked at. Knowing this helps provide you with some excellent insights that you can use to form better test ideas to optimize your website.

Ultimately, before anything is changed or tested on your web pages you should be gathering visual insights to help you improve your decision making and what needs testing. Don't just guess at they are doing, go on a hunch, or always do what your HiPPOs think because this will result in sub-bar optimization efforts and may even have a negative impact.

These visual analysis tools come in many forms. Click heat maps are the most basic type, which show you exactly where visitors click on all of the pages on your website. Next there are eye flow heat maps, which show (and predict) where your visitors are looking—which is often different than what they click on. Last, and impressively, they also come in the form of video sessions of your visitors using and clicking around your website.

While you can get some understanding of what your visitors are clicking on in web analytics tools by using link tracking, this doesn't really substitute for good visual-based analysis, particularly if not all your links are tracked or have distinctive names, making it hard to tell which link visitors are actually clicking on.

Tuesday: Check Click Heat Maps for Your Key Pages

There are several benefits to using click heat map analysis tools to visually understand what your visitors are clicking on. First, they can tell you if your visitors are clicking on what you want them to ideally click on, for example your important calls-to-action. This may sometimes be very different from what you expect them to be clicking on.

Another good benefit of using click heat maps is to analyze how visitors use your main navigation links—for example, your header and left-hand navigation menus or your related links sections. This way you can understand which links are the most popular and which ones don't seem to resonate with your visitors. Based on the results of this, you can optimize your navigation options to better engage and convert your visitors.

Click heat map analysis will ultimately help you understand what needs testing and improving on your pages. For example, if visitors don't seem to be clicking on your important links, test placing them in more visible locations, and try testing the wording of the links in case your visitors don't understand what they are for or what they mean.

It's important that when considering doing a test on any page on your website, you should first look at a click heat map to see which links and elements on it are most and least popular with your visitors. This will give you additional insight into which page elements you should focus on and test, and will improve the efficiency and results of your testing efforts.

This click heat map analysis is particularly important to run on and understand for the pages that relate to your conversion goals and use cases.

Next, you will learn about the different click heat map reports and tools that are available for you to evaluate and make use of.

The first and most primitive of these is Google Analytics In-Page Analytics report (`www.google.com/analytics`), which enables you to see an overlay of link click percentages on any of your pages. You can see an example of this tool in action in Figure 4.3.

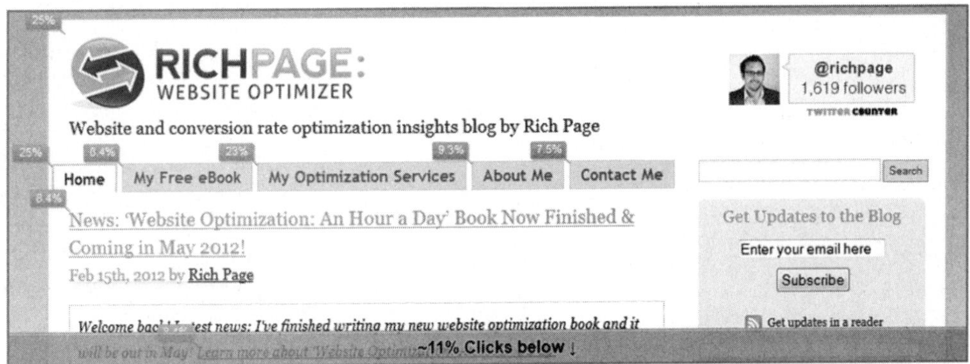

Figure 4.3 Screenshot of the Google Analytics In-Page Analytics report

You can also analyze clicks for each of the different visitor segment groups you set up in Chapter 2 to see how clicking patterns vary. This is important, because visitor click patterns are going to vary depending on where the visitor comes from, or the characteristics of them.

This is a rather primitive visual analysis report though, relying on simply showing percentage usage metrics for each link instead of better color coded heat maps, but it will give you some good basic details. On the plus side, it is simple to make use of because it requires no downloads or plugins to be able to view these clicks on your website.

In more advanced analytics tools they usually offer more visual click analysis functionality, with greater emphasis on showing heat maps of clicks. This makes it much easier to visually decipher what people are clicking on the most, with the brighter the color of the heat, the more people clicking in that area.

In Adobe SiteCatalyst this is known as the Click Map tool, which requires you to download a browser plugin to do this visual analysis. This useful tool also allows you to turn on revenue related click analysis (if you use that in Adobe SiteCatalyst) and helps you understand revenue per click, and total revenue generated from each link.

For a more powerful tool that is dedicated to click tracking visual analysis, you should try using Crazy Egg (`www.CrazyEgg.com`). In addition to offering powerful click heat map visual analysis (see Figure 4.4 for an example), they also offer some other great features. The tool lets you run visitor segmentation on your clicks to see what particular groups of visitors click on (but much fewer segments than Google Analytics offers). They also offer scroll map visual reports that show you on average how far visitors scroll down any of your pages and have some great options for generating automated email reports to help keep you in the loop better regarding this visual analysis.

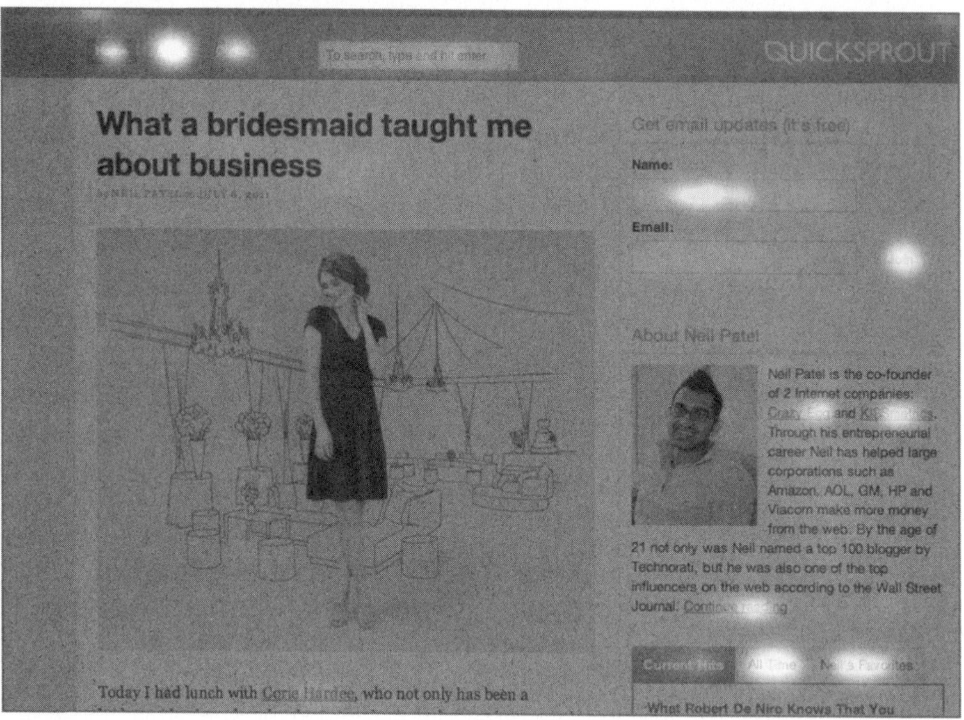

Figure 4.4 Screenshot of the Crazy Egg Heat Map tool

Wednesday: Use Eye Tracking Tools to Understand Visitors' Eye Flow

Knowing what visitors are clicking on is a good start for understanding visitor behavior, but you really need to know what your visitors are *looking at* too. This can often be different than where they are clicking, and depending on what they look at first it can have a major impact on your ability to engage and convert them.

Ideally you want to design your pages so that your visitors look at your most important content first, such as key images and calls-to-action. Unfortunately, many websites have too much content that distracts the visitor's eye away from these more important elements (with marketing banners and ads being a major offender).

Therefore it's essential that you analyze how your visitors currently look at on your website, particularly on your key conversion pages, and based on findings run tests on your page elements to improve what they are looking at first.

Up until recently it was fairly hard to get this visitor eye flow insight without having to do expensive laboratory-based eye-tracking tests. However, over the last few years some great improvements in web technology have made this much cheaper and easier to understand, with two great tools in particular that you can use.

The first tool that you can make use of to understand your visitor's eye flow is from Gazehawk (`www.Gazehawk.com`). In order to use this you simply submit your website that you want reviewed for eye flow (or upload images of web pages you want reviewed), and then their testers begin using your website while their eye movements are tracked and recorded using webcams. You can either use their testers or find your own visitors to do this—all they need is to have a webcam to able to participate. The tool then aggregates your testers' eye flows and generates eye flow heat maps so you can see what visitors are looking at, which you can see an example of in Figure 4.5.

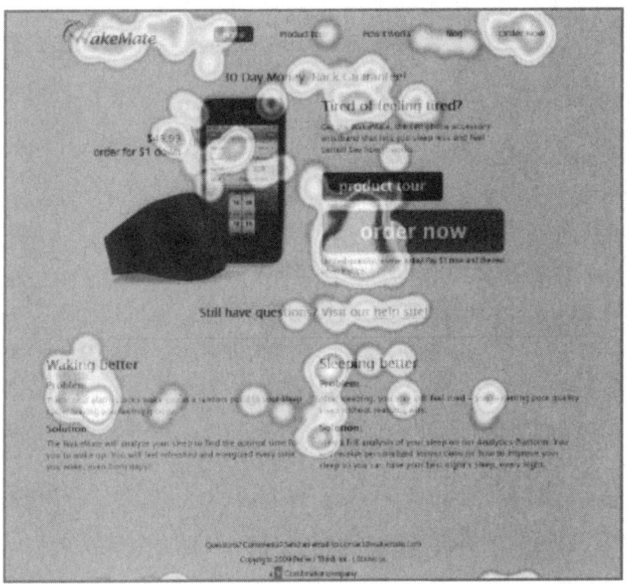

Figure 4.5 Screenshot of the Gazehawk Eye Heat Map tool

They also then give you live replays of what your test visitors looked at, so you can replay at your leisure to get even more insight. Basic tests start from $500 for 10 test participants, which sounds expensive, but that is much cheaper than traditional eye flow laboratory tests, which usually cost in the thousands.

Another simpler eye flow tool you can use is available from AttentionWizard (`www.AttentionWizard.com`). Instead of actually putting your web pages in front of testers' web cams, they are put through this tool's proprietary algorithm to predict what page elements your visitors are likely to look at the most. It then generates a great heat map of the results, complete with the flow and order of things they look at (for example what they look at first and last). This is done almost instantly and is great for getting a quick prediction of what your visitors might be looking at. In Figure 4.6, you can see an example of this eye flow analysis.

This tool is much cheaper than Gazehawk's because it doesn't use real people and prices at the time of writing start from $27 per month for 10 heat maps per month.

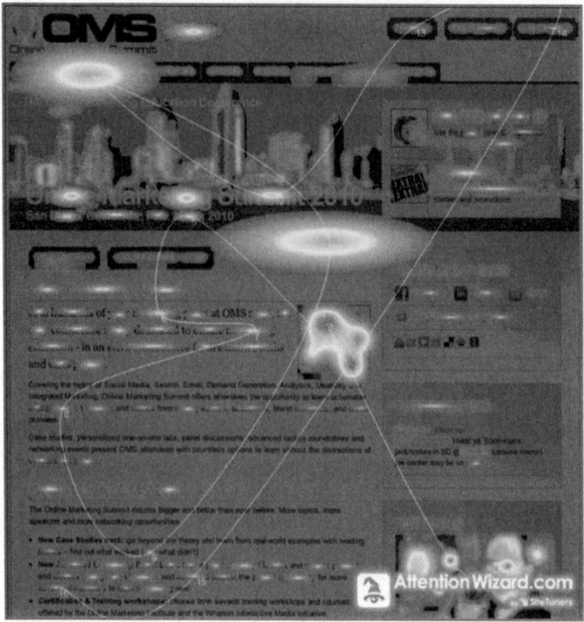

Figure 4.6 Screenshot of AttentionWizard Eye Heat Map tool

It is also important to try and predict visitor click and eye flow patterns before you launch something and not just after you launch something. Remember it's much cheaper and easier to get feedback to act on it early in the website development phase, rather than trying to test and change a live website. Both of these eye tracking tools are essential for helping with website prototyping and wireframe development of new websites, web pages, or new site features.

As another option to gain visitor eye flow analysis, if you have a higher level of budget, you can consider renting or purchasing an eye tracker machine. These allow you to do unlimited eye flow tracking experiments with as many people as you want. You just need to recruit people to participate and find a lab where you can use the machine on them. There are several companies to evaluate that offer these machines, such as Tobii (`www.tobii.com`).

Thursday: Use Visitor Recording Tools to Gain a Complete View of Your Visitor's Experience

Don't you wish you could stand over the shoulders of your visitors and actually see what they are doing on your website, without them knowing you are there? You would be able to see how they actually navigate your website (not just how you think they do) and what pages and elements they get stuck on or engage with the most.

Luckily there are now a few website tools that allow you to do this by recording your visitors' mouse movements and clicks, all without you needing to be there in person or needing to use expensive web cams. The visitor isn't even aware they are being recorded, and they don't have to download anything to be recorded, either.

The pioneering tool to offer this visitor recording ability is called ClickTale (`www.ClickTale.com`), but there is now a cheaper, simpler tool called Userfly (`www.Userfly.com`), in addition to a more expensive but more robust offering from Tea Leaf (`www.Tealeaf.com`).

The visitor recordings these tools gather can be searched and categorized in many ways (by page seen or by entry point, for example), and you can also change the speed of the replay to make it faster to watch. The tools also offer aggregate reporting so you can understand how visitors interacted with your web page forms, the most clicked and engaged elements of your pages, and the average progress they make through your conversion flows. These aggregate reports are great because it means you don't have to sit through every single recording to get an overall impression of these important aspects of your website.

You can see a sample screenshot of this visitor recording from ClickTale.com in Figure 4.7. As you can see in the figure, ClickTale shows the playback controls, where the visitor has clicked (marked by circles), and where the mouse currently is (with a circle around the mouse pointer).

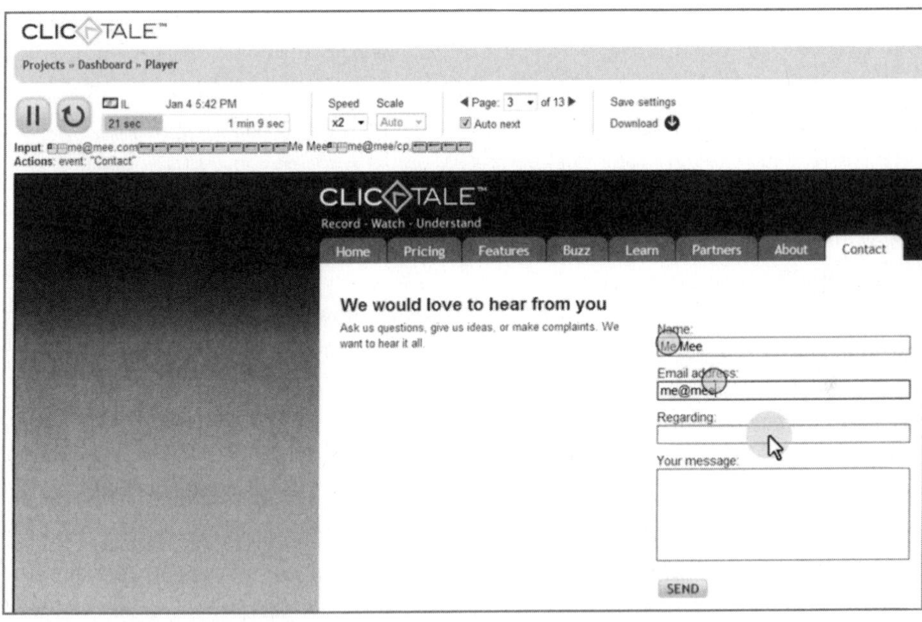

Figure 4.7 Screenshot of ClickTale visitor recording playback

There are several insights you can learn from these visitor recordings that you wouldn't be able to learn from your web analytics tool or click heat map tool. For example:

Learn which page elements your visitors hover over the most but don't click on. Running replays for this helps you see if your visitors are pausing for a while before clicking on something, possibly indicating confusion or hesitation. Or perhaps they are thinking something is clickable when it actually isn't, which is something you should try to remedy when this occurs on any of your pages.

Learn how far, on average, your visitors scroll down your pages. Running replays and reports for this can help you see how engaging your pages are, and if your visitors are often not getting to important content that you may have lower down on some of your pages.

Helps you understand how visitors interact and attempt completing your web page forms. Running these replays and reports is very useful on your conversion-related pages where you are asking the visitor to fill in forms—for example, your sign-up or shopping cart pages. This helps you understand and optimize which fields of the form your visitors most frequently abandon your page from and most often leave blank.

Another great thing you can do on the more powerful visitor recording tools is to set up email alerts to inform you of any visitor issues with any pages relating to your key conversion goals.

Friday: Implement Tools and Gather and Review Visual Analysis for Insights

Today you need to begin to implement at least one or two types of these visual analysis tools on your website. Before you decide on which ones to try using, you should first review with your IT department each of the tools to find out which ones are easier to implement from a technical standpoint. Depending on how strict your IT department is, you may get some pushback relating to some of these tools, because they require continual data capture from your pages. If this occurs, you should set up a meeting with them to make them understand the importance and real benefit of using these tools.

After you have chosen one, set it up, and gathered at least a few weeks' worth of data, you need to start spending time reviewing all this visual analysis reporting. This is important because there will be an abundance of it, and you need to generate some common visitor patterns and insights from it. To help you do a better job with this, you should categorize your results by page, and spend more time on ones that relate to your conversion goals. Then while you are reviewing the results you should start documenting a list of patterns and insights to try testing and optimizing on your website. The first time you do this visual analysis review of the results you should spend considerable time on it (ideally dedicate a few days). You should then perform some brief visual analysis on your key pages every month or two after this and see if you notice anything new that may be worth testing and optimizing.

Last, every time you launch new page functionality or content on your website it's important that you run this visual analysis on the related pages to see what you can learn from and then test and optimize.

Week 10: Generate Insights from Visitor Satisfaction and Feedback Tools

As previously discussed, it's important to try and understand *why* your visitors do *what* they are doing in order to gain ideas for testing and optimizing. Today you are going to learn another way to do this by making use of additional tools to listen to the needs, feedback, and experiences of your website visitors.

Monday: Learn the Importance of the Voice of Your Visitors and Asking for Feedback

As stated before in this book, your website really would be nothing without your website visitors. And it's important to remember that they are pickier and more web savvy than ever before, usually having a wealth of choice on the internet and growing expertise and expectations of browsing websites.

These website visitors usually know exactly what they want from a website, what they don't like, and what they prefer. These visitor viewpoints are unfortunately quite often different from the viewpoint that your website decision makers have, particularly your HiPPOs. And if your visitors don't like what they see, or can't accomplish what they came to your website to do, they can simply leave your website and go to one of many other potential competitor websites. This then has a negative impact because of the missed potential conversion from this unsatisfied lost visitor.

Therefore, rather than just presuming you know what is good for your website visitors or listening to your HiPPPOs demands all the time, it's critical that you ask your website visitors for their opinions and feedback, listen to what they say, and then act upon it by testing and optimizing pages relating to the feedback. Many of the best companies in the world have learned the importance of acting on great visitor feedback and have been very successful as a result of this. Apple and Zappos are two great examples of companies really listening to their customers, adapting their companies based on the feedback with impressive results.

Asking for feedback also makes your visitors feel more wanted and more involved with your company and ultimately helps build a better relationship between you and them. This can have the great effect of increasing the amount of engaged repeat visitors that you have, often resulting in higher levels of conversion from them, too.

Tuesday: Survey Your Website Visitors to Gain Feedback and Insights

One of the best and easiest ways of gaining feedback from your visitors is to set up surveys on your website and ask them a series of questions about their experience of visiting your website. These surveys come in two main forms: short and simple health-check surveys about your website and more in-depth surveys about particular aspects of your website. Today you will first learn about these types of surveys and then review the tools available to you and begin surveying your visitors. After you have gathered enough results from your surveys, the analysis from them provides invaluable ideas to help test and improve your website and also helps indicate what needs fixing most urgently.

Set Up a Simple Survey and Ask Three Very Important Feedback Questions

One of the most effective surveys you should run on your website is one that is short and to point, yet yields the most insight from your visitors. This type of survey should ideally have less than five questions to help ensure higher survey completion rates and less chance of the visitor getting frustrated by having to complete a very long one.

When setting this short survey up, it's important to always include three specific questions that are particularly effective at gaining insight and feedback from your visitors:

- What is the main reason you visited this website today?
- Were you able to complete the task you came to this website for? If not, why not?
- Would you recommend this website to a friend? Please provide reasons why.

These three simple questions help form a quick health check of your website, in particular the second question, which you should turn into a "task completion rate" success metric. As discussed earlier, this is because if people can't complete the task they came to your website for, then they probably won't be happy, and there is a good chance they won't come back.

In addition to these three questions, you should also include a question that you can use to gather specific feedback about an area or feature of your website. This can be changed or rotated for each survey you run depending on new features being launched or the current area of your website that you are looking to generate test ideas for.

As a fifth and last question you should also include an open-ended question. This allows your visitors to vent or rave in detail about anything you may not have directly asked them a question about in the survey.

You need to run this type of short feedback survey as soon as you can to start forming some great visitor insights, and to get a significant sample you should get at least 100 hundred results before you analyze the data. Depending on how quickly you get feedback coming in, you could wait until you have at least 200 responses to really make this analysis worth your while.

Once you have gathered enough responses, you need to analyze the results to look for patterns and common themes. To help you do this you can export the text of your survey responses into a text file and then import them into a word cloud tool like Wordle (`www.Wordle.net`) for easier analysis. This will help you understand what survey feedback is most common that you should act on first without having to focus on every single piece of feedback you get.

After you have done the analysis, you should then rerun this survey several times per year to gain new insights, and ideally you should permanently feature a link to one of these types of surveys on your website to constantly gather and monitor feedback.

Set Up In-Depth Surveys to Gain Additional Feedback

In addition to the shorter survey just discussed, you should also periodically set up and run longer surveys to gain feedback and insight for specific areas or features of your website. For example, if you have just launched or redesigned major content or functionality on your website, you could ask feedback related questions about that. Ideally you should use this survey on the pages that are related to what you are trying to gain additional in-depth feedback about.

This survey can be quite long, but to ensure you get reasonable completion rates (about 20%) you should try and keep the questions to fewer than 20. To help increase survey completion rates, you should try and split up your survey questions into multiple pages and include a progress bar.

Evaluate and Set Up Tools to Survey Your Visitors

There are several tools you can use to run your website visitor feedback surveys. If you have a fairly small website or a limited survey budget, a good tool with a free version you could try is 4Q (`www.4Qsurvey.com`). This tool is great for asking a limited set of questions as in the shorter type of survey just discussed, and you can also integrate your results into Google Analytics to perform great analysis on the visitor characteristics of your survey respondents.

Another lower-budget survey tool you can use is called Survey Monkey (`www.SurveyMonkey.com`), which offers more advanced functionality, including question logic and branching that allows you to show related questions depending on the visitor's previous question answers, and multiple different types of question formats (for example matrix style, multiple choice etc.). It also offers the ability to customize the look and feel of the survey to match your website.

Ideally you should try and use a more advanced survey tool though. There are several you can choose from including Adobe Survey (`http://www.omniture.com/en/products/analytics/survey`), Opinion Lab (`www.OpinionLab.com`) or Foresee Results (`www.Foreseeresults.com`). These advanced survey tools offer greater flexibility in survey setup by allowing usage of rules and logic and also offer alerts based on results. They also offer advanced results analysis, including the ability to filter based on the page that visitors completed the survey from—important because reactions and feedback can heavily vary depending on the page the user takes the survey from. This means you can gather feedback for each of your pages and sections of your website rather than just feedback for your website as a whole.

These more advanced surveying tools also have great options for launching the surveys to ask for feedback. Instead of immediately showing the questions to a visitor upon arriving at a website and risk not getting good responses, they instead ask visitors if they would like to participate in a survey after they have spent more time on the website. This works by reminding the visitor to complete the survey as they are about to exit or by leaving a pop-up survey window open on their desktop or browser while the visitor is browsing the website. See Figure 4.8 for an example of this pop-up survey in action.

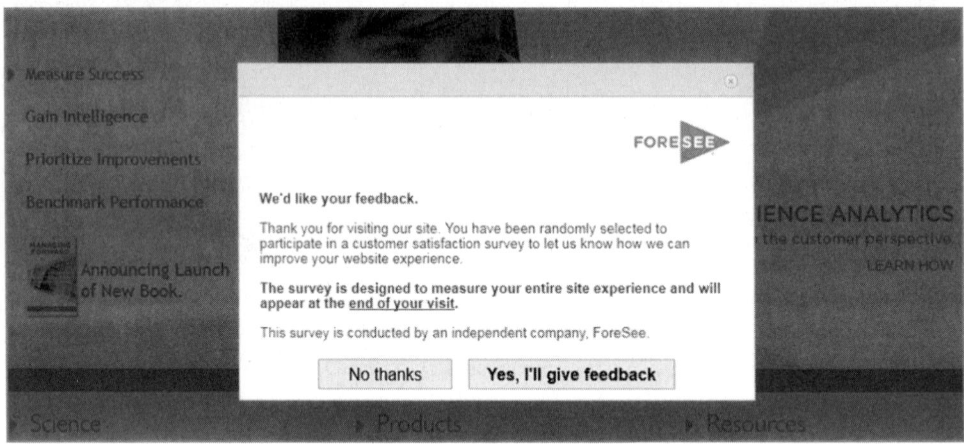

Figure 4.8 An example of a ForeSee Results survey pop-up

Another great newer, reasonably priced survey tool you can use to help gain even greater visitor insights is called KISSinsights (`www.KISSinsights.com`). This unique tool helps you gather shorter but more specific visitor insight in the most contextual and most important moments rather than showing longer general website surveys on all of your pages. The tool enables you to do this by automatically popping up a single question survey on specific important pages that you are targeting. For example, you could ask a shopping cart feedback question just on your shopping cart pages, or ask a pricing feedback question just on your product pricing page. This allows you to ask for quick and specific feedback without overwhelming your visitors with long website surveys and ensures the visitor has actually seen the page you are asking feedback about. Figure 4.9 shows an example of what this survey tool looks like in action.

This unique feedback tool is definitely worth trying on your website to gain feedback and test insights, especially because they have a free trial and their paid plans start at just $29 (at the time of writing this).

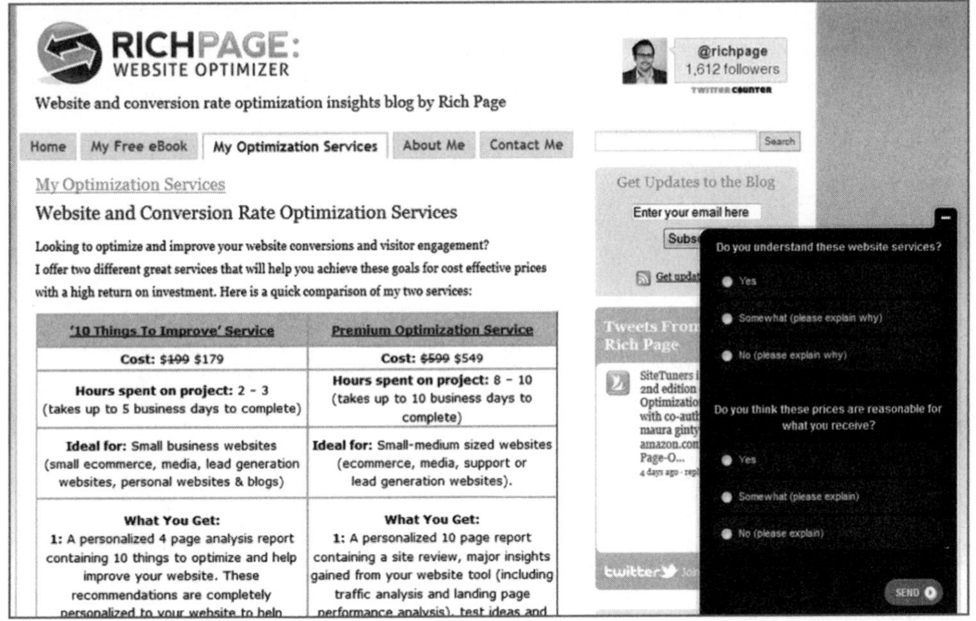

Figure 4.9 Example of a KISSinsights survey pop-up

Other Website Survey Best Practices

To ensure greater success, there are also several other best practices you should adopt when running feedback surveys on your website that you will now learn about.

First, you should always have a "give feedback" link available on all pages of your website, because doing this allows for your visitors to give feedback any time they want, whether this is to give praise or to complain about something. A link in your footer is a great place to have this permanent survey link in addition to more prominent modules on your pages that visually ask your visitors for feedback. Some websites even go so far as to have open text comment boxes in the footer of their websites to encourage more feedback.

Don't Annoy Your Visitors with Surveys

Don't use a pop-up survey asking visitors for feedback immediately as they enter your website, as this could annoy them and cause them to exit your website. Remember they usually won't be able to give you good feedback until they have used your website a few times anyway—definitely not after seeing one page. Instead of this you should ask them if it's okay to ask for feedback after they have completed using your website. You should also limit the number of questions you ask to ideally less than 20, as the more you ask, the more likely the visitor will get frustrated halfway through and abandon it.

In order to get more survey responses to gain possible insight from them, you should try offering an incentive to your visitors for completing the survey, for example, by offering a coupon or special promotion if they complete the survey.

You also need to make sure you have enough survey results for each survey you run in order to make sure you can gain a representative, unbiased sample of feedback. Anything less than 50 visitors will mean you will risk not getting enough of a realistic, representative and valid response.

Another best practice is to include ratings questions for your website in several categories—for example, ratings out of 10 for overall website rating, and ratings for website features and website design. The results of these ratings should ideally be included in your weekly analytics website reports so you can monitor and understand the current rating level of your website. Several survey tools offer this built-in page rating functionality and is something that many feedback rating tools also feature (which will be discussed in more detail tomorrow).

Wednesday: Use Website Feedback Rating Tools to Gain Further Insight

Many tools have recently appeared that help increase your ability to generate, organize, and analyze this all-important feedback from your visitors. These great, relatively inexpensive tools help visitors submit website and product improvement ideas and complaints and give ratings for particular elements of your website.

One of the first tools you should know about is called Get Satisfaction (`www.GetSatisfaction.com`) and in particular is great for any website that offers a product or service. Not only does it offer good functionality for collecting feedback about what you are selling and identifying problems on your website, it also allows for visitors to rank and rate other visitors' feedback. This makes giving feedback a democracy and helps website owners prioritize which feedback is most important to act on first. Figure 4.10 shows a screenshot of the Get Satisfaction pop-up in action. As you will see, it's very intuitive for the visitor to offer feedback and to see what other ideas and feedback are most popular from other visitors.

You could also try using UserVoice (`www.UserVoice.com`) for a slightly cheaper but less advanced tool that offers similar powerful feedback and support options.

For a slightly different perspective on feedback generation, you could also try using the feedback tool from Kampyle (`www.Kampyle.com`). It allows visitors to submit ratings for different features and aspects of your website (that are fully configurable in the tool), and even goes as far to let visitors leave their contact details after giving feedback so you can reply to them if need be.

All these tools also have great options to make it easier for visitors to see how to give feedback, with all of them having icons and widgets that stay visible on screen as they scroll, either showing a button in the bottom right or showing as a tab on either side the of the browser. In Figure 4.11, you can see an example of this tab that Uservoice.com uses in the bottom right of the visitors' browser.

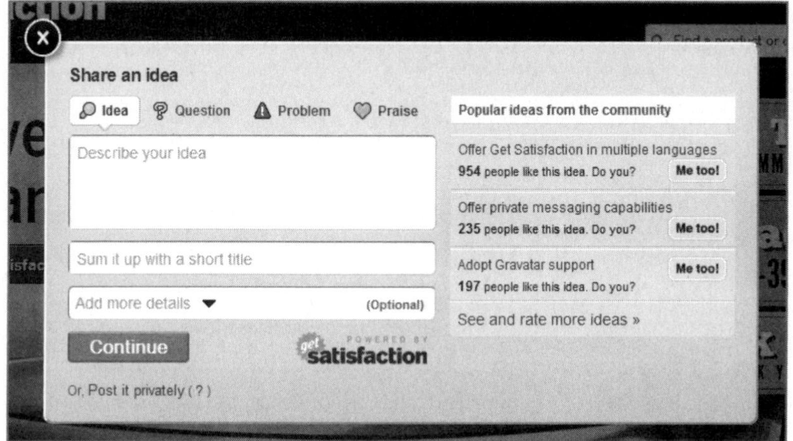

Figure 4.10 Example of a Get Satisfaction survey pop-up

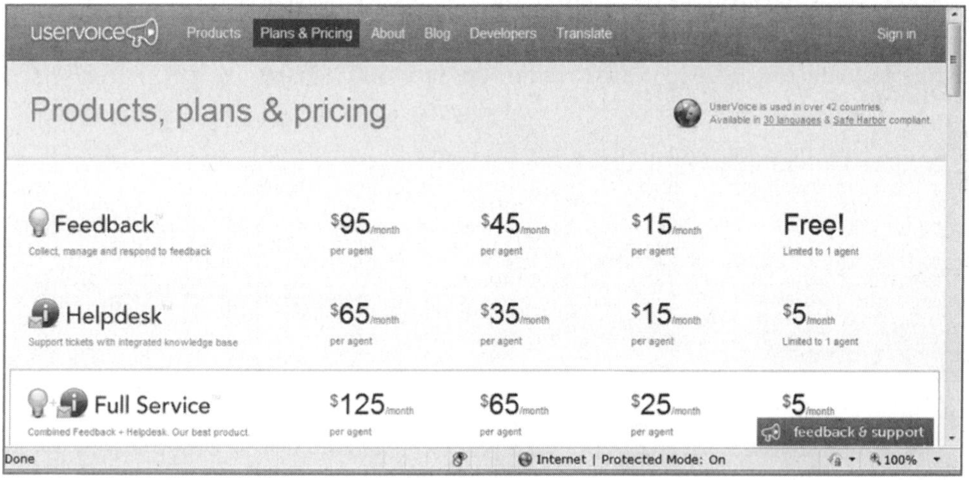

Figure 4.11 Example of a UserVoice feedback tab in bottom right of browser

Once you have chosen and set up one of these feedback tools on your website, spend considerable time reviewing and analyzing the ratings and comments you initially receive. As with the other feedback and survey tools that have been covered, make sure you receive at least 50 responses to ensure a representative and valid sample to review. You then need to look for any patterns regarding the ratings or feedback received and use these to generate ideas for testing and optimizing your website.

After you have done this the first time, as discussed earlier you should then try and add your website feedback ratings to your web analytics reports each week and monitor them for trends. You should also review your latest responses in depth on at least a monthly basis to look for new insights.

Thursday: Gain Feedback on the Usability and Task Completion Rate of Your Website

Unfortunately for you and your online business, website visitors are getting smarter and more demanding every day, and the website usability bar of websites is being continually lifted by new standards and best practices. Because of this, regardless of how good your website looks, if visitors find your website too hard to use in comparison to other websites, they can easily go to Google and find a competitor website that offers better usability instead. This obviously has negative impact on your ability to engage your visitors, let alone convert them.

Historically, in order to gain usability feedback from your visitors you usually had to run expensive usability labs and focus groups. While these often gave some good feedback, they were limited in that they only represented a small sample of your audience. This meant that results were sometimes biased and unrepresentative, unfortunately resulting in website changes that had little positive impact on visitors.

Due to the recent shift and focus toward improved website usability, luckily there are now several usability feedback tools that you can use to gain usability feedback from a much larger and representative population of your website visitors, all without needing to run expensive focus groups or usability labs.

The first and simplest usability tool you should try using is UserTesting.com (`www.UserTesting.com`). This tool offers a great way of understanding how visitors interact with your website in great detail and how easily they complete tasks you give them. You simply pick the number of testers you want to review your website and their demographics (for example age, gender, income and web expertise). You can even recruit testers from your own website to make sure they are from the exact target market you are looking for. You are charged a small fee per person who is tested (just $29 if you get at least three to test your website), so this ends up being much more cost effective than running usability labs.

After you have picked your testers, you then submit a list of tasks that you want feedback on for your testers to try and complete. You also make use of the option to ask your testers a set of questions at the end for you to gain additional feedback.

After the tester has reviewed your website and answered the tasks and questions you pose, you get a visual recording of them interacting with your website and answering your questions, complete with audio of them talking through your website. This allows you to look for and optimize any common issues your visitors may have, and will also often give you great ideas for testing and optimizing your website. See Figure 4.12 for a screenshot of this tool in action and the tester giving feedback.

To make best use of this tool, get at least 20 testers (any less and you risk getting unrepresentative or biased responses) to try and complete the major use cases you created for your website earlier in this chapter. After they have finished your test, review their responses and look for patterns and insights from them, in particular taking note of common issues they have with any of your use cases. This will help form some great ideas for testing and optimizing the pages relating to these use cases, and will usually help increase your conversion rates and success metrics.

Figure 4.12 Example of a tester giving feedback using UserTesting.com

To help you gain considerably more task completion feedback from a wider audience of your current website visitors, you should consider using a tool called Loop11 (`www.Loop11.com`). This usability tool enables you to get many more task completion feedback responses for a much cheaper rate than UserTesting.com (at the time of writing this is $350 per 1,000 visitors being tested).

A benefit of using this tool is that you can gain feedback from your actual visitors on your website rather than having to recruit them from other places (like you would need to do with UserTesting.com). The visitor also doesn't need to install anything in order to respond to your task completion questions; they just get a pop-up asking if they would like to participate, and a bar appears at the top of the website asking tasks for them to respond to. You can see an example of this bar being used on Amazon.com in Figure 4.13. All you have to do is submit a list of tasks that you want to see if your visitors can complete, and you should start getting responses immediately.

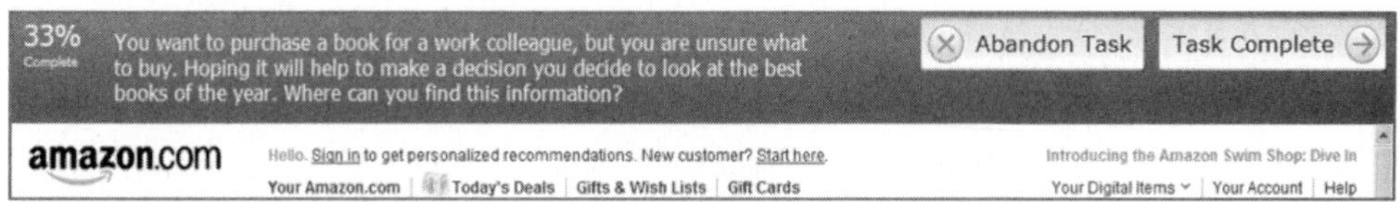

Figure 4.13 Example of a tester giving feedback using Loop11.com

While you don't get an audio and video recording of each respondent as with UserTesting.com, this tool importantly takes UserTesting.com's task feedback and analysis feature to a higher level. It actually measures and reports on how many visitors complete each of your tasks and at what completion rates, so you can run analysis on which use cases are most problematic.

Run Your Use Cases as Tasks in a Usability Tool for Visitors to Complete

One of the best uses of a task completion usability tool like Loop11 is that you can put your use cases to the ultimate test and ask your website visitors to complete them.

To do this, take the major use cases you created earlier in this chapter and turn each one of them into a task in a tool like Loop11, and run the tool to see how easy it is for your visitors to complete them. Test your use cases on at least 50 people from your website, and then from the tool report findings, note down the percentage completion rates for each of your use cases in Table 4.2.

▶ **Table 4.2** Visitor use case completion grade table

	Use Cases for Your Website	Visitor Use Case % Completion Rates
1		
2		
3		
4		
5		

If any of your use cases get below 70 percent completion rate from your visitors, you need to pay particular attention to testing and fixing pages associated with them. This really is a great exercise to perform, because fixing any major use cases that are hard for your visitors to complete will mean your visitors will be happier, more engaged, and convert more often (increasing your conversion rates).

There are several other tools that you can also use to analyze this use case completion rate from your website visitors, for example Usabilla.com (`www.usabilla.com`) and UserZoom.com (`www.userzoom.com`). Both of these tools also offer other tool functionality, like mockup and wire framing options, or surveying and online card sorting options.

Pitfalls of Visitor Usability Testind to Avoid

To ensure that you get reliable actionable feedback from your visitors when using these usability tools, it's key that you involve enough people in each round of usability tests. One common mistake is to only involve a small number of visitors, which often results in biased or extreme feedback that might not actually reflect your regular website visitors. This is particularly problematic if your visitors don't fit your target market, and haven't been to your website before (or at the very least a competitor website).

Therefore, it's important when doing usability testing that you get feedback from at least 20 people per usability test, and make sure you are picking visitors who fit the types of visitors usually on your website. Some tools allow you to pick and recruit your own participants, and I suggest you make good use of this to ensure you get highly relevant and targeted results from your own website visitors.

Gain Feedback from Usability Experts

The next tool that you should consider using allows you to obtain usability feedback from experts rather than your website visitors. This tool is called Concept Feedback (`www.ConceptFeedback.com`) and helps balance out some of the visitors' feedback (who may not necessarily suggest how to fix or improve things the best way) with opinions and feedback from experts.

You can get feedback from experts in multiple categories, from design and usability experts, to website strategy and conversion rate experts. It is also offers free options to ask for feedback from the general expert community on their website. Once you gain this expert feedback (usually within 48 hours), it offers great built-in options for easily sharing and reviewing this feedback with your design, marketing, and IT teams.

The expert feedback results from this tool are great to complement the feedback generated from your other usability and feedback tools and should help provide some great ideas for testing and optimizing your website.

Use Usability Tools Pre-launch in Addition to Post-launch

One last best practice is to not just use these usability feedback tools on your live websites; it's particularly important to also make use of these tools before you launch new websites, launch a redesign, or offer a new feature or functionality. You can get great feedback regarding wireframes, mockups, and images from these tools (not just live websites), allowing you to gather and act on feedback much more quickly and cheaply than on a live website.

Ultimately you shouldn't just presume that your visitors are going to like what you launch or change, no matter how pretty or cool it may look. If they don't like it, they may start using a competitor's website instead, so you should always get feedback from visitors before you launch or change something.

Friday: Make Use of Web Chat Tools to Gain Additional Insight

Today you will learn about making use of web chat tools to help with your website optimization efforts. Not only do web chat options provide a great real time support mechanism for your visitors, but they allow you to ask feedback related questions of your visitors in real time. The responses from your visitors enable you to analyze them for any patterns or issues that they mention most often and help you discover great insights for testing and optimizing your website. Another benefit of web chat tools is that you can modify your questions immediately depending on the context or what the visitor is currently doing (as opposed to traditional survey tools, which aren't able to be this dynamic).

Web Chat Tool Best Practices

Not only should you offer web chat button options on your website for visitors who need to get help and support fast, but you should proactively seek feedback using chat pop-up requests. You should have specific questions to ask your visitors that are geared toward helping improve your website, not just general questions like "Can I help you?" or questions about your products or services. For a few examples of questions, you should try asking visitors if they are finding what they need, and if not, what your website could offer to make it easier, or you could ask them if they find anything problematic or lacking about using your website.

You could also try asking your visitors questions regarding particular tools or sections of your website that you are looking for feedback about, in addition to feedback on conversion related pages like your shopping cart or registration pages.

However, as noted earlier with survey pop-ups, you shouldn't be too intrusive with these web chat pop-up requests. In particular you should avoid making use of these within a few seconds of a visitor arriving on the home page or any other major page. This is because you may pop up the chat tool to a new visitor who won't be able to give you good feedback yet, or may get frustrated with the popup and leave. To increase the chances of them responding favorably, ideally you should wait at least 20 seconds before popping on this page, and do so with good reason only.

Once you have asked feedback questions of a significant amount of your website visitors (which should ideally be at least 50), you should then take a look at the text chat logs and try and look for patterns or common issues that are mentioned. Again, you could export all the data into a word cloud tool like Wordle to help you find most commonly used words and phrases. You should make note of any particularly common issues and themes because the pages related to these make great candidates for testing and optimizing.

You should also use best practices for placing web chat buttons on your website. At the very least you should make sure they are in a consistent place on your website so that your visitor always knows where to find them if needed, but more important, you should also place them in areas where they are likely needed the most. For example, while your visitors are in your shopping cart or signup process, their anxiety levels are likely to be much higher, and placing prominent web chat buttons in a highly visible spot on these pages is a great way for the visitor to get help to address any concerns they may have.

Web Chat Tool Providers

When looking at web chat tools there are several options for you to start evaluating today, in particular two good and popular options from BoldChat.com (www.BoldChat.com) and SnapEngage.com (www.SnapEngage.com). Both of these offer a wide variety of web chat service levels that cater to both small business and large enterprises, starting at a very reasonable $19 per month for a basic level at the time of writing.

Both of these chat tools also sync with your CRM tools (customer relationship management), so you can manage and record your visitor chats and associate them with sales records and other customer details. Another great feature of these tools is that many of them allow you to co-browse your website with your web chat users, so your visitors can show you anything they may be having issues with or have a suggestion on. SnapEngage even allows you to use your own instant messenger accounts to chat with your website visitors instead of having to download software to talk to them (see Figure 4.14).

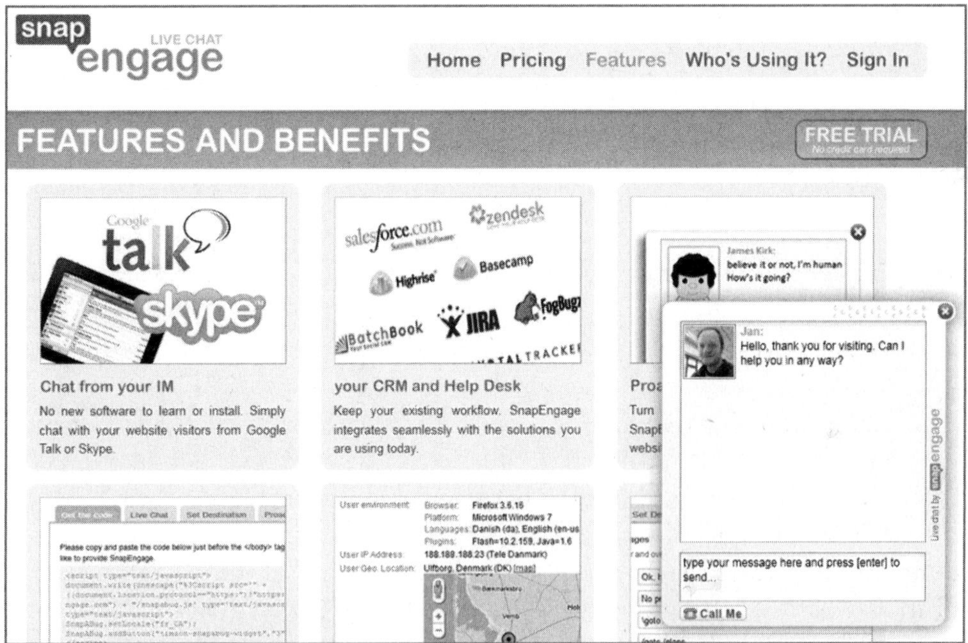

Figure 4.14 Example of a SnapEngage web chat pop-up request

There is also a built-in limited functionality web chat tool in the Woopra (www.Woopra.com) web analytics tool (which may also give you another reason to evaluate this newer analytics tool). If you are looking for an even more robust full enterprise-level web chat tool, you could consider using LivePerson (www.LivePerson.com).

5 Build the Foundation of a Better Converting Website

Before you can begin effectively optimizing your website, you first need to learn important web design and usability foundations. Applying these will mean your visitors will find it easier to navigate and make better use of your website, and increase the chances of them engaging and converting. These foundations apply to any kind of website and will help build a solid foundation to maximize the impact from your website optimization efforts throughout the rest of this book.

Chapter Contents

Week 11: Understand and Improve Your Website's Layout

As you began to learn about last week, it is very important that you design and create a highly usable website that your visitors can easily use and engage with. This will increase the chances of them converting and coming back in the future. Don't just make it look good—if you ignore usability conventions that your visitors have now grown accustomed to seeing you will risk losing them to a competitor website that does a better job with this.

This week we are going to continue discussions around the importance of website usability for optimizing your website, and focus on improving a particular aspect of it—your website layout. Applying best practices for this will ensure that your website is optimally laid out and more usable, enabling your visitors to find what they are looking for more easily without issues.

Monday: Understand the Impact of Your Web Page Fold

One of the most important layout considerations you need to understand is how your web pages look "above the page fold" and what your visitors can see there. This is the area that is visible in a visitor's web browser without them having to scroll vertically to see more and sometimes represents all they see before judging your website, particularly if they are a first-time visitor.

What the visitor sees above the page fold can have a major impact on your conversion rates, because they might not see your most important conversion-related content and calls-to-action if they are lower down. This is supported by a 2010 study by Jakob Nielsen that found that web users spend 80% of their time looking at content above the page fold. For more details on this study you can visit this page: `www.useit.com/alertbox/scrolling-attention.html`

While this isn't as much of an issue for well-known brand websites because visitors will often scroll more (like Amazon.com or CNN.com), this is problematic if your website is much newer or less well known because many of your visitors won't know what to expect lower down on your pages. Therefore, today you will learn about some best practices to ensure your website doesn't make this mistake by not showing the most important content above the fold.

Learn the Most Common Page Fold Area Size

To understand the potential effect of the page fold, the first thing you need to do is learn what the most common page fold height is.

The most common screen resolution height is 1024 × 768 pixels (according to recent general web statistics at the time of writing), but you need to cater to a lower common size because a significant portion of people still browse on 800 × 600 screen resolution, particularly the older, less tech-savvy generation.

This visible page fold height gets even smaller when you take into account the room that is taken up in many Internet browsers by extra toolbars (as you can see in Figure 5.1). Therefore, to ensure that a large percentage of your visitors see your important content above the page fold, you should use a slightly lower height as your page fold area—500 pixel height would be considered safe to use.

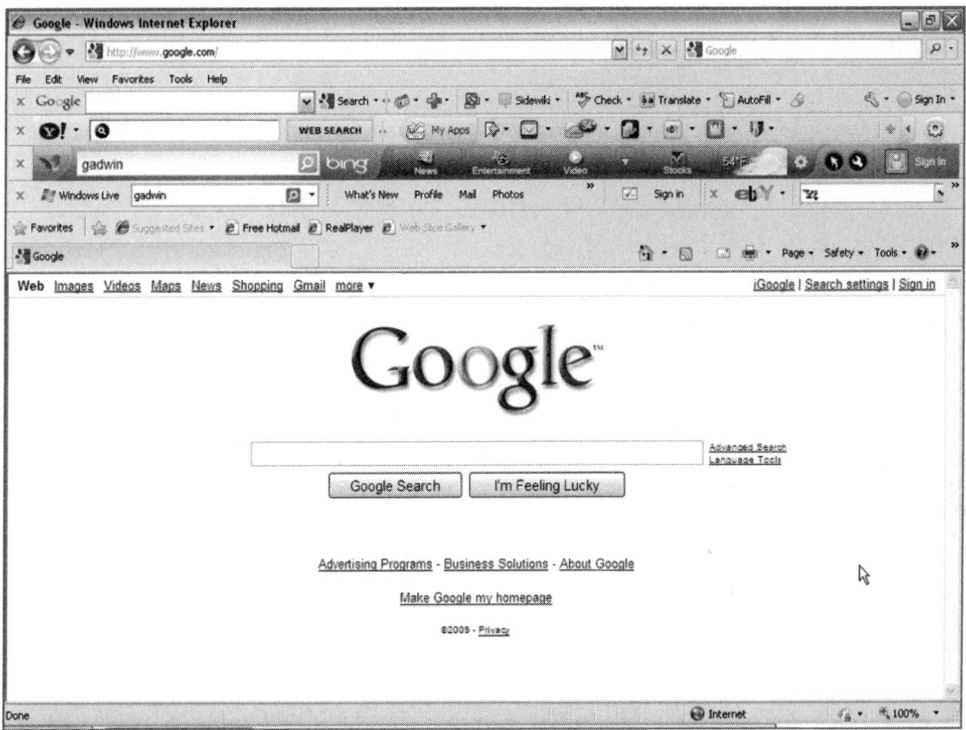

Figure 5.1 A browser with too many toolbars turned on

Display Your Most Important Content above the Page Fold

To ensure that your visitors see your most important content, you should always display your most important information above the page fold, particularly your calls-to-action and supporting text and images. This is essential for your top entry pages like home pages, paid search landing pages, and product pages. This is particularly bad if it's the visitor's first visit to your website because they will often judge your website in less than three seconds and leave if they don't find what they are looking for.

One great quick way to check if your key pages are following this best practice is to use Google's free Browser Size tool (`http://browsersize.googlelabs.com`). For any page that you want to submit and review, this overlay tool shows color-coded percentages of the page that your visitors are likely to be seeing above the fold. You should try to fit your most critical information and calls-to-action in the colored area that denotes more than 90 percent. Figure 5.2 shows this tool in action, so you can see the percentage areas.

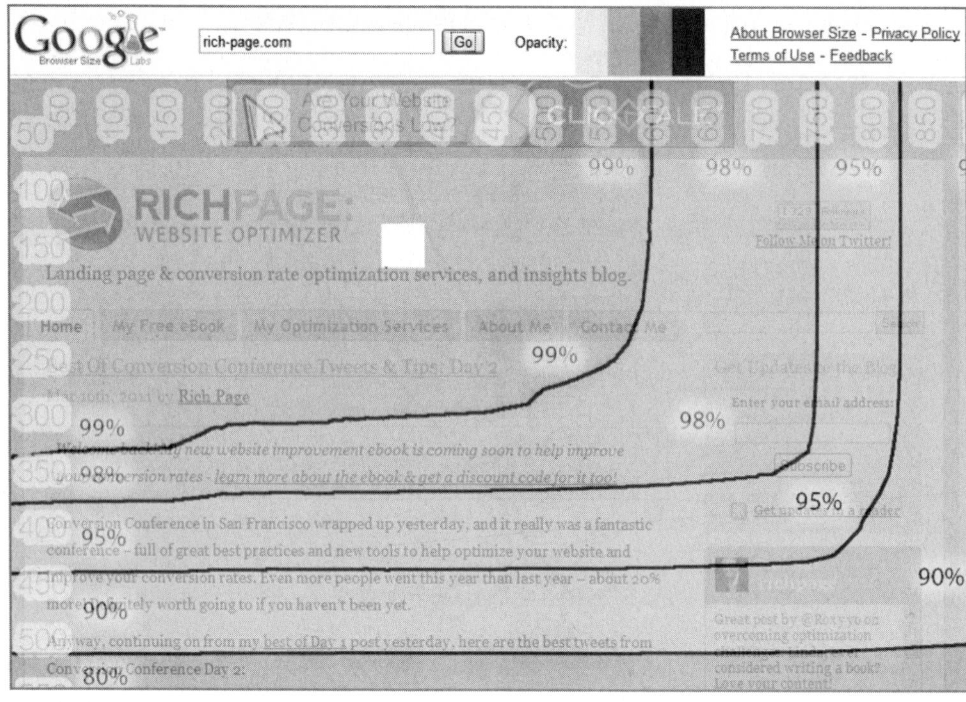

Figure 5.2 Google's Browser Size tool in action

Scrolling Can Impact Your Visitor Engagement

Although many visitors do scroll down on websites quite often now, you should try and make your web pages as short as possible, so it's easier for visitors to view the whole of your pages. Even if you have a media website, you should try and split long pages into separate, shorter pages to make it easier to read them (also having the benefit of increasing page views per visit, which can help increase ad revenue).

E-commerce website pages can be longer (apart from the homepage which should remain more concise), because they have to convey more per page, particularly on product pages and category pages, and visitors won't mind scrolling as much on these pages because they will expect them to be longer.

If you are only selling one product or service, you could test using a longer "sales letter" type of page that contains all the key information needed to convert the visitor with a major call-to-action at the bottom—these often convert quite well for some products.

Last, you should never make your visitors have to scroll horizontally on your regular website. This is because you run the risk of them not realizing there is more content to the right of your pages, as occurs on some trendy media websites like `glo.com`. The only time you might want to experiment with offering this is if you have a version of your website just for tablet devices, which are more suited to horizontal scrolling by hand swiping.

Tuesday: Understand the Impact of Your Website Design on Eye Flow

Regardless of how good you think your website looks, if you don't understand the impact of website design on your visitor's eye flow this can have a big negative impact on your conversion and visitor engagement rates.

If you don't understand how visitors usually read and scan websites, in addition to what can impact their eye flow, you may inadvertently cause friction to their eye flow or distract them from key content like calls-to-action. This reduces the likelihood of your visitors engaging and converting.

Therefore today you will learn about how your visitors read and scan websites, and then understand what can impact and distract their eye flow. This will help you test and create pages that flow better and result in a higher number of conversions.

Understand the F-Shape Reading Pattern on Websites

To understand the effect of visitors' eye flows and how to lay out your pages better, you need to understand how visitors typically look at websites. Studies have shown that they typically look at the top left of the page first and scan horizontally, and then they look down slightly and scan again horizontally to the right. They then typically scan down the rest of the page, mainly keeping to the left of the page. This is known as the *F-shape reading pattern*, a term that was coined by Jakob Nielsen. An example of an F-shape reading pattern heat map is shown in Figure 5.3. You can read more about this at `www.useit.com/alertbox/reading_pattern.html`.

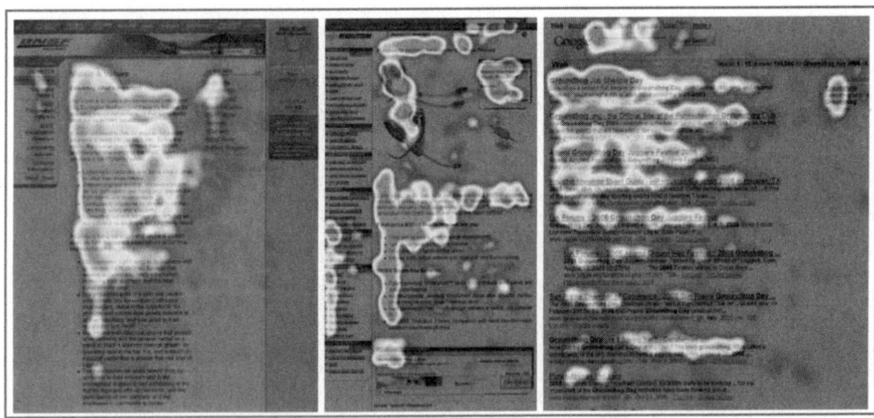

Figure 5.3 F-shape reading pattern examples

This reading and scanning pattern ultimately means you need to convey your most important wording and imagery at the top-left of your website. Headlines and sub-headlines are particularly important to make good use of in this location, and you will learn about how to make effective use of these in Chapter 6.

It also means you shouldn't rely on using the right-hand side of your pages to show key information because your visitors won't look there very often.

Understand the Influence of Using Images, Videos, and Other Graphical Content on Eye Flow

One of the things that can have a huge influence on your visitor's eye flow and where they look on your webpages is the usage of images, videos, and other graphical content.

Careful and planned placement of images and graphical elements can actually help guide the visitor's eye flow through the most important parts of your pages, eventually increasing the chances of them clicking on the main call-to-action on your pages. If you don't do this, your less important images and graphical elements will distract and detract your visitor's eye flow away from these.

The best way to understand the impact of your visitor's eye flow is to use eye tracking tools that were discussed in Chapter 4, such as Gazehawk and AttentionWizard and analyze what your visitors are looking at, particularly on key conversion-related pages. Based on what you observe, you should test rearranging graphical elements on your pages to refocus the flow so that your visitors end up looking at your key call-to-actions more often.

In Chapter 6, you will learn much more about how to optimize your usage of images, videos, and interactive content to help increase your website conversion rates further.

Use White Space Effectively in Your Design

Having empty space on your website is often criticized by web designers who like to ensure their website real estate is maximized and covered as much as possible. However, this isn't always true, because when used effectively, white space can help draw the visitor's eye toward important page elements like calls-to-action. It can also break up some of the intensity of pages and make them look less crowded to reduce confusion.

Therefore, next you need to review your website and make sure it doesn't look too crammed, remembering to put yourself in the shoes of your visitor and getting feedback from them if possible. Then you should try testing increasing spacing slightly around key page elements, particularly around key calls-to-action, to see what positive impact that hopefully has on your conversion rates and success metrics.

Note: You can use eye flow tracking tools discussed in Chapter 4 to help you here too, and test to see if eye flow improves by using more white space around your key page elements.

Wednesday: Check Your Website in Different Browsers and Resolutions

Slight variances between website browsers and screen resolutions can have a dramatic impact on how your website looks and functions, which can potentially reduce your conversion rate. Therefore, it's important to ensure your website works well and looks good in all major browsers.

Not only are there now many different browsers you need to check your website in, but there are now a wide variety of screen resolutions you need to check too. It's now fairly common for some visitors to browse websites with very large screen resolutions (with many tech savvy visitors using widths higher than 2000 pixels), and this can play havoc with your carefully planned web page layout and flow, particularly if your website auto expands to fill the screen width.

Today, you will learn some best practices to help negate the impact of different resolutions and browsers on your website and conversion rates.

There are literally thousands of different combinations of browsers and screen resolution sizes that you should check your website in. Doing this sounds like a very daunting and time-consuming task to have to perform regularly, but luckily there are now several great tools that can help you or your design team do this checking in an automated fashion.

For example, the CrossBrowserTesting.com tool (`www.crossbrowsertesting.com`) checks how your website looks in any combination of browser and resolution that you want to check. It also gives you image thumbnails of each of the versions checked, so you can review and understand potential issues. This tool is also very cost-effective, with monthly plans starting at just $29 per month and a free one-week trial at the time of writing.

There are also a couple of other effective but limited functionality browser-checking tools that you can use to check what your website looks like in any browser (but not screen resolution size unfortunately). For example, Adobe BrowserLab (`http://browserlab.adobe.com`) and BrowserShots (`www.BrowserShots.org`) are currently free and well worth using.

At the very least, you should check what your key pages look like in the most common browsers and screen resolutions, in particular your home page, checkout or signup pages, and product or service pages. Then fix any of the major issues with them and recheck what they look like again to ensure that they are fixed in all combinations.

Thursday: Learn Other Website Layout Best Practices

Today you will learn about some other best practices for the layout of your website. This includes optimizing the layout to work better on smaller screen width resolutions, avoiding use of auto-expanding websites, and always centering your website.

Optimize Your Website to Work on Smaller Screen Widths

If your website isn't optimized to work well on smaller browser resolution sizes, visitors using them may miss important content to the left or right on your website like calls-to-action or other functionality, and thus negatively impact your conversion rates.

Therefore, you should design your websites so that the most important content and elements of your website are visible on a resolution width of 800 pixels (800 × 600 pixel resolution), which is the narrowest browser width that a small percentage of your visitors is likely still using.

To check this, simply change your monitor's screen resolution so that it has a width of 800 pixels and then check all of your pages to see if any key page elements to the left or right can't be seen because of this narrower width. You can use Google's Browser Size tool to get a good idea of this too (as discussed earlier).

It's particularly important to check for any page width issues on your key conversion-related pages, such as your shopping cart or registration pages. If you do find issues, you should ideally move the important elements that are not being seen to more prominent central spots.

Avoid Using Auto-Expanding Width for Displaying Your Website

Sometimes it's seen as fairly "cool" to have your website expand to fit the width of your visitor's browser, no matter how wide it is, and many web designers still like to spend considerable time designing websites that do this. This is also sometimes referred to as using *liquid layout.*

Unfortunately, this expanding website design can often have negative consequences on key aspects of your website, such as module and text layout, which often unintentionally damages your website conversion rates without your realizing it. Key issues with auto-expanding width websites on very wide resolutions are the huge amount of white space this causes, and separation of key calls-to-action and supporting modules.

If your website does auto-expand to fill browser width, it's important that you check for this potential impact. This can simply be done by changing your screen resolution to a very wide one like 1600 pixel-width (one of the more common larger screen widths), and then checking your pages to see if any of your page layouts look broken or don't flow as well. Again, its most important to check your key pages because issues on these will have a bigger impact on your conversion rates.

For an advanced way of checking the impact of this, you could set up a visitor segment in your analytics tool for visitors using this width and see if they experience lower conversion rates than average.

Once you have reviewed what your web pages look like in this wider view, you should try to fix any layout of flow issues you uncover, or consider redesigning your website in the future so that it uses a fixed-width instead.

Ultimately though you should try to use fixed-width design for your website to limit potential negative impact, and to have more control over the layout of your pages and how they look and flow for visitors on many different screen sizes.

Horizontally Center Your Website

Not only should you always try to use a fixed-width for your website, you should also make sure your website is designed so that it is centered across the visitor's web browser. If you don't do this and instead left justify your website (pushing it against the left hand side of browsers), this can have the effect of making your website look very small and unbalanced, particularly when a visitor is looking at your website on a very wide screen resolution. While fixing this won't have a big impact on conversions alone, it is one of the smaller things that can contribute to a more usable and better converting website.

It is also important to check how your website looks on mobile devices. This is due to the huge recent rise in mobile website browsing, a subject that will be covered in greater detail in Chapter 7.

Friday: Check How Your Email Marketing Efforts Look

Your email marketing efforts can have a significant impact on your website's conversion rates because they often form a considerable, highly targeted, and highly convertible traffic source to your website.

Therefore, you also need to consider the layout of how your marketing emails look and render in different email providers, and fix any issues you see.

In particular, you need to check what your emails look like in email preview panes, because the page fold is usually significantly smaller in email readers, and you need to make sure your most important content can be seen there.

Another important thing you need to check for in particular is to make sure your emails look good when visitors have images turned off by default (the default setting on many email clients like Outlook). Instead of risking having your images and important image call-to-actions in them not show, it is best to make use of plain text on background images to achieve a similar effect for users with images turned off.

You should also check how your email marketing efforts look in different email providers, such as Gmail, Yahoo Mail, Hotmail, and Outlook. This is because your emails can look different or broken across some of these email providers, which can have a negative impact on getting some of your most important visitors to your website and ultimately lower your website's potential conversion rates.

You will learn much more about these email marketing optimization best practices in Chapter 8.

Week 12: Improve Page Load Speed

Do you remember having to use slow dial-up Internet access? Remember how painful it was, in particular the frustration of finding a website that took forever to load? Unfortunately, this issue is rearing its ugly head again, despite the widespread usage of high-speed Internet connections. This is in part due to web designers who increasingly use slower loading but "cool" new interactive media elements but have little understanding of the impact that this has on visitors and conversion rates.

When you combine this with the fact that many websites are built with bloated or inefficient programming code, this can make matters even worse for page load times. Therefore, this week you are going to learn about improving the speed of your page load time to make your visitors happier and improve your conversion rates.

Monday: Understand the Negative Impact of Slow Page Load

Slow-loading web pages can have a surprisingly negative effect on your conversion rates because many of your visitors will not wait for them to load and abandon them prematurely. This was echoed in a recent study by Forrester Research that found 40 percent of consumers would abandon a page if it took more than three seconds to load.

Visitors are often quick to judge these offending slow-loading websites, often without giving the website a second chance in the future. This quick judgment is even more likely to occur when they arrive on your home page, especially if it's their first visit.

Often this slow-loading page impact happens without online marketers even realizing it. This is because many offices where websites are built have the fastest Internet connections you can get (which are much faster than home high-speed Internet connections), so page load speed issues are often overlooked. It's also important to understand that website visitors are even pickier about waiting for pages to load when browsing websites on mobile devices, because they have much slower Internet connections. This will be discussed in more detail in Chapter 7, where you will learn about mobile website optimization.

Finally, another emerging impact of slow-loading websites is the negative impact on your rankings within Google search results. Recent studies have shown that Google lowers rankings for websites that are particularly slow at loading, particularly for their paid search listings. This obviously is going to have a major impact on your conversion rates if you are highly reliant on Google for driving quality traffic to your website.

Therefore, during the rest of the week, you will learn how to check your page load performance, key issues to look for, and how to fix any offenders that you find.

Tuesday: Check How Fast Your Web Pages Load and Diagnose Issues

Remember that offices where websites get built usually have the fastest Internet connections possible and are much faster than regular home Internet connection speeds. Just because your website pages load fast on your office network doesn't mean they will for your website visitors in their homes.

Therefore, today you will check how fast your web pages load at more common Internet connection speeds, and then use tools to diagnose any issues.

To do this, you can use the advanced settings of a tool called Web Page Test (`www.webpagetest.org/`) to check your page load times on different connection speeds. This is particularly important to do for your home page, because visitors are even more sensitive to slow load times here.

Next you need to diagnose if you have page load issues. To help you do this, there are several free tools to help diagnose a litany of potential common page load issues on your website. These issues can be in the form of slow-loading third-party applications, slow-loading external JavaScript calls, and bloated website programming code or CSS files. Here are some of the tools you can try using:

Google Analytics Site Speed Report (`http://analytics.blogspot.com/2011/05/measure-page-load-time-with-site-speed.html`**)** This report reveals load times across all of your pages. It also reports on average load times for the major types of website browsers. To access this report, just go to the Content section in your Google Analytics account and click Site Speed Report.

Google Page Speed (`https://developers.google.com/pagespeed/`**)** This is a great tool from Google that analyzes your website load times and gives you a load time grade. More important, it generates some prioritized suggestions for ways that you can make your website pages load faster. This doesn't require that you use Google Analytics or any custom code either. Ideally you should ensure you get a grade of at least 80 percent on this tool, and fix any of the high priority issues that the report diagnoses. See Figure 5.4 for an example of the speed test results page.

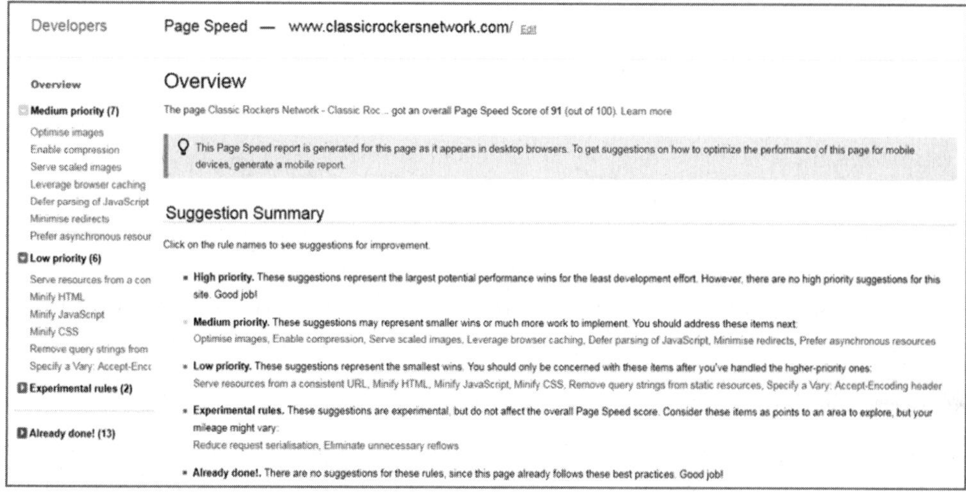

Figure 5.4 Example of Google Page Speed results

OctaGate SiteTimer (`http://octagate.com/service/sitetimer/`**)** This simple tool shows you how long it takes all of the elements of your web pages to load, so you can spot and fix problematic files or code that loads the slowest on your pages.

Yahoo's Yslow Tool (`http://developer.yahoo.com/yslow/`**)** If you are a web developer, this diagnostic tool is essential for discovering page load issues. This is a FireFox plug-in that tests your website against common things that slow your website down. For example, it helps check for bloated JavaScript and external script calls and reports back on key offenders.

Once you have used some of these tools to detect your web page load-time performance, note any major issues you find and try to address them as soon as possible. You will probably need to get some help from your IT department to do this, as many of the issues may be very technical in nature.

Over the next few days you will learn about some particularly problematic things that cause slow loading pages, and some ways to overcome them.

Wednesday: Limit and Optimize Your Usage of Slow-Loading Website Elements

One of the major culprits of slow-loading web pages is the overuse of visual or interactive elements created with excessively long and bloated JavaScript, HTML5, Adobe Flash, or other website code. Examples of these potentially problematic page elements are interactive or dynamic content (that allows visitors to control and fine tune their experience), image sliders, video players, and intro splash pages. If these slow-loading elements are found frequently on your website, they can often frustrate visitors and can give them reason to leave your website prematurely.

Entertainment-related websites are common offenders of slow page load, because they usually contain multimedia like video and audio, in addition to slow loading "cool" elements.

To reduce the risk of visitors leaving your website due to slow-loading elements, you should consider rebuilding slow-loading elements so they load more quickly— for example, using different technology or more efficient code. And if your website has an intro page, you should run a simple A/B test that compares the engagement and conversion rates of your website with and without this intro page.

Another common solution is to offer two different versions of the website to your visitors, a high-bandwidth version and a low-bandwidth basic version. You can either let the visitor chose the version they want, or better yet, detect their level of connection speed if possible and automatically choose the best version based on their connection speed level.

You should also be sure to focus on the visitors who are browsing your website on mobile devices, because they are going to usually have a much slower connection. As you will learn in Chapter 7, the best solution to this is to create a separate lighter mobile website that doesn't feature these slow-loading elements and therefore loads more quickly.

Thursday: Reduce the File Size of Your Images and Videos, and the Length of Your Page Code

Other major causes of slow-loading pages are pages that include images and videos that are unnecessarily large in size or pages built with bloated, overly long code or pages that make inefficient calls to other website services. Luckily it is fairly quick to fix these and improve your website load times, and today you will learn how.

Reduce Image and Video Sizes

First, you should check the file sizes of the images and videos on your website. You may be surprised at how large some of them are! By reducing the file size of these you can often shave vital seconds off your web page load times and make your visitors much more happy and engaged.

It's fairly easy to reduce the file size of images by using simple web design tools to compress file size, often by as much as 50 percent, but be careful that you are not reducing their quality too much so they look noticeably poor. You should also save them as files that are optimized for website use—don't use TIF files or other formats that are more appropriate for print use. And don't be tempted to take the easy way out and just scale down your website images by using smaller dimensions, because even though they will look smaller, it can still take up as much bandwidth to download them.

Another way to reduce file size is to use photo-editing software to crop images so they become smaller in dimensions and therefore file size too.

You should pay particular attention to the backgrounds of your website if you are using images (including advertisements), because these can often be very large in file size. Ideally, you should not use a very large image as your background but instead make use of a smaller repeatable image and tile it horizontally and vertically on your website.

Reducing video file size is a little bit harder, but there are some decent video compression services available, such as WinSoftMagic (`www.winsoftmagic.com`). You should also consider shortening your videos, or splitting them up into multiple videos, so they will load more quickly.

Improve Website Code Efficiency and Reduce Size

To speed up your page load times you should also reduce the size and improve the efficiency of the code that your website uses. First you need to diagnose potential code issues using the tools discussed yesterday if you haven't already done so. Due to the technical nature of these code-based load time issues, I suggest that you get help from your IT department to run tests, interpret the results, and fix any issues that are diagnosed.

One thing to consider in particular is to optimize the usage of third party JavaScript code tags on your webpages, like the ones you use to track and test content for your visitors. While individually they are usually fine, if you have many of them on your pages it can slow down load time. There are now several services that you should consider using to manage these tags and speed up load times, such as Adobe's Tag Manager (`www.omniture.com/en/products/platform/tag-manager`) and Tag Man (`www.TagMan.com`).

Friday: Optimize the Delivery of Your Website Content

An alternative to tweaking code on your website to decrease page load times is to use a service that will optimize the delivery of your website content from your website servers.

This is known as *content delivery optimization*, and it helps in several ways. Most important, it compresses your website code so that it loads more quickly and efficiently. It also caches your website on your website servers, which means that your pages don't have to be completely loaded again when a visitor returns to your website, greatly increasing the perception of a faster-loading website.

There are several services from companies like Akamai (`www.akamai.com`) that provide this type of delivery optimization, and most large websites will usually use a service like this to improve their website load times. Unfortunately, these services can be costly, but they are often worth investing in to speed up your website load times.

It's particularly important to do this content delivery optimization if your website has extremes in your peak traffic flows or has content that is highly seasonally influenced. This is because it reduces the risk of your website not being able to handle this high volume of traffic and crashing (having the worst possible impact on your conversion rates and visitor perception).

Much of this content delivery optimization is highly technical, so I suggest that you get some technical help from your IT department to pursue options like this. You can even try and do this in-house to produce similar effects and benefits if you have the necessary technical resources available.

Week 13: Optimize Your Navigation Menus and Links

In online marketing, there is a lot of emphasis placed on attracting and driving visitors to websites, which is definitely important to do. But unfortunately often too little emphasis is placed on helping your visitors move *around* your website once they get there, and helping them complete the task that they came for in the first place.

Even with the advance in understanding of website usability best practices, website navigation menus and related links are still often poorly designed with little consideration for the visitor's needs and wants, often with poor choices of links presented in them. This makes it unnecessarily hard for visitors to find what they are looking for in an effective, quick manner.

This week, to help you lay a better navigation website foundation and improve how well your visitors move around your website, engage, and convert on it, you will learn how to optimize your navigation menus and links.

Note that there is also another major method that visitors navigate through websites, which is through the usage of internal search tools. However, because of the importance of site search and the ability to generate insights from this, it will be covered in more detail next week.

Monday: Learn the Importance of Navigation Menus and Links

If your website has poor or confusing navigation menus and links, it will be much harder for your visitors to find what they are looking for or to complete the task they came to your website to achieve. If this is the case it can often mean that they will seek out another website that is easier to navigate than yours and won't return to yours as much, having a negative impact on your ability to engage and convert them.

It's not just optimizing your header navigation menu either—you also need to make sure your visitors can make good use of secondary left-hand navigation menus and related link sections to get around your website better and more efficiently.

Therefore it is essential that you spend time reviewing and optimizing your navigation menus and links on your website to ensure you are better meeting the needs of visitors.

Luckily, there are many different ways for you to optimize your website navigation menus and links that you will learn through the rest of this week.

Lastly, don't forget about the increased number of your visitors who will be visiting your website on mobile devices, because you will need to optimize and make your navigation links work better on these much smaller resolution screens. You'll learn about this in more detail in Chapter 7, which covers mobile website optimization best practices.

Tuesday: Optimize the Contents, Usability, and Location of Your Navigation Menus

One of the key ways that your visitors navigate through websites is via the use of navigation menus that persist across all pages of a website. Today you'll learn some best practices and test ideas to help improve the ones on your website.

Position Your Main Navigation Menu at the Top of Your Website

It is now so common to see main navigation menus at the top of websites that it has become a website standard to show this menu in this location, as opposed to the left-hand side of your website.

The top navigation menu should ideally be in the form of a bar that spans the width of your website and should be tall enough to be easily noticeable and interacted with. You can offer a supporting secondary left-hand navigation menu if you have an e-commerce or media website that has many broad and deep categories to navigate.

There has actually been a recent trend of several major e-commerce websites moving their top menu to the left, using fly-out mega menus instead. Amazon.com was one of the first to change to this style, and others like Staples.com and Walmart.com have followed suit (perhaps because they think if Amazon is doing it, it must be the right thing to do, which is not always the case). While these certainly are fairly usable, the jury is still out on whether these are more effective than advanced drop-down menus at the top supported by a secondary left-hand menu, which will be discussed next.

Use Additional Left-Hand Navigation Menus for Deeper Websites

On websites that have particularly deep hierarchies, you should also use a left-hand navigation menu to support your top navigation menu. This will allow visitors to more easily explore and understand what deeper subcategories are available to browse. To improve the visitor's ability to do this more quickly, you should make your left-hand navigation menu instantly expandable (accordion-style) when clicked on, without needing a page refresh. You can see an example of this type of expandable left-hand menu in Figure 5.5.

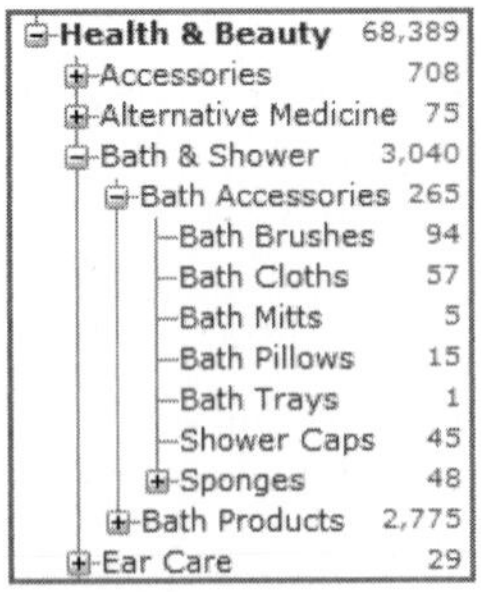

- **Health & Beauty** 68,389
  - Accessories 708
  - Alternative Medicine 75
  - Bath & Shower 3,040
    - Bath Accessories 265
      - Bath Brushes 94
      - Bath Cloths 57
      - Bath Mitts 5
      - Bath Pillows 15
      - Bath Trays 1
      - Shower Caps 45
      - Sponges 48
    - Bath Products 2,775
  - Ear Care 29

Figure 5.5 Example of an expandable left-hand navigation menu

These menus also take up less room than fixed menus that are fully expanded already. This means you can make more use of the left-hand sidebar to show additional promotions.

Make Sure Navigation Content Is Easy to Read and Understand

When labeling the links in your navigation menu, you should make sure your visitors can easily read and understand them. This helps reduce possible confusion and friction when they are using them, because it is very frustrating for a visitor to have to click each main link in the navigation menu to find out what each leads to.

First, you need to make sure your navigation bar is sufficiently big enough so that the links are easily readable. To ensure this, ideally the links should be at least 14 or 16 point font size and should contrast well with the background color of the menu to make them easier to read.

For the language level of your links, you should use high-school grade language (and in general on your website), and also refrain from using jargon or techy words. Therefore, go ahead and set up a test to remove or correct any offending navigation links—you will likely see an increase in click-through rates on your navigation menus.

Your navigation menu should also act as a signpost system that lets your visitors know where they are at all times on your website. This is particularly important for when visitors arrive deep within your website from search engines.

To help do this you should be visually highlighting the current page that a visitor is on in the navigation menu. This is often best achieved by inverting the color and font of the tab, or by using a pointer or colored indicator at the bottom of the tab. Surprisingly, many large websites fail to do this, including websites like Target.com and OfficeDepot.com.

Wednesday: Optimize Your Usage of Navigation Drop-Down or Fly-Out Menus

Websites that have many categories and sub-categories need to offer more than just a standard main navigation menu. If you only have static menus that don't expand, your visitors will have to click on each category to find the subcategories within them. This can be frustrating and time consuming for them.

Having a website that offers advanced drop-down or fly-out menus that contain links to all subcategories and other important links is a much better experience for visitors. By using these it means they can instantly see what subcategories are under each main category, and it gives them a great quick overview of what your website offers just by moving their mouse on these dynamic menus.

Today you will learn best practices that can help you optimize your drop-downs and fly-out menus so they are more usable for your visitors.

Check How Easy Your Navigation Menus Are to Interact with and for Any Potential Issues

If you have drop-down or left-hand fly-out menus that are designed with poor usability you may frustrate your visitors when they use them, possibly causing them to leave your website. Sometimes they are hard to interact with, scroll over, and even break entirely in some browsers. Therefore you need to check how easy it is to use them and fix any issues you find.

In particular, you should check if your mouse can easily fall off your drop-down or fly-out menu when using it, and also check to see if they get obstructed by other page elements. These are both particularly frustrating to visitors when they occur.

Test Advanced Navigation Menu Functionality

You should also test improving the functionality and usability of your menus by showing larger drop-down or fly-out menu areas that include advanced navigation options. The benefit of these is that you can include more tools and promotions in them than normal menus, which will greatly assist visitor navigation and engagement.

In these advanced menus, you should test showing search boxes that relate to the navigation tab currently rolled over, promotional items or modules, and relevant imagery or icons. The ElectronicArts.com website has a particularly good example of this advanced menu, which can be seen in Figure 5.6. Another example is ESPN.com, which has a great dynamic menu that even includes the ability to include personalized content in it (like favorite team-related content).

These advanced functionality drop-down menus can also help make your website stand out from the crowd of competing websites, and encourage repeat usage.

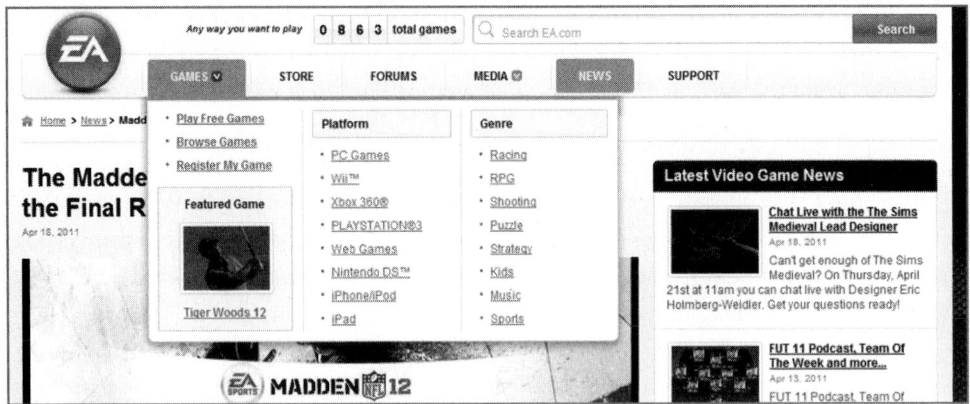

Figure 5.6 Example of a good advanced drop-down menu

While this may take a while to prototype and create, I suggest you develop one of these advanced types of menu and test it against your current navigation menu. Don't forget to get feedback from your visitors on your current and proposed new navigation, too.

Test the Order of Long Drop-Down Menu Links

If you have drop-down menus that have many navigation options in them (more than five), you should test what order you display the links in them to better influence your visitors to convert to your goals. Don't just display them in a random order; you should think which ones are most important to show visitors first. In particular, you should test moving your links higher for pages that have greater relevance to your conversion goals.

If none of your links have higher priority from a conversion standpoint, you should test putting your items in alphabetical order because this will make it is easier for your visitors to read and understand all of the options available. This is also particularly important to do if you have long drop-down menus with more than seven drop-down items.

Thursday: Improve Your Usage of Website Navigation Links

Next, you need to optimize the other major ways that visitors will navigate around your website in addition to your navigation menus, from basic links to related links. Here are some best practices for you to optimize these other ways of navigating on your website.

Optimize and Use Related Links on Your Pages

A key principle to follow is to never let your visitors dead end on your pages without offering suggestions for where they should go next. If you don't do this, your visitors will often just read what you are showing them and simply leave because they are either satisfied or don't know what to click on next.

This is particularly important for media and blog websites that have many articles for visitors to read. This is because rather than letting them leave after reading an article, you should show them links to related articles to engage them further. When they use these related links, it will increase page views per visit, which will then in turn increase ad revenue from the additional ads seen per page (which, as discussed in Chapter 2, are key success metrics for these two types of websites).

One of the best ways of ensuring this doesn't happen is to make better use of related links at the end of your pages, which is where the visitor's eye flow will naturally end up. Don't just place these in the right-hand rail of your web pages, because visitor's eye flow often doesn't end up looking there due to the high frequency of banner ads usually found there.

Examples of related links to test can come in the form of most popular content, or related items, categories, or sections. To see a good example of how this can be done on a media website, take a look at Figure 5.7, which shows how FamilyFun.com includes related links on its article pages.

Figure 5.7 Example of good related link options at the bottom of a page

Therefore, to take advantage of this go ahead and work with your design team to come up with a few styles for displaying related links. To understand what usage and versions of these engages the most, you need to test each of these related link styles, along with the links that you are showing in them and the location of them on your pages. This will improve your engagement rates and likely have a positive effect on your conversion rates.

Don't Make Your Visitors Guess Which Links Are Clickable

It's important to make sure that your website visitors know what links are clickable on your website. If you don't do this, you will decrease the ability to influence what your visitors click on and make it harder for them to find related content links, which is particularly problematic if they relate to your conversion goals.

Unfortunately, too many websites still make their visitors guess what links are clickable on their web pages, often using links that don't stand out and barely look any different than normal website text or using bold text that looks the same as links.

This is particularly problematic for your visitors who aren't very web savvy and will have less of an understanding of what might be considered a link.

To make it more obvious and to confuse your visitors less, go ahead and make your text links underlined and a different color from your regular text (with blue being a great color to use because it is a website usability standard). While it may sometimes be hard to convey this point to your graphic designers (who often like to be very creative and cool regarding the style and color of their links), a great way to prove this is by testing your current style of links against more obvious and underlined links in order to see which gets higher click-through rates.

Friday: Learn Other Best Practices to Help Visitors Navigate Your Website

In addition to the navigation best practices already discussed this week, there are also several other, smaller best practices that you should test using on your website, including using breadcrumb trails and better footer navigation links. Today you will learn about these best practices, which will help visitors navigate your website better and increase the chances of them engaging and converting.

Have a Helpful Mini-Navigation Link Area in the Top Right

To aid visitor navigation you should always place a mini-navigation link area in the top right-hand area of your website that contains useful links.

This should include account and help related links such as shopping cart, contact, help, FAQ, and login and register links. Visitors often now expect to see links of this nature in this location and may be frustrated if they can't find these important links.

This mini-navigation area should use simple text links, and be much smaller than the font in your main header navigation menu to help deprioritize these links slightly. Icons like shopping carts are useful visual representations too.

This link area should also look consistent and be available on every page of your website so that your visitors notice it more easily and can access it any time. Figure 5.8 shows a good example of how a mini-navigation area in the top right of a website page can be used effectively.

Figure 5.8 Example of a helpful mini-navigation area in the top right

If you haven't already got this useful link area on your website, test adding it to your website and see if it helps increase visitor task completion rates and overall conversion rates. And if you already have one, test to make sure you are using the types of links that are listed above, and test the presentation of this link area.

Make Your Website Logo Clickable, Sending Visitors to Your Home Page

A simple thing you need to do next is make sure your website logo is clickable, redirecting the visitor to the home page after clicking on it. Many website visitors will now expect this to happen when clicking on website logos and will be frustrated if they can't do this, particularly if they also can't find a "home" link in your navigation. This provides an easy way for your visitors to get to your home page and also means you don't waste space by adding the "home" link into your navigation menu.

Use of Breadcrumb Trails to Aid Visitor Navigation

Another simple yet effective way to aid your website visitor's navigation is to place a breadcrumb trail set of links that shows the visitor context of where they are in relation to the rest of the website. This isn't necessarily a highly clicked set of links, because it is more of a visual guide to visitors—think of it as a signpost system to help your visitor understand where they are on your website.

This is particularly useful for your visitors who have arrived deep within your website from a search engine and may not know where they are in the context of the rest of your website.

In terms of format and location, these breadcrumb links should show the locations that are higher up in the hierarchy of where the visitor is, plus the page they are currently on. Using a forward chevron or arrow between the links is a good way to indicate the depth of pages above where they currently are. Ideally this should be placed at the top of the main content area of pages, just below the header navigation menu and just to the right of the left-hand menu if you have one of those. Figure 5.9 shows a good example of how breadcrumb links are used on Amazon.com.

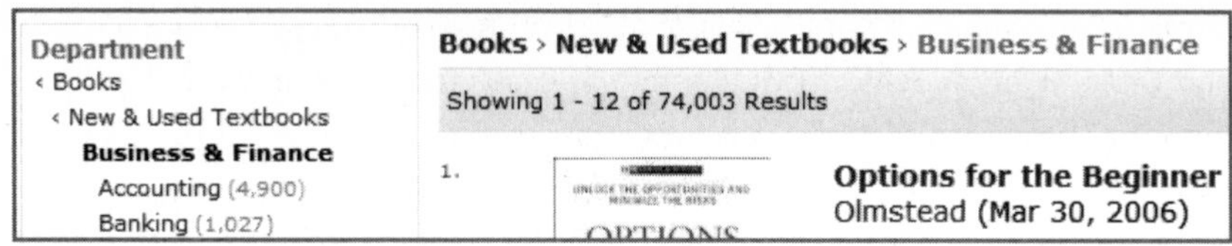

Figure 5.9 Example of good breadcrumb trail usage

Optimize Your Footer Navigation Links

Another way to optimize the way that your visitors navigate your website is not only to have a footer link area on your website but to optimize the format and contents of it.

Don't just have a single row of links to things like your contact page, privacy policy, and site map. Instead, make your footer area much more of a navigational aid to your visitors by making it taller to include lists of the major sections and subsections of your website and your major calls-to-action (like register, sign up, learn more, etc.). Figure 5.10 shows a great example of an optimized footer from Shoes.com that even includes a newsletter signup area.

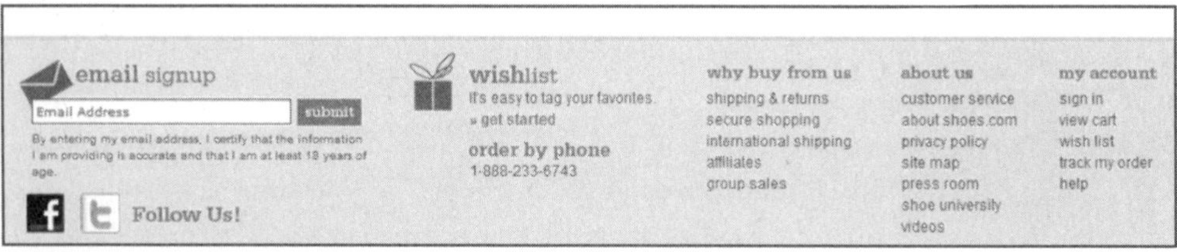

Figure 5.10 Example of an optimized footer link area

Therefore, you should test creating a few different versions of your footer area with these extra links and see which versions help increase click-through rates on it.

Test Different Navigation Options for Logged-In or Repeat Visitors

A more advanced best practice to improve your navigation is to offer different navigation links to different types of your visitors, and not just have a "one size fits all" navigation menu. This meets your visitors different needs better and often results in increased engagement and conversions.

For example, if your return visitors often log in, they are more likely to prefer seeing prominent log-in and account-related options, and not links that are trying to get them to sign up (which they already have done). This would be particularly good to do on the home page because that is where repeat visitors often come back to.

To do this you will need to set up visitor segments in your testing tool for visitors who are new, returning, or who frequently log in and then target different navigation options to them to better engage them.

Depending on your exact business model or value proposition, you could test offering different navigation links for any type of visitor group that you want to show different options to, not just whether they want to log in or not. I suggest thinking about what navigation needs your different types of visitors will have, and then trying to create, test, and target different variations to them. This will likely result in higher visitor engagement rates and higher overall conversion rates.

Week 14: Optimize and Learn from Your Internal Site Search

An internal site search tool is extremely valuable to offer to visitors on your website, not just in terms of offering them a very important way to try and find what they are looking for, but also because the keywords being searched for can provide some excellent feedback and insight that you can learn from to help you optimize your website.

If you don't offer a very good internal site search tool, your visitors will find it harder to find what they are looking for and abandon your website more often, and you won't be able to gather intelligence regarding what they were trying to find. Therefore today you will learn best practices to optimize and learn from your internal site search.

Monday: Offer a Good Internal Search Tool

The most important thing you should do is to make sure you are already offering a good internal search tool to visitors on your website and understand some of the options available to you to add or improve this internal search functionality.

Use Built-In Search Tool Functionality or Build It Yourself

The simplest approach to offering an internal site search tool is to use built-in functionality that your website platform already has. This is because many websites are built on a platform that has the option to turn on and use internal search functionality. Often these are fairly limited in functionality though, and you will need to evaluate how good your tool is, in particular the usability of the tool, how well you can customize how it works and what reporting is available.

Another option that you might consider is to build your own search tool. Depending on the complexity of your website and how much development resources you have to available to do this, this can sometimes be cheaper than using a third-party search tool (which options for will be discussed next). Unfortunately it's hard to build an internal site search tool that matches the number of options and flexibility that an internal search tool provider offers.

Choose a Search Tool Provider

The best option is for you to choose a new search tool provider and plug that into your website. While this is often a more expensive way of offering an internal search tool, doing this usually gives the most flexibility in how your tool works and what it offers. Here are some options available to you:

Google Site Search (`www.google.com/cse/`) This free internal search tool is the simplest to use because it makes use of existing Google search technology to crawl and index your website, allowing visitors to search your website. However, there are not many options to customize your search results and optimize this tool.

Fusion Bot (`www.fusionbot.com`) This mid-range internal site search tool offers a variety of service plans and functionality (including a free option), so it is a good solution for a wide variety of budget levels.

Adobe Search&Promote (`www.omniture.com/en/products/conversion/search-and-promote`) This excellent internal search tool from Adobe is expensive but offers the highest amount of flexibility and functionality with your search results page. This enterprise level tool also has particularly good options to promote and optimize anything you want to feature in your search results, and you can set up rules that automatically optimize what is shown on your search results to increase conversion rates for any of your goals.

Note: To implement an internal site search tool you will need to work with your IT department. They should be able to help you choose one that will work the best with your website and set it up correctly.

Tuesday: Optimize Your Internal Site Search Location

If your visitors can't find what they are looking for and then can't easily locate your internal site search input box, you will increase the chance of them leaving your website. Therefore, today you will learn best practices so that your visitors will find your internal search box more easily.

Place Your Internal Search Tool at the Top of Your Webpages

First, you need to make sure that your internal search box is not only on every page on your website but in an optimal and standardized location. Depending on the type of website you have, visitors will expect to see it in a different location in your navigation header menu area. For websites that are very search driven like e-commerce websites, it needs to be more prominently placed in the center of your webpages. On most other types of websites, you should still show it at the top, but deprioritize by showing it in the top right instead.

Don't just bury it away in the right-hand or left-hand column of your website either, particularly because visitors often do not look there due to the "banner blindness" issue. You should also make sure it's big enough for your visitors to see and easily interact with, and it is clearly labeled as an internal search tool, with a submit button next to it.

Don't Place Something Else in the Top Right That Looks Like a Search Input Box

Make sure you don't confuse your visitors by placing other input boxes (such as newsletter signup boxes) in the same spot where they would usually find your internal search input box.

This is problematic because visitors will often naturally start typing a keyword search in an input tool box in the upper right of your website purely if it looks like a search input box and will be frustrated when they get no search results, possibly causing them to leave your website prematurely. Also, ideally you also shouldn't put two input boxes into your website header area, as this may confuse the visitor even further as to which one is the internal search input box.

For an example of this confusion, Figure 5.11 shows a website that has a search box in the top left and a newsletter box in the top right.

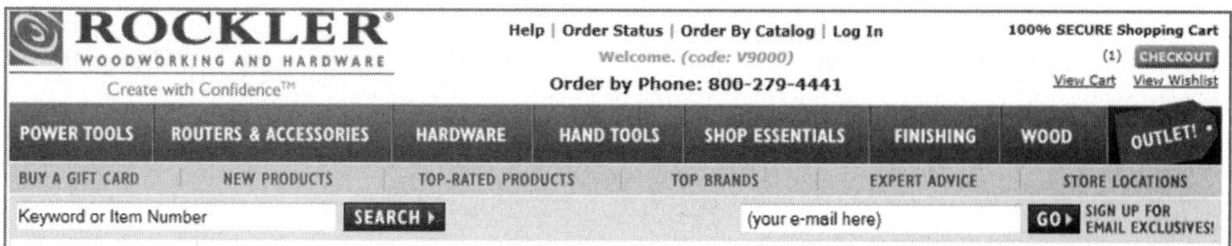

Figure 5.11 Example of internal search input box location issues

Wednesday: Optimize Your Internal Site Search Functionality and Usability

Today, you will learn some best practices for making your internal site search more powerful and more usable. This will result in much greater visitor usage of this tool and more engagement and conversions from them as a result of using it.

Offer Auto-Predict Results in the Internal Search Box

An increasingly common, smart way to improve the usability and power of your internal site search tool is to offer auto-prediction results in the search input box, much as Google now offers for their search input box on their website.

This functionality allows users of your search tool to get search suggestions while they type, helping them to understand what they might want to search for, and also to make it more efficient and quicker to enter their search query.

Figure 5.12 shows an example of auto-predict in action on Buy.com.

Therefore, try to introduce this auto-predict functionality into your internal search tool box, either by upgrading your tool or by building this functionality into it.

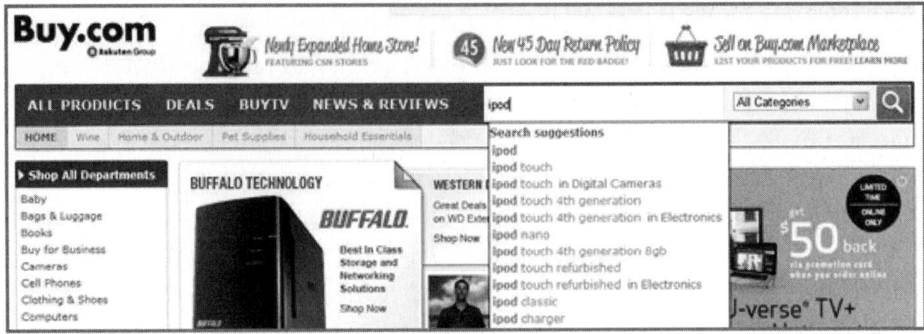

Figure 5.12 Example of auto-predict in a search entry box

Ensure Search Box Default Word Content Disappears When Users Begin Typing There

You need to make sure that when a user begins typing into your internal site search tool box the default word content disappears. For example, many internal search input boxes contain default words like "keyword" or "type search here" or "search." If this doesn't happen, it results in them struggling to easily enter a search term in the box, and often results in bad search results due to it also containing the default search box words. This can potentially cause them to prematurely leave your website out of frustration.

Add Additional Search Filter Functionality for E-commerce Search Boxes

If you have an e-commerce website, you should add search filter options next to the input box to allow visitors to search within particular product categories.

This helps the visitor refine their search to only a particular category that they are interested in and will help them find what they are looking for more quickly. You should offer this by showing a filtered drop-down menu adjacent to the search box, adding options to search within the music or electronics sections of your website for example. Amazon.com does a great job of offering this, as you can see in Figure 5.13.

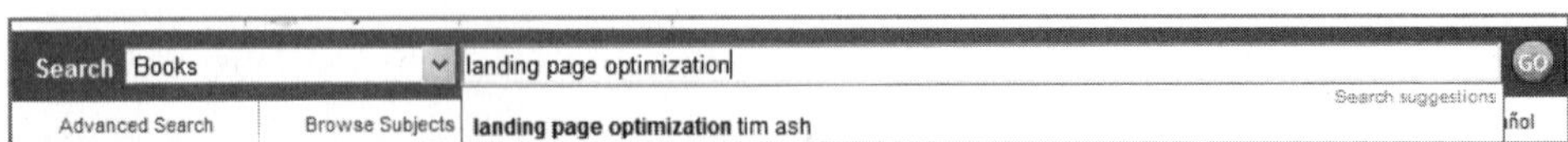

Figure 5.13 Example of adding search filter boxes

Thursday: Optimize Your Internal Site Search Results

Many website marketers and owners think it is good enough to simply offer an internal site search tool and often don't pay much attention to the actual results it generates for visitors. Far too many websites' internal search results lack relevance and quality or just inundate the search user with hundreds of results to weed through. Therefore, today you will learn some best practices to ensure a positive visitor experience with your search results, and help increase engagement levels and conversion rates from these searchers.

Offer an Advanced Internal Site Search Option

Rather than just offering a basic search tool box on your website that only lets visitors search by keyword or only a few search criteria, you should give your visitors the option to run an advanced search to find exactly what they are looking for much more easily.

This advanced internal search tool should offer a greater number of search criteria, for example by content category or price range, and the ability to do Boolean searches that allow visitors to use "and," "or," and "not" logic. For an example of a website with a good advanced search tool, take a look at Figure 5.14, which shows the Advanced Search page at Cars.com.

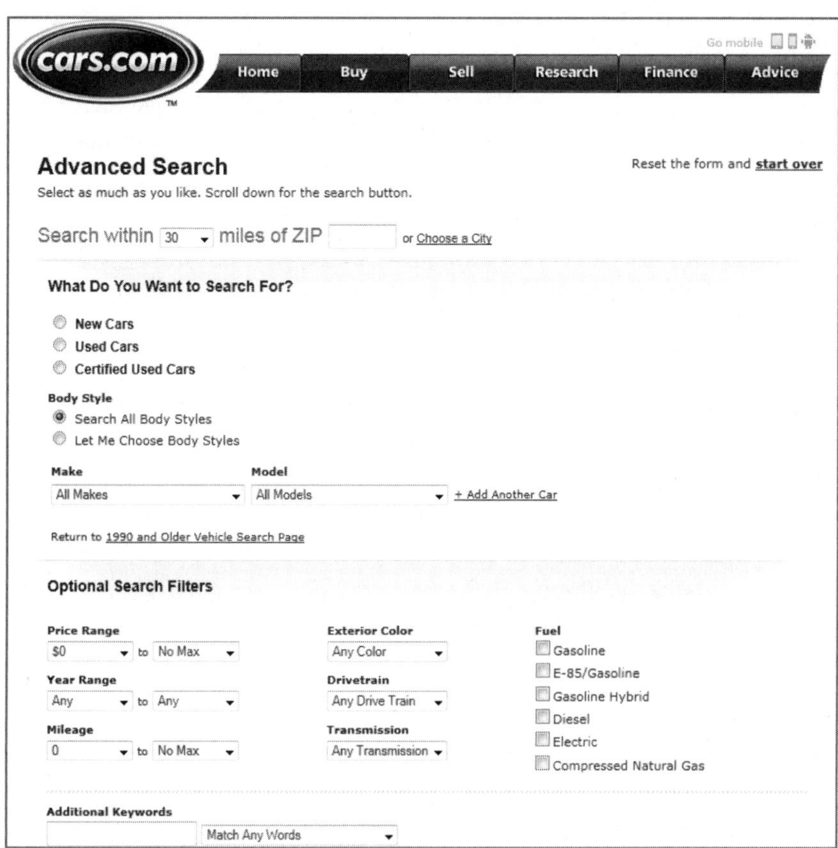

Figure 5.14 Example of a good advanced search page

So that your visitors can easily find and use this advanced search page, ideally you should have a link to this advanced search right next to your search input box.

It is particularly important to offer this advanced search tool on websites that are very search driven, such as websites where visitors are searching for something specific like a car to buy, a place to live, or someone to date. If you don't offer advanced search options on websites like these, visitors may get frustrated and go to a website that has better search options instead.

Use Featured Keyword Results to Promote Conversion-Related Items

When a visitor runs a search on your website, this shows an increased amount of engagement with your website. Therefore, it's a good opportunity to try and influence what they click on next in order to help increase conversion rates on your website.

You can take advantage of this by showing featured keyword listings that promote items that will increase the chances of them converting (but still relate to what they were searching for). For example you could show them promotional products or ones that are on sale relating to their search query.

These featured promotional searches should be shown in a separate box at the top of the search results. However, don't go over the top with usage of this, and always make sure what you are promoting is relevant to what the user has searched for; otherwise, you may risk them getting alienated or frustrated by what you are trying to promote to them.

If your current internal search tool doesn't offer this functionality, you should consider upgrading your tool to one of the advanced tools discussed earlier that has options for this, such as Adobe Search&Promote.

Make Sure Your Internal Search Tool Adjusts for Spelling Mistakes and Acronyms

You should understand that your visitors might not always know how to spell what they are looking for or know the most common name for what they are looking for. Rather than not showing any related search results when this occurs and risk potentially losing your visitor because they didn't find what they are looking for, you should optimize this. This involves building logic into your internal search tool that recognizes common misspellings and acronyms and then shows results for the corrected search results instead. Most good internal search tools will offer this great functionality.

Figure 5.15 shows an example of how auto-correction is used on Amazon.com.

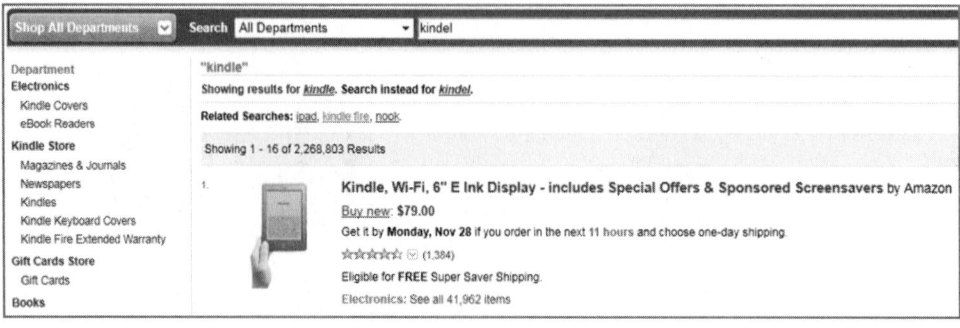

Figure 5.15 An example of auto-correcting a misspelled search entry

Make Sure Your Tool Includes Customer Support–Related Keywords

Many website visitors use internal search to try and obtain information about support topics but often fail to get related results that they are looking for and potentially leave your website. This is because often internal search tools are only set up to crawl and index products and services and not additional help articles or forum topics.

Therefore, you need to make sure you have relevant results for common customer support keywords like "shipping," "phone number," and "returns." Most internal search tools should allow you to choose what you would like to crawl and include in your search results, and if you cannot do this, I suggest you upgrade your search tool.

Allow Visitors to Refine Internal Search Results to Find What They Need

The next thing you need to do with your internal search tool is to make sure that users can easily refine their search results to narrow down and find exactly what they are looking for. This is because your visitors will often search for something broad first and then want to narrow it down by filtering the results by price or subcategory for example.

This is best done by offering search-refining filters in the left-hand rail of your search results page—for example, by category of the search results or by the newest first. You should also include a search box at the top of the search results page that allows visitors to search for something else or modify their search keywords. In Figure 5.16, you can see that REI.com does a great job with this in their internal searches and also offers a featured result area right at the top of the search results.

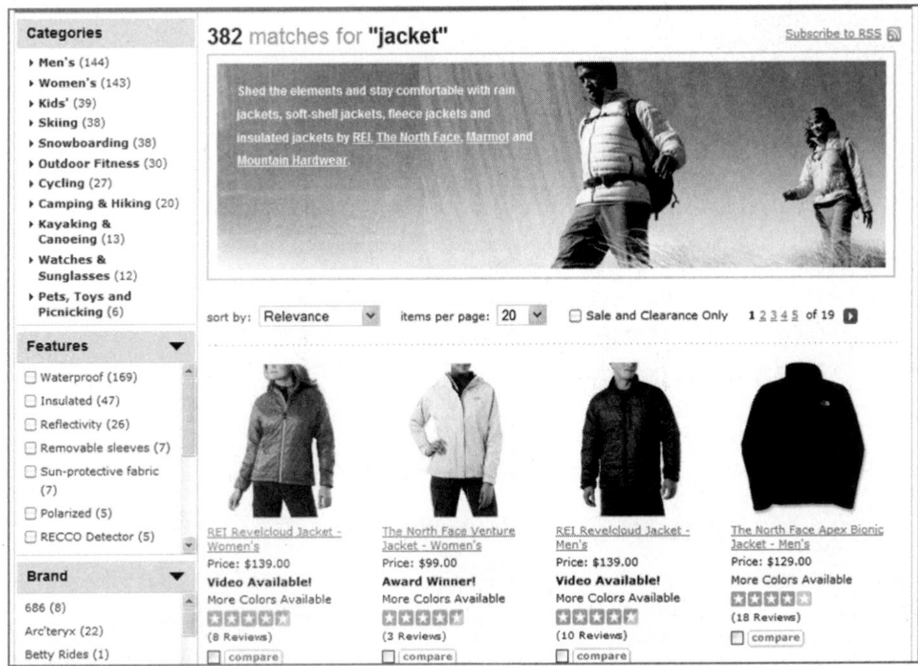

Figure 5.16 Good example of search results filters

You should also allow your visitors to customize how their search results are displayed, including the option to change the number of results shown per page. Depending on if your internal search is very product oriented, you should also give your visitors the option to show the search results in a grid format instead of a more traditional list view. You can also learn much more about how to optimize e-commerce search results and browse pages in Chapter 7.

Don't Let Visitors Dead End If There Are No Site Search Results

When a visitor runs an internal search that has no search results, you should always show them a few recommended options or next steps instead. This increases the chances of them clicking on something on your search results page and not abandoning your website because they couldn't find what they were looking for.

For example, you should show them something they might be interested in, like your most popular content or categories on your website. As an example, Zappos .com is very good at handling an internal search that has no results, as you can see in Figure 5.17.

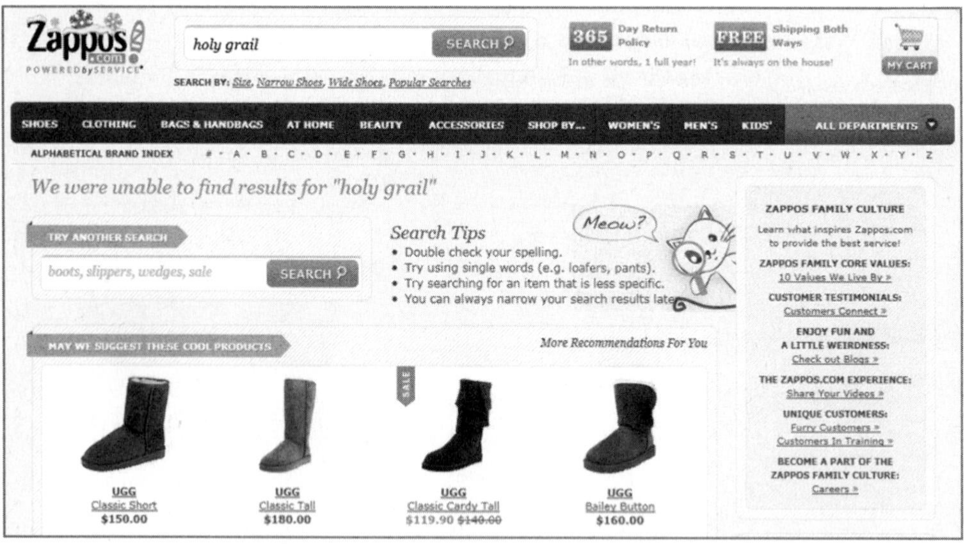

Figure 5.17 Handling an internal search with zero results

Therefore you should test making some improvements to your internal search results page by adding additional useful links if no results appear.

Friday: Analyze Your Top Internal Keywords for Additional Insights

Not only is the internal search tool an essential navigation method for your visitors, their keyword search queries also form a goldmine of information to help you better understand visitor behavior and intent. These insights can then help you form better test plans to optimize your website.

If you aren't currently tracking what your visitors are searching for on your website, then you are going to be missing some great additional insights. Therefore, today you will learn how to analyze your keyword search reports to gain better insights.

Ensure You Are Tracking and Reporting on Your Internal Keyword Searches

First of all, in order to analyze and gain insight from your visitors' internal keyword searches, you need to make sure all of the internal keywords being searched for are being tracked by your web analytics tool. This is configurable in most good web analytics tools and is usually tracked by signifying a URL parameter that contains the keyword that was searched for. For example, if you use Google Analytics, follow the instructions at `www.google.com/support/googleanalytics/bin/answer.py?answer=75817&topic=12627` to set this up.

Once you have set up this tracking, you then need to run and monitor reports for the top internal search keywords on your website. This is usually fairly simple to do in most analytics tool by running a fairly standard report. For example, in Google Analytics you need to run the Site Search Overview report, which is found under the Content report section. See Figure 5.18 for an example of this report.

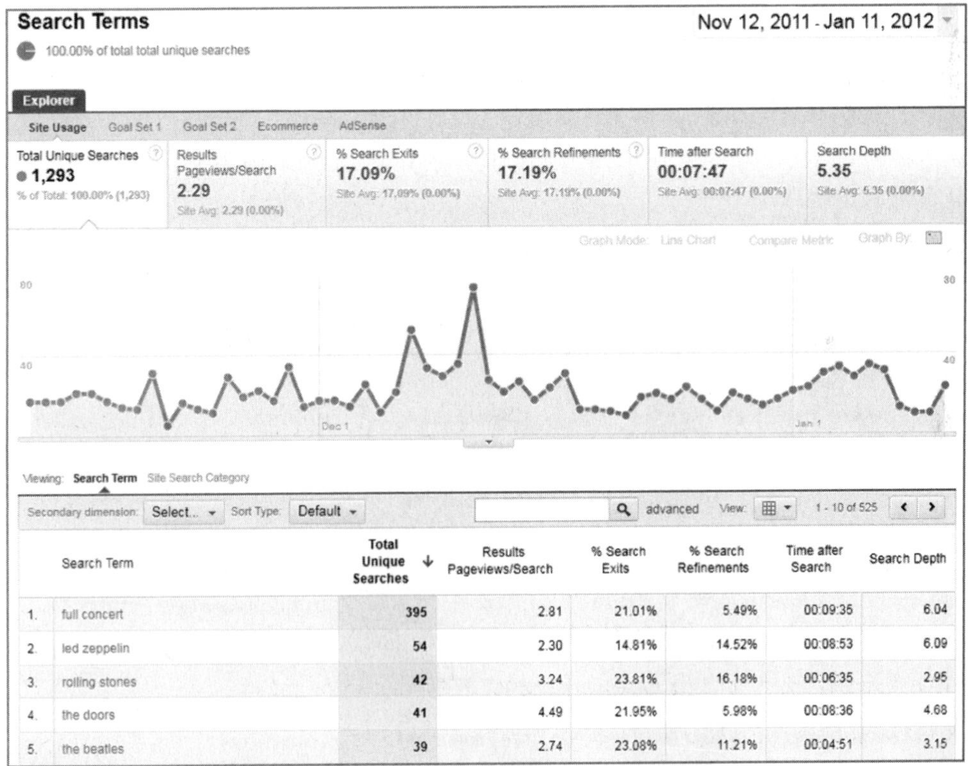

	Search Term	Total Unique Searches	Results Pageviews/Search	% Search Exits	% Search Refinements	Time after Search	Search Depth
1.	full concert	395	2.81	21.01%	5.49%	00:09:35	6.04
2.	led zeppelin	54	2.30	14.81%	14.52%	00:08:53	6.09
3.	rolling stones	42	3.24	23.81%	16.18%	00:06:35	2.95
4.	the doors	41	4.49	21.95%	5.98%	00:08:36	4.68
5.	the beatles	39	2.74	23.08%	11.21%	00:04:51	3.15

Figure 5.18 Example of a top internal searches report

Check for Popular Internal Search Keywords That Yield Poor Results

When you are looking at your internal search keyword reports, just having some very popular internal searches doesn't mean users are happy with the results that are generated when they search for these. Sometimes they will be searching for something that yields either none or very few results or results that have low relevance or quality. When this occurs they will be frustrated and may often leave your website because they can't find what they are looking for.

To understand and gain insight into this, use the internal search tool on your website to search for your top keywords shown in your report and check if any of them yield zero, few, or poor search results. If you find keywords like this, it usually means one of two things. First, it can mean you need to create additional content relating to these search keywords so that it better satisfies your visitors' search queries (and these keywords can often provide great ideas to expand what your website should offer).

Second, if these poorly performing keywords are not relevant to what you offer on your website (or plan to offer), it can be an indicator that your visitors are confused about what your website offers and expects to find. If this occurs you should try to address this by explaining better to your visitors what they can find on your website.

Another good simple indicator you can use to see which of your keyword searches may have poor results is to look for the number of visitors that immediately exit after searching for a keyword. In Google Analytics this is known as the "% Search Exits" metric, and is shown as standard on their internal search reports. The higher this percentage for a keyword, the more likely it offers zero, low, or poor quality results.

Check for Page Locations That Result in Most Internal Search Usage

You can also gain some great insight from looking at which pages your internal search is most often used on and the corresponding keyword searches that are run on them.

For example, if your product page has many searches run from it, this could indicate that your product page isn't giving all the information that visitors need and that you should test placing the missing information on it that they are searching for. This should result in higher visitor satisfaction with the product page and higher conversion rates.

In most web analytics tools you can find which pages your internal search is mostly common run from to find these insights. In the example of Google Analytics, you can find this by running a report called Search Pages to see a list of top pages that your internal search is used on.

Make Content Relating to Your Top Keywords More Prominent

Internal search reports can also provide some valuable insight into what content you need to make more prominent for visitors on your website. If you see keywords heavily dominating your top-searched keyword reports, this is a good indicator of your most popular content that relates to these.

Therefore, you should consider testing making links to the related pages of these keywords more prominent on your website, for example, by adding them to your main navigation and top entry pages. By doing this, visitors who don't use your internal search can find this very popular content without having to run a search, and you may increase engagement and give your conversion rates a slight boost.

Understand Influence of Internal Search Usage on Conversion

One last good but advanced thing to do with your internal site search data is to help you understand how influential your internal search is on your conversions.

This can be done by setting up a visitor segment in your web analytics tool for any visitors who run an internal search on your website (usually defined by someone seeing your internal search results page). You can then see the conversion rate for this segment of internal search users and compare it to the overall conversion rate for all of your visitors. Refer back to Chapter 2 to learn more about how to set up visitor segments like these.

If you see a much higher percentage of visitors converting when using your search tool, you should make your search tool even more prominent on your website. This would result in more usage of the tool, and because these users convert higher, there would be an increase in conversion rates for your website. To make it more prominent you could make your search box slightly bigger and more obvious, or add additional search boxes to more visible areas on common entry points like your home page.

6

Learn the Power of Influence and Persuasion on Visitors and Conversions

Visitors to your website are not robots—they are real people with real emotions, feelings, and thoughts, and they do things on your website for a reason. In this chapter, you will gain a more thorough understanding of these reasons and what makes your visitors click, so that you can better influence and persuade them to convert for your website goals.

Chapter Contents

Week 15: Influence Your Visitors by Optimizing Your Calls-to-Action, Headlines, and Text

You are probably spending considerable effort and money attracting visitors to your website, but how do you better influence them once they arrive and get them to do what you want them to do? This week you will learn more about this and focus on improving your usage of calls-to-action (CTAs), headlines and text to influence and convert more of your visitors for your goals. This week is one of the most important to understand and utilize in this book, because these elements are often some of the biggest influences on the conversion rate and success metrics on your website.

The marketing principles of AIDA, which describe the key phases that a potential buyer goes through (attention, interest, desire, and action), are particularly appropriate to use and influence this week, because you can use your headlines, subheaders and text to attract attention, raise interest and desire, and then use your CTAs to influence your visitors to take action (where the all-important conversion point occurs).

Monday: Review and Optimize Your Headlines and Subheaders

Your headlines and subheaders are often one of the few things that a visitors' eye will be drawn to and read on your web pages first. This is because they stand out more than other text, and are usually found in the first part of the F-shape reading pattern that you learned about in Chapter 5.

If they are not compelling and don't engage your visitors to want to continue reading, then there is a smaller chance they will stick around and convert for your goals (this is particularly true for first-time visitors). This is therefore going to have a seriously negative impact on your conversion rates.

Today you'll learn some great best practices to optimize your website headlines and subheaders in order to better engage and convert your visitors.

Keep Your Headlines and Subheaders Simple and Concise

First you need to make sure your headlines and subheaders aren't too long. Ideally your headlines should not span more than one line and definitely be shorter than 40 characters, but your subheaders can be slightly longer (ideally less than 80 characters though). The shorter you can make any of these the better because it will make it easier and quicker for your visitor to read and understand them.

You should also try testing simple direct statements for your headlines and subheaders, because they can often work better than clever or elaborate ones that your marketing team may have created.

To test the impact of improving these, come up with a few simpler and shorter variations on your current headlines and subheaders and run a test to see which ones perform better for lifting engagement and conversion rates. For an example of direct and short headline or subheader, see the HubSpot.com landing page in Figure 6.1.

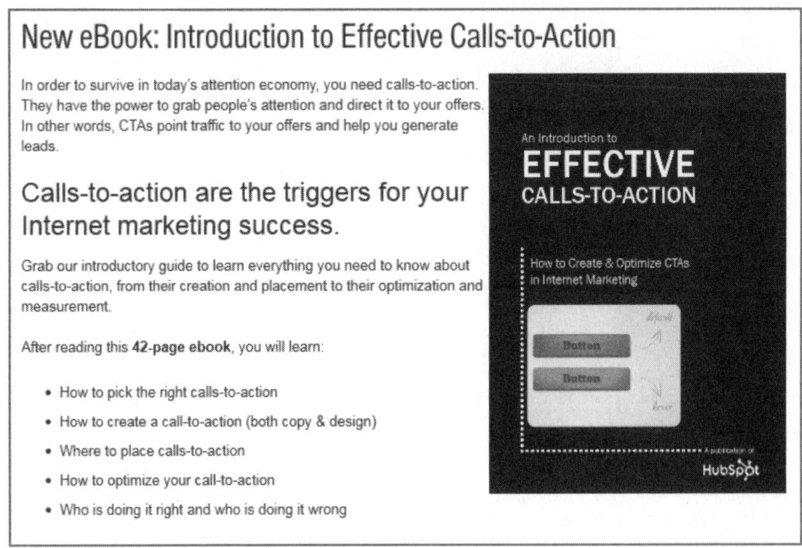

Figure 6.1 Example of a short and direct headline

This is particularly important to do for any pages that are associated with your conversion goals such as product pages, and also your home page.

Pose Provocative Questions

To spike the interest and curiosity of your visitors, you should test posing provocative questions for headlines that relate to them (for example, "Unsatisfied with your website conversion rates?"). These are more likely to catch the visitors' eye and get them reading the rest of your page content.

For a good example of this in action, see the Autoglass.com home page in Figure 6.2, which asks "Chipped Windscreen?" as a strong way to influence their visitors to click on their auto glass repair CTA. Go ahead and put yourself in your visitors' shoes and think of common questions that they might have, and then try testing a few of these in the form of headlines on your pages to see which ones engage and convert better.

Solve for a Need

You will get many more people reading your pages if your headlines solve one of your target audience visitors' likely common needs. Again, try putting yourself in your visitors' shoes and think of what needs they will likely have, and then test a few different variations for your headlines. For example, you could test using something like "Reduce the Bounce Rate of Your Home Page in 5 Easy Ways."

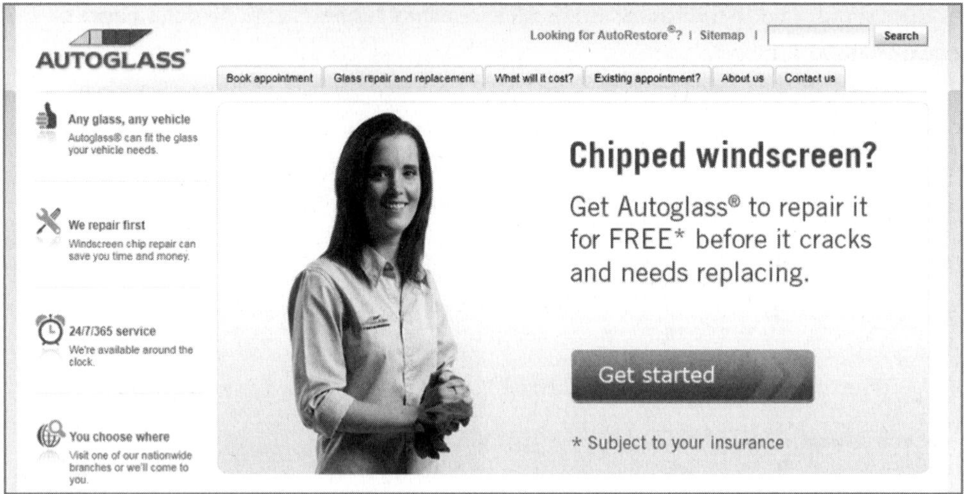

Figure 6.2 Example of a provocative question headline

Try "How-To" Wording

Visitors are often more engaged with headlines that offer to help them do something, particularly in the form of "how-to" guides. You should test changing a few of your headlines to this type instead, and you should also test incorporating step numbers into the headline. This makes it sound easier to understand and digest for the visitor. For example, you should test styles of headline like "How to Easily Lower Your Cable Bill" or "5 Steps to Improve Your Email Productivity."

Create a Sense of Urgency

Another tactic to test using on your headlines and subheaders is to create a sense of urgency in the wording of them. This will often make your visitors act and convert more quickly because they will fear they are going to miss out if they delay. This works particularly well if you are selling a product or service.

If possible, in the wording try and use specific numbers of stock items that remain, or specific time frames that remain, as this adds more realism to how scarce they are. For example, you could use something like "Act Now Before This Limited Offer Ends on December 31" or "Hurry, Only 3 Left in Stock."

Personalize Your Website by Using the Visitor's Name and "You" Wherever Possible

Studies have shown that people love seeing their name and respond better to something that includes it than something without it. To take advantage of this you should test personalizing your website and your emails by adding the reader's name into the header or subject line. This will increase the chances of them engaging with it and reading more. In addition to this, test adding references to "you" in your website or email to make it more personable instead of using "us" and "we."

Here are some examples of headlines and subheaders that make them seem more personal: "Dave, are you ready to improve your website?" and "Emily, have you seen our latest hot fashions yet?" You will learn more about this text optimization tactic and others on Friday of this week.

On Headlines for Paid Search Landing Pages Repeat Wording from the Ad Just Clicked On

To increase the chances of your visitors engaging and converting after clicking on a paid search ad, on your paid search landing pages you should test repeating and using some of the wording from the ad in the headline on your pages. This helps ensure continuation of messaging—if you don't do this and your ad doesn't relate well to your landing page you will lower your chances of converting visitors.

This can sometimes be achieved dynamically using your testing tool to pull this wording from the ad and show on your landing pages—please consult an optimization and testing expert in order to try and run this advanced technique.

Tuesday: Review and Optimize Your Call-to-Action Buttons and Links

After you have engaged your visitors to stay on your page by utilizing better headlines and subheaders, next you need to persuade them to take action by using influential calls-to-action. These usually come in the form of buttons or links, and their action should be aligned to convert for your website goals and use cases.

Your CTAs often have one of the biggest and most critical impacts on your conversion rates, so it's essential that you spend considerable time testing and improving them. Therefore, the rest of this day is going to focus on best practices for them.

Make Sure Your CTAs Are Optimally Located

It is very important to always suggest what your visitors should do next on your pages—don't just leave it up to them to decide and risk them leaving your website. To influence this, you need to place your CTAs in several key areas of all your pages.

The first key area to place them is high up in your main content area, above the page fold (as discussed in Chapter 5). This increases the chances of them being seen—don't just bury them away at the bottom of your page or in the sidebar of your website. This is particularly important for your pages that relate to your conversion goals, like product or service pages.

Next, if you have an e-commerce website, your CTA buy buttons should not only be placed on your product pages above the fold, but your buy and learn more CTA buttons should also be placed next to anywhere you list a product on your homepage, category, browse, and search results pages.

Then if you have longer article, lead generation, or service pages, you need to make additional use of them at the end of these pages. This is because your visitors' eyes will often end up there after they read the page so it is a logical place to show them options for what to do and click on next. For a good example of this, see Figure 6.3 for how SEOmoz.com does this on their longer service description page.

Therefore you should go ahead and review your website for your current usage of CTAs, and then run tests to move the location of them to try and increase conversion rates. This is particularly important to do on your home page and pages that relate to your conversion goals like product and service pages.

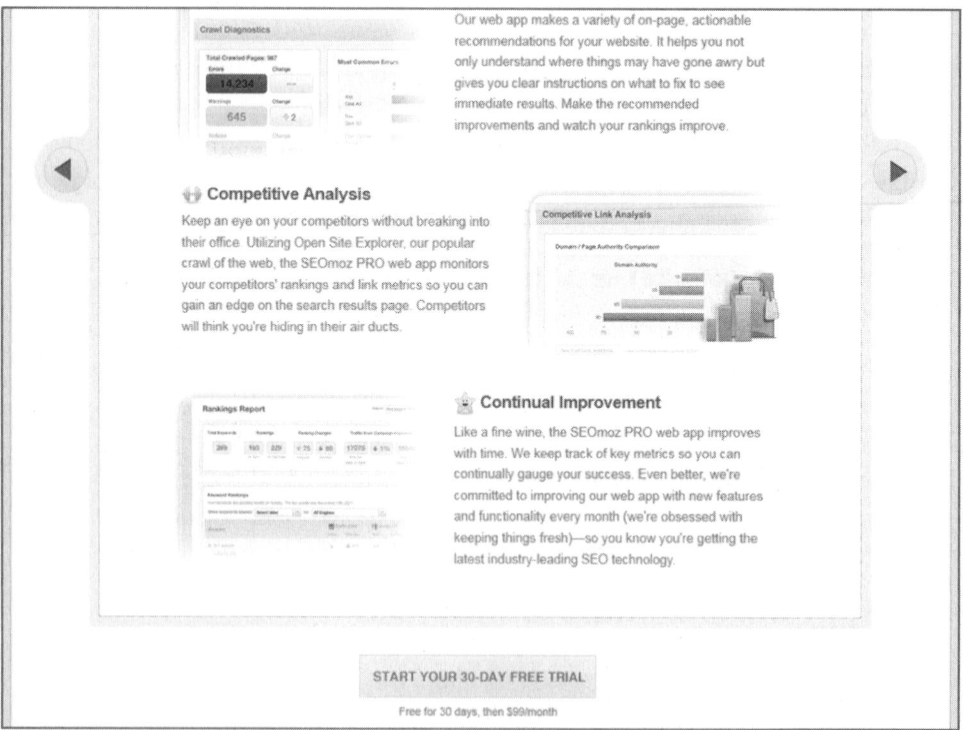

Figure 6.3 Example of a good CTA at the bottom of a service page

Test the Format of Your CTAs

How you format and present your CTA buttons also has an extremely big impact on your conversion rates. You should therefore spend considerable time testing different variations of the size, style, color, and wording of them to get the highest conversion rates possible. Here are some important elements to test:

CTA Size

Many websites make the mistake of having very small CTA buttons or links that don't attract visitors' attention. Make sure they are big enough for your visitors to notice, but don't make them too big and obnoxious. As a guide, you should aim to balance the size of your CTAs with the rest of your supporting copy and website elements on each page.

I definitely suggest you test increasing the size of your CTAs to make them slightly bigger, as this is often a quick and simple way to increase conversion rates.

CTA Style

There are several tactics for you to test regarding the style of your CTA buttons and links. Here are some things you can try testing, with some examples in Figure 6.4.

- Test using a button versus a link for your CTA, and vice versa. Don't just presume one will work better than the other.
- Test using a button with an arrow in the design of it to help draw the visitors' eye.
- Test adding other icons in the design of buttons to help stylize and make it stand out.
- Test using a button with a beveled effect or a shadow so that it stands out more, which helps make the button look 3D versus flat.
- Test using a rounded rectangle for a button (or even more circular shapes), as this style gives more of an impression of a button and makes them more intriguing to push.

Figure 6.4 Example of different CTA button styles

CTA Color Scheme

Here are some best practices to use when testing the colors of your CTA buttons:

- You should test making your button colors stand out from the rest of your color scheme, but don't make them clash or become too garish.
- Greens, oranges, and more neutral colors should be tested, but test many other versions of colors too because sometimes even basic colors like gray can lift your conversion rates.
- Although some experts say to stay away from using red buttons because that color is associated with danger and warning, sometimes using it can have positive results on conversions and is worth testing.
- Don't go for subtle variations of colors; always try and come up with a few bolder variations to test against, as these radical changes often stand out more and can have a higher potential impact on your conversion rates.

CTA Wording

The wording of your CTAs is one of the key things to help trigger action and the all-important conversion, and, depending on how well you use them, can have a major impact on your website conversion rates. Here are some best practices, along with examples in Figure 6.5 to use in your CTA tests to help lift your conversions:

- Rather than using very generic and uninspiring words like "submit" or "click here" on your buttons, you should test making the wording action-based instead. You could test using words like "get started," "start your free trial," "try it for free," or "see our low-cost plans." Using words like these can often make a huge difference on your conversion rates.
- Test adding additional supporting text right onto your button to help convey benefit or reduce risk. This text should be smaller than the main CTA wording, and adding this can often help increase conversion rates.
- Don't just make small changes to your CTA wording, and ideally you should try testing three to five significantly different versions of button wording.
- If you are using paid search landing pages, you should also match your CTA wording on those pages with the wording in the ad that was seen prior to your visitor arriving on them. This way you help to continue the messaging from the ad they clicked on and help increase conversion rates.

Figure 6.5 Example of different CTA button wording

If you run into issues from your web design or branding teams not allowing you to test variations of your CTAs using these best practices, refer back to Chapter 3 where you learned ways to help overcome these.

Wednesday: Learn Other Best Practices for Improving Your CTAs

Today, you'll learn about some other CTA best practices that you can test using on your webpages to help increase your conversion rates:

Emphasize the More Important CTA Buttons If You Have Multiple Types per Page

If you have CTA buttons for multiple things on one page, you need to prioritize and put more emphasis on the ones that are going to entice visitors to complete your most important website goals. Don't just give them all the same size and treatment, even though it might look nice in terms of website design, because it will confuse the visitor as to which one they should click on.

Make Sure Your CTA Buttons Are Legible and Easy on Your Visitors' Eyes

On your CTA buttons and links, you definitely shouldn't use fonts that are smaller than 10-point size, because visitors will find them harder to read and they won't stand out very well. Ideally, your CTA text should be bigger than your regular page text.

You also shouldn't use nontraditional fonts or colors that are hard to read—stick with common fonts like Verdana and Arial and colors that are not garish or loud. In other words, don't let your web designers use trendy looking fonts and color combinations, because even though they might look cool to them, they can often have negative effects on your CTA click through rates, and thus your conversion rates.

Therefore, to see which ones convert better, try creating a few different CTA buttons that feature bigger text and are more easily readable.

Test Placing Risk Reducing or Benefit Statements Next to CTAs

Another thing you should test is placing small wording right to the side of or below your CTAs that reduces the risk of purchase and better explains the main benefits of doing so. This is good because it can often help propel the hesitant customer forward and improve conversion rates further.

Here are some examples of this risk-reducing and benefit-highlighting wording that you should test placing next to your CTAs, with some examples of buttons in Figure 6.6 that use this great tactic:

- It's free!
- Money back guarantee included.
- No commitment needed.
- No credit-card details required.
- Takes less than 60 seconds.
- Your transaction is 100% safe and secure.

Figure 6.6 Examples of CTA buttons with risk reducers and benefits

Look for Inspiration on Your Competitors' Websites and Google Search

To find inspiration for your CTA tests, you should look around some of your competitor websites and see what they are doing with their CTA buttons and links. Don't blatantly rip off the same wording and styles from them though, as this is likely to cause problems.

For other CTA messaging ideas, try running a Google search for terms relating to your website to see how other competitors are phrasing things in their search results.

Based on all these best practices for improving your CTAs, go ahead and create some more variations on your current CTA buttons and links and start testing to see which have the best impact on your conversion rates. You should be able to increase conversion rates by a couple of percentage points at the very least, and you will check the impact of these in the final chapter. Don't forget to involve your marketing team on coming up with these variations, as they will often have great ideas to increase conversion rate lift even further.

Thursday: Shorten Long Sections of Text and Convey Key Points

Over the next couple of days, you will learn some best practices to optimize one of the simplest conversion influencers of your website, and that is your website's text.

First it's important to understand that website visitors don't read text on websites the same way they do on other media like newspapers and magazines. Instead of reading all of the text on pages, they will typically scan them to see if they can find what they're looking for, and then, if they're interested, they might read more. Therefore, today you will learn how make it easier for visitors to scan and be engaged by the text on your web pages.

Shorten Long and Dense Sections of Text

To help your visitors read and scan your content more easily you should review your website for any particularly long and dense blocks of text and make them shorter and easier to read—short, chunked paragraphs work the best.

To do this, test taking out any unnecessary wording to help reduce the word count (to help you do this, think whether each paragraph is really needed by putting yourself in your visitors' shoes). To reduce the amount of text per page you could also test splitting your text up into multiple pages and have pagination links at the bottom of each page in the article. Doing this will also help increase page views per visit for media websites and helps increase ad revenue.

This is particularly important to test and improve on your home page and top entry pages, as long blocks of text on initial entry pages will not engage your visitors very well and will increase the chances of them bouncing from them prematurely.

Convey Key Points Using Bullet Points

Another great way to optimize the usage of text on your website is to make use of bullet points instead of blocks of text, particularly when conveying benefits or highlighting something important. This helps make your content easier for your visitor to digest, and helps better convey your more important wording. So go ahead and look through your website and see what text you could possibly try testing turning into bullet points instead.

Ideally, you should make the wording for each bullet point fairly short, and not longer than one or two sentences. You should also restrict your sets of bullet points to less than five per section, because if you are using any more than this you lose your ability to emphasize the more important bullet point contents. You should then test the order of them to see which points resonate most with your visitors and improve conversions.

You can also test stylizing the bullet point icons to make them stand out more (try using arrows or stars at the beginning of each bullet point). Another thing you can test is the usage of elements of bold and different font colors within each bullet point text.

Figure 6.7 shows a great example of a bullet point list style to test using on your website text that incorporates all these best practices, and a great one being used on PayPal.com.

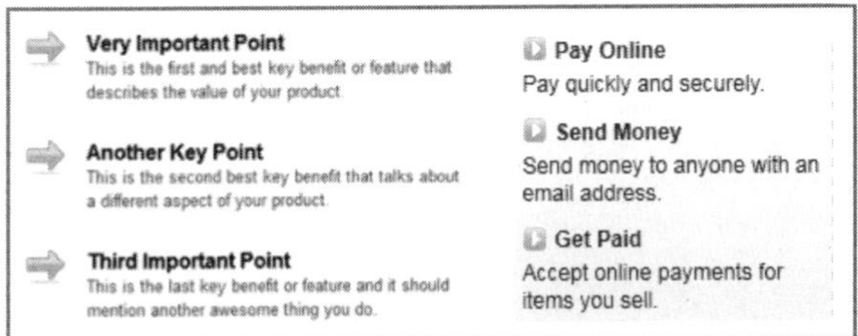

Figure 6.7 Examples of bullet point style lists

Use Other Ways to Emphasize Important Words and Points

In addition to condensing your text and making use of bullet points on your webpages, you can also use some best practices to draw visitors' eyes to particularly important words on your website. These words should be the key ones that are associated with trying to convert your visitors, like benefits or risk reducers, for example. Here are some best practices to try testing on your web pages:

- Test using **bolded font**, *italicized font*, and different font colors to draw the eye.
- Test using yellow text background highlights to help draw the eye better, just as if you were using a yellow highlighter pen when taking notes on paper.
- Try using hand-drawn arrows, underlines, circles and asterisks, and even hand drawn signatures (these can work particularly well on long lead generation or product sales pages, but don't overuse them).

Friday: Make Sure Your Website Text Is Easy to Read, Understand, and Relate To

The next thing you need to do to optimize your website text is improve the style and voice of your writing and make it easier for visitors to read, understand, and relate to.

This will help increase the chances of them being influenced and engaged by it. Today you will learn some great ways to do this with your website, which will also work well on your email campaigns too.

Focus Your Text on Your Visitor, Not Your Website

First you should make your text more centric around your visitors and their needs and not around you and the owners of the website. This has the effect of making your text less sales-like, and more personal and relatable to your visitors, ultimately helping to persuade and convert them better. Many websites make this mistake with the voice of their text, but luckily it is a fairly simple one to fix.

The best way to fix this is to review your website text, and test changing your text to focus on words that relate to your visitor like "you" and "your" rather than words that relate to the owners of the website like "we" and "our." Here are a couple of examples of saying a similar thing both ways; which one would engage you more? I'm sure you would choose the second one, as your visitors probably would too.

- Website owner voice: "Our website features the best new products that we proudly created."
- Website visitor voice: "You will love the new products here designed to benefit you."

An additional tactic you can try is using their name if possible. If the visitor is logged in to your website and you know their name, you should test dynamically combining their name with key parts of your text. Here is a simple yet effective welcome message that includes the visitor's name and visitor centric text: "Welcome back Dave, You will love the new products here designed to benefit you." This tactic works very well for personalizing email subject lines too.

Focus on Benefits, Not Just Features

To help focus your text even more on your website visitors, you should add text that explains the *benefits* of using your website, products or services, *not just the features* of them. This often has a great impact on improving conversion rates.

This is important to do because features can sometimes not provide much meaning if there is no context or the visitor doesn't understand the need for the features. Examples of benefits are if your website offerings meet a need or save the user time.

So that you can understand the difference and power of using benefits, Table 6.2 gives you a few examples of benefits and how they differ from features.

After you have understood this, you should create a few examples of benefits for using your website and products and then test placing them prominently on your website.

▶ **Table 6.2** Examples of features versus benefits

Features	Benefits
Available in small, medium, and large	Saves you time
Available in 3 different colors	Customizable to meet your needs
Comes with 5 premium tools	Lasts longer than other brands
10 megapixel zoom	Reusable

Simplify Your Website Text and Make It Easier to Understand

To make your text even easier for *all* types of your visitors to understand, you need to simplify the language level you use for your text. To do this you should aim to use a level that will appeal to the most common level of language of visitors to your website. Doing this ensures that the bulk of them will understand everything that you are talking about on your website and increases the chances of them being influenced by it and not alienated by it.

A good best practice is to use high-school level language on your website and to avoid business school language. This also includes the removal or translation of any industry jargon or "techy" sounding words that you might have on your website.

Go ahead and reread the text on your website, put yourself in your visitors' shoes, and ask yourself, "Will most of my visitors understand what we are talking about?" After you have identified any language they might not understand, test either simplifying the text or removing it. While doing this in isolation won't impact your conversion rates very much, when combined with other text best practices you have learned here, it will likely increase your conversion rates.

Optimize Your Font Colors and Sizes

It's important to realize that your choice of font size and color can have an impact on your conversion rates and can easily be optimized. Too many websites make it hard to read text by having font size that is too small or poor choice of text color on background colors, potentially causing visitors to prematurely exit.

Best practices here include providing high contrast between your text and the background color (for example black text on white background is easier on the eye and better than gray text on black background), and not using a font size smaller than 8 point because this will cause friction for visitors and increase chances of them not reading and leaving your website.

You should also test increasing the line spacing of your paragraphs to 1.5 lines. This should add to the readability of your text and help increase the chances of visitors reading it.

If your website is a media or publishing site with many articles, you should add a text resizing option at the top of your articles. This is particularly useful for older readers, and for visitors who are looking at your website on a mobile device (due to smaller screen resolutions). Figure 6.8 shows an example of how to show this text resizing option at the top of an article page.

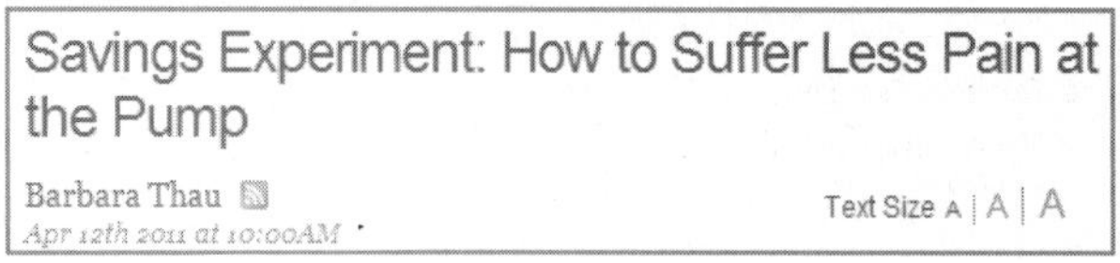

Savings Experiment: How to Suffer Less Pain at the Pump

Barbara Thau

Apr 12th 2011 at 10:00AM

Text Size A | A | A

Figure 6.8 Example of a text resizing tool on article pages

Don't Let Search Engine Optimization Paralyze Your Text Optimization

You may get pushback about making these website text changes from your search engine optimization (SEO) team. Yes, there is a balance of using a certain amount of text to aid with SEO purposes. However, most SEO ranking factors have nothing to do with the words on your page, with most now coming from offsite linking from other websites (having quality links to your website from trusted, authoritative and topically relevant websites is the key).

As long as you have the right keywords in your URL and browser title and some mentions of your keyword in your text, you shouldn't need to write huge long keyword-stuffed paragraphs anymore to help rank your website better in search engines.

And not having to worry about this SEO impact means you can have more freedom to tweak and test the all-important wording on your website to help better engage and convert your visitors.

Week 16: Influence by Optimizing Your Images, Promotions, Videos, Rich Media, and Advertising

This week is going to focus on optimizing your usage of images, videos, rich media, and advertising to help influence visitors on your website, because combined, these factors can often have a significant impact on conversion rates without you realizing it. You will learn several best practices this week to help improve your usage of these and help to engage and convert your website visitors better.

Monday: Optimize Your Usage of Images

Far too often, websites use too many images, use ones that are not needed, and don't make use of images correctly when they are most needed. A great photo used in the right place can be worth more than a thousand words, yet a poorly used photo in the wrong place can actually have a negative effect. Today you will learn some best practices to apply to your images to help better influence and convert your website visitors.

Limit Your Usage of Images

First, you need to avoid using too many images per page. If you are using more than four images per page, it is likely to clutter the page and confuse the eye flow of your visitors, making it hard for them to understand what to look at first. This may result in them prematurely abandoning your website. This is particularly important to avoid on your home page, as visitors will unfairly judge the rest of your website based on this.

Test Key Image and Photo Elements

Next, you need to see whether your usage of images and photos on your website actually adds value for your visitors and aids in converting them to any of your website goals. What you show in them and the size of them, can have a significant impact on this. Depending on what you are trying to achieve with each one, and what message you are trying to convey, you will need to test many elements of them. So instead of just picking photos and images by gut feel and intuition, here are some things that you should test when selecting and using them:

Test the size of your photos and images. First of all you need to test different sizes of your key photos and images to find the optimal size. If they are too big, they can overwhelm pages and detract from key CTAs or other important content. But if they are too small, they can be missed or ignored, and it is especially very bad to have small screenshots of products. It is particularly important to test the size of images and photos on your homepage and your service and product pages (which you will learn about later today).

Test people in your photos and what they are doing. Using people in your photos is an important way to influence your visitors but is often done poorly. Depending on what you want these people to help you convey, here are some things that you need to test combinations for to see what engages and converts your visitors best:

- Gender
- Age
- Ethnicity
- Apparel (for example, business attire, academic, or casual)
- Facial expression (for example, smiling versus looking confused)
- What they are doing (for example, sitting, pointing, or shaking hands)

You should also consider doing a professional photo shoot to get some quality photos of exactly what you are looking for. While this is not usually cheap, it is certainly worth the investment to help improve photos and influence and impress your visitors better.

Pay Attention to Your "Hero Shots"

Hero shots are large website images or photos that usually focus on marketing a product or service and are usually designed to convey an offer or engage visitors further. They are usually used on key pages like the home page, often in the form of a slideshow rotator that a visitor can click through or watch it scroll through automatically. These rotators are great for featuring more than one thing at a time in this hero shot area.

Unfortunately, the usage of hero shots is often abused, and all too often a poor choice of hero shot detracts from other more important CTAs on the page.

However, a carefully selected hero shot in the perfect spot can help support your call-to-action and get your visitors to convert for your goals much more quickly. Here are some things to test regarding your hero shots to help you improve them:

Test adding a message and a clickable CTA button on your hero shot. This can help support your hero shot further and usually will help increase conversions.

Optimize the size and balance of the hero shot in relation to the rest of the page. You should consider the rest of the elements on your page, and don't overpower everything else on your page.

Test usage of different types of people in your hero shot. You should also test using people in your hero shot using the elements you just learned about because this can have an impact on influencing your visitors and conversion rates.

Test where people are looking or what they are doing with their hands. If your hero shot contains people, ideally you want to have them looking or pointing to the area that you want your visitor's eye to flow next.

If you are using an image rotator, limit the number of hero shot slides. If you use more than five different hero shots in your image rotator this will dilute the power of your more important ones, and also reduce the chance of your visitors seeing all of them. Don't just use this as a dumping ground for latest new promotions; always be sure to remove older, less relevant content in your image rotator.

Figure 6.9 shows an example of well-designed hero shots within a short image rotator, with overlaying text and a good CTA.

Include More Photos or Screenshots of Your Products or Services

If you are selling products or services, you need to allow your visitors to see many photos or screenshots of them. This will help your visitors visualize what your product or service looks like better and increase the chances of them buying it. Just having one photo certainly won't be adequate, and some of your better competitors will most likely have more.

On product pages, you should show one main photo, with thumbnail photo links below it to allow your visitors see more photos of it (ideally, at least three more; around ten is good). You also need to have photos that focus on specific features of the product, and ideally have images of it in use by the consumer (for example, wearing it or using it).

Figure 6.9 Hero shots in an image rotator

If you don't have enough photos of your products, as discussed earlier, consider doing a photo shoot to get some that meet these best practices just mentioned.

On service pages, you should show at least three screenshots that each convey a major feature of your service (more depending on how many features you need to convey).

Your Product Photos Should Allow Visitors to Zoom and Interact

Remember that websites have an immediate disadvantage over traditional stores in that website visitors cannot pick up an object to examine it better. Therefore, rather than just showing one sized image for your products and hoping that satisfies your visitors, you should at the very least allow the visitor to zoom in to see a bigger version of the photo by clicking on it.

Ideally you should take this a step further and let your visitors zoom in on different elements and parts of the product. This can be done by using a pop-up that magnifies the area of the photo the visitor is hovering their mouse over. Make sure you use a higher quality image when zooming in—this zoom-in view shouldn't be blurry. Figure 6.10 shows an example of this type of product zoom in action.

Bear in mind there are also some tools out there than can help automate this photo manipulation and resizing process, such as Adobe Scene7 (`www.scene7.com`).

To take this image viewing even further, you could try and offer a way of panning around the image so the visitor can see more angles of the product. While this is usually costly to implement, this is particularly important if you are selling products that are high fashion or have many product features that need to be shown and emphasized. Selling cars online is the perfect example of when this is needed most.

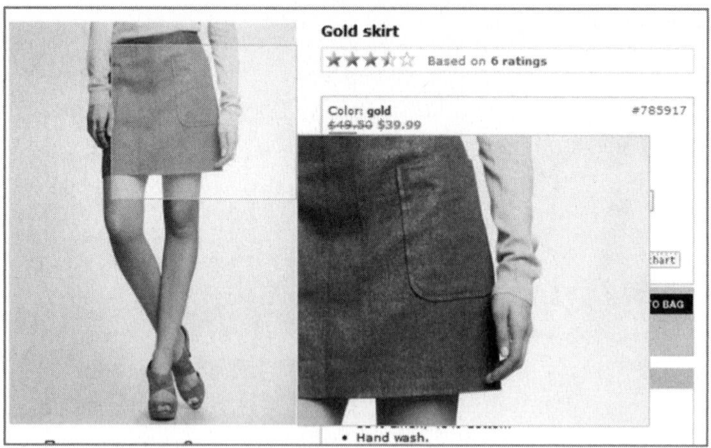

Figure 6.10 Example of zooming in on different areas of an image

Allow Visitors to See User-Submitted Photos of Your Products

You should also consider showing visitors photos of your products taken from other visitors and offer options for them to submit their own photos. Not only does this help with increasing the number of photos you can show, but it also helps improve the social proof of your product and increase the changes of it being purchased. This is because if visitors see many other visitors using the product, it will increase the chances of them buying it (as discussed earlier).

It's also good to allow visitors to submit photos because sometimes they will take and upload better (or more unique) photos than those you currently have on your website!

Amazon.com does a particularly great job of offering this, as you can see in Figure 6.11.

Figure 6.11 Example of offering user-submitted photos

Tuesday: Optimize Your Promotional Banners

One of the simplest and easiest ways to influence what your visitors click on your web pages is to create and promote banners relating to your conversion goals. These could be in the form of promoting your hot new product, a free download, or showing your latest deal, and you should be making use of several of these on your website to help drive conversions.

These promotional banners are excellent candidates to test and optimize to improve click-through and conversions. Today you will learn how to do this by combining many of the best practices found in this book already and some new ones. And when creating versions to test, you need to remember to go for some more radical changes instead of subtle changes, because this will improve the chances of bigger conversion rate lifts.

Test the Contents of Your Banners

What you actually show in your promotional banners will have the biggest impact on visitor engagement and conversion levels. Therefore, you need to test many different versions of the following elements to find the one that works the best:

Test the imagery in your banners. It's important that you test the imagery being shown in your banners, because as you learned yesterday, this can often have a big impact on your conversion rates. Therefore, you need to use those best practices you just learned when using imagery in your promotional banners.

Test the CTA of your banners. One of the most important things to test in your promotional banners is the CTA that you use in them. Depending on how big your banner is, you should ideally include a button for your CTA to entice visitors to click on it.

Test headlines and text in banners. Other than testing the imagery and CTA of your promotions, the next most important thing to test is the wording in them, particularly the headline. Come up with a few variations of this to test using the best practices you learned about in Week 15.

Test the Overall Style of Your Banners

After you have figured out what you want to test in your promotional banners, you need to think about the overall style of your banners, and come up with a few versions to see which engages and converts the most—for example, the color scheme, whether it looks 3D or flat, and the border of the banner. This is where you will need to have great web designers to come up with a few engaging styles for you to test.

Test Animated versus Static Banners

Using animations in your promotional banners is important to test. Done well and selectively, this can help draw the eye and engage. Done poorly, it can irritate and cause your visitors to leave your website if you have too many per page. Ideally you should limit your animation to two or three animation steps and carefully plan the series of them so they end up with a great CTA on the last slide. The animation should auto-repeat, just in case the visitor missed it initially (important if it's not immediately seen above the fold).

Go ahead and come up with a few animated versions of your banners and test to see if they engage and convert better than static ones.

Test Location and Size

Next, you need to test the optimal location to place your promotional banners. First, they should be fairly contextual and relate to the page they are found on. You should also test the size of them, because if they are too small, they may go unnoticed, or if they are too big, they may overpower more important content and CTAs on your pages. Go ahead and use a real estate test to check for the best conversion influencing areas to show your promotional banners, then do follow up tests on the actual size of them.

Use Content Affinity Targeting for Your Banners

In Chapter 4, you learned about the power of using affinity targeting to increase relevance of your content to your visitors and to get great conversion lifts. This is an excellent thing to test doing with your promotional banners on your home page and category pages and will increase the chances of your visitors engaging and clicking on them. Refer back to Chapter 4 for how to do this.

Use a Tool to Automate Creation of Your Banners

Designing many different versions of promotional banners to test often takes a considerable amount of time and cost and results in many different versions to manage. To relieve these issues, you should consider using a good asset management and manipulation tool like Adobe Scene 7 (`www.scene7.com`).

This tool dramatically improves these issues by dynamically changing elements of banners including text and images without needing to actually create separate files. The tool then tests them to find the best combination that most engages or converts your visitors.

You can also integrate it with Adobe Test&Target to show groups of visitors targeted messages in your dynamic banners (like content affinity targeting just mentioned) and also to improve the options for testing different versions.

Make Sure to Clearly Continue Messaging on the Next Page

Regardless of what you test for your promotional banners, if you aren't continuing the message of the banner onto the next page, you will frustrate the clicker and increase the chances of them leaving your website prematurely. Consequently, you should make sure that the next page you are sending your visitors to clearly shows details of what they just clicked on. And don't just bury this away on the page either—it should be visible above the fold.

One last point to cover today—all these best practices for promotional banners will also work well for testing ad banners placed on other websites to drive traffic to your website, and increase the chances of visitors converting after arriving.

Wednesday: Optimize Your Onsite Advertising

If you have a media or publishing website (like NewYorkTimes.com or AOL.com), you are going to be heavily reliant on using advertising on your website for generating revenue. Even nonmedia websites like e-commerce websites are starting to diversify and increase their revenue stream by using more advertising on their websites.

Unfortunately though, usage of ads can have serious implications for your visitor engagement and conversion rates, which many websites are often unaware of. However, there are certain types of advertising that can be used that are better for a visitor experience and ones to definitely avoid, which will be reviewed today.

Note that this onsite advertising is different than the promotional banner ads that you learned about yesterday, as these onsite ads being shown aren't created by you, and are ads for other businesses shown in standardized locations like the header or side bar.

Avoid Using Intrusive and Annoying Ad Units

First, let's discuss some particularly intrusive ad units that you should avoid using. Even though you may generate slightly higher revenue from them, they will often frustrate your visitors, and as a result of this increase your bounce rates and eventually reduce your repeat visit rate. Here are the ones you should avoid using:

Expandable Leaderboard Banner Ads These types of intrusive horizontal banner ads are usually found high up on webpages and automatically push your website content down significantly to make room for the ad or cover up key elements of the page. This often causes confusion for visitors because of the ad pushing down other elements of the website and is a very bad experience when they cover navigation or other key page elements. See Figure 6.12 for an example of this push down banner on the ESPN.com home page.

Interstitial Page Ads These whole-page ads are quite common, and are designed to give maximum exposure to a single ad or promo, showing up between some pages on websites. Unfortunately these interrupt the visitors' flow and often cause premature abandonment, particularly if these are shown immediately upon entering a website or if there is no obvious way to skip or close the interstitial page.

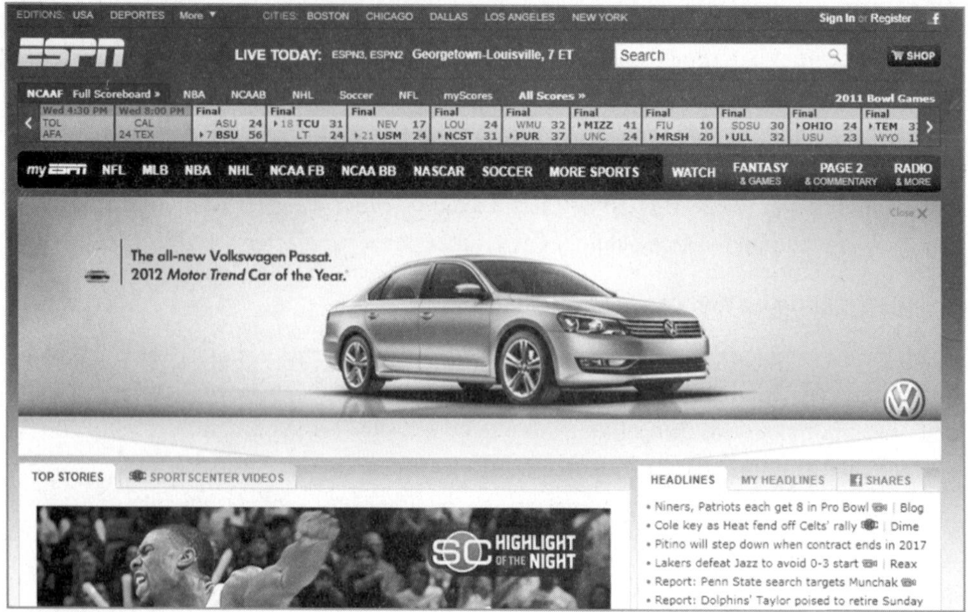

Figure 6.12 Example of an expandable leaderboard banner ad

Pop-Up Ads These ads pop-up over web pages and are designed to gain exposure to the ad by interrupting a visitor's eye flow and concentration. These are particularly frustrating for visitors when the ad covers important text and links and ones that are particularly hard to find the close button for. Figure 6.13 shows an example of one of these.

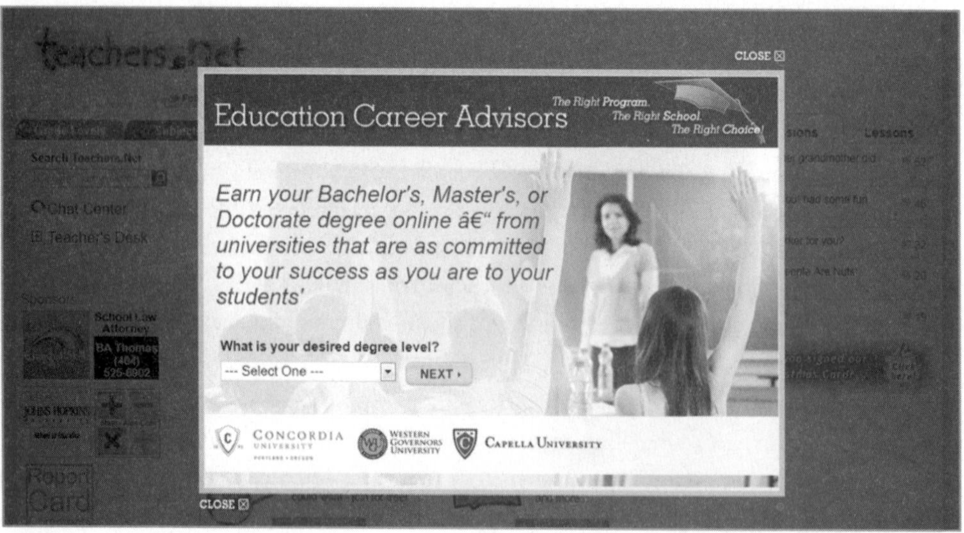

Figure 6.13 Example of a pop-up ad

Dynamic pop-up ads that actually move across web pages are particularly frustrating for visitors as they are often hard to turn off and should be avoided.

Irrelevant Auto-play Videos and Ones That Are Hidden with Auto-play Sound Auto-play videos often end up irritating visitors if they aren't very relevant to the content or if they can't find where the video is playing to stop it or mute the audio. This is particularly bad for auto-play videos that are not shown above the page fold, and also ones that are hard to mute.

Test Using Less-Intrusive Ad Types

To reduce the chances of annoying your visitors and increase the chances of generating advertising revenue, you should test using these less-intrusive ad types instead:

Contextual Text Link Ads These are text link ads that relate to the content on the page and were made very popular by Google Adsense (`www.google.com/adsense`). Implemented well, these can provide related links that add value to visitors and increase revenue for the website.

You could also try using Kontera.com (`www.kontera.com`), which has a great "In-Text Advertising" solution where they scan your text and show related popup links for products and services.

However, bear in mind that using these will often increase the exit rates of your pages because they take visitors away from your website and don't go overboard with these, as it will also be harder to influence your visitors to click on your links that you want them to.

Sponsor Logos on Content Advertisers are starting to understand that visitors rarely click on traditional banner ads now, and as a result they came up with a better solution to advertise their products in a more natural, contextual way, by sponsoring related articles or content. These usually allow the advertiser to have their logo on the article or site, often with related links to the sponsors' websites too.

Background Takeover Ads These newer types of ads form the whole background of websites and, if done well, can help drive good click through rates without irritating the visitor too much, as long as they aren't overly animated and don't clash with your website color scheme very much. Figure 6.14 shows an example of a well-executed background ad on Disney.co.uk for Lego that matches the leaderboard banner ad promotion.

Figure 6.14 Example of a background takeover ad

Thursday: Optimize Your Video Usage

Due to the recent trend of increasing internet connection speeds and the rise in online viewing of videos, movies and TV, there is a tremendous opportunity for websites to use video to help convert visitors and generate revenue. Currently there is much emphasis on performing search engine optimization for videos so they rank higher in search engines, but very little focus on optimizing usage of these so they engage and convert better. Therefore, this is great for you to capitalize on, build competitive advantage, and ultimately increase your engagement and conversion levels. Today you will learn how to do this.

Create Demo and Review Videos of Your Products and Services

If you are selling something on your website, a great way to help influence your visitors to buy from you is to create and show demos and reviews of your products or services. These videos should ideally be relatively short (less than three minutes) and be of relatively high quality yet not take too long to buffer and load.

These should be placed on your product and service related pages, with a thumbnail of the video right next to where you show photos of the product or service, or have a direct link to the video that makes the video appear in place of the image. For a good example of this in action, Figure 6.15 shows how ASOS.com offers demonstration video options on their product pages right below the main photo.

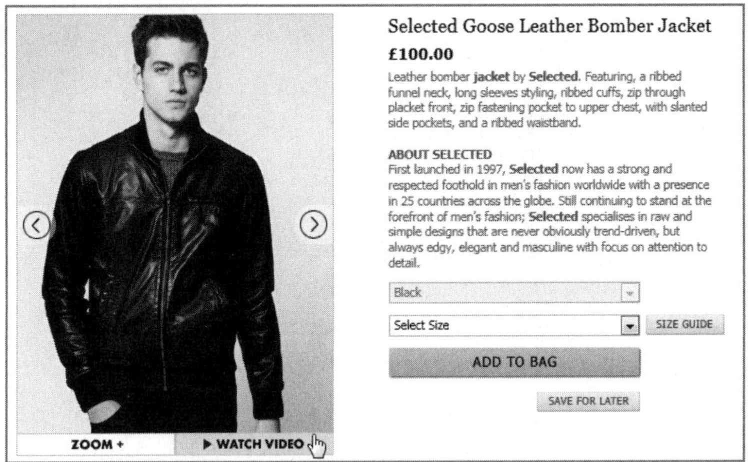

Figure 6.15 Example of product demo video options on a product page

Create How-To or Guide Videos

"How-to" and guide videos are ideal to show if your product or service needs a certain amount of explaining that text or images alone can't deliver very well. They also help provide a much deeper level of understanding to your visitors.

These videos should highlight the benefits and features of using your product or service and can be slightly longer than traditional demo or review videos. To help increase your conversion rates from them, you should always include a few built-in CTAs on the last frame of the video where they can learn more, or buy your product or service.

These videos should be prominently shown on your home page above the fold, on your top entry pages (particularly your paid search landing pages), and on your product and service pages. In Figure 6.16 you will see a good example of how HubSpot.com uses a "how-to" video on their landing page to convey benefits of using their service.

Best Practices for All Kinds of Videos

No matter what you are trying to achieve with videos on your website, there are several best practices that you can use to help engage and convert your visitors better.

Use Video Compression Services to Make Your Videos Load Quicker Videos can often be a major cause of slow-loading webpages, which can often result in visitors prematurely abandoning your webpages. Therefore you need to pay particular attention to the file size of your videos and compress them to smaller sizes so they load quicker. You can use video compression tools and services to help you do this, as discussed in Chapter 5.

Figure 6.16 Example of a how-to video in action

Include Related Videos or a CTA at the End of Videos You shouldn't just end your video without providing options for what visitors should click on next, because this will increase the chances of them leaving your website prematurely.

If you are a media website that wants to increase video views, you should include related videos (like Figure 6.17 that shows what YouTube shows at the end of their videos), or if you are using the video to help sell something in particular you should include a CTA to learn more or make a purchase.

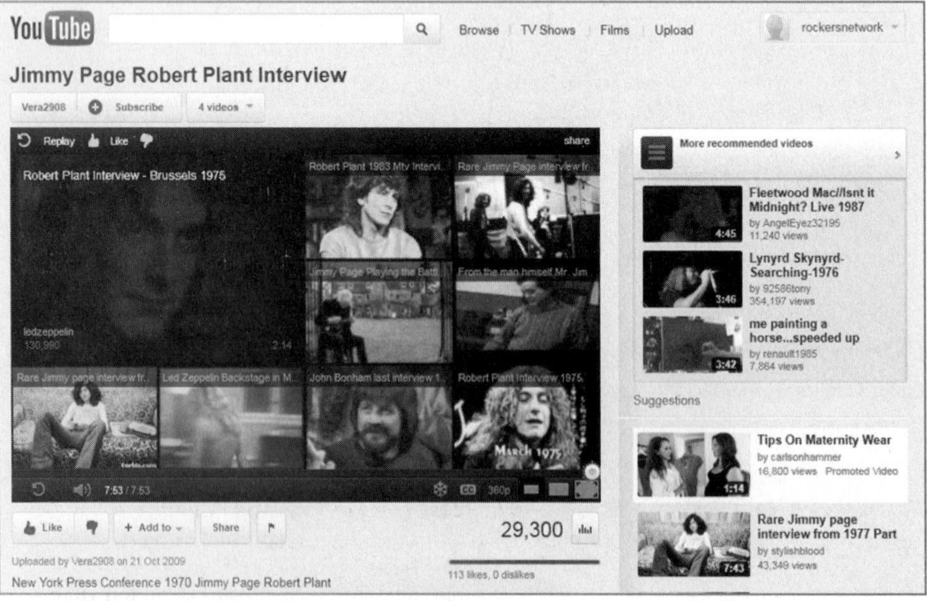

Figure 6.17 Example of related videos at the end of a video

Go ahead and test adding relevant CTAs or related links at the end of each of your videos to see which ones engage and convert the best.

Avoid Showing a Long Ad at the Start of Your Video Unless you have a media website that relies on advertising for your revenue, you should not put a video ad at the beginning of your videos because this will frustrate your visitors and often cause them to abandon watching your video.

If you have a media website, you can use these ads, but they should be no longer than 30 seconds and should give the visitors the option to skip the ad after five seconds has elapsed of it; otherwise, you will risk frustrating your visitors.

Include Social Sharing Options in the Video Player To increase the number of other people watching your videos and engaging with them, you should allow your video viewers to easily share your videos with others. In particular, you need to offer embedding options so that visitors can embed your videos on their own blog, website, or social network and add social network sharing options. The best way to do this is to offer options for this right at the bottom of your video player.

Analyze Your Video Metrics to Optimize Performance

Don't just hope and presume that the video content on your website is working well; instead you need to actually monitor its usage and optimize its performance. Many advanced web analytics tools have built-in video tracking metrics and reports, but unfortunately many of the free or cheap analytics tools don't offer this so you will need to either upgrade to an advanced tool or use a specialty video analytics service like Oculu (`www.oculu.com`).

Here are some of the most important video-related metrics that you need to understand and then measure and optimize for all of your videos:

- Video starts (ideally, you should measure auto-started versus user-started)
- Video completion rate (a great indicator of visitor satisfaction of your videos)
- Videos viewed per visitor (a good indicator of how engaging your videos are)
- Video views by page location (useful if you have the same video playing on multiple pages)
- Ad video starts and completes (important to know if you are showing ads in your videos)
- Participation (attribution) of a video view on conversions (it's good to understand how important your videos are for causing conversions on your website).

Friday: Use Rich Media Website Greeters to Increase Engagement and Influence

There are specific rich-media techniques involving human interaction and dynamics that you can use to help increase visitor engagement and better influence what they do on your website. Today you are going to focus on using this powerful technique on your website, much the way store visitors feel more engaged when a store assistant greets them and tells them what is on sale and asks if they need any help.

This works well because studies have shown that people are more likely to engage if human dynamics or interaction is present. And on websites, showing human elements like talking faces is also usually much more engaging for visitors than text or images that don't move. To help you engage your visitors this way, there are two common ways of showing human-related rich media: animated and real-video website greeters, which you will now learn more about.

Test Using Interactive Animated Website Greeters

The first way that you can test showing this human-related rich media is to create an interactive animated website greeter that greets and engages your website visitors. There are several tools now available that let you create these and allow you to customize what the spokesperson looks and acts like, and what the script should be of what they say to your visitors.

Two major examples of websites that provide these services are SitePal (`www.sitepal.com`) and CodeBaby (`www.codebaby.com`). Both have hundreds of pre-created animated greeters for you to choose from and customize to fit the needs of your website better.

Although more expensive than SitePal, CodeBaby offers some essential advanced functionality to help increase your conversion rates further. In particular, it gives you the option to show related pop-up boxes right next to the greeter, containing links to help direct your visitors to pages relating to your conversion goals. These are essential for helping visitors understand what they should click on first and are a great way to increase conversions from the home page in particular.

See Figure 6.18 for an example of this animated spokesperson from CodeBaby, including the related links to the left of it.

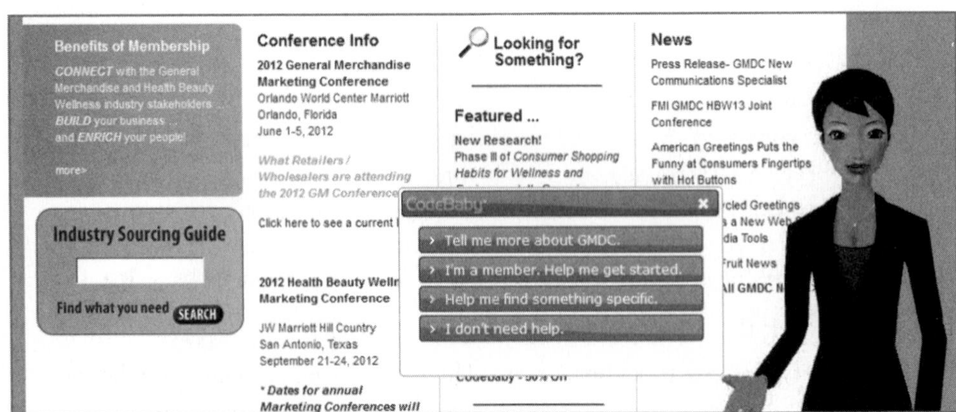

Figure 6.18 Example of an animated greeter

Test Using Video of Real Human Greeters

The next way of showing these human greeters is similar to the interactive animated greeters that were just discussed, but they actually show video of real people instead.

To help you create these, there are several options. The easier and cheaper option is to use a pre-created video greeter from a service like Tweople (`www.tweople.com`), which even has options to customize the greeter by recording and showing someone from your company instead. The second option is to create a more customized video greeter using an agency like Innovate Media (`www.innovatemedia.com`). See Figure 6.19 for an example of one of Innovate Media client's video greeters used on a banking website.

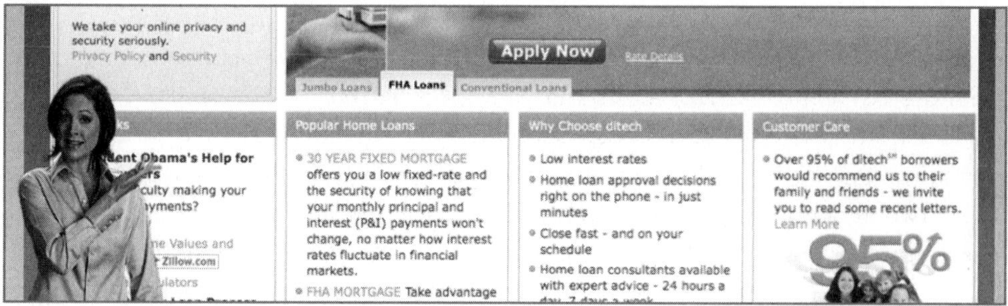

Figure 6.19 Example of a video human greeter

Another good reason to use video greeters is because you can measure the performance of the video and optimize it. In particular you should measure the completion rates of your video greeter to see how often visitors see the whole thing rather than just ignore it.

I suggest you evaluate animated and video greeters to see what fits your needs and budget better. Once you have picked a service, test tweaking what the greeter says in order to try and increase engagement and conversion rates further. For example, you could test asking the visitor a question rather than just a simple one-directional statement.

It's also important to test where these greeters show up on your website and under what circumstances. These usually work very well to show to first-time visitors, particularly on your home page. Don't just simply use these on every page of your website and for every visitor though, as this will annoy your visitors by seeing them too often and may result in them abandoning your website prematurely.

Week 17: Harness the Power of Social Proof, Reciprocity, and Scarcity

This week you will learn about influencing your visitors by using the power of social proof, reciprocity, comparison, and scarcity. These influence and persuasion theories are discussed in the book *Influence: The Psychology of Persuasion* by Robert B. Cialdini, Ph.D. (HarperCollins Publishers, 1998), which is a must-read for any budding website optimizer. Many marketers in the offline world have made great use of these theories, and you can adopt these same principles in order to influence and persuade your website visitors to complete more of your goals, and therefore, increase your conversion rates.

In particular, social proof works very well, and this will be covered during the first few days. Social proof (sometimes referred to as social validation) is a marketing approach and theory that has been used for many years with great success. This principle basically states that if your product or service seems to be well-liked and many people seem to be using it, this strongly influences the likelihood of other people using it and their positive perception of it too. For example, if someone is given the choice to dine in a restaurant that has few people in it versus one that is nearly full, then they are far more likely to pick the one that has more people in it. But more surprisingly, psychologists have found that this is also more likely to result in a better review of the restaurant, even if the food or service isn't in reality that great.

The same applies to websites; visitors are far more likely to engage with a website if they see signs that many other people are using the website (seeing positive comments, reviews, testimonials, etc.) and are also more likely to have a positive association with it.

Monday: Build Social Proof by Optimizing Your Testimonials

Testimonials are a very powerful form of social proof. But it's not enough to simply have them. How and where you display testimonials can have a major impact on conversion rates. The following are best practices you can apply or test.

Show Testimonials with Photos of Real Customers

One of the simplest things you can do to help optimize your testimonials is to obtain pictures from some of your customers that have given them, and clearly promote these alongside their testimonial. This is because testimonials with real photographs bring authenticity to them and are perceived as more trustworthy than those without. They also draw the eye. Consider asking customers to provide photos to use on your website, and then test adding them to your testimonials and see their likely positive impact on your conversion rates.

Show Video Testimonials

Video is highly engaging for many website visitors now, so you could consider using videos of your testimonials in addition to just photo and text testimonials. This makes them even more relatable and believable.

Go and ahead and get in touch with some of your best customers and ask them if you can record them giving an interview about their experience with your website. You could also offer them an incentive for doing this, like a credit or discount. From this interview, you should be able to edit it into a short good video testimonial to use on your homepage or other key pages. In Figure 6.20 you can see a good example of usage of video testimonials on the home page of IntuitGoPayment.com.

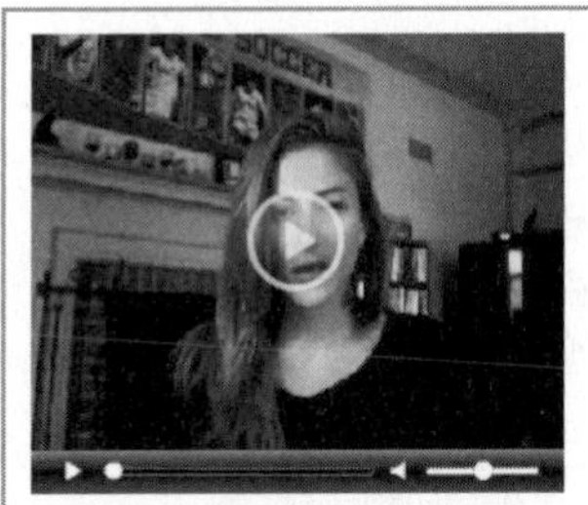

Everybody's using it.

Artists, girl scouts, contractors — it works for everyone. Hear what people are saying about GoPayment.

See more videos

Figure 6.20 Example of a video testimonial

A word of caution: although videos can help improve conversion rates, if they are intrusive or annoying, they can have the opposite effect. Always allow visitors to easily turn off sound from your testimonial videos, and you shouldn't use "auto-play," which can frustrate visitors who are unsure of how to turn the sound off.

Obtain and Include Many Relevant, Impressive Testimonials

The more testimonials you can obtain from your customers, the greater the chance of finding a really impressive one that will have a much greater impact on social proof than just a regular generic testimonial. Showing an outstanding testimonial in comparison to a generic uninspiring one can sometimes make the difference between your visitor purchasing or not.

A great idea to find more testimonials is to search through tweets on Twitter (`www.twitter.com`) that mention your website. If you find positive tweets about your website there, you should send the tweeter a message asking if you can make use of their tweet as a testimonial on your website, and ask them if they would mind expanding on it for a testimonial, too.

Show Testimonials on Your Home Page

Your home page is one of the most powerful places to promote your testimonials, because this is a very common entry point for first-time visitors, and they will need social proof to give them a reason to stay on your website. Showing testimonials here also maximizes the chance they will be seen, as there's no guarantee a visitor will click deeper into your website to a page that has one.

Remember to place these testimonials above the page fold, just in case your visitors don't scroll down any lower and leave prematurely. If you have a home page image rotator area, you could try featuring one of your best testimonials as one of the slide contents, as you can see in Figure 6.21 for the SurveyMonkey.com home page.

Figure 6.21 Example of a testimonial on a home page

Show Expert Testimonials

Another way to add even more credibility and social proof to your testimonials is to obtain and display ones that are from experts in your industry. These should come from someone who is very knowledgeable about what you are selling or promoting, and the more famous they are, the more this will amplify the positive effect. Go ahead and obtain a few of these and then test displaying them above the fold on your home page and other key pages to see the likely positive impact on conversion rates.

For a good example of this, in Figure 6.22 you will see SEOmoz.com making use of expert testimonials on their home page.

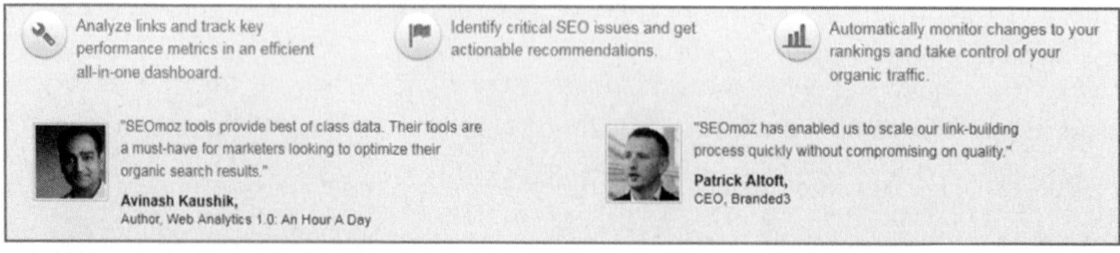

Figure 6.22 Example of expert testimonials

Tuesday: Build Social Proof by Optimizing Your Usage of Ratings and Reviews

Having reviews and ratings of the content on your website (whether it is products, services, articles, videos, or other) is another very important way to build social proof and influence visitors. To put it simply, the more reviews and ratings that your website and its content has, the more it will likely increase the social proof of your website. To help build social proof even further, today you will learn how to best show these ratings and reviews, and how to attract more of them.

Show Visitor Ratings for Content on Your Website

One of the quickest and simplest methods of improving social proof for your website is to begin gathering and showing ratings for the products, services, articles, videos, and other content on your website. These ratings are usually submitted by visitors directly or when they are submitting a review for your content. They usually come in the form of showing a rating out of 5 or 10 for each item, most often visually illustrated by stars (or check marks or other icons). Or in its simplest form this can be illustrated by showing a thumbs-up or thumbs-down.

There are also a number of tools that you can use to bolt on this rating (and review) functionality to your website, including Power Reviews (`www.PowerReviews.com`) and Bazaar Voice (`www.bazaarvoice.com`). Work with your IT department to explore these options in more detail and to help pick one that will be easier to implement on your website.

Not only do these ratings give visitors a great quick indicator of the quality of the content, this is also a quicker method for visitors to provide feedback than having to provide a more detailed review of the content.

Ideally this rating should be shown prominently in several key areas. First, it should be shown on product pages near your price or main image. Figure 6.23 shows a good example of how REI.com shows this rating on a product page.

You should also show these ratings on your category, browse and search results pages, as this will help your visitors decide on which products they want to click on to learn more about. For an example of this, see how BestBuy.com does this in Figure 6.24.

Don't forget to allow your visitors to sort these browse pages by top ratings to make it easier for them to find your best content. (You'll learn more about this in Chapter 7, when you'll review best practices for these types of browse and search results pages.)

To build social proof even further, next to the actual rating of your product or other content, you should also show the number of ratings that it receives. If these numbers of ratings get high (over 100 for example), it conveys to the visitor that many people are engaging with your content, thus increasing the chance that they will also engage with it (as long as the ratings of your content are fairly positive). This concept of showing numbers of interactions to build social proof will be discussed more tomorrow.

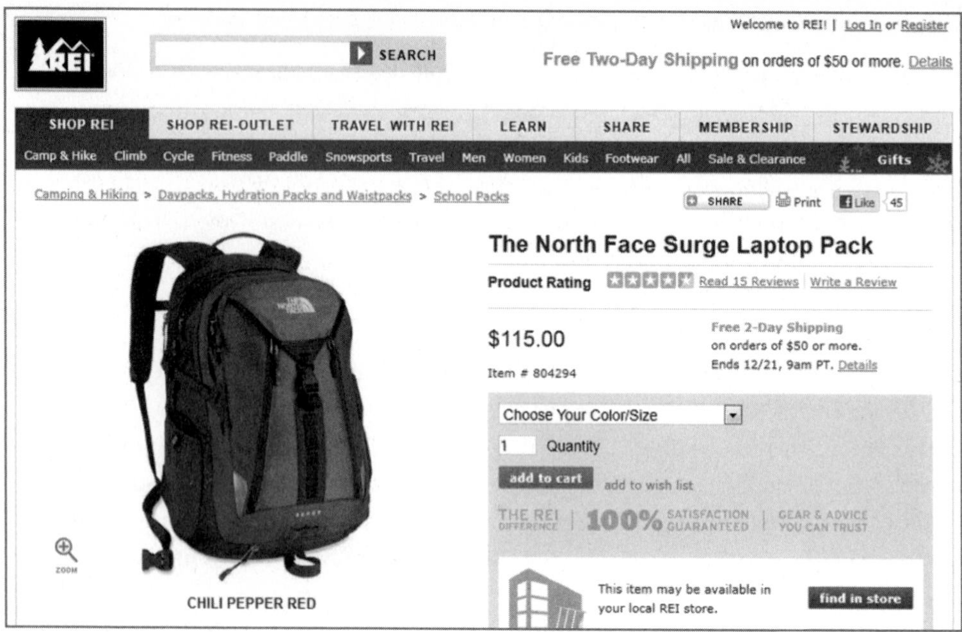

Figure 6.23 Example of ratings on a product page

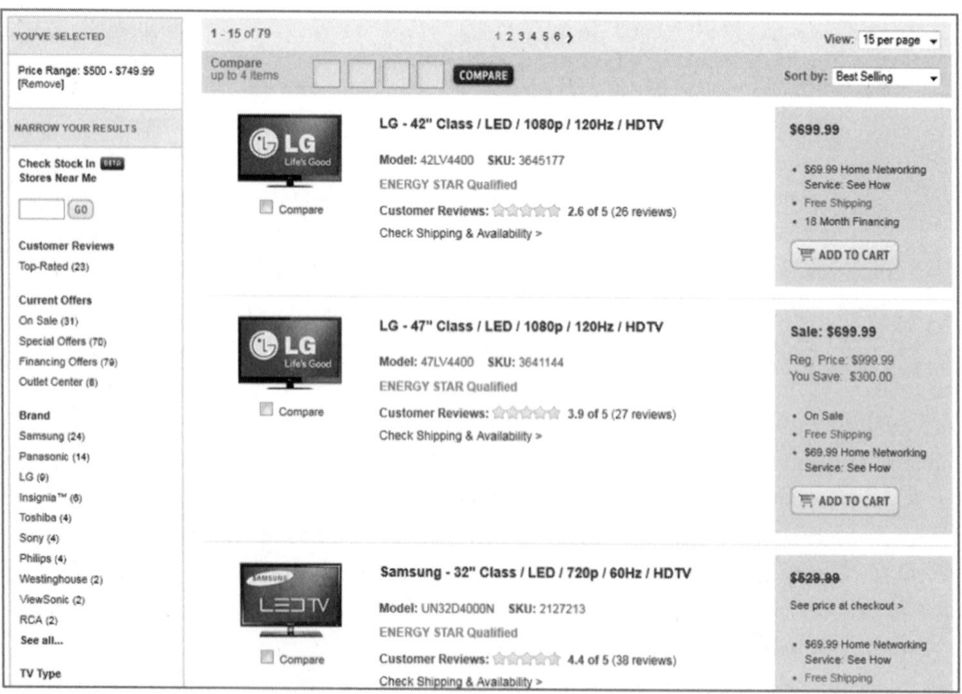

Figure 6.24 Example of ratings on a browse page

Improve the Usability of Your Review and Rating Process

In order to increase the number of reviews and ratings and help build more social proof, you should make it as easy as possible for your visitors to submit them.

First of all, to encourage more reviews and ratings you should clearly promote that visitors can (and should) submit their own reviews and ratings. This is best done by having review and rating submission links on your content pages, and ideally these should be placed next to the area where you show the average rating for the product, and also right by the area on your page where you show your current reviews.

However, you should also check to see how easy it is for your visitors to use your review submittal form, and you may want to remove fields that aren't very important or non-mandatory. If the review submission form is on its own page, you should also check the exit rate for this page to see if it's causing problems for your visitors. Many analytics tools offer form completion tracking so that you can also see exactly which fields your visitors get stuck on, and then optimize or remove them to increase your review form completion rates.

To make it even easier for visitors to submit a review, don't make it mandatory for them to have to create an account before they can do so. To reduce the likelihood of fake reviews, you could add fields to the submission form that prove the submitter is human, such as using a CAPTCHA or asking a simple math question (that you will learn more about in Chapter 8).

Get More Visitors to Write Reviews by Offering Incentives

Some visitors may be reluctant or shy to leave reviews of your products, particularly because this often takes time. One of the best ways to help reduce this reluctance and increase the number of reviews you get is to offer an incentive for visitors to review your products or services, such as offering a discount, gift certificate, or potential contest prize.

Ask Visitors to Rate Products Purchased from Your Website

Asking for a review from a visitor who has just bought from you is a simple way to generate more reviews to increase your social proof. This is the best time to ask them for a review because they will be much more likely to offer an opinion shortly after buying, rather than just hoping that they remember to review the product in the future. Don't send this trigger email too quickly though because you will need time for the product to be delivered and interacted with first. You will learn more about how to optimize emails like this in Chapter 8.

Let Visitors Rate Other Visitors' Reviews

To give your reviews even more social proof, you should allow your visitors to rate reviews depending on how helpful they found them and then show how many people thought the review was helpful. This can simply be done by posing a question right at the end of the review to the reader if they found it helpful, with two buttons for yes or no. Then next to the review, you should state how many people found this review helpful. Amazon.com does a great job of doing this, as you can see in Figure 6.25.

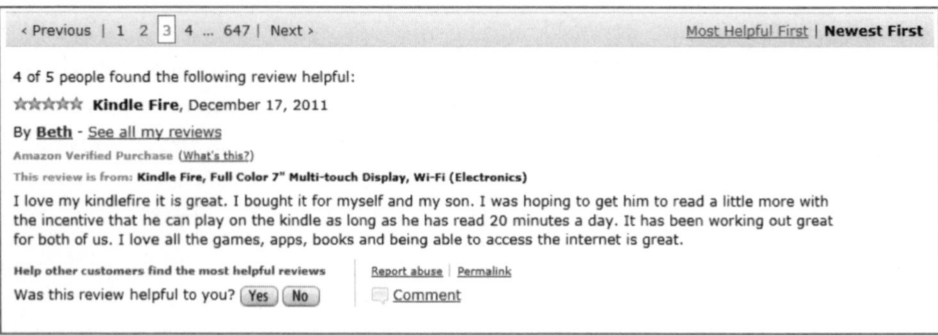

Figure 6.25 Example of rating each review

Doing this also lets visitors sort and filter through reviews better, and will also help to reduce the negative social proof impact from unfairly negative reviews on any of your content, and vice versa it can also increase the impact of great positive reviews.

Wednesday: Other Best Practices to Help Improve Your Social Proof

Today, you'll learn some best practices that you should implement to increase the level of social proof on your website and thus increase conversions.

Optimize Your Website for Social Sharing

Don't forget about the power of a recommendation from a friend or colleague. Not only does this help build social proof for your products, services or other content, it also helps because people are much more likely to come to your website if they know one of their friends is also using it. This traffic is also often much more targeted and qualified and will have a greater chance of converting. Because of this you should make it as easy as possible for your visitors to share your website and its content with their friends, family, and colleagues.

Use Social Networking Buttons and Links to Increase Social Sharing

A great way to do this is by having buttons that allow your visitors to share any of your content on Facebook (the Like button) and Twitter (the Tweet button). Ideally you should place these share buttons on all of your content, particularly at the end of your articles and adjacent to your photos and videos or your products and services, as this will increase the chances of visitors using them.

When placing these two share buttons on your website, don't forget to choose the option to show the number of times the content has been shared on the button, as this helps build social proof too (as you will learn about in the next section).

CNET.com has a good example of doing this, plus showing other social network sharing buttons, as you can see in Figure 6.26. They also use another best practice to make the sharing buttons stay in place as the visitor scrolls down, so they are always visible.

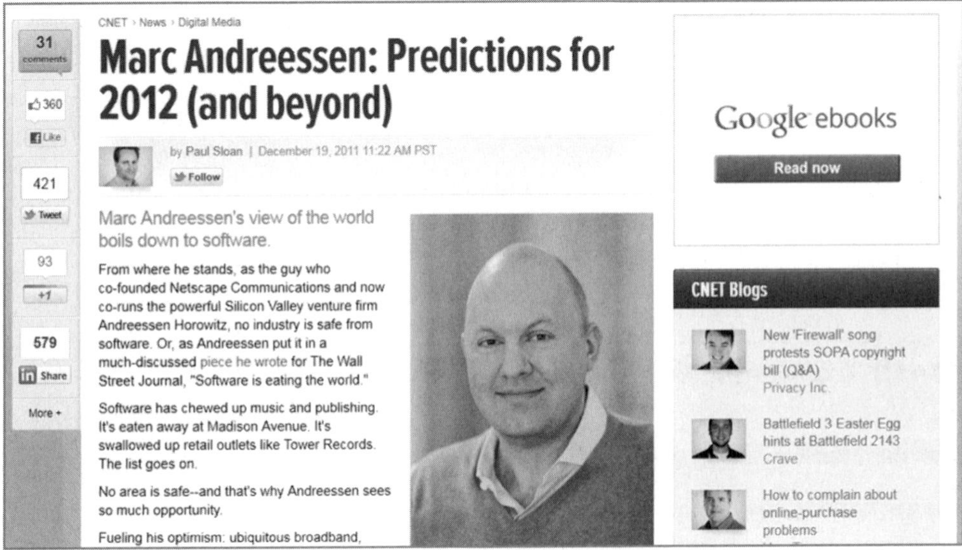

Figure 6.26 Example of prominent social sharing links

Use Traditional Refer-a-Friend Options

Don't forget to offer refer-a-friend links on your web pages too, where the visitor can quickly and easily send a message to their friends recommending the current page they are on at your website (or your website as a whole). You could try testing adding links and promotions to refer-a-friend options on your login related pages, product or service pages, and also in the footer of your pages.

To encourage this refer-a-friend activity even more, you could try running a referral contest, with prizes going to the people who refer your website to the most friends. Or you could offer a discount to the person doing the referring as a reward for doing so. NetSpend.com has a great example of this incentivized refer-a-friend tool on their website, as you can see in Figure 6.27.

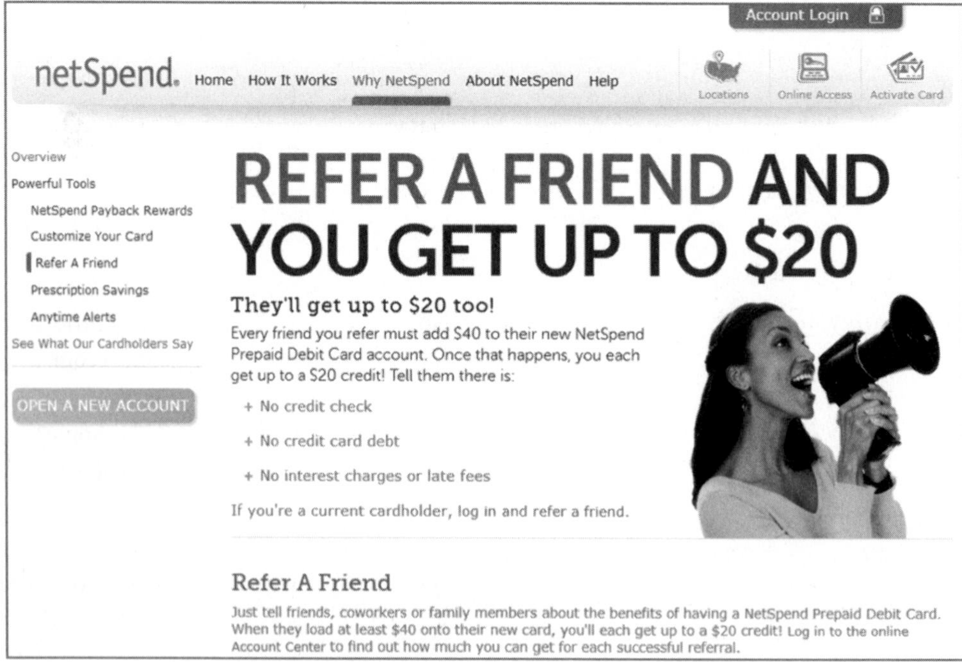

Figure 6.27 Example of a refer-a-friend promo and incentive

Show Usage Numbers to Illustrate Social Proof

Clearly showing the number of customers or users your online business has is a powerful way to build social proof for your website, particularly if you have a high volume of satisfied ones. To take advantage of this, get some good usage statistics about your online business and then run a test to show these on your home page and other key pages above the page fold in a few different variations.

For some ideas, you could test prominently adding text like "Now loved by over *X* satisfied customers" or "Downloaded over 100,000 times." Even something as simple as stating how many years your company has been in business will help.

A particularly great example of this can be seen on the Basecamp.com home page in Figure 6.28 where they use several numbers to illustrate just how much their service is used. This also prominently features the logos of their big clients, which also helps build social proof, as you will learn about next.

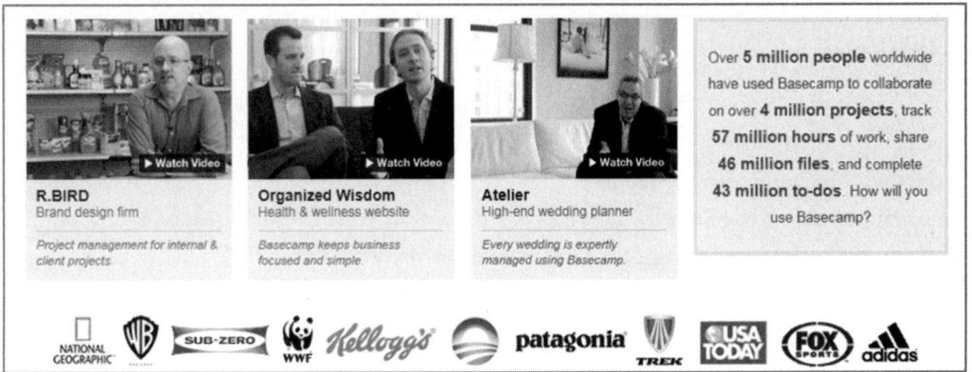

Figure 6.28 Examples of customer usage numbers

Show Client Logos to Build Social Proof

If you are selling products or services, one of the best ways to improve social proof is to show logos of clients you have, particularly if you have large clients with recognizable logos.

Test the power of this by adding your most major clients' logos to your home page and product or service pages above the fold, in either a column or row, labeled as "Our Clients" or similar wording.

In Figure 6.29, you can see a good example of this in action on the AWeber.com home page, which also uses a good header for the section to explain the significance of the logos and provides a link to see who else uses their services.

Figure 6.29 Example of a client logos module

You should also make the client logos clickable, and send the clicker to a page that shows more details regarding your top clients, ideally with testimonials from some of them. You might also want to test graying the logos out if they appear too distracting, because this may increase focus on other key calls-to-action and increase conversions.

Show Media Mentions and Press Releases to Build Social Proof

Another way to build social proof is to show examples of the media talking about your online business. If you can get some good news agencies to run press releases about you and you show that on your website, visitors will more likely think your website is well-liked due to it being mentioned in the news.

If you don't have anything great written about your online business from the press (and check Google news for this), I suggest you run some press release campaigns regarding something newsworthy, or engage with some press release professionals to help you. There are several services that can help with this, like PRweb.com (`www.PRweb.com`) and PRnewswire.com (`www.PRnewswire.com`).

Once you have obtained some great media mentions, you can do two things. First, you can take the best quote from one of the press releases, and test featuring it on your home page and make it clickable to the full article on your website. Second, you can also test showing the logos of the media websites that have written about you, as in the example in Figure 6.30, and link each of their logos to the article that mentions your website.

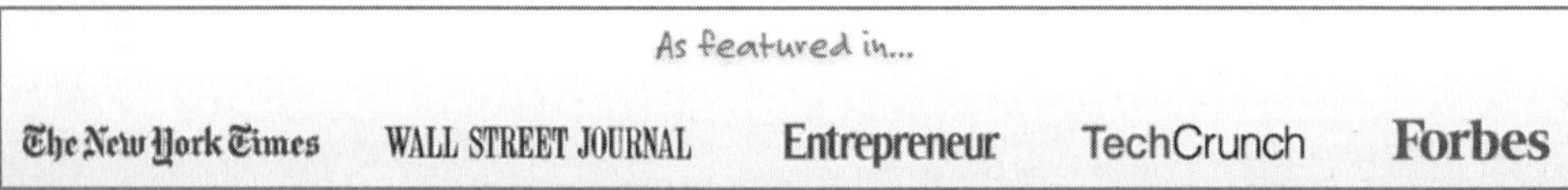

Figure 6.30 Example of logos from media mentions

Thursday: Use Scarcity to Influence Your Visitors

A powerful, unique approach to influence visitors to buy from your website is to introduce scarcity tactics. This theory works on the premise that if something seems unavailable (or is about to be), people often want it even more.

These scarcity tactics have worked very well historically in the offline world—for example, Apple not creating enough supply for iPhones, which caused huge long lines at stores and major publicity, and how Disney deliberately releases their movies in short time frames only. These tactics can also work very well in the online world when designed to make your visitors think that if they don't buy or sign up now your product or service offered will sell out very soon.

There are several examples of websites that do a good job of this that you should model. First of all is Amazon.com, which uses these scarcity tactics to show if any of their products are low in stock. They always clearly state on their product pages if there are only a few left in stock; as you can see in Figure 6.31 where they state in red "Only 1 left in stock—order soon."

Figure 6.31 Product showing limited stock scarcity tactics

Booking.com also does a very good job of showing scarcity on their hotel pages. They show next to each type of room in their hotels whether there are fewer than five remaining, with last-chance wording if there is only one room left. Combining this scarcity tactic with their approach of popping up a message stating how many other visitors are currently looking at the page (as you can see in the example of Figure 6.32) apparently does a very good job of increasing the conversion rates of Booking.com.

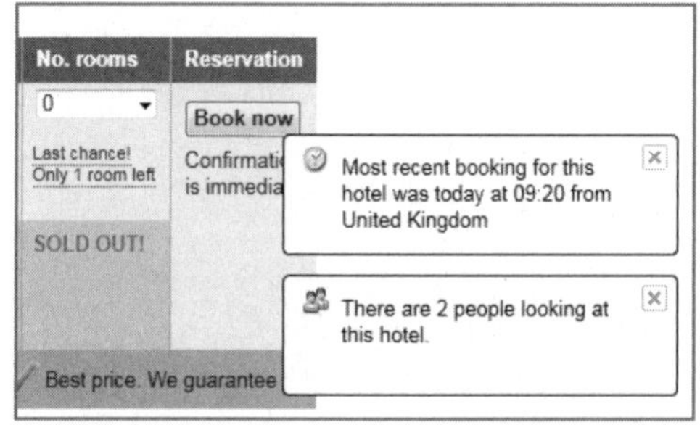

Figure 6.32 Other limited availability scarcity tactics

Orbitz.com and several other travel websites are also taking advantage of these scarcity tactics by clearly stating if there are only a few tickets left for each flight.

As a few examples to test on your website, if you are selling products test showing the number of items of your products that are currently in stock, and if this is low, show additional messaging urging them to buy before it sells out. Or if you have a sale or promotion running, you should clearly state how many days are left until it's finished. If done well, you are likely to see a good conversion lift from using tactics like these.

Friday: Influence Your Visitors by Using Reciprocity

Next you will learn about the theory of reciprocity to help influence your visitors better. Essentially, it states that if you give someone something for free (or very cheap), they will often feel obligated to return the favor and reciprocate by buying from you in the future.

Clever marketers have been using this to great advantage for many years. An example of an offline organization using this theory with great results are the Hare Krishna who give out free small flowers to strangers in train stations, who then feel obligated to return the favor by talking to them and donating to their organization.

This theory can often work well online too. To test this theory on your website, try offering your visitors something of value for free, such as a guide, a whitepaper, a free upgrade on shipping, or a free upgrade on their initial service level. This should have a good effect of increasing conversions in the future. If you don't already have something of value to give away for free on your website, try creating something like an e-book containing tips or advice.

In Figure 6.33 you will see a good example of a website, HubSpot.com, using reciprocity by giving out free e-books to visitors.

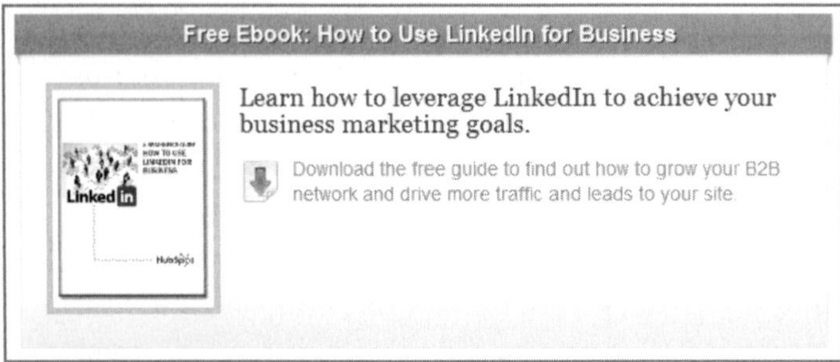

Figure 6.33 Reciprocity using a free e-book

You could also test asking for the visitors' email address to send them the free item. This is good because depending on if they agree to receive future emails, it's a great way to market to them and get them to come back to your website, hopefully reciprocating and converting for one of your goals.

Week 18: Influence by Making Your Visitors Feel Safer and Building Trust

One of the strongest emotions that website visitors often have (and yes, even for your website) is a feeling of fear and anxiety just before they purchase or sign up for something. This is because they often feel they might be spammed or worse still, their credit card or personal details stolen or used for fraudulent purposes. As a result of this visitors are often wary of giving details like this, having a significant negative impact on website conversion rates.

Recent studies echo this too. In an August 2011 report by Harris Interactive and McAfee, 84 percent of online consumers had some level of concern when giving their personal information online, and the number of consumers who believe that most websites are safe has actually fallen over the last two years, now down to about one-third.

Even though online and data storage security measures have improved greatly, this resurgence of security and safety concerns has been caused by an increase in online fraud, the growing fear of personal identity theft, and the rise of phishing fake websites that trick visitors into giving their account or credit card details.

And these security issues aren't limited to just e-commerce websites. Any type of website that requires registration or any of the visitors' personal information is prone to these security concerns from their visitors.

One of the best ways to help ease your visitors' security fears (and therefore increase conversions) is to influence their perception of how secure and trustworthy your website is. This week you will learn some great best practices to help you achieve this.

Monday: Optimize the Display of Security and Trust Seals and Symbols

One of the best ways to increase levels of trust and to make visitors feel safer is to prominently display logos and seals that visitors associate with higher levels of trust and security. For example, in the same Harris Interactive/McAfee recent report, 75 percent of online consumers indicated that they would choose to shop on a website with a trust or security symbol than one without.

When website visitors see these security and trust symbols, they are much more likely to complete the checkout or signup process, thus greatly increasing conversion rates. Today you will learn how to optimize and make better use of these seals and symbols so you influence and convert more of your visitors.

Test Using Different Types of Security and Trust Seals on Your Website

There are various types of security and trust seals that you can use to relieve your visitors' anxiety and increase conversion rates, as described here:

Security Seals These seals are obtained when you upgrade your website security level using Secure Sockets Layer (SSL) technology. This SSL encrypts any personal information or credit card details being submitted, so that only the sender (the customer) and the receiver (the online business) can use them. Providers of these also run frequent vulnerability scanning to ensure no data breaches occur.

There are several leading providers of these security services, including VeriSign (`www.VeriSign.com`), GeoTrust (`www.GeoTrust.com`), and McAfee (`www.McAfeeSecure.com`). Obtaining these secure services isn't cheap, but it is highly recommended to do so, particularly because of the positive conversion influence that occurs when showing the related security seal on your website. You should work with your IT department to implement SSL on your website and therefore make use of these important security seals.

Privacy Seals Visitors are often apprehensive about giving their personal information online because of the rise in personal identity theft. A great way to relieve some of this anxiety is to prominently show privacy certification seals on your website. This will usually result in an increase in conversions, particularly when related to sign-ups or registrations where personal information is requested from the visitor. The best way to get these seals is to evaluate and use a vendor who will certify your website, for example TRUSTe (`www.truste.com`).

Business Approval and Accreditation Seals The next type of seal to use on your website to improve the level of trust it conveys are ones that inform the visitors that your business is approved and accredited. It is particularly important to show these if your website and online business is small or not well-known because your new visitors probably won't know your website very well and will be more likely to not trust it.

If your website is based in the United States, the first main way of obtaining one of these seals is to register your online business with the Better Business Bureau (`www.bbb.org/us/bbb-online-business/`). This seal will often be commonly understood by visitors and will often help build trust. You could also try obtaining a seal like this from BizRate (`www.BizRateInsights.com`), which offers services to get your online business rated and accredited.

Table 6.1 shows some examples of these types of security and trust seals and symbols.

▶ **Table 6.1** Examples of security and trust seals and symbols

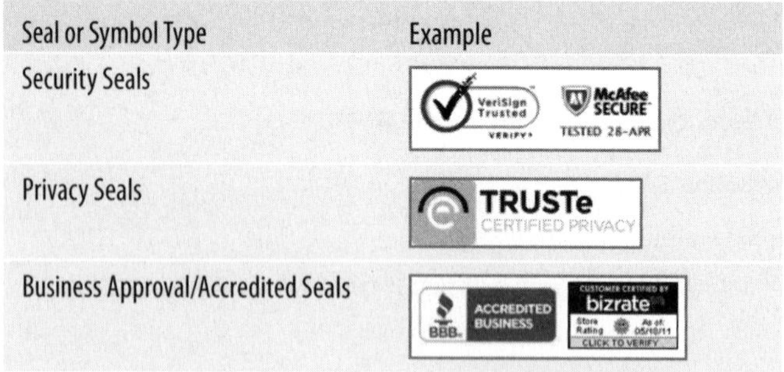

Seal or Symbol Type	Example
Security Seals	VeriSign Trusted VERIFY · McAfee SECURE TESTED 28-APR
Privacy Seals	TRUSTe CERTIFIED PRIVACY
Business Approval/Accredited Seals	BBB ACCREDITED BUSINESS · CUSTOMER CERTIFIED BY bizrate CLICK TO VERIFY

Obtaining these trust and security seals can be relatively expensive, and if you are looking for a cheaper alternative to obtain them, there is a great new option available. This is offered from a company called SafeSite Certified (`www.SafeSiteCertified.org`), which realizes the impact these security and trust seals have on conversion rates and wants to make these even more accessible for companies to use on their websites. Not only do they offer seals like the ones discussed previously, but they also offer functionality to test different styles of the actual seals to see which colors or styles have the most impact on your conversion rates.

As another cheaper way of doing this, you could create your own home-made seals or badges that show lock icons or secure messaging and then test adding those to key pages on your website to see their conversion rate impact.

Optimize the Placement of Your Security Seals and Trust Symbols

Careful placement of these trust seals and symbols on your website can have a great positive influence on your visitors' fears, and therefore increase your conversion rates. Rather than just burying these away out of visitors' eyesight in the footer of your website, you will now learn about many more influential places that you should test showing them.

Here are some best practices to help test and optimize the locations of these on your pages:

On e-commerce websites, test placing security seals near your checkout buttons. Visitors typically have the most apprehension and anxiety about completing their purchase just before they start checking out—usually on the shopping cart page. Therefore, you should test placing security seals near your checkout button on this page, as this will likely have a great impact on reducing this issue and increasing your conversion rates. Surprisingly, few websites do this, so this also represents a great way to gain competitive advantage over your rivals' websites.

Place security seals prominently on the first page of the checkout, registration, or signup flow. Another high-impact area to show security seals to reinforce your commitment to security and trust is on the first page of your checkout, registration or signup flow. You should run some tests that add your seals to several different locations on these pages, and see which locations have the highest impact on increasing your checkout completion rates. In Figure 6.34, you can see that REI.com does a great job of this on its first checkout-related page (the login page), with "The REI Guarantee" section in the right-hand rail that includes the VeriSign security seal logo.

Figure 6.34 Example of a well-placed security seal in checkout

Display your seals right by the credit card fields on your billing page. Website visitors also typically experience increased anxiety if they are asked to enter their credit card information during a checkout or signup process. If you are selling something on your website, you should test placing your security seals right next to the credit card fields in order to reduce this anxiety and increase your conversion rates.

Test placing different types of security and trust seals in your website header. Another great place to test showing one or two security seals is in different locations in your website header. Your business accreditation logo and security seals often work well there in particular. Therefore, go ahead and test a few different combinations of types of seals and locations in your header to see what increases conversion rates the most.

Tuesday: Make Use of Supporting Text and Pages to Build Trust and Security

Before visitors decide to purchase on your website, they will often want to learn more detailed information about your security policies—for example, what you are doing to protect them and their information and what happens if a security breach occurs. And while having a great impact, your security seals alone might not be good enough to convince all of them to purchase on your website, and some won't even understand what they mean.

To help address this and further reduce their purchase or signup fears, you will need to show additional security and trust related text on your pages, and make them easy to understand. Today you will learn how to do this.

Show Security-Related Text in Addition to Seals

The first thing you need to do is add prominent text that verbally reinforces your website's high level of security and helps build trust. This is particularly good for visitors who might not immediately understand or realize the significance of the security and trust seals on your website (for example, what a "VeriSign Trusted" website actually means). Go ahead and test adding a few variations of this security-related text adjacent to your security and trust seals to see which ones increase your order completion rates the most.

If you have an e-commerce website, the most critical place to display security and safety wording is on the shopping cart and checkout pages. Using text like "Your transaction is 100% safe & secure" and linking this to a page or popup that explains your security policies will likely result in an increase in conversion rates. See Figure 6.35 for an example of this text next to a security seal.

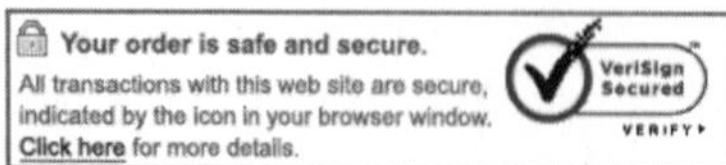

Figure 6.35 Example of security text next to a security seal

You should also test placing words like "Secure" or "Check out securely" right under your checkout or signup button, because this very quick test could have a great impact on your conversion rates. Then you should test making this wording link to a security details page so the visitor can learn more about how safe your website is (which will be discussed next).

To make your visitors feel more secure about clicking the checkout button, you can test labeling the button with security building wording like "Checkout Securely" or "Secure Checkout" (as opposed to just "Checkout"). For example, the checkout button on the Norton.com website is called "Continue to Secure Checkout," as shown in Figure 6.36.

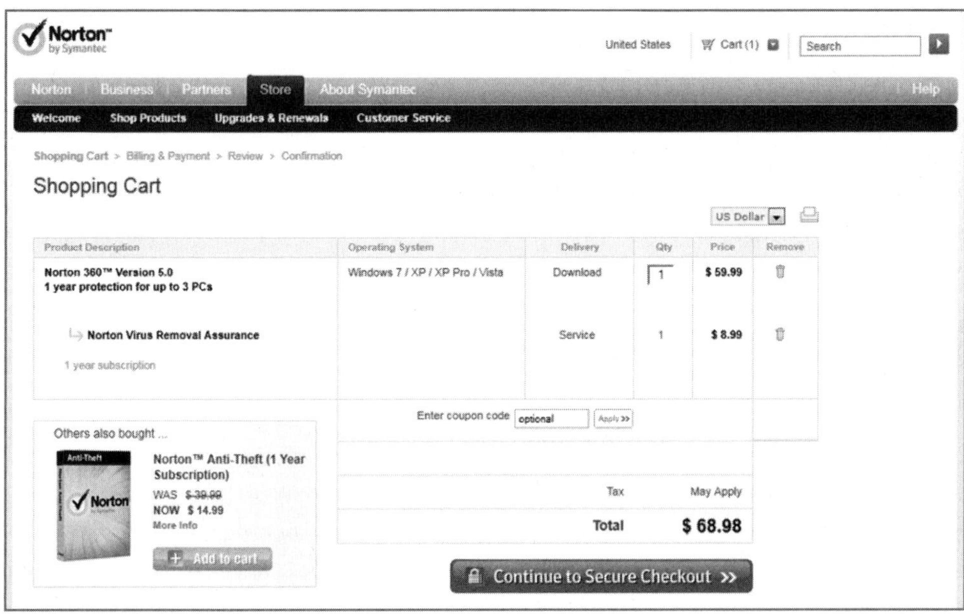

Figure 6.36 Example of security wording in a checkout button

Create a Security and Privacy Page and Prominently Link to It

To help your visitors understand more about your security and trust policies, go ahead and create a page that shows the full details of this for your online business and website (if you haven't already got a page like this). Use language for these policies that is easy for visitors to understand and relate to, and not overly technical either.

It's important that you prominently link to this page from the footer of your website and in your help and support section because this is where visitors will expect to see it. You should also link to it in the same places where you show your security and trust seals and symbols, where visitors may most often want to know more about these details and your policies.

Create Pages That Detail Your Guarantee, Money-Back, Shipping, and Return Policies

Visitors are much more likely to trust and buy something from a website that clearly states its guarantee and return policies, just in case they aren't happy with their purchase.

If you don't already have pages on your website that explain your guarantee, money-back, shipping, and return policies, then you need to go ahead and create these. They will help reduce purchase anxiety and apprehension in your visitors, particularly if your policies regarding these seem generous and fair to them.

To maximize the influence of these, optimize the layout and messaging of them using best practices and test ideas you learned through the earlier weeks in this chapter, such as using bullet points for key points. Don't just have these pages formed of long blocks of hard to read text.

To promote these policies you should test placing text links to these pages across your website, particularly on your product or service pages and checkout related pages. You should also place links to these in your footer, site map, and support pages because visitors will most often expect to see them there. If some of these policies are part of your unique value proposition (like Zappos.com does with its free shipping and returns), then you should use promotional banners for these too.

You should also reduce the risk of purchase for your visitors, which is a subject you will learn about tomorrow.

Wednesday: Reduce the Risk of Purchasing for the Visitor

The more reasons you can give your website visitors to assure them there is low risk and that they won't regret purchasing or signing up for something from your website, the higher your conversion rates will be. These reasons to reduce potential purchase anxieties are called risk reducers, and you will learn how to make great use out of them today.

Test Offering a Money-Back or Exchange Guarantee

A great risk reducer to build trust and increase product- or service-order rates is by including a money-back and/or exchange guarantee. The time period for returning or exchanging a product can be anywhere from 7–90 days, although 30 days is most common. Test different types of guarantees to see which influences conversion the most, and if you already offer a guarantee, then test offering a better one.

You should test clearly, stating this guarantee on your home page, your product or service pages and your checkout pages, as it will often have the most impact on these pages.

You also ideally need to promote this guarantee in the form of a visual seal too, which will draw your visitors' eye to the guarantee and increase the chance that they will be influenced by it. Test creating a few different styles to see which one impacts your conversion rates the most. Figure 6.37 shows some examples of this type of seal.

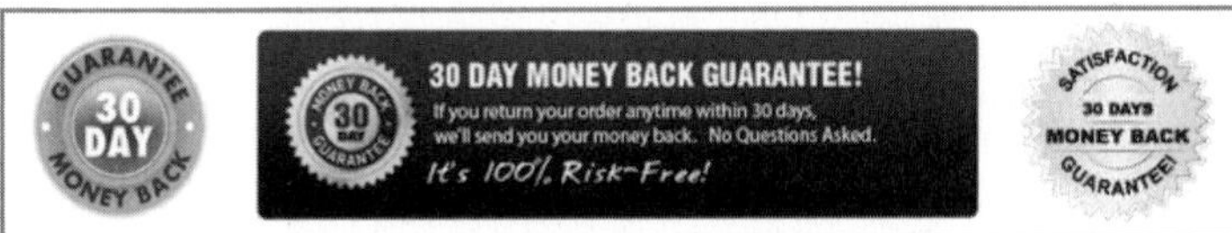

Figure 6.37 Examples of guarantee seals

Test Free Shipping Offers

If you are selling products on your website, another way of reducing risk is to offer free shipping for your visitors. Many online businesses now offer this on an occasional basis or on a permanent basis like Amazon.com does (free shipping on certain products with a minimum order of $25). This can be offered in a variety of ways, either free shipping on everything, or with a minimum purchase and/or on particular products only.

If you don't currently offer free shipping, test offering this for a limited period on your website to see if it improves conversion rates. It will usually improve your average products per order too, so also check for that metric when analyzing results.

If you already offer free shipping, you can test two things. If you have a minimum purchase required for free shipping, test lowering this, for example, from $50 down to $25 (if your business allows for this). You can also test increasing the number of products free shipping is available for if it currently is not offered on many. When evaluating test results for these, in addition to checking for conversion rate lifts, you also need to check if there are any negative impacts on your profit levels and average order value.

Offer Free Returns

Another risk reducer that you can use if you are selling products on your website is to offer free returns, or at least do a trial run offering free returns. As long as your business model allows for this and can support it, it can really help reduce purchase anxiety. Often the money you have to spend on the shipping associated with these free returns can be outweighed by the additional levels of revenue.

This works particularly well for clothing websites that have to work against not being able to let their customers try on the clothes before they buy. Zappos.com is an example of an online business that has done very well by offering this, and it has become a very popular and well-known feature and unique value proposition for their website.

Test Improving Your Free Trial Details

Offering a free trial is a great risk reducer. If you have a website that offers one of these for its products or services (or is thinking about it), you should test the messaging for your free trial to increase conversions. This will help increase the number of visitors responding to this offer.

In particular you should test clearly stating that there is no obligation or commitment to purchase or sign up (if indeed that is the case) because visitors can often be wary if your offer seems too good to be true. You should also state that if the visitor isn't happy during their trial they can cancel at any time (with no hidden fees).

If your business allows it, test increasing the length of your free trial if it is currently fairly short. Increasing it from 7 days to 30 days may result in a significant lift in purchases.

Restate Your Risk Reducers in Your Shopping Cart

Before they decide to go through with their purchase, the shopping cart page is where visitors will need the most reassurance that their risk of purchasing is low. Therefore, you should prominently restate some of the risk reducers that were covered above on this page. Test adding them to the footer or the sidebar of your shopping cart to achieve this. As you can see in Figure 6.38, ASOS.com does a very good job of this by clearly showing two of their risk reducers (free returns and free next day delivery) in the footer of their checkout page.

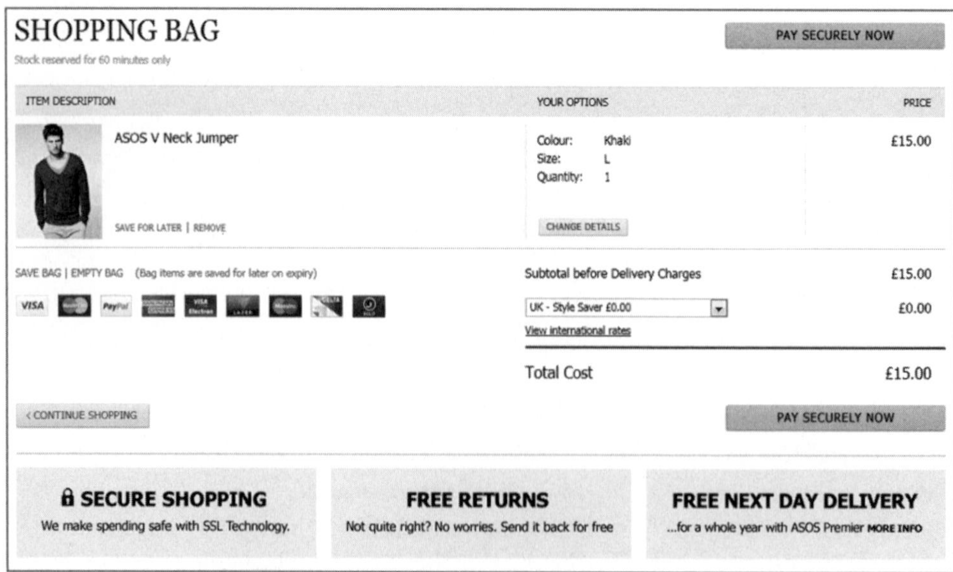

Figure 6.38 Example of risk reducers on a checkout page

Thursday: Optimize Your Customer Support and Contact Options

Another way to build your website visitors' trust and sense of security is to provide customers with support and contact information when and where they are most likely to need it. Today you will learn some best practices to take your support options a step further, past just offering email and phone support.

Clearly Promote Your Support and Contact Pages

First you need to make sure that your visitors can easily find your support and contact options. Don't bury links for these pages on your website; they should be visible on every page on your website so that visitors can make use of them at any point. The best place to show the link to your support page is in the top-right and footer of every page in addition to a link for your "contact us" page in the footer of your pages. These are standard places that visitors will expect to find these.

Offer a Web Chat Option

Not only is offering a web chat option for your visitors a powerful way to gather feedback from them (as discussed in Chapter 4), it's also a great way for visitors to get immediate support and help relieve any possible issues they may have. It's particularly valuable for visitors who don't like chatting on the phone as well as for visitors who don't want to have to wait for support via email.

To gain best use of this web chat option you need to test offering this above the fold on your shopping cart or registration pages, because these pages are often a source of problems and anxiety for visitors. A recent study by BoldChat supported this and found that 76 percent of website visitors would initiate a web chat in response to issues they were encountering during the checkout process. Test being proactive with web chat on these pages, too, and pop up a chat dialog box if visitors seem to be idling for more than 10 seconds on them (don't do it any quicker as this may annoy your visitors though). You should also show this web chat option on your contact and support pages.

To find out how to best display a web chat option, you should test different versions and styles of chat buttons in the header of these pages or in the right-hand rail, and see which version increases usage of them the most. For more information about web chat tool options and best practices, please refer back to Chapter 4.

Offer Support Forums and FAQ Pages

Another support best practice is to offer self-service methods for visitors to get answers to their questions and concerns. Offering FAQ (frequently asked question) pages and support forums empowers them to find their own answers, and is a great option for those who don't have time to call or request help via email or phone.

Offering this support method also cuts down on your more traditional support-related expenses like call center costs, which can be very expensive.

On these pages, be sure to mention things like your return policy and money back policies, because as discussed earlier, visitors will often want to know this information before purchasing. You should also list the top 10 FAQs and provide your visitors with a way to search for specific forum or FAQ topics. Be sure to link to these pages from your support and contact pages.

Ideally, you should also track how often these self-support mechanisms are used. If they aren't being used very much (low page views), this is an indicator that you need to optimize the usability and functionality of them.

Friday: Learn Other Best Practices for Increasing Levels of Trust and Security

Today you will learn some other effective best practices for improving your website's level of trust and security, thus reducing visitors' anxiety and improving your website conversion rates.

Clearly State Your Privacy Policy Regarding Email Addresses

Most websites will usually ask for a visitor's email address for one reason or another—for example, to register for a profile, sign up for a newsletter or purchase something. Unfortunately, visitors are wary of providing this information due to concerns about getting spammed. And if you can't get a visitor to give their email address to your online business, your future conversion rates are going to be significantly impacted because you won't be able to market to them via email.

In order to help relieve this anxiety and build the trust needed for the visitor to give you their email address, you need to clearly state that your website won't spam, rent, or sell email addresses. This should be stated in close proximity to your sign-up forms, with a link to a page that explains your privacy policy regarding this.

In Chapter 8, you will learn more about best practices relating to email marketing and how to encourage your website visitors to provide their email addresses.

Allow Visitors to Provide Their Credit Card Details over the Phone

As mentioned earlier this week, website visitors are often apprehensive about providing their credit card details online. To try and convert these visitors, in your checkout pages you should provide them with an option to complete their purchases over the phone instead.

Some large online businesses are apprehensive about showing their phone number on their website or making it very visible, because the costs of running a call center can be very expensive as opposed to handling support online. However, it is definitely worth testing the conversion rate impact of offering a phone number in your top right hand corner of all pages and your shopping cart page. To help you do this there are now great new tools to consider using that allow you to track usage and attribute conversions from a support phone number on a website, for example Mongoose Metrics (`www.mongoosemetrics.com`).

Only Ask for Personal Information That Is Necessary

Due to the increase in personal identity theft, many website visitors are reluctant to disclose particular personal information like their phone numbers and addresses. This information should only be necessary on a checkout page if the visitor is having something shipped to them. If you have phone number and/or address fields on your signup or registration pages, you should test removing them to see if this increases your conversion rates. Also, if you do require information like this, you should always include tool tip text next to each field that explains why it's needed to allay concerns from visitors.

Optimization Best Practices and Test Ideas for Different Page Types and Flows

Now that you have learned some essential website optimization fundamentals that will help kick-start your efforts, in this chapter you will discover and start to use best practices and test ideas for many different types of pages. This includes the all-important home page, product and service pages, and other key conversion flow related pages like checkout. You will also learn the importance of optimizing the mobile versions of your webpages.

7

Chapter Contents

Week 19: Focus On and Optimize Your Home Page

This week's focus is on one of the most important aspects of your website, your home page. It is critical to spend considerable time testing and optimizing this page for two major reasons. The first reason is because it often forms the all-important first impression of your whole website, and just as a book often gets judged by its cover, millions of websites get judged by just by looking at their home page. Worse still, this judgment usually occurs within very few seconds, often as few as three seconds (as some studies claim). And who really wants their website judged wrongly or unfairly?

Second, depending on how well your home page is optimized, this can have a major impact on the number of downstream conversions on your website. In the extreme, if the visitor leaves your home page immediately (which is known as a bounce) then obviously there is zero percent chance of them converting in that visit. A well-optimized home page will act like a welcoming committee and inform and guide the visitor through their choices, ultimately increasing the chances of them engaging and converting for your website goals.

This week you will learn some great best practices to make sure your home page is judged well by your visitors and engages and converts them the best it can.

Monday: Learn How Your Home Page Is Being Judged and Check the Bounce Rate

The first thing you need to do this week is to learn how your home page (and therefore website) is likely being judged and how to get a better idea of its performance by checking the number of visitors currently bouncing from your home page upon arrival.

Understand How Your Home Page Is Being Judged and Perceived

As mentioned in the introduction, it is critical to test and optimize your home page because it is a page where your visitors will often judge the whole of the website. This becomes even more important when you consider that your home page is often one of the most common entry points to your website, so it is often the first page your visitors see and react to.

Even if they arrive at your website on another entry page, visitors will often go to the home page to get a better idea of what your website is about. Therefore, if your home page doesn't do a good job of conveying benefit and value of your website to your visitors and they badly judge it, they are much more likely to leave it and not convert for your goals.

So that you can get a better idea of what your visitors might be thinking, first you will learn some common judgments, perceptions, and associations that visitors can have about a website just by looking at its home page. Here are some common negative ones that visitors may have, which you need to make sure doesn't happen:

- The visitor doesn't like the layout or organization of the website.
- The visitor doesn't understand what they can do on the website.

- The visitor feels overwhelmed with choices or content.
- The visitor hates seeing so many ads.
- The visitor thinks the website doesn't look trustworthy or safe.

In contrast, here are some positive associations that visitors can have about a website after looking at just the home page, which you need to try and convey:

- The visitor thinks the website looks professional, credible and safe.
- The visitor enjoys the color scheme and design of the website.
- The visitor understands what they can do on the website.
- The visitor understands the clear choices they can click on first.

Any of these judgments and perceptions by your visitors can be formed very quickly, so it's vital to understand what they may be thinking in the critical first three to five seconds. To help you obtain this feedback about your home page, other than using some of the page-specific feedback tools that were covered in Chapter 5, there is a specific tool that will help you. It's called FiveSecondTest (`www.FiveSecondTest.com`) and allows you to gather feedback based on a user's five-second experience of your home page (or any page you want to submit to them for testing).

To make use of this tool you simply submit your home page and create a few questions that you want users to answer, and they will be shown these after they have been shown your home page for five seconds. Ideally you want to ask questions such as "What was the one thing you remembered the most?" or "Based on this home page, what do you think you can do on this website?" The tool then gives you some great options for reviewing your question answers, including a word map where you can more easily see the most common words used in them.

This is a very low-cost tool, with even some free options, so I suggest you get a set of responses about your home page using this tool—at least 20—to give you a better idea of what they are thinking. This will then give you some ideas of how to optimize and correct any misconceptions by tweaking your home page.

Check Your Bounce Rate to Understand Your Home Page's Current Performance

One of the best ways to see if your visitors are judging and perceiving your home page negatively is to see how many of them are immediately leaving upon arriving on it. When this occurs, this is known as a bounce, and the percentage of these occurring on your homepage can be understood by using the bounce rate metric. The higher this bounce rate is, the more this suggests that your home page is being judged poorly and has problems that need testing and optimizing.

You can find out how your homepage is currently performing for this very useful metric by looking at a pages report in your web analytics tool. Simply add in the bounce rate metric for this report (and to understand how this is calculated and how this differs from exit rate, see the upcoming note), change the date range to the last 30 days, make sure your home page on this report, and then note down the bounce rate for it.

What Is the Difference between Bounce Rate and Exit Rate?

Both of these are very useful engagement metrics, but there are slight differences for when you should use each one.

Bounce rate for a page is the percentage of visitors who directly arrive on it from an *external source* only (like an email), then immediately leave without seeing another page (and is defined as single access visits ÷ entries × 100). It's great for helping understand initial reaction to a page. However, it only works for entry pages, so don't use it on pages that rarely get directly arrived on like a thanks page; otherwise, it will give you a false result.

Exit rate for a page is the percentage of visitors who leave it after arriving from *any* source, whether that's from another page of your website, or any external source like a search engine (and is defined as exits ÷ visits × 100). It helps paint a bigger picture of where your website is leaking most visitors and, unlike bounce rate, it can be used on any page—it doesn't have to be a common entry page for it to work.

In terms of interpreting your home page bounce rate percentage, if it is below 25 percent that means your home page is doing a very good job already; if it's between 26 percent and 50 percent, there is definite room for improvement. If it's over 50 percent then you have some major issues that need addressing.

To help you improve this bounce rate metric on your home page, over the rest of the week you will learn best practices to do this and help engage and convert more of your visitors. But first, you need to see if there are underlying traffic source issues causing higher bounce rates on your homepage.

Check Bounce Rates for Major Traffic Sources to Your Home Page

Sometimes it might not be the design or contents of your home page that causes visitors to bounce. Instead, sometimes this can be due to having low quality sources of traffic for it. For example, your home page may be search engine–optimized for the wrong keyword, and therefore causes visitors to bounce because they aren't finding what they expected.

Therefore, you need to dig a little deeper and see if any of your major traffic sources bounce particularly high. The best way to do this is by applying filters by traffic source on your homepage bounce report that you just pulled. Many of the most common ones should already be there for you to use and filter your report. In Google Analytics, you simply have to change the filter in the drop-down list and check organic search or paid search, for example (as you learned about in Chapter 2). You should then make sure you have visitor segments built for each of your major traffic sources, and then apply each of them. When applying these major traffic source segments, note any sources of traffic that have a particularly high bounce rate.

Once you have found problematic high-bouncing traffic sources, you should then figure out what is causing this traffic to bounce at a high rate and attempt to address the issue with that source of traffic (for example fix the link messaging of the source or fix any poorly performing keywords).

Tuesday: Find Out What Your Visitors Click and Do on Your Home Page

You should *never* presume you know what your visitors are doing on your homepage and what links or page elements your visitors are clicking on, even if you helped create or design it. This is because visitors may instead be often doing or clicking on something you don't really want them to or intend them to. Therefore, today it's important that you find out exactly what your visitors are doing and clicking on your home page to give you better insights.

First you need to understand what they are clicking on by making use of click heat map tools that you learned about in Chapter 5, either by using the tools built into your web analytics tool, or a dedicated tool like CrazyEgg.com. Go ahead and run a click heat map for your homepage for the last seven days of traffic and note down patterns you observe.

If you notice a high percentages of clicks on nonessential links on your home page and few clicks on what you actually want your visitors to click on (which match your use cases you created in Chapter 4), this represents a sign of a poorly performing home page.

I also suggest that you check if your visitor click patterns vary depending on whether the visitor is a first time or repeat visitor. Often you might find that repeat visitors are clicking on particular things (especially login buttons), whereas new visitors often are more exploratory and click on a broader set of links.

Next you need to get some feedback regarding what your visitors are looking at on your home page—this can be different than what they are clicking on. To do this you should use a visual recording tool like ClickTale (which we reviewed in Chapter 4), gather some recordings about your home page and then analyze the results to gain insights. Again see if repeat visitors do different things than first-time visitors.

Last, you should get some good visitor feedback about your home page—their feedback is excellent for gathering ideas to test and optimize it. This feedback can be obtained using visitor feedback tools like UserTesting.com, and also by using page-specific survey or feedback tools (as reviewed in Chapter 4). Go ahead and ask them questions regarding what they think of your homepage, for example what they like and don't like, and how they would like it to be improved.

Now that you have begun to better understand what your visitors click and do on your home page, for the remainder of the week you will learn some best practices to start testing and optimizing it.

Wednesday: Shorten and Declutter Your Home Page

Far too often, website home pages become dumping grounds for online marketers, who simply add new promotions, features, or news to them without any thought to the visitors' experience and what they want them really to do or click on. Worse still, they often don't switch out old content for this new content, so the page gradually gets longer and more cluttered. This then unfortunately has the negative effect of confusing visitors about what to click on or look at first.

In fact, one of the *key* reasons for visitors to abandon a home page is because they are overwhelmed with choices and don't know what they should do next. Therefore, today you focus on this to make sure your home page isn't guilty of this.

First, you need to go ahead and take a look at the length of your website's home page. Unless it's a media website that focuses on showing many news pieces or articles, your home page should be fairly short. By short, ideally you shouldn't need your visitor to scroll very far down to look at the main contents of it, and your most important calls-to-action (CTAs) should be above the page fold (as discussed in Chapter 6). E-commerce website home pages can be a little longer because they need to feature different types of products and deals that they offer, but these should be limited to no more than two or three times page fold height.

Next, you need to understand which elements can be removed from your home page. To do this you need pull up that click heat map report that you just looked at that shows you what visitors are clicking on the most on your home page. If visitors aren't clicking on a major element of your home page, chances are that you can remove this feature (or test redesigns of the module if it's something that relates to one of your major goals or use cases).

Based on what you find, you should then run a quick inclusion/exclusion test to determine the impact of removing, one by one, some of the least-clicked modules and links on your home page. This test will help identify several things with low impact on conversion to take off your home page to help shorten and declutter it.

To give your home page a start in the right direction, here are some prime candidates to test removing or shortening to declutter and improve perception of your entire website:

- Old website/company news or old press releases
- Large numbers of promotional banners (focus on and restrict to just two or three)
- Long lists of products that you sell (restrict to 5–10)

- Banner ads (for home page only—particularly the leader-board banner)
- Long blocks of text images that don't add value or help visitors decide what to click
- Job postings or information
- Company management or investor information

Thursday: Give Your Visitors a Few Clear Choices to Meet Their Needs and Your Goals

Now that you have learned how to declutter and shorten your home page, next you need to learn how to focus it so that it meets the few biggest needs of your visitors better. This is because your home page should act as a springboard to get your visitors off the home page and deeper into the section of your website that most meets their needs. This is best achieved by showing them prominent links and buttons on your home page that allow them to easily choose from and start doing what they want to do on your website.

If you have an e-commerce or media website, this is usually solved by having good navigation menu category options, a prominent search box, and links to your latest deals and products or content (refer back to Chapter 5 if you want to revisit how to optimize these links and navigation items).

If you are a lead generation website or are only selling one main service or product, ideally you should offer your visitors no more than three main choices, because any more and you will risk confusing them as to what they should click on. To understand which choices to promote to them, you need to revisit the five major use cases that you developed for your website back in Chapter 4.

First, you need to run a test to see which three of your five use cases engages your visitors the most on your home page. To do this, create a simple button for each of your five major use cases, and then run a multivariate test with these buttons shown above the fold to find the combination of the three use case buttons that gets the highest click through rates.

Second, once you have determined your three most valued use case and CTA buttons to add to your home page, you should test the copy, presentation, and location of them to see what engages your visitors the most. Ideally you need to place these above the fold and make them fairly prominent, with some graphical treatment.

Don't just simply forget about the other two major use cases, though; you should also clearly place links on your homepage to these. Just don't make them as prominent as the three most engaging ones you found through testing.

Swapalease.com has a particularly great example of offering three main CTAs for their important use cases on their home page, as you can see in Figure 7.1.

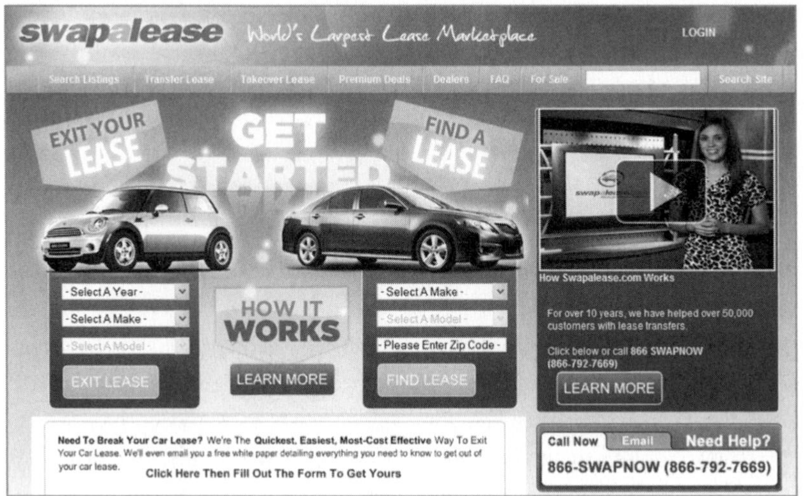

Figure 7.1 Example of a home page with three clear calls-to-action for major use cases

Friday: Learn Other Testing Ideas for Your Home Page

Today you will learn about several other test ideas and best practices that will work for any kind of website home page.

Test Adding Social Proof Elements to Your Home Page

To help influence your visitors better, you should make use of social proof best practices on your home page. As discussed in Chapter 5, there are several types that you can use, some of which will work particularly well on your home page. The first one that often influences well is to test showing customer/sales numbers, such as the number of satisfied customers you have or number of products available/sold. The second type of social proof that will usually work well on your homepage is to test adding some expert reviews or testimonials from customers, ideally in the form of a video.

Optimize Usage of Content Sliders

Next you should try optimizing usage of a content slider at the top of your home page. These are very popular and are often great for highlighting promotions, product or content. Used well they can better engage and convert your visitors for your goals, but used poorly they can annoy visitors. Here are some test ideas and best practices for using these, which are usually found at the top of a home page:

- Test the height and width of these (don't have it use all of the "above the fold" page space, as this will push down other important content).
- Test adding good CTA buttons to your slides in it, and test the imagery used (particularly people in them), as discussed in Chapter 6.
- Test using targeting in the slides to meet the needs of your first time and repeat visitors better; as discussed shortly.

- Test offering tabs, links or thumbnails to help visitors understand the contents of your slider, and offer navigation buttons.
- Don't make them too long or rotate too quickly or visitors may miss an important slide; limit number of slides in them to five, and three seconds per slide is recommended.

Always test usage of these though—sometimes it may even be better to just show a strong static promotion instead of a rotating slider. For a good example of content slider being used on a home page, see the example in 7.2.

Figure 7.2 Example of a good content slider on a home page

Use Real Estate Tests to Find the Optimal Order of Major Page Elements

After you have figured out which of your home page elements are most important to show on your home page (as discussed earlier), you need to run tests to find out which positions on your page have the greatest influence on conversion. Rather than just adding new things to the bottom of your page, or guessing at which order to place your new elements, you should run a real estate test to find the best order. For example, you could test moving up the latest deals module, or move down marketing/news-related items. You should then do follow up A/B tests to improve the contents of these high influencing elements to lift conversions even further.

Target Relevant Content for New and Repeat Visitors and Repeat Purchasers

Rather than offering a "one size fits all" home page, you should target major visitor segments to show them more relevant content that will meet their needs better (as discussed in Chapter 4). This is best targeted and shown in highly visible modules on your page (such as content slider just discussed), and will often result in more engaged visitors who will convert at a higher rate.

On your home page you should target new visitors by showing helpful content, such as first-time user information, or entice them by offering coupons for their first purchase. You should also try to target repeat visitors by showing them content relating to their favorite category (called content affinity targeting, as you learned about in Chapter 3).

You can also test targeting repeat purchasers by showing them upsells or new products that relate to what they purchased.

Remember that you can't do this targeting in Google Website Optimizer. This forms a major reason for you to upgrade your testing tool if you have that tool, to one that does offer targeting.

Test Adding a Navigation Sidebar on Your Home Page

If you don't currently offer a left-hand navigation side bar, you could also try testing adding one that contains your major site sections, newest content, and most popular content. Many home pages make great use of these to aid and improve visitor navigation.

Week 20: Optimize Your Product, Service, Lead Generation, and Other Key Pages

No matter what type of website you have, you are more than likely going to have at least one category page, product or service page, lead generation page, or a pricing list page. These are key pages that influence a visitor's decision making process and the performance of them can have a significant impact on your website's conversion rates. Therefore, today you are going to learn about how to best test and optimize these pages to help further increase your conversion rates.

Monday: Optimize Your Product Pages

Your product pages are another of the most important pages to optimize because they have such a big impact on your conversion rates and success metrics. Today you will learn how to analyze the performance of your current product pages, and more important, some great ways to test and optimize them. If you don't have any product pages on your website, you can skip ahead until you find a type of page that your website has.

Identify Your Current Product Page Performance

Before you learn about test ideas for your product pages, it's important to understand how they are currently performing. The easiest way to determine performance for product pages is by looking at the number of visitors who exit your website on a product page, which is known as the *exit rate.*

It's important to look at this metric, because as discussed last week, bounce rate would only indicate performance of your product page for visitors who directly arrive on it from external sources. Exit rate takes into account the performance of the page no matter if the visitor came from another of your pages first, or arrived from an external source.

The higher this exit rate percentage, the more it means your visitors aren't being engaged and influenced to purchase from these page and the more it needs optimizing.

To find this exit rate for your product pages, log in to your analytics tool, run a pages report and find your product pages (or product page template or grouping), and then add in the exit rate metric. Pick a date range of the last 30 days to give you a better current understanding of page performance.

To give context to your current exit rate metric, below 25 percent means your product page is performing well, between 26 percent and 50 percent, means definite room for improvement and over 50 percent means there are some major issues that need addressing. Note down this current exit rate because you will be revisiting this in later months to see how your efforts to improve it are faring.

There are other more advanced and complicated ways to measure performance for product pages, such as determining the ratio of product page visits to clicks on "Add To "buttons, or setting up and analyzing a conversion goal that includes your main product page as the first step and the order confirmation as your last step.

If you have too many product pages to analyze individually, you may be able to set up additional analytics tracking to analyze them as one group (or content type). This involves some extra tagging on them to signify them as a product page content or page type—consult an analytics expert if you wish to set this up. Analyzing them as a group is better than analyzing just one or two, because individual product page performance may be skewed by the price or interest levels per product.

Learn Test Ideas and Best Practices for Product Pages

Now that you understand the current performance of your product pages, here are some test ideas and best practices to begin optimizing them:

Provide a good overview of your product. A common reason why visitors do not complete their online purchase is because they don't have all the necessary details they need for them to make the purchase. To ensure they get the information they need, it's vital that you provide a great overview of your product on your product pages. This information should be fairly prominent and should not be buried away too far down the page. Here are some key things to test prominently showing (if you don't already show these clearly):

- A bullet point list of product features/details (or a few short paragraphs)

- Technical details (size/weight/product specification)
- Options available (state any different colors available or sizes etc.)

Focus on the benefits of your products. While it's important to add product features to your product pages, it's even more important to prominently state the benefits of using them, too. This will help give visitors a better understanding of why they need your product. Refer back to Chapter 6 where this was discussed in more detail, and based on those best practices, go ahead and run a test to add benefits to your product page or improve how you are stating your existing ones.

Test how you display your product. It's very important to show your visitors images of what you are selling, particularly because visitors can't tangibly touch your product as they can in a store. You should, at the very least, have one or two photos of your product and place these in the top left of your page, but you really need to use the product image best practices you learned in Chapter 6, like offering zoom functionality and multiple types of photos. You should also test creating videos for some of your key products and place a prominent link to them on your product page.

Consider testing your product prices. A great way to influence conversion is to actually test your product prices. This works particularly well if you have some control and flexibility of your prices. If you can, try testing increasing and decreasing your price for each of your products by 10–20 percent and see what impact that has on your conversion rates and profit levels.

Remember that higher prices may mean fewer sales and lower conversion rates, but it means higher profit margins, and on the flip side, lower prices may mean lower profits but higher conversion rates and higher revenue. Therefore, testing your price will help you determine your optimal price and maximize your profits and revenues. Don't forget to make sure your tested prices carry through from your product page to your checkout because you will confuse visitors by having two different prices if you don't do this.

Test how you display your sale or discount prices. Clearly showing your price on your product page is obviously the most important element, but you should also test how you are displaying product savings for your visitor (if they are on sale). Some visitors prefer to see savings in the form of a percentage (for example "saves you 25%") and some prefer to see actual monetary savings (for example "saves you $15"), or you could test showing both.

You can also test different colors and sizes of showing the savings to see what has the most impact on conversions. There is also a great new tool that you can use to show customized savings to visitors, depending on their traffic source, called Runa.com (`www.Runa.com`). For an example of a product page that does a good job of showing savings, take a look at the OfficeDepot.com product page in Figure 7.3.

Figure 7.3 Example of showing savings on product page

Clearly display related promotions. Showing related promotions or deals on your product pages is often a great way to increase conversions. For example, if some of your products qualify for free shipping, you need to state that near your price (just like Amazon.com does). Another promotion to mention would be if you offered a limited free trial. You should test placing these promotions in different places (like above the page fold) to help lift your conversion rates, but don't force them down your visitors' throats too much.

Clearly state stock levels. You should also clearly show stock levels for each of your products on your product pages. If you don't do this and the visitor orders a product that is out of stock, you will run the risk of frustrating them if you have to later inform them of this issue. It's also important to mention estimated restock dates if your products do go out of stock, rather than just annoy your visitors by saying your product is "out of stock." Also, as discussed in Chapter 6, items with low stock can help create a sense of scarcity and result in higher conversions.

Clearly state your return or money-back policy. Your visitors will be more apprehensive about ordering from your website if they don't know your return policy or your money back policy. Clearly stating this on your product pages (and FAQ pages) will help reduce this purchase anxiety and help increase the chances of them purchasing. Showing a seal to visually highlight this will also help draw the visitors' eye and increase the chances of them being influenced by it.

Test your calls-to-action, particularly the buy button. As discussed in Chapter 6, testing CTAs is one of the best ways to increase your conversion rates, and is especially true on your product pages. In particular you should test using different text, styles, size and color for your buy buttons. For example, there are many other ways to say "buy," for example "order now" or "add to cart," and while these may seem very similar, slight differences in the wording of these buttons can impact your conversion rates, as can the color, size and style of the CTA button.

Test showing recommended product options. Not only is showing recommended related items on your product pages good for suggesting additional products to your visitors, but it is a great navigational aid to your visitors if they didn't find quite what they were looking for. You should also try testing showing recommended upsell options, for example showing accessories for products or related warranties.

To see what influences your conversions the most you should try testing the location, size and number of these modules that show recommended items, the number of products in them and how their details are displayed (prices, titles, thumbnails etc.), and also the title of the modules (for example "Recommended for You").

Don't make these too prominent or large though, because you need to give more prominence to the current product that you are trying to sell on the page. To help you control, automate, and optimize usage of recommendations like this, you should consider using a tool like Adobe Recommendations (`www.omniture.com/en/products/conversion/recommendations`).

Offer product reviews and ratings. As discussed in Chapter 6, it's particularly important to add reviews and ratings to build social proof, and it is most critical to show these on your product pages to increase conversion. If you don't currently show ratings and reviews, you should introduce this functionality onto your product pages (using something like PowerReviews.com or Bazaarvoice.com), and as you build up the number of reviews, it will gradually have a positive impact on your social proof and conversion rates.

Test using tabs for different types of information. Another thing you could try testing is adding tabs to show information on your product pages. This has the effect of making your pages shorter and better organized and acts as a good way for visitors to easily browse more details about the product, such as technical details or return shipping details and other policies. For a good example of a product page that makes good use of tabs, see how Macys.com does this in Figure 7.4. As you can see, this website also shows the average rating in the header for the reviews tab, which is a great additional usage of tabs.

Run inclusion and exclusion tests to de-clutter your product pages. As discussed in Chapter 3's testing strategies, a great way to better focus your pages and to remove elements that aren't influencing conversion is to run inclusion/exclusion tests—don't just presume everything you currently have on your product pages is needed to convert your visitors. Go ahead and review your product pages and identify a few less important elements to consider testing for removal. Finding and removing elements that don't contribute much to conversion will help de-clutter and focus your product pages better, and usually has a great impact on increasing orders from these pages.

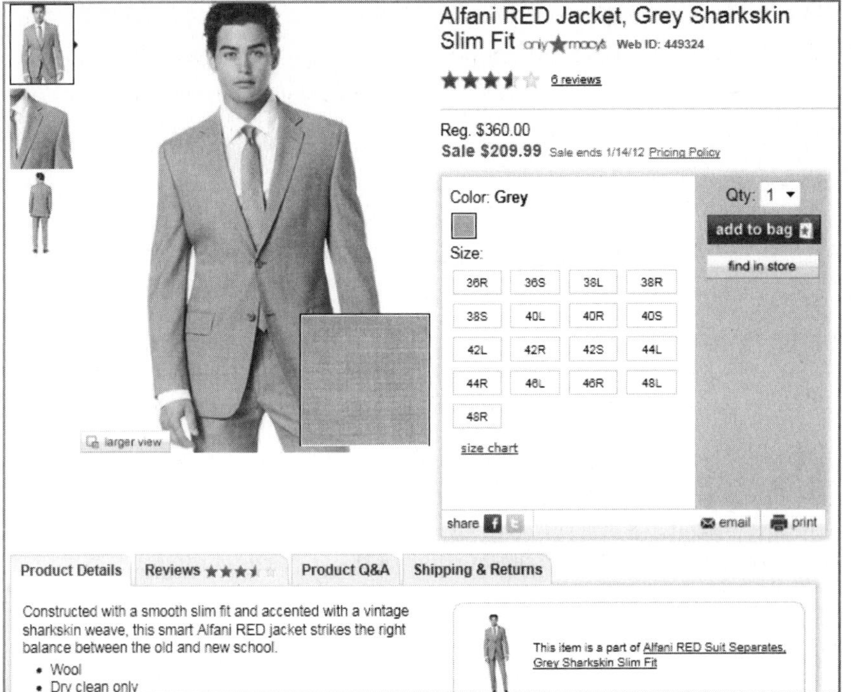

Figure 7.4 Example of a product page with good usage of tabs

Tuesday: Optimize Your Service Pages

Many websites sell services instead of physical products. These can be either web-based services (like an email tool) or offline based services (like bank services). These types of websites have pages that describe the service being sold, and are often called "features" pages. These service pages require different best practices to optimize, and today you will learn how to best do this and optimize them. If you don't have any service related pages on your website, you can skip ahead until you find a type of page that your website offers.

Identify Your Current Service Pages' Performance

Identifying your service pages' performance works very similar to identifying current performance of product pages that was discussed yesterday. Please refer back to that and follow the same best practices, and determine the exit rate for your service pages for the last 30 days. You can use a similar exit rate grading system to understand your service page performance too (with over 50 percent indicating many problems that need fixing). You then need to note this current rating down because you will be revisiting this in the last chapter to understand how your optimization efforts have fared for these pages.

Test Ideas and Best Practices for Service Pages

Here are some specific best practices and things to test in order to optimize your service pages:

Provide a good overview of your service. As discussed yesterday for product pages, it's essential that your service pages prominently show a good overview, including a bullet point list of features and service levels. Checklists can work very well for service pages, and you can try using a matrix-style table to compare your services to those offered from a competitor.

Focus on the benefits of your service. Benefits are even more important to show on your service pages, because unlike products, services are not tangible and are harder to describe the features of. Therefore, you need to use the best practices found in Chapter 5 to prominently show the benefits of using your service on your service page.

Test the screenshots or images of your service. It's very important to test and optimize how you show screenshots or images of your service, so that visitors can see it in action. Visitors will rarely buy a service if there are no screenshots of images of it in action. In particular, you should test adding more than just one image (three to five is a good number to test), and test the quality and size of the screenshots. You should also test the location of the screenshots.

Test including a demo video of your product. A great way to convey the benefits and features of your service is to create a short promotional video and test adding this to your service page above the fold. To set this up and optimize this video, refer back to Chapter 6 where you learned about optimizing videos.

Consider testing your service prices. As discussed yesterday for optimizing your product pages, if you are able to, you should also test the cost of your prices to influence conversions. For example try increasing and decreasing your price by 10 percent to see what impact that has on conversion rates.

Test how you display your sale or discount prices. As also discussed for optimizing your product pages, if your service is on sale or being discounted, you should set up tests regarding how you display your sale or discount prices, such as percentage savings versus monetary savings.

Clearly state your guarantee and money-back policy. Your visitors will be more apprehensive about ordering from you if they don't know your guarantee or money-back policy. Clearing testing stating this on your service pages will usually help reduce this risk and help increase the chances of them purchasing. Test showing a guarantee seal on this page too, as this will help draw your visitors' eye to this so they are more often influenced by it (as discussed in Chapter 6).

Test your calls-to-action and headlines. On your service pages, a great headline with a powerful supporting CTA button can really help improve your conversion rates. Therefore, go ahead and test headlines using the best practices you learned about in Chapter 6, and test your signup CTA buttons—in particular the wording, styles, colors and location of them. It's important to test having a couple of these buttons present on this page, ideally one above the page fold, and then one toward the bottom if your page requires scrolling.

Test showing testimonials and reviews. As discussed in Chapter 6, reviews and ratings help build social proof, which in turn helps improve conversion rates. For services, reviews from industry work very well in particular, so you should try and obtain some and test prominently showing them on your service page.

For an example of a good service page that contains many of these best practices mentioned above, see Figure 7.5, which shows the services page on SEOmoz.org.

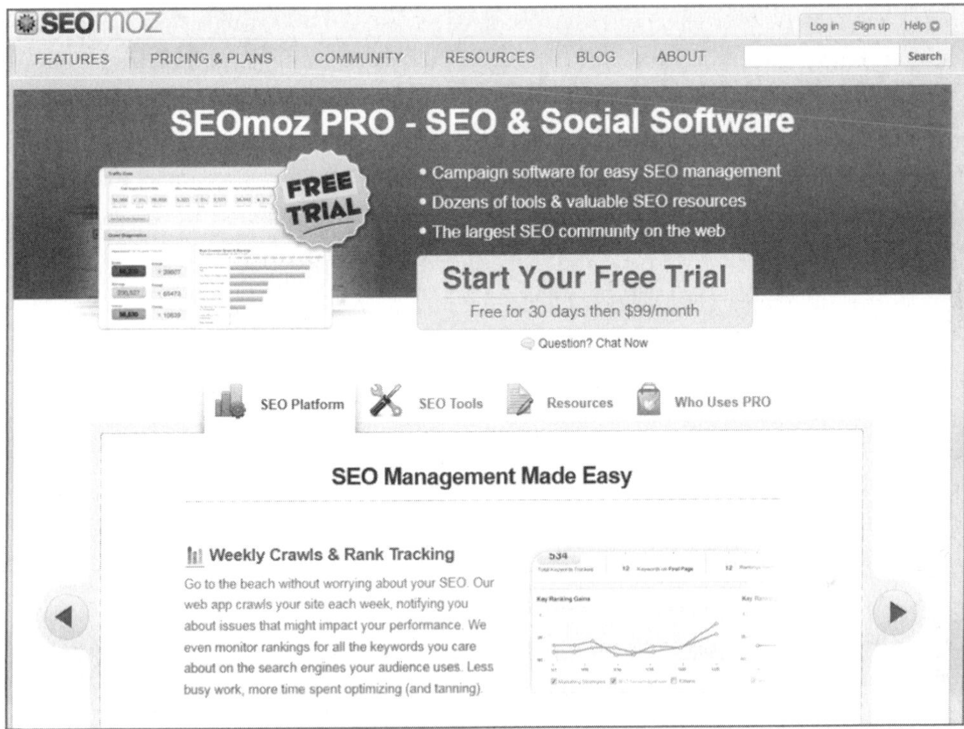

Figure 7.5 Example of a service page using many best practices

Wednesday: Optimize Your Lead Generation Pages

Another very important type of page to optimize is lead generation pages. These pages have a main goal of trying to get visitors to sign up for something using a form, which represents a lead for the receiving online business to then try and convert, hence the name "lead generation." These types of pages are fairly common on several types of websites, and many marketers create paid search landing pages specifically to drive traffic to and generate leads from. Today you will check the performance of these pages and then learn some best practices and tests to optimize them.

Check the Performance of Your Lead Generation Pages

Just as you needed to do for your other key pages reviewed so far, first you need to understand the current performance of your lead generation pages. This helps you set a benchmark that you can later revisit to see how well your optimization efforts have fared. So go ahead and log in to your web analytics tool and find the exit rate for your lead generation pages, and use a date range of the last 30 days. If you are pointing traffic directly to them, you should also use bounce rate to determine performance.

Best Practices to Test and Optimize Your Lead Generation Page

First, let's review some general things you need to test and optimize for your lead generation pages. Most of these things you need to test and optimize for these pages have already been covered in detail in earlier chapters. The only additional thing you need to pay particular attention to is the actual form on your page, which you learn about shortly. Try testing some of the following things:

- Test using bullet point lists of benefits and features instead of long blocks of text.
- Test shortening your page and make sure your CTA is above the page fold.
- Test showing a great testimonial, if possible with video.
- Test which supporting image or hero shot you use.
- Test the headline and subheaders.
- Test showing number of customers to build social proof.
- Test showing client logos and media mentions to build social proof.
- Test showing risk reducers like guarantees or free trials.
- Test different color schemes including background and header.
- Test adding a demo or sales video about your product or service.
- Test offering something for free as incentive to complete the form (such as a coupon, free trial, or e-book).
- Test removing elements that may be distracting (using an inclusion/exclusion test).
- Test moving the form to a separate page, and instead focus on a bigger CTA button to begin the signup process on another additional page.

A good example of a landing page that uses many of these best practices can be seen in Figure 7.6 at Intuit.com. They even tested moving the signup form to an additional page and replaced it with a call-to-action button instead, as just mentioned.

For another example of a unique well-designed lead-generation page, see Figure 7.7. This has a particularly eye-catching design that might help contribute to improved conversions.

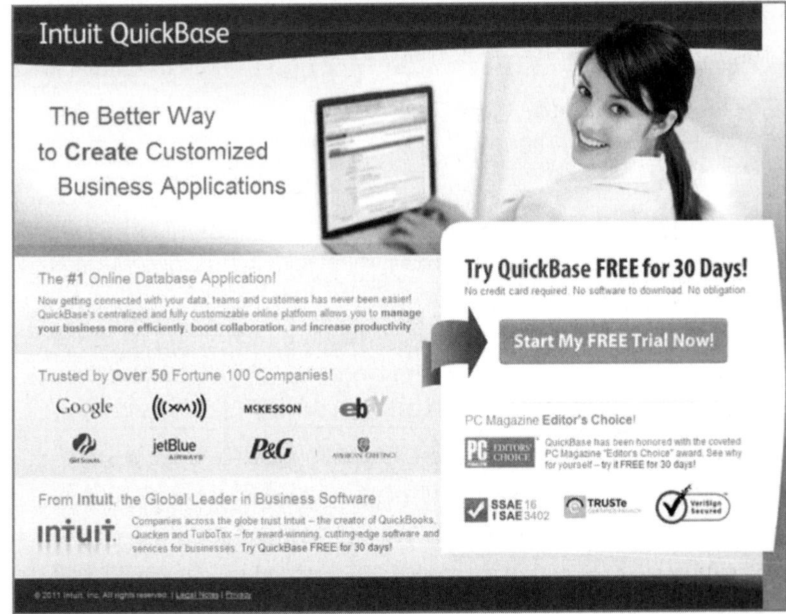

Figure 7.6 Example of a good lead-generation page with a button instead of a form

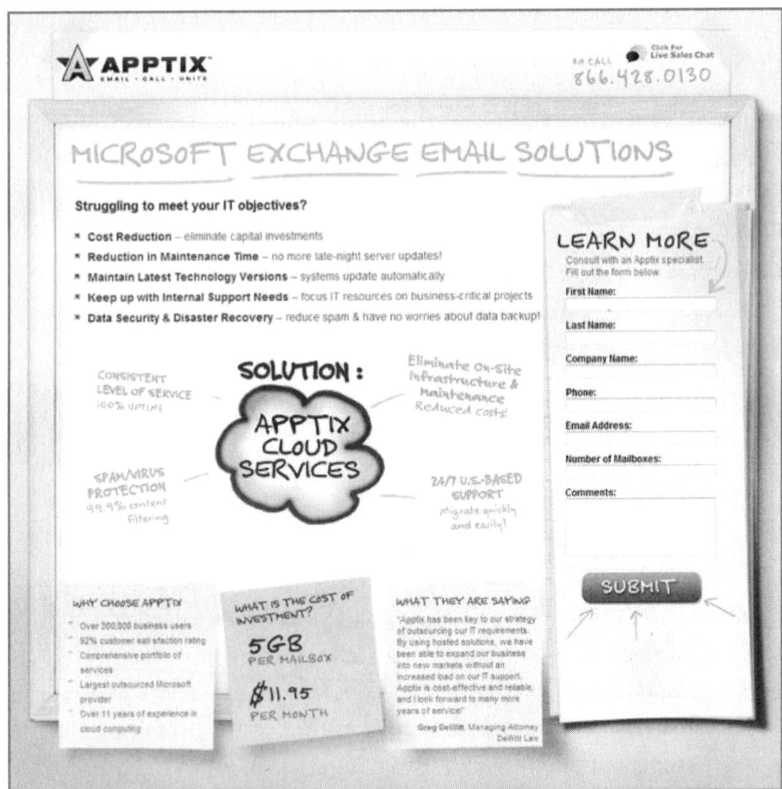

Figure 7.7 Example of a good lead-generation page with a unique design

Other Best Practices for Paid Search-Landing Pages

There are also specific things you should do if you are using paid search to send traffic to your landing pages. Driving this kind of traffic to these pages can result in very high conversions on your website because the traffic is so targeted, particularly if you use the following best practices:

Create a separate landing page specific to paid search. First of all, don't send your paid search visitors to your main lead generation page that you can navigate to on your website. You need to create a separate dedicated lead-generation landing page that is not a part of your website's link structure or site map and point to that directly from paid search instead. This gives you more flexibility for testing and optimizing it without affecting other global page elements that may be on your lead-generation page.

Test removing navigation links to help visitors focus on the page. Second, you should test removing header navigation and other unrelated navigation from your paid search landing lead-generation pages to increase your conversion rates. Doing this eliminates potential distractions for your visitor to click on and better focuses them to convert by completing the form on the landing page. If you need to show extra information, you could test showing this in tabs on this landing page (as discussed for product pages earlier this week).

Continue paid search ad messaging on the landing page. Last, make sure you use the same wording in your paid search landing page that was found in your paid search ad. This helps continue the messaging (scent-trail) and will ensure that visitors remain engaged. Far too often, online marketers use paid search ads that direct visitors to a generic page that doesn't mention the wording in the ad the visitor clicked on. This often results in preventable page abandonment when the visitor arrives because they can't find what they were looking for.

Ideally, you should build a landing page for each paid search ad that you use and match the wording in both. If you have a search team expert in your company, ensure that you work closely with them to ensure this occurs.

Best Practices to Test and Optimize Your Lead-Generation Forms

To increase the conversion rates of your lead generation pages it's important that you spend considerable time testing the actual form on these pages. This will often have the biggest impact on optimizing these pages and generating more leads from them. Here are some things you should test doing in particular to optimize your form:

Test the location of your form. Test running a real estate test on your form to see which location most increases form completion rates. In particular you should test moving it above the page fold if it isn't already. Typically forms tend to convert better when in the right hand side of pages because of how people read, and they will want to read details before they use the signup form, but you should test several locations to find the best converting one.

Keep your form short and limit number of fields. Ideally you should keep your form as short and simple as possible. Just because you might want extra information from visitors to help qualify and complete a sale doesn't mean they will like giving it to you. Test removing some less important fields from your forms and ones that aren't mandatory, as this is likely to increase your conversion rates. To figure out which ones to remove, you should ask yourself if you really need each of the fields and figure out which ones aren't as important to keep, and then test the impact on conversion when removed. If you need more fields to gain information from the visitor, you could test asking for additional details on the next page after they have submitted or ask them at a later point.

Test placing email privacy text near your submit button or email field. Testing adding this email privacy text can help increase form completion because it is likely to reduce anxiety from the visitor, as discussed in Chapter 6. This privacy text should state that you won't sell or rent their email, or spam them. You could also test putting a privacy policy link near your submit button to try and increase conversion rates.

Test adding a powerful call-to-action at the top of your form. A great way to lift form completion rates is to test adding a large CTA headline at the top of your forms and then test different wording options to see what has the best impact on form completion rates. This needs to match and support the overall CTA button and messaging found on your lead-generation page.

In Chapter 8, you will learn more about testing and optimizing forms that are longer, such as registration and signup forms, and also about specific details for testing and optimizing newsletter forms.

Try a Testing Tool Specific to Optimizing Lead Generation Pages

You could also try using a testing tool specifically designed to help improve conversion rates on lead-generation pages. This tool is called UnBounce.com and was mentioned in Chapter 2. It allows you to make use of great lead-generation page templates that already make use of many of the best practices mentioned throughout this day. This tool also allows you to easily test many things like different page layouts, button types, and text to see which versions convert better. It's fairly low cost, and you don't need any website programming knowledge to create or test these lead capture pages.

Thursday: Optimize Your Category Pages

Many websites have category pages of some sort, particularly ones like e-commerce or media websites that feature many types of products or content.

Offering these general category pages allows visitors to better explore what your website offers, and they are vital for showcasing the different things that a visitor can do in each subsection of your website. Today you will learn some best practices to test and optimize these pages, both for general websites ones, and ones specific to e-commerce websites.

Understand Your General Category Pages Performance

Just as you needed to do for your other major types of pages you learned about in this chapter, you first need to understand the current performance of these types of pages. This helps you set a benchmark that you will revisit in the last chapter to see how well your optimization efforts have been faring. Therefore, go ahead find your exit rate for your category pages in your analytics tool.

Best Practices to Test and Optimize Your Category Pages

Here are some best practices and test ideas that will help you optimize the performance of any type of category pages:

Use a left-hand sidebar to aid navigation. You should test placing navigation links in a left-hand sidebar on your category pages. These should provide visitors with better options to explore each category and should include links for sub-categories, most popular content, and new content. If you are selling items, you can also show links to different brands or price levels so that visitors can browse that way, too.

Showcase new and most popular content. You should also test including promotions and new and most popular content on category pages that relate to the category the visitor is browsing. Show banners and text links for these above the page fold on your category page to give them more exposure. Don't use too many of these modules though, and you should also run real estate and inclusion/exclusion tests on them to find the optimal placement and number of them.

Test placing an introduction at the top of your category pages. Placing a text or visual overview at the top of your category pages helps introduce the type of products or services being offered in each category. This is particularly useful for products and services that are complicated or aren't immediately obvious as to what they are and therefore need some explanation.

Target visitors to show them recommended items. Category pages are great to show your repeat visitors recommended items relating to their previous purchases or most frequently seen content. This is because visitors on these pages are often looking for suggestions on what to buy or look at. Refer back to Chapter 4 to learn more about other affinity content targeting best practices that you can use on pages like this.

For a good example of a category that showcases many different things and includes personalization, see the example of Amazon.com in Figure 7.8.

Add a third column to feature promotions or featured content or products. If you don't already use a third column on your category pages, you should consider testing adding one. This will give you extra space above the page fold to promote other important items. Ideally you should show account related details here, and use targeting that will show them content that most relates to what they have previously browsed or purchased.

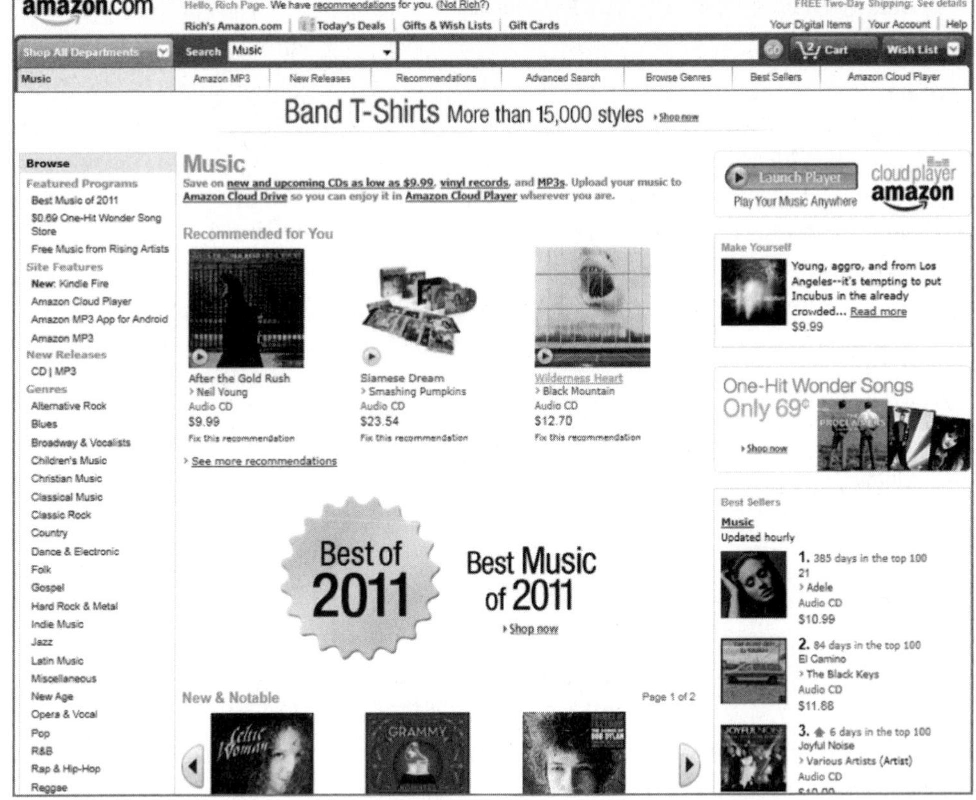

Figure 7.8 Example of a good category page that includes personalization

Best Practices to Test and Optimize Your E-commerce Category Pages

If you have an e-commerce website, your category pages are very important to optimize. This is because optimized usability and functionality of these pages will help your visitors explore and find what products they are looking for much quicker and help increase conversion rates. These e-commerce category pages are also often the same type of page as used for internal search results pages on e-commerce websites.

In addition to the general category best practices just discussed, here are some things that you need to do to optimize these e-commerce category pages in particular.

Show Products in a Grid or List Format and Offer the Ability to Change Display Options

The more traditional way of showing products on category and subcategory pages is to use a grid format, which ideally should contain no more than 20 per page and have clear pagination links. You might also want to try testing showing results in a list format—much as Amazon.com is now doing instead of a grid layout.

Your e-commerce category pages should display details for each product by using an image and the name of the product and also have a CTA button for the visitor to click on to learn more or buy the product (and the name and image should also act as product links too). You should also show the price of the product and any relevant savings.

You need to test all of these elements to find the style that increases conversions the most, in particular the size of the thumbnails. If they are too big it will be hard for visitors to scan many products per page, and if they are too small they won't be able to see the product image well enough. You should also be sure to test the CTA button for different wording and styles to see which versions increase conversions the most.

To help visitors decide on which products they want to click and learn more about, you should also show your star ratings next to each of your products. This will help increase click-through rates in addition to help build social proof for your products (refer back to Chapter 6 to revisit best practices for these ratings).

For a good example of an e-commerce category page that exhibits many of these best practices, see the example of Staples.com in Figure 7.9. They even offer the ability to switch between list view and grid view, and offer "quick view" functionality (which will be discussed shortly).

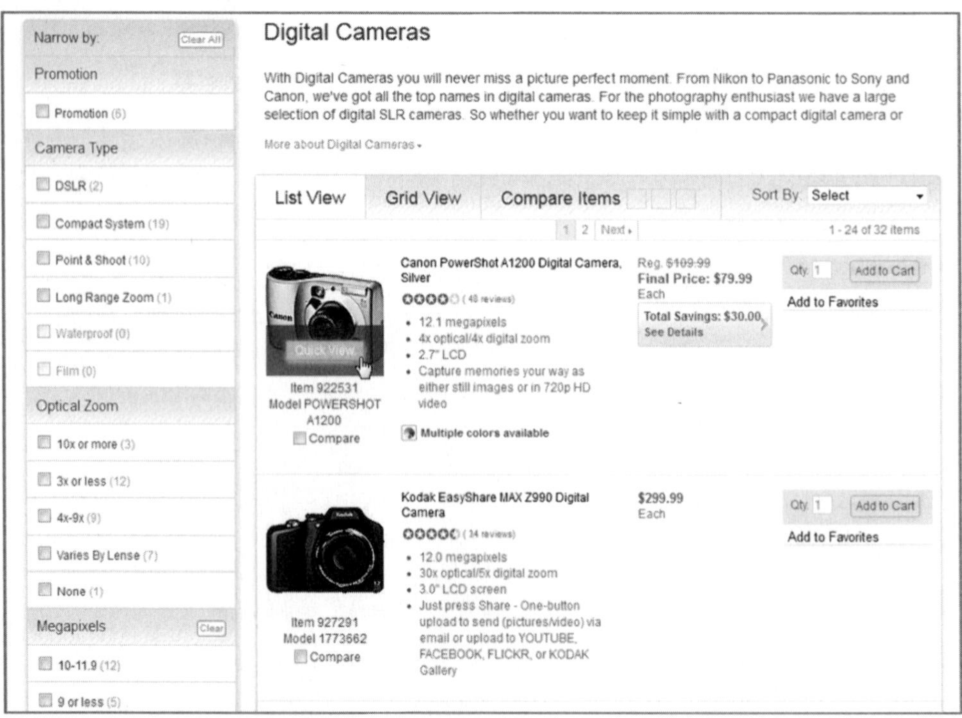

Figure 7.9 Example of an e-commerce category page designed with best practices

You could also go further by allowing visitors to personalize how the products are displayed by changing the number of products seen per page (including a "show all" link), the size of the image thumbnails, and if possible, an option for showing the products in list format instead of grid format (more like traditional search results pages).

Add Functionality to Filter and Sort Products Shown

You need to include functionality that allows visitors to filter and sort the products they are seeing on your category pages. This will greatly enhance their ability to find exactly what they are looking for more quickly and increase the chances of them converting and purchasing.

Depending on exactly what you are selling, there are many of these filters you will need, such as subcategory, brand, prince range, color, size, and average rating. This filter functionality can be shown in two ways, by using checkboxes in the left-hand sidebar, or by using multiple drop-down menus just above main area where you are showing your products. You should also allow visitors to use multiple filters at once and give them options to easily clear and reset the filters they are currently using.

In addition to filtering, you also need to have clear options that allow the visitor to sort the current selection of products being shown on the page. Depending on what you are selling, this should include criteria like sorting by lowest and highest price, highest customer rating, and newest. Again, this filtering option can be added in the left-hand side bar or placed in a drop-down menu at the top of the products.

For an excellent example of offering this filter and sort functionality on an e-commerce category page, see how Nordstrom.com is now doing this in Figure 7.10.

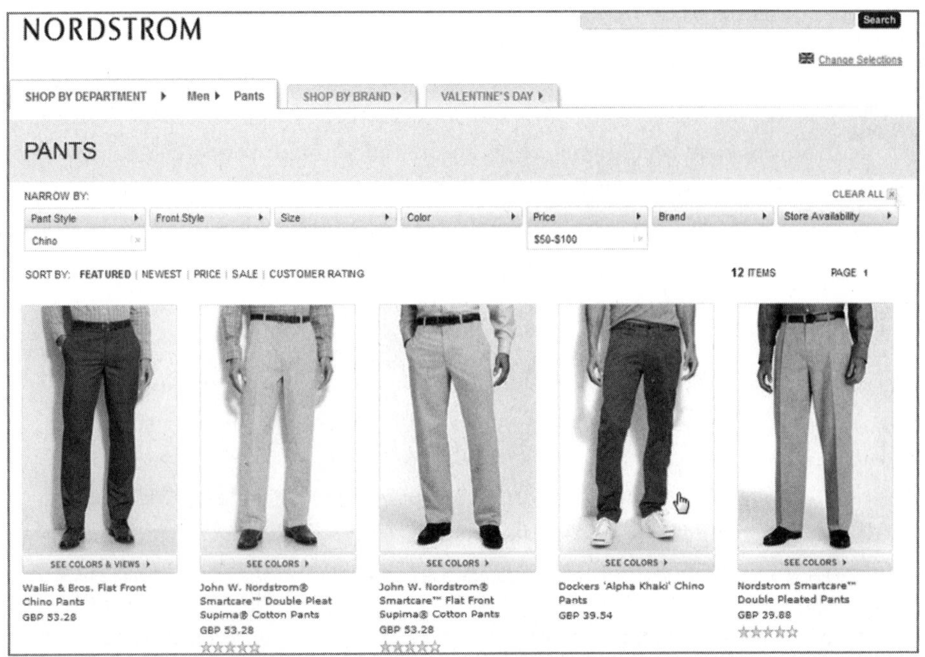

Figure 7.10 Example of good filter and sort functionality on an e-commerce category page

Use Quick View Functionality to Make It Easier to See Extra Details

Rather than your visitors having to click and visit separate pages for each of the products they want to know more about, you should enable them to see key extra information while staying on your category page. This should come in the form of adding a quick-view button for each product that pops up a box showing a larger image and extra key details about the product. You should test how this quick-view box appears, either by hovering over the button or product image or by clicking on the button to see which version helps increase conversion rates. To see an example of this quick-view button on an e-commerce category page look back to Figure 7.9.

Friday: Optimize Your Pages That Compare Product or Service Options

If you are selling something with different price and features options and you have a page that compares these, it's important that you optimize these pages, too. The goal of these pages is to provide good decision-making information to visitors; never just simply state all your different options and leave it up them to decide which level to sign up for. Not helping the visitor choose may cause anxiety for them and cause them to leave because of a lack of understanding of the best option to pick. Today you will learn some best practices to help influence their decision and increase conversion rates on these pages. If you don't have these types of pages on your website you can skip ahead to next week.

Check the Performance of Your Product or Service Options Page

In the same way you did for your other key pages reviewed earlier this week, first you need to understand the current performance of these types of pages. This helps you set a benchmark that you will check in this last chapter to see how well your optimization efforts for this page have been doing. So go ahead and log in to your web analytics tool and find your exit rate for this page.

Best Practices to Test and Optimize Your Product or Service Options Page

Here are some best practices and test ideas that will help you optimize these types of pages, including an example of a well-designed one:

Visually indicate most popular plans or service levels. You should test stating this on your most popular plan to aid decision making for your visitors (and it doesn't have to be the actual most popular, it can be whichever service level you want them to sign up for—but be realistic about promoting the most expensive one). You can also test visually supporting this in many ways, by changing the size of the containing box, changing the color, or adding an indicator at the top of the box that states which one is the most popular, or saves them the most money.

You could also test showing whether particular plans or service levels are best suited for different types of users (like beginners or advanced users), as this helps visitors self-select the one that most needs their needs.

Create names for each plan or service level. Giving each of your service plans different names will help your visitors understand the quality or grade of your plans or services better, for example "pro," "gold" or "premium." This will make it easier for them to decide which level they want to pick, so go ahead and test this.

Use pop-up help for feature or benefit details. Don't just let your visitors guess or presume they will know or understand what each of your service level or plan benefits are, because often they will not fully understand. To ensure they understand each benefit or feature better, you should test making sure you show help links so they can learn more about each one. This is best done using pop-ups that contain the help details when a visitor hovers over a help link or question mark.

Clearly show risk-reducing statements. This is a great page to show and reinforce risk-reducing statements that you are using on your other pages. For example, test showing your "free trial" or money-back guarantee details. As discussed in Chapter 6, these have a great impact on conversions.

Try and restrict to just three service levels or plans that you offer. The more options you have to choose from, the harder it will be for your visitors to decide. This is because research has shown that the more choices you present to someone, the more chance that they will be confused and not pick anything (known as the paradox of choice). You should also test having more than two options as two doesn't give the visitor enough choice.

Test switching the order that you display your plans or service levels. You should test reordering your plans or service levels so that the most expensive is shown to the left or highest, and the least expensive to the right or bottom. This is because visitors often will choose the first or highest option, so doing this will often increase revenue generated from your signups (even though it may reduce conversions though).

Add clear call-to-action buttons for each plan or service level. Adding CTA buttons for each service level or plan should entice the visitor to click and sign up. For example, if you are showing features in columns for each level, test adding these at the bottom of each plan, rather than just having one "signup" button for all. Don't forget to test the wording, style, color and size of these CTA buttons too.

For a good example of a service comparison page that contains many of these best practices, see how ClickTale.com does this in Figure 7.11.

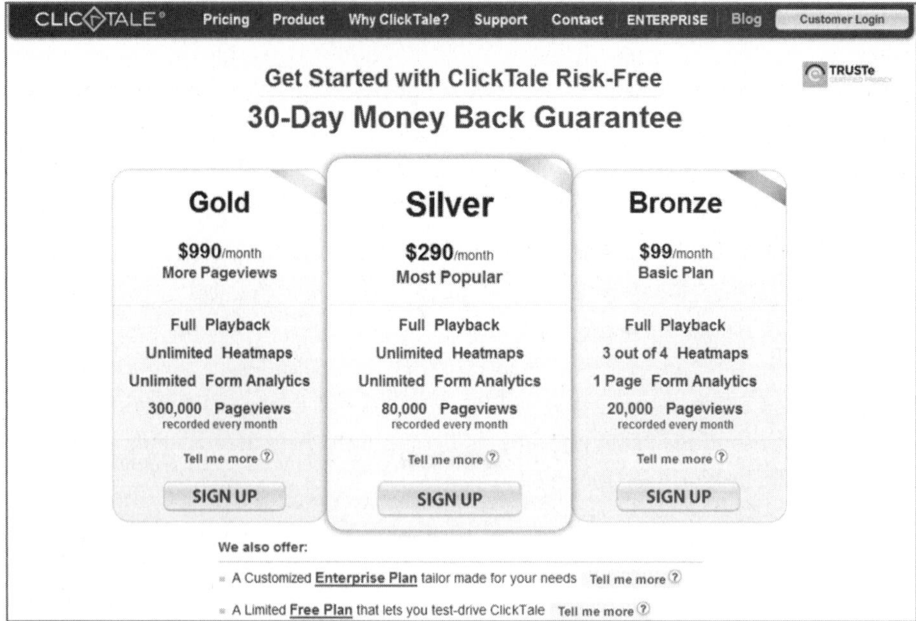

Figure 7.11 Example of a good service comparison page

Week 21: Optimize Your Shopping Cart and Checkout Flow

This week, you'll learn how to best test and optimize your shopping cart page and checkout flow. This is critical for e-commerce websites and can have a major impact on many key success metrics including shopping cart abandonment rate, number of products ordered, and the website's overall conversion rate.

If you have a website that is not related to e-commerce, and you are not selling any products or services, you should skip ahead to Week 22.

Monday: Check Your Shopping Cart and Checkout Flow Conversion Rates

First of all, today you need to check how well your shopping cart and checkout pages are currently performing and converting. This will help you understand which pages of your flow are problematic and need optimizing the most. This will also form a benchmark that you will then revisit in the future to determine how successful your optimization and testing efforts have been.

You will now learn about four great success metrics to help you understand and measure shopping cart conversion rates in your analytics tool.

Check the Exit Rate of Your "Item Added to Shopping Cart" Page

A simple way to check your performance of these pages is to check your exit rate for the first page in the checkout conversion flow. This is the page that visitors see after they have added items to their shopping cart and is usually called the shopping cart page.

An exit on this exact page means they are abandoning your checkout process prematurely and that you need to optimize it (as you will learn about on Tuesday). If the exit rate is very high for this page (above 70 percent), it means your visitors are usually not influenced enough by this page to continue to purchase the products they added to their cart.

To find this, log in to your web analytics tool, look up this page in your pages report, and then add in the exit rate metric (and change to the last 30 days). Even if you use a pop-up message to signify additions to the cart instead of a page (that will be reviewed later), you can still tag that pop-up page with analytics code and measure the performance of it in the same way.

However, realize that this rate is likely never going to be very low (less than 25 percent) because quite often visitors will add another product to their cart in a later visit before purchasing all at the same time or simply may not be quite ready to purchase the items added yet.

Check the Exit Rate of Your Order Review Page

This is the final page that visitors see before they confirm their purchase. To find the exit rate for this, look for this page in your analytics pages report, change the date range to the last 30 days and pull in the exit rate metric again. Ideally there should be a low exit rate because if they have gone this far down the checkout path, there should be few reasons for them to leave it, unless they see something wrong.

If the exit rate for this page is high (above 30 percent), it means visitors are wary about something they have seen (or not seen) on it and have abandoned it prematurely; therefore you need to optimize this page (which you will learn about on Thursday).

Check the Checkout Completion Rate and Shopping Cart Abandonment Rate

The checkout completion rate metric represents the percentage of visitors who start and *complete* your checkout process. The inverse of this is called the "shopping cart abandonment rate" metric, and is the number of visitors who *leave* your shopping cart checkout before completing it.

No matter which definition you use, it represents the simplest but most important and revealing metric to help analyze your shopping cart checkout performance. It can be calculated in a web analytics tool by using a calculated metric (checkout completion rate is the number of visits to order completion page divided by the number of visits to "add to cart" page, then multiplied by 100 to get the percentage). Some tools even allow you to define this metric when implementing the tool.

You can also find this checkout completion rate metric in the web analytics' funnel or fall-out report for your checkout pages, which you will learn about shortly.

Calculate this conversion rate now using data from the last 30 days and see how it is currently performing. This will also set a benchmark for you to revisit in the last chapter to understand how your optimization efforts have fared.

Ideally you want this checkout completion rate to be fairly high. Anything below 60 percent means you have great opportunity to test and optimize your checkout pages, and below 25 percent means you have major things that need optimizing and improving urgently.

Next you should set a target for what you want this completion rate to be. However, bear in mind there is no definition of a perfect percentage rate because every online business is different and will vary depending on many things, like your website's value proposition and number of competitors you have. The main goal is to set a target for and improve your current percentage rate; even small percentage point improvements can yield some amazing increases in revenue.

Check the Funnel Report for Your Checkout

This goes funnel report goes deeper than checkout completion rate and helps you understand which pages of your flow your visitors are most often dropping out of and where they are going. This is great for understanding which pages of your checkout flow are most problematic, helping you identify which ones to pay extra attention to optimizing.

This report is available in the leading web analytics tools. For example in Google Analytics you find this by looking at the Funnel Visualization Report, which is found under the Goals section of the menu. In this report, for each stage you will see the percentage of visitors who are converting to the next page of your checkout flow, and at the bottom it will show the percentage that completes the checkout (the checkout completion rate as just discussed). In Adobe SiteCatalyst this is called the Fallout Report, and it gives you more flexibility in which pages you want to include in this report.

Figure 7.12 shows an example of a Google Analytics Funnel Report for a conversion flow.

Go ahead and run this report in your web analytics tool and analyze the last 30 days of data. In particular you should always look for the page that has the highest drop-off rate because optimizing that will give you the biggest lift in your checkout completion rate.

Now that you can better understand how your shopping cart and checkout is currently performing, you will learn some best practices and test ideas to help improve these pages and these success metrics.

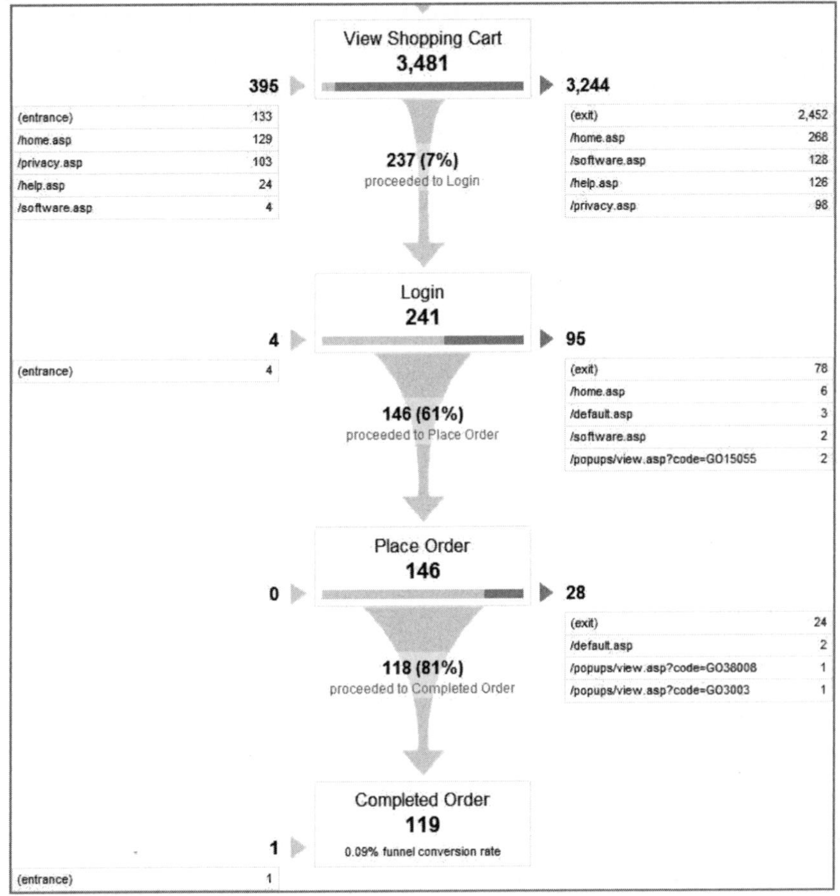

Figure 7.12 Example of Funnel Report in Google Analytics

Tuesday: Optimize Your Shopping Cart Page

Once a visitor has shown enough interest in your one of your products to add it to their shopping cart, this signifies the start of the all-important checkout flow. If your shopping cart page is not fully optimized and easy to use, visitors will abandon this critical first page of your checkout flow. This therefore means your checkout completion rate will be reduced, regardless of how well you optimize the rest of the pages in your checkout—the abandoners won't even see them.

To maximize your checkout completion rate (and therefore your overall website conversion rate), today you will learn best practices and test ideas to optimize your shopping cart page.

How Easy Is Your Shopping Cart to Customize?

In order to implement the best practices that you are about to learn, you need to make sure you are using a shopping cart that is easy to customize. If it is very time intensive or expensive to customize by implementing these upcoming best practices, then you should consider switching your shopping cart to another provider that is more flexible (such as customcart.com). This will make it much quicker and easier to test and optimize your checkout flow and its completion rate.

Make It Obvious to Visitors That They Have Successfully Added Items to Their Cart

Websites far too often don't do a very good job of clearly indicating that the visitor has added something to their shopping cart. This often frustrates visitors, who may accidentally add multiple versions of the same product to the shopping cart or may not understand where they have been taken to after adding the item to the cart.

To prevent this frustration and increase the chances of your visitors continuing to checkout, you should always at the very least send them to your shopping cart page after they click the buy button, with clear messaging saying they have added an item to it.

As another solution, you can test using a pop-up box to inform them of this and a summary of their cart contents. This is good because this enables them to continue to shop without having to see the shopping cart each time, and it may result in a greater number of products per order. Make this pop-up clearly visible, in the center of the screen ideally, and don't just pop it up in the top-right corner as visitors may miss this, particularly if the pop-up doesn't stay up for long.

Clearly Show Shopping Cart Items and Allow Visitors to Manipulate Contents

Visitors are going to want to check the current contents of their shopping cart and easily adjust its contents by removing items or changing quantities if need be.

To do this you need to clearly state the products currently in their cart (with links that take the visitor back to the product page for each item if they need reminding). You also need to allow them to easily delete items or change quantities (ideally by using update and remove links or buttons on this page). In case they aren't ready to buy all of the items in their cart yet, you should also show a link or button next to each cart item that allows them to save it for later purchase. Buy.com does a great job of offering all of this functionality in their shopping cart, as you can see in Figure 7.13.

ASOS.com takes this functionality even further by allowing visitors to change sizes and colors of the items in their shopping cart, all without having to leave this page. This apparently had a great impact on lifting their conversion rates, so you should try and test implementing this type of functionality to change cart item details too, if relevant to what you are selling.

Your Shopping Cart

Product	Availability	Qty.	Price	Order Summary
Greatest Hits Save for Later	Usually ships within 1 business day	1 remove	$9.27	Subtotal: $85.10 Proceed to Checkout
William & Catherine Save for Later	Usually ships within 1 business day	1 remove	$17.84	
Toshiba SD7300 DVD Player Save for Later	Usually ships within 1 business day	1 remove	$57.99	
		UPDATE QUANTITY CHANGE		

Figure 7.13 Example of a shopping cart that is easy to check and change contents for

Don't Surprise Visitors with Total Costs, Taxes, or Hidden Fees Later In Checkout

One way to frustrate your visitors and potentially cause them to abandon the checkout is to not fully show upfront all costs associated with your order. To prevent this from happening, your shopping cart page should always display your total cost with a breakdown of charges, including estimated taxes and shipping costs and any other less-obvious costs (for example surcharges or non-standard taxes if you have them).

Provide Clear Calls-to-Action for What Visitors Should Do Next

There are two important things you need to clearly highlight on your shopping cart page so that visitors know what to do next. First and most important, you need to clearly show a button that allows the visitor to proceed to checkout. This button should ideally be above the fold, and repeated below the contents of the shopping cart so there is a greater chance of them seeing it.

Second, many visitors won't be ready to check out at that point because they want to continue shopping. Therefore, you need to also show a button on your shopping cart that states "continue shopping." Don't make it as prominent as your checkout button though, as ideally you obviously want to get them to check out at that moment.

Keep Your Shopping Cart Simple and Without Distractions

The main thing that your shopping cart needs to do is to show enough details to satisfy your visitors into checking out, and to not distract them with other things that may result in them not completing the purchase. Therefore, you should run inclusion/exclusion and real estate tests to understand which elements and locations on your shopping carts have the most impact on your conversion rates.

In particular, test removing unnecessary links or promos, particularly for competing promotions, and test removing unrelated promotional ads if you have them on this page. The only thing that often works well is to include recommendations for related items—this often increases the average number of products per order, as you will learn about shortly.

For an example of a very busy shopping cart that is filled with ads and promotions, all competing for the visitor's attention, see ToysRus.com in Figure 7.14. This shopping cart could be easily improved just by running inclusion/exclusion tests to removing these and focus the page better.

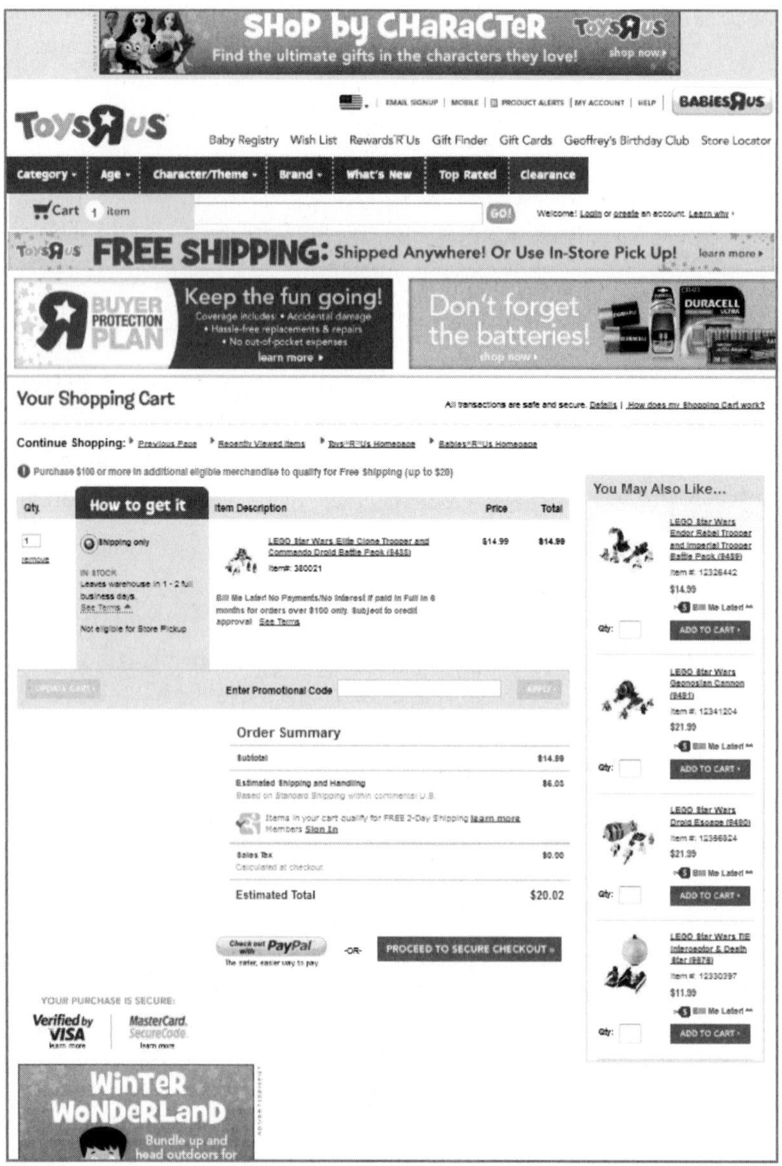

Figure 7.14 Example of a shopping cart with many distractions

Place Trust and Security Seal and Text on Your Checkout Page

As discussed in Chapter 5, adding trust and security seals and related text on your checkout-related pages helps to relieve visitors' security anxiety at a point when it is most likely to be high. Therefore, the first place you should test adding these is on your shopping cart page, in particular testing placing a security seal and text right by your checkout button. This quick simple test will likely improve your shopping cart completion rate, and you should also try testing several different types of seals and text, and their locations, to see which variation has the highest impact on checkout completion rates.

Make Good Use of Related Product Recommendations

To increase revenue for your online business, you should try and influence the average number of products per order from your visitors. To help increase your visitors' products per order you should test placing related product recommendations on the shopping cart page.

There are a couple types of recommendations you can test making that will usually work better on this page than other pages. First you can test showing items that are complementary or an accessory to the items in the cart, and you can also try showing items related to those in the cart, particularly ones that are currently on sale. Amazon.com does a great job of doing this on their add-to-cart page, as you can see in Figure 7.15. REI.com also does a great job of this by showing related cheaper products like accessories, which have found to convert higher than showing more expensive items.

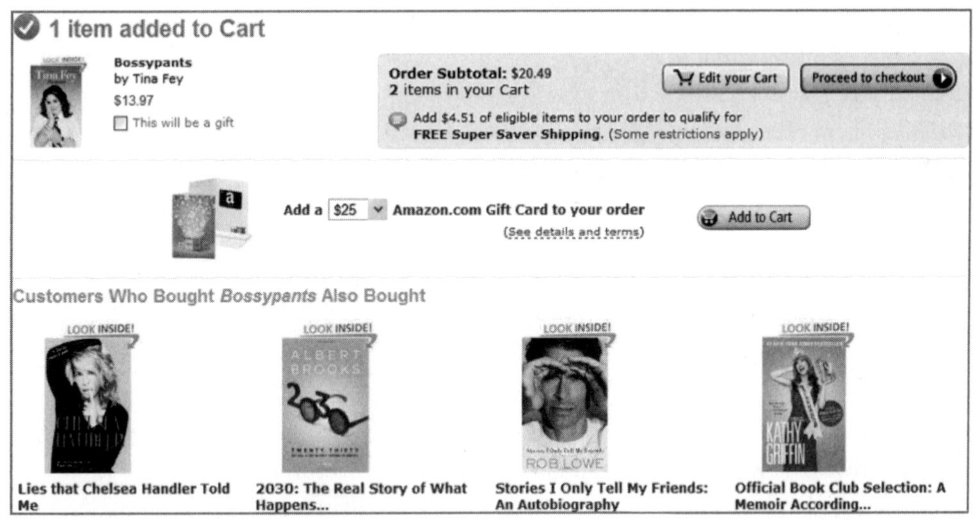

Figure 7.15 Example of recommendations on a shopping cart page

The key thing is to always show relevant products for these recommendations. Showing irrelevant ones will have the opposite effect on conversions because you will end up annoying visitors who think that it seems to salesy. Instead you should always tell them why they are seeing the products being recommended, ideally by showing and testing a descriptive title for this recommendations box (as Amazon.com also does).

As you learned earlier, there are some great tools to help you create and automate running these recommendations, such as Adobe Recommendations and Monetate.

Wednesday: Optimize Your Checkout Flow

So your visitor has decided to begin the checkout after adding something to their cart. Congratulations! However, there are still many hurdles that you need to clear before they successfully (and happily) check out and buy your product. Unfortunately many websites have poor checkout flows, and having just one poor performing element of it can result in premature checkout abandonment. Today you will learn some best practices and test ideas to help get more visitors through your checkout and increase your conversion rates.

Don't Make Visitors Have to Register before They Can Purchase

Visitors may not always want to sign up for an account on your website before purchasing something, and if you force them to, this may reduce your checkout conversion flow. As a result, you should always allow visitors to check out without the need to register.

To do this, on the first page they see after the visitor clicks on the checkout button (this usually is the "login or register to continue" page), you need to show a CTA that lets them check out as a guest. This should be in the form of a button that says something like "check out as a guest" or "check out without an account," along with support text. On this page you should also show options that allow existing users to log in and options for new visitors to create an account.

OfficeDepot.com does a great job of making it easy for any type of visitor to understand their options for checking out, as you can see in Figure 7.16.

If your visitors are checking out as a guest, you should then offer them the chance to create an account after they have finished checking out, and explain the benefits of doing so (for example, it remembers your details to save you time buying in the future, it offers newsletters and coupons, and so on). Registering will usually increase the chances of them coming back, and often gives you the ability to send them marketing campaigns (if they opt-in to them), so you should try and influence them to do this.

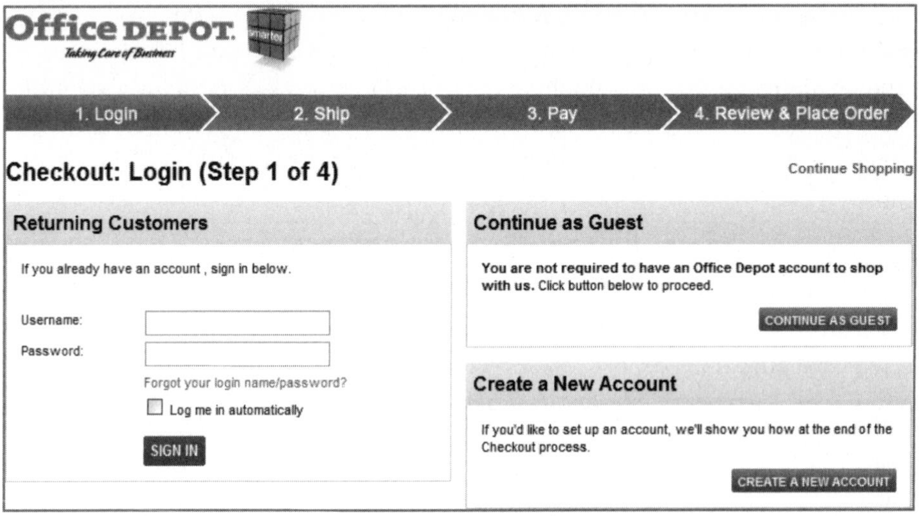

Office DEPOT
Taking Care of Business

1. Login > 2. Ship > 3. Pay > 4. Review & Place Order

Checkout: Login (Step 1 of 4)

Continue Shopping

Returning Customers

If you already have an account , sign in below.

Username:

Password:

Forgot your login name/password?

Log me in automatically

SIGN IN

Continue as Guest

You are not required to have an Office Depot account to shop with us. Click button below to proceed.

CONTINUE AS GUEST

Create a New Account

If you'd like to set up an account, we'll show you how at the end of the Checkout process.

CREATE A NEW ACCOUNT

Figure 7.16 Example of good visitor checkout options

Show a Progress Bar at the Top of Your Checkout Pages

You should always show a checkout progress bar at the top of each of your checkout pages. This helps your visitors by letting them know how many steps are in your shopping checkout flow, and what step they are currently on. For this you should show the step number for each step, and arrows pointing to the right between each step so visitors can understand how many steps are ahead of them. Look back to Figure 7.16 to see a good example of this progress bar on OfficeDepot.com.

If you have many steps in your checkout flow (more than four or five), you should consider testing reducing and condensing them to fewer pages, because this often can increase checkout completion rates—visitors often don't like having to go through many steps. Combining the billing and shipping pages into one page is a great way to reduce checkout length and is definitely worth testing.

Conversely, if you have only one or two pages in your checkout flow but they are longer and contain many fields, you should test splitting these up into three or four pages, as this may seem less overwhelming for visitors and increase your checkout conversion rate.

Display Customer Support Options in Your Checkout Flow

Your visitors' purchase anxiety levels are usually the highest during your checkout pages, and you need to help relieve this by showing support options on these pages. To do this and help improve your checkout completion rates, you should test clearly showing your support phone number and email address on these pages and, ideally, also test showing a live chat support option for immediate support help (as discussed in Chapter 5).

Make It Easier for Your Visitors to Complete Your Forms

How good is your error validation when visitors are filling in the forms in your checkout pages? Many checkout flows are abandoned purely because a visitor gets an error message while filling it in and doesn't know how to remedy it.

To help improve this, when your visitor makes an error you need to highlight the field in red that they need to fix, and also show a prominent message at the top that explains what is wrong and how to fix it. You should use friendly sounding easy to understand language (like "you forgot to enter your ZIP code") and never use technical sounding error messages or error numbers.

You should also remember to test removing unnecessary or non-mandatory fields to see what impact that has on your checkout completion rates.

In Chapter 8 where optimizing forms is discussed in more detail, you can learn more about these topics, including example screen shots.

Improve Your Billing and Shipping Address Sections

The billing and shipping pages are two areas of the checkout flow that often represent a big source of frustration for visitors and often result in premature checkout abandonment. Here are some best practices to help reduce the chances of this occurring, therefore improving your checkout completion rates:

- Allow visitors to copy their billing address to their shipping address, and vice versa, because this makes it quicker and easier to complete these sections. This is best achieved by having a checkmark next to both billing address and shipping address sections asking the visitor if they want to use the same address for both. You can see an example of this in Figure 7.17.

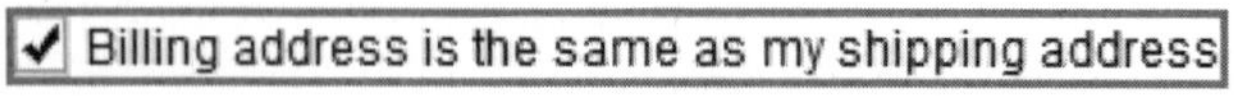

✔ Billing address is the same as my shipping address

Figure 7.17 Example billing address same as shipping option

- Offer newer, additional purchase methods other than just credit cards and virtual checks. In particular you should test adding installment payment options like BillMeLater (`www.billmelatersolutions.com`), which are proving very popular and often help increase checkout completion rates.
- A particularly troublesome billing related field is the credit card security ID field (often known as CVC code), and many websites fail to explain what this is very well, thus causing checkout issues. Therefore, right next to this field you should show an example of what this is and where the visitor can find it on their card. This can also be achieved by having a help link next to this field that pops up an image with more details (see Figure 7.18).

Figure 7.18 Example of a credit card security ID image explanation

- Allow the visitor to store their main shipping address (and other addresses) in their account to use in their future visits. Doing this helps repeat purchasers complete the checkout process quicker and easier and is particularly great for visitors who often ship to different friends and family and also ship to work and home addresses.

Thursday: Optimize Your Order Review and Confirmation Pages

The last two pages of your checkout flow are also very important to pay attention to and optimize. These are the order confirmation and review pages where your visitors review their order before placing it and where you confirm their order. Today you will learn some test ideas and best practices to optimize these pages.

Optimize Your Order Review Page

The order review page is essential for you to optimize because it can make or break your order for two main reasons. First, if you don't show them something they expect (or don't expect), and second, visitor purchase anxiety will be the highest at this final point of the checkout process. To increase the chances of them placing their order and to relieve their anxiety, you need to clearly show all of the following things on this page:

- Items and quantities being ordered
- Total costs (including shipping and tax)
- Shipping destination
- Estimated shipment and delivery dates (particularly important for holiday periods)
- Customer support options

If you don't show all this information that visitors will want to double check (and give them options to easily edit), there is a much greater chance of the visitor abandoning the checkout early. And don't confuse or irritate them by showing them things they don't expect to see either, such as unexpected additional fees or costs, delays with shipping, or stating items are out of stock.

Optimize Your Order Confirmation Page

The order confirmation is often largely overlooked by online marketers, because the all-important conversion has finished upon load of this page. However, this page represents not only a way to communicate about their current order, but a high potential place to continue to engage the customer and help increase future conversion rates from them.

Instead of simply stating to the visitor that they have completed their order, here are some ways to test and optimize this page:

- Always thank the visitor for their order (simple, but effective).
- Include a reference number so the visitor can track their order.
- Tell the visitor how they can track their order (if it's being shipped).
- Add an area that features product recommendations and upsells relating to the product the visitor just purchased.
- If you have coupons for future orders, test showing them here.
- Show options for the visitor to create a full account, including benefits of doing so.
- Show options to sign up to your newsletters or product updates.

You should also optimize your order confirmation emails with the same type of messaging, because they form a more permanent record for visitors to refer back to and check. This will be covered in more detail in Chapter 8 where you will learn about email optimization best practices.

Friday: Learn Other Advanced Shopping Cart Best Practices

Today you will learn about some other newer and more advanced technologies and best practices to help lift the checkout completion rate of your shopping cart even further.

Test Ways to Retain a Visitor's Shopping Cart Items

Most shopping carts only remember added cart items when the visitor comes back if they were logged in at the time of adding them. Consequently, many items added to carts may be forgotten if they weren't logged in, reducing chances of them being purchased in the future.

To get around this, you should use shopping cart functionality that remembers any items that they added, whether they were logged in or not. This is called a persistent shopping cart and uses cookies to remember shopping cart contents. E-commerce websites like Amazon.com and Buy.com do a great job of offering this. To implement this, you will have to consult your IT team to see if they can create this functionality, or consider evaluating another shopping cart that offers it.

If you are already using a shopping cart that offers this advanced functionality, test increasing the length of the cookie expiration associated with it so that it remembers longer. This is because, depending on which cart you are using, some expire within a few weeks, negatively affecting your chances of your visitors ordering products added to cart if they come back after that point.

Test Using Shopping Cart Recovery Automated Emails

Website visitors who place products into shopping carts and leave before purchasing them are very hot prospects to convert in the future. Unfortunately, though, many websites don't do anything or very little about this and let this potential purchase and conversion go to waste. To increase the chances of getting these visitors to come back and finish their purchase, you should test use shopping cart recovery automated emails.

These automated emails work well because they allow you to easily inform visitors if they still have items in their shopping cart and encourage them to come back and finish the order. Some good tactics to use in these emails are using wording stating that prices may change or that items may go out of stock soon if they don't finish the order. You could also test going for a simpler approach and ask them if they had an issue with their shopping cart, using wording like "Oops—was there a problem with your shopping cart?" Usage of advanced emails like this will be covered in much more detail in Chapter 8.

Week 22: Identify Other Key Pages and Flows for Optimization

Every website is different, with its own value proposition. As a result, it means that depending on your exact website, you will likely have many other important conversion influencing types of pages and flows that need to be identified and optimized.

Today you will learn how to make advanced use of your web analytics tool to analyze and find these other types of less common flows and pages. Once you have found good candidates, you should then use the best practices from this book to test and optimize them and increase your website's conversion rates even further.

Monday: Identify Issues with Top Entry Pages and Optimize

Today you will focus on analyzing the pages that visitors most often arrive on your website, which are called entry pages. Regardless of how they relate to your main conversion goals, your top 20 entry pages are very important to optimize because they form a considerable amount of traffic to your website for you to influence and convert for your goals. If you don't optimize these pages, your visitors may leave your website before you have a chance to influence them, thus having a negative impact on your conversion rates.

The best way to understand if there are issues with these top entry pages is to understand how often your visitors are immediately leaving your website upon arriving on it (known as a bounce as previously discussed). This can be easily determined by running a Top Pages report for the last 30 days of data, and then pulling in the entries and bounce rate metrics. If you need to calculate bounce rate manually, you need to take your single access metric and divide that by your entries metric, then multiply that by 100 to get a percentage.

Then go ahead and review your top entry pages for any pages have a relatively high bounce rate, which is considered anything above 40 percent. Make a note of any of these pages because they form excellent optimization candidates to better influence and convert your visitors on (using the general testing best practices and ideas found in this book).

You should also realize that some pages will naturally have a higher bounce rate though, like media or publishing websites where visitors often just come to read articles they find in search engines and then leave. However, you can try and manipulate your visitors to stay longer by using related links as you learned about in Chapter 5.

Last and very important, quite often, because of how your website may be being linked to or ranked in search engines, some of your top entry pages may not be ones that relate closely to your conversion goals. If some of your problematic entry pages don't really relate to your goals, you should consider adding related CTA links on them to try and drive visitors into pages that will help influence and convert them better.

Tuesday: Identify Issues with Top Exit Pages and Optimize

Now that you have found your most problematic entry pages to your website, you need to find your most problematic *exit* pages; in other words the pages that your visitors most commonly leave your website from. These pages are great candidates to optimize, because doing this will mean your visitors will stay on your website longer and stand a higher chance of engaging and converting for your goals.

Rather than using and finding the bounce rate for these exit pages, you need to use the exit rate metric instead. This will give you a more complete picture of which pages your visitors are most often leaving your website from; bounce rate only works for entry pages (only pages that your visitors directly land on from an external source).

To find your top exit pages you need to run a Top Pages report in your analytics tool. Change the metrics to include visits and exit rate on this report and then re-sort your pages using the exit rate metric to find the highest percentage exiting ones. Don't forget to use 30 days as a date range because this will give you a better current understand of exit page performance.

However, sorting this will often show many pages with very little traffic that aren't great candidates to optimize. To fix this, before you do that re-sort, you should export the top 20 visited pages from your Top Pages report into Microsoft Excel and then re-sort them in Excel. Doing that means it will rank your top 20 visited pages by the highest exit rate. This way you can prioritize which ones needs optimizing first.

Exit rate is often a default metric on top page reports for analytics tools, but if you need to add this manually to your report, you need to calculate this metric. This is done by taking the exits metric and dividing that by the visits metric, and then multiplying that by 100 to get a percentage.

Once you run this top 20 highest exited pages, note any pages with exit rates of higher than 40 percent because these are great candidates to optimize to make sure that visitors don't leave so soon. Note down ones associated with any of your conversion goals in particular, as optimizing these will have an even greater impact.

In order to optimize these pages, if they are associated with any types of pages discussed in this book so far (or in the rest of the book), then use the test ideas and best practices for that type of page. If they aren't mentioned in this book, one simple way to try and keep your visitors on your pages longer is to use related links at the bottom of these pages. As discussed in Chapter 6, these act as a great way to improve visitor flow to make sure visitors don't leave if they don't know what to do next.

You should also make sure you find the exit rate for common through-flow pages like category pages and search results pages to see if these are problematic. These pages should never have high exit rates because if well optimized, they should act as filters for your visitors to drill down and find what they are looking for and should not be exited from very often.

Note: You should also realize that visitors will always have to exit your website at some point, so you are never going to have perfectly low exit rates for all your web pages, no matter how hard you try. The main point is to reduce your current exit rates.

Wednesday: Identify Issues with Your Other Top Conversion Flows

For the rest of this week, you will learn how to find other pages that, when optimized, will have a great impact on your conversion rates. These all involve using advanced analysis reports and best practices in your web analytics tool.

Today you will learn how to identify issues with your top conversion flows, other than ones like your shopping cart, registration or signup flows discussed in this book. While these are usually the most common types of conversion flows on websites, if you have a more unusual website that has a unique approach to selling or engaging your visitors, sometimes you may not be fully aware of your top ones.

The best way to find your other top conversion flows is to find which series of pages most often result in reaching your goal completion page(s).

You can do this in advanced analytics tools by running a top paths report (or similar report) that shows you the most common visitor paths on your website and drop off rates, and then customize this to focus on your conversion related pages. To customize it, you need to use your main conversion event pages as the last page (whatever defines conversion success, like a thank you page), and then add wild cards to the two or three previous steps. As an example of doing this in Adobe SiteCatalyst, you would use the PathFinder Report and use a "precede pattern." You then use the wild card for any previous pages, and for the final page of the flow use the one that constitutes conversion success. It will then show you the most common flows to your conversion success page. You can do a more basic version of this in Google Analytics using the Reverse Goal Path Report, but it doesn't show you the drop off rate between the pages.

After you have found your other top conversion flows, you need to identify which pages of your flow have the highest drop off rate because they are great candidates for optimizing. Doing this will result in an increase in overall conversion rates for your website, much like after optimizing other conversion flows like shopping checkout pages. The first page of the conversion flow is usually the most important page to optimize first, because if you don't fix that, it doesn't matter how good the rest of your conversion flow pages are because many of your visitors won't even see them.

To help you understand what these other more unique top conversion flows might be for your website, here are some examples of ones that may occur quite often:

- Newsletter signup that involves many visitors seeing a newsletter example first
- Service signup that involves many visitors seeing a demo page first
- A product page that involves many visitors from a subcategory page first

Thursday: Look for Issues with Traffic Sources Leading to Your Conversion Flows

One thing that is often neglected by online marketers is taking their top website conversion flows a step back to examine possible issues with traffic sources. This is because if the visitor arrives on your website from a search or other external source expecting to see something in particular, and they then don't see it, they will often abandon your page prematurely, no matter how good it is. This is often referred to as message continuation or scent-trail issue, and you need to make sure it doesn't happen on your website.

It is important to find these traffic source scent-trail issues because if you fix any ones leading to your top conversion flows, then you will get more visitors deeper into these flows and convert more of them.

The first traffic sources you need to evaluate for scent-trail issues are ones relating to your search engine top keywords and then your top referring websites. We will now discuss these in more detail.

Check the Performance of Top Search Keywords to the First Page of Your Top Conversion Flows

One of the major culprits of scent-trail traffic source issues are caused by badly performing search engine keywords. This can be caused by either web pages that have been optimized for the wrong keyword, or keywords that have poor results descriptions in search engines.

To find these poorly performing keywords, particularly for the first pages of your top conversion flows, you can do a couple of things. In Google Analytics, they now have a new report called a Goal Flow report that you can use, as highlighted in Figure 7.19. In this report, you simply change the first step to become your top search engine keywords.

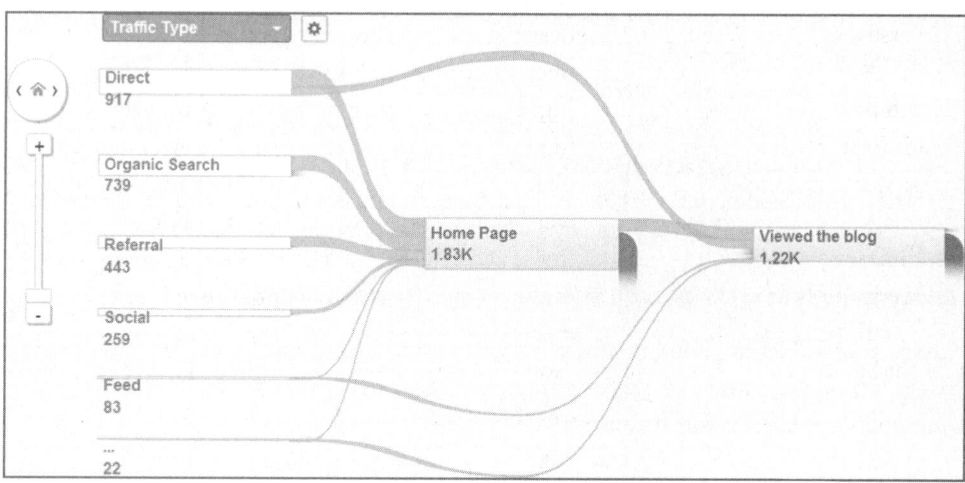

Figure 7.19 Example of a Goal Flow Report in Google Analytics

Next, you should take these top keywords that show up in this report, and then search for them on Google (and Bing) to see how relevant your web pages are for each of these keywords (checking for scent-trail and message continuation issues). Look for the keyword wording of the listing to make sure it's relevant, in addition to the actual page it's pointing to.

If you find problematic pages, you need to do more SEO on them so they rank for a more relevant keyword, or improve the wording associated with the keyword in the search results so that it's more relevant (and compelling) to click on.

This is particularly important to check for your paid search keywords, because you don't want to be wasting money on these ads. You can also check keyword issues in Google AdWords for ones that have alerts on low quality, because these are probably not converting well and bouncing too, requiring fixing.

As the second way of doing this analysis, in some advanced analytics tools you can even determine the influence of each keyword on any of your conversion goals. For example you can do this advanced technique using the order participation metric in Adobe SiteCatalyst, and pull that in on your top search keywords reports. This means you can take an even better look at which of your keywords are not influencing your goals very much, and see if there are any SEO issues with them that can be fixed.

Check the Performance of Top Referring Websites to the First Page of Your Top Conversion Flows

Next, you need to do a similar thing, but instead of checking for the top keywords arriving on your first conversion flow page, you need to look for issues with referring websites. To do this in Google Analytics, simply change the first step in your Goal Flow Report to focus on referring websites instead of keywords, or run a manual report to find the top referring websites in analytics tools that don't offer this type of advanced report.

Then check each of these referring websites to see if there are any scent-trail issues—you may find that they are linking to a poor choice of page on your website, or using link wording that sets incorrect expectations. If you find any offending referring websites, you should contact them and get them to tweak the link wording to become more relevant, or the page they are pointing to so that it links to a more relevant page.

Friday: Identify Other Pages with High Impact on Conversion to Optimize

Today you will learn about an advanced way of finding high impact conversion-related pages to optimize, and also some examples of other pages that are likely to have high potential to influence conversion.

Use Participation Metrics to Find High-Impact Conversion-Related Pages

If you have an advanced web analytics tool, you can understand which pages most influence your conversion rates; in other words, which pages are most often seen by visitors before they convert. Because these influential pages that you can find are so often seen before conversion occurs, any tests and improvements you make to them will have a greater impact on increasing your conversion rates.

One way of doing this is by using advanced metrics called *participation metrics* to find out which pages are most often associated with conversion. This process of finding influential pages is often called *attribution analysis*.

You can run this attribution analysis using participation metrics in several advanced web analytics tools. For example, when you set this up in Adobe SiteCatalyst, each conversion that occurs on your website is worth 1 unit, and this gets split up and credited to any pages that were seen by the visitor in the lead up to conversion. For example, if your visitor saw five pages in the buildup to purchasing, each of the five pages would get 20 percent of the conversion credit, which would equate to 0.2 conversion credit.

For each of your pages the conversion credits are then totaled up by the tool to give you a participation metric rating—the higher this is, the more often the page is seen on the path toward conversion, and therefore the more influential it is on your conversion rates. To help you understand this metric better, the tool also shows this as a percentage across all of your pages.

This great participation metric can be set up to work on multiple conversion goals, including orders, leads, signups, and even on revenue.

To set up these advanced metrics and report on this, you will have to work with your web analytics tool vendor, because each tool has a slightly different way of doing this. For an example of how this works in Adobe SiteCatalyst, visit this link: `http://blogs.omniture.com/2010/03/11/summit-topic-3-participation/`. Bear in mind also this can't be done in Google Analytics.

If you can set this up, you should pull in your participation metric on your top pages report (for the last 30 days), and then re-sort your pages by this metric. This will reveal to you the pages that currently participate most in your conversions—and you may find pages that you may have thought would have had very little impact, but turn out to have high impact.

Once you find these top conversion influencing pages, you can try and optimize these even further to get even more juice from your conversion rates.

Examples of Other Potential High-Impact Conversion Pages

To help you think of some good examples on your own website, here are some suggestions of often ignored, but potentially high-impact conversion related pages:

- Logout page
- Login page
- Account-related pages

These examples all are typically seen after an initial conversion has occurred, so little conversion attention is often placed on these. You can influence your conversion on these high trafficked pages by promoting and linking to your other conversion related pages, for example by showing related products, deals and promos (and using targeting works great here to increase the relevance to visitors).

Week 23: Optimize Your Website's Mobile Experience

The recent growth of the mobile web continues to explode with the ubiquity and popularity of smart mobile phones, with a growing percentage of users now getting their Internet fix via these instead of their regular desktop or laptop computer.

Mary Meeker, a leading Internet analyst at Morgan Stanley, even went so far as to state that "Within the next five years, more users will connect to the Internet over mobile devices than desktop PCs."

Unfortunately though, websites viewed on these smart mobile devices are fraught with many usability and conversion related issues because of the smaller screens viewing them. Because of the slower connection speeds on these too, visitors are also usually much quicker to exit from slow loading mobile websites to find a faster loading one.

Therefore, to help reduce this potential negative impact, this week you will learn and start using some best practices to build and optimize a mobile website to satisfy this growing population of your mobile visitors.

Fortunately for you, many websites are currently doing a very poor job of optimizing their mobile website version (or don't even use make use of one), so adopting these best practices can help form a great competitive advantage, and have your competitors' website visitors coming to your mobile optimized website instead.

Monday: Check the Percentage of Mobile Traffic, Conversion Rate, and Bounce Rates

Today you will learn how to check how much mobile traffic your website currently gets, and understand how your mobile website visitors are currently performing in comparison to your regular website visitors.

First, you need to check the current percentage of your visitors that are using your website on a mobile device; you may be surprised at how large this percentage is.

To find this mobile visitors percentage rate, you need to look at your mobile reports in your analytics tool and pull the number of mobile visits to your website in the last 30 days. Then divide that by the overall number of visits to your website in the same period, and multiply that by 100 to get a percentage.

To help give you an idea of what is a significant mobile visitor percentage, a recent study by ComScore in late 2011 found that 7 percent of all U.S. website traffic is driven by smart mobile phones and tablets, with two thirds of that coming from smart mobile phones. Therefore, around 5 percent is an average number of mobile visitors on your website, and over 10 percent can be considered a significant number.

Next you need to understand how these mobile visitors' conversion and bounce rates compare to the rate of your regular website visitors. To do this you need to first create a visitor segment in your web analytics tool for the visitors who use your website on a mobile platform (using the steps discussed in Chapter 2).

Once you have done this, you should check your website conversion rate for this mobile visitor segment and see how it compares to your normal website conversion rate. If it is much lower, this is an indicator that your mobile visitors are having issues and therefore the mobile version of your website needs optimizing.

The next thing you need to find out for this mobile visitor segment is the bounce rate for your top 10 pages. Simply pull a Top Pages report for this mobile visitor segment, then pull in the bounce rate, and then see how these compare to the bounce rates of regular visitors to those pages.

This can help you understand any pages that are problematic for your mobile visitors in particular, and will help you understand which are in need of optimizing the most. This is very important to check and compare for your conversion flow related pages like your checkout flow, signup or registration pages.

Tuesday: Check What Your Website Looks Like on Mobile Devices

It's important to understand that your website can look very different on the small screens of smart mobile phones. Depending on how your website scales and resizes on them, it can have disastrous consequences on usability for your website, thus having a major negative impact on your conversion rates. There are also several non-standard browsers on less popular mobile phones that can have even worse effects on this.

Therefore, today you need to check how your website looks on mobile platforms to uncover any potential issues like these that your visitors might be having.

Luckily there is a great tool called MobiReady.com (`www.MobiReady.com`) to help you automate checking your website on the many leading mobile browsers (like those found on Blackberry, iPhone and Android phones), and also provides you with detailed error reports.

Even if you have already tweaked your website so that it looks better on smart mobile phones, it is still important to recheck this because mobile browsing standards often change very quickly.

Also bear in mind that if you have a high proportion of visitors that are iPhone and iPad based (over 10 percent) and if you have critical website elements like navigation built with Adobe Flash, you may want to consider rebuilding these with another technology like HTML 5 or JavaScript. This is because at the time of writing this, Adobe Flash content unfortunately doesn't work on those devices.

Ultimately, even though you can make some tweaks to your website so that it works slightly better on mobile smart phones, you need to go a step further and create an alternative mobile version of your website that your mobile visitors will see. This will meet their needs much better, and will increase the chances of them engaging and converting on it. You will learn how to create and optimize this over the next few days.

Wednesday: Understand the Need for a Mobile Version of Your Website

As just discussed, rather than just fixing your website so that it looks a bit better on mobile phone browsers, you need to build a separate alternative version that better meets the needs of your mobile visitors.

To help you understand the reasoning of why you need to have this separate mobile version of your website, consider the negative impact of visitors having to use your regular website on a smaller mobile phone screen.

First it's much harder for your visitors to navigate and use your website on a smaller screen with no mouse. This means it's much more difficult for them use important parts of your website like navigation menus, buttons and forms. Second, it means they have to rely on zooming in and out (often by pinching the screen) to see all of your web page content in detail.

And when you combine that with the problem of much slower internet connections on mobile phones causing much slower loading pages, browsing your full website on a mobile phone is really not good for your visitors (and therefore not good for your website conversion rates either).

Now that you have hopefully realized the importance of creating this separate alternative mobile website version, today you will understand some options for doing this.

Use a Tool to Help You Create a Mobile Version of Your Website

A great way to dip your toes in the world of mobile website optimization is to use a tool that will convert your regular website into an additional mobile version too. This is often much cheaper and quicker to build this way, although it won't give you as much flexibility as building your own custom mobile website (which you will learn about tomorrow).

There are several levels of functionality (and therefore price) of these tools. On the lower cost but lower functionality end is MoFuse.com (`www.MoFuse.com`). For a more customizable tool but with higher cost, there is Mobify.com, (`www.mobify.com`) which gives you greater control and flexibility, easy deployment and great tracking options. See Figure 7.20 for an example of a mobile website version of alibris.com created using the Mobify.com tool.

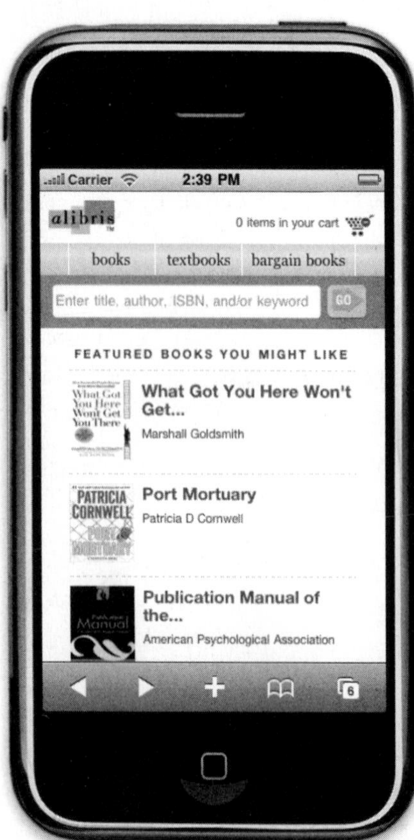

Figure 7.20 Example of a mobile website version built by Mobify.com

And if you have a blog for your website, there are also specific tools that you can use to create a mobile version of your blog, such as WPtouch Pro (`www.bravenewcode.com/store/plugins/wptouch-pro`).

Detect Mobile Visitors and Redirect Them to a Mobile Version Instead

Regardless of how you build your mobile website version you need to make sure your mobile visitors automatically get redirected to it. Most tools used to create mobile website versions will handle this for you, but if you are building your own, you need to handle this yourself.

The best way to show your mobile website version to the right visitors is to automatically detect if the visitor is using a mobile device to view it, and if so, immediately redirect them to your mobile version. This acts sort of like having a traffic cop who redirects visitors to the right place. This can simply be done by using JavaScript to detect visitors on any mobile platform and redirect them to the mobile version of the website.

As an advanced technique, you may also want to consider redirecting your tablet device visitors to a tablet-specific website version that caters to the unique finger swiping navigation capabilities of these tablets.

Thursday: Optimize the Mobile Version of Your Website

Today you need to learn several best practices for optimizing your mobile website version to better meet the needs of your visitors and convert more of them.

Some of the tools you just learned about will allow you to implement some of these, particularly the more expensive tools like Mobify.com; however, many of these best practices will require you to custom-build your own mobile website. In the long run you should aim to build a custom version by either gathering enough resources to build this in-house, or gaining the budget to outsource the creation of this to an agency. This is even more important to custom build if you have a high percentage of mobile website visitors.

Use a Single Column Layout, Auto-expand Width and Larger Fonts

One of the most important things to do is to make sure your mobile website looks better at a lower resolution. To help you do this, there are three best practices that will also ensure greater usability for your visitors. First you need to limit your mobile website to a single narrow column, and to never make a visitor have to scroll horizontally.

Second, unlike regular websites, your mobile website needs to auto-expand to fill the width of mobile browser resolutions (called responsive web design). This is important because this width can vary hugely between smaller-screen smart phones like the keyboard-based Blackberry phones (as low as 320 pixel width) and the large screens of the iPhone4 and Android phones. However, avoid being tempted to use responsive web design across mobile and your regular websites, as you really need to build separate versions that cater to each type of visitor's needs better.

Last, to make your mobile website version text more readable, you also need to make sure you are using larger fonts than your regular website—this is very important when you consider how small the screen is. Often you can achieve this by using responsive web design, so the smaller the resolution, the larger the font is automatically scaled up.

Optimize the Speed of Your Mobile Website

As discussed earlier this week, visitors are even pickier when it comes to waiting for web pages to load on mobile browsers than on regular browsers and often give up if it takes longer than a few seconds to load.

The best way to optimize and improve the load time of your mobile version is to make it very light in terms of code and design, with minimal usage of images and visual design aspects. Making use of simple CSS code is a great lighter way to achieve a good website design without needing images, and you should also avoid using slow loading visual elements built with JavaScript or Adobe Flash, as these will take much longer to load on mobile websites.

You should also use the web page load time analysis tools that were mentioned in Chapter 5 to measure how fast your mobile pages are loading and to identify any issues to fix.

Focus Your Mobile Pages on Search and Navigation

Given the small screen size and lack of ability to use a mouse to interact with pages on most smart phones, it is much harder to navigate through mobile website versions. Therefore it's critical that you simplify and improve the navigation options on your mobile website to compensate for this.

One of the most important elements to prominently show on all of your mobile pages is a search input box, either at the top (important on home pages) or at the bottom of pages. In the tool box you should also use auto-predict search functionality and spelling correction to assist visitors with their ability to search without a traditional keyboard.

Next you need to make sure you show simplified single-column navigation options that allow the visitor to easily see your category pages, ideally by using drop-down menus because they take up less space. On the home page more space can be devoted to this navigation menu, and you can use icons to help your visitors visually identify categories. For a good example of this, see the Staples.com mobile website in Figure 7.21.

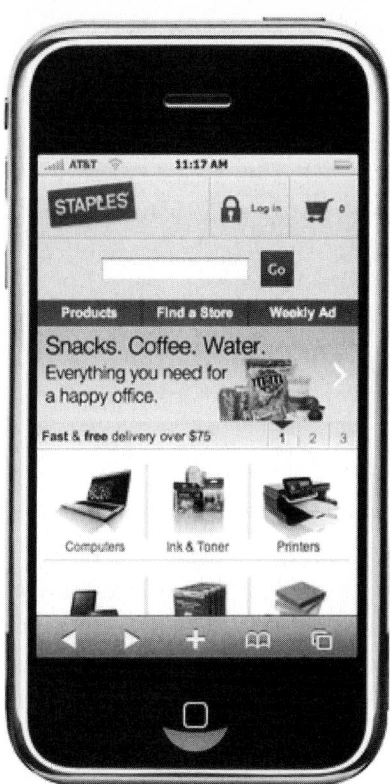

Figure 7.21 Example of a mobile website with good search and navigation options

These best practices are particularly important to apply for mobile website home pages, because if visitors can't immediately understand how to navigate or use a search, they will leave and try and find a mobile website that does a better job with this.

And on your interior mobile pages, you should also make sure you add breadcrumb navigation links at the top as a way of navigating because these are much more useful here than on regular websites.

Think Functional Rather Than Pretty, and Think Clean

Don't waste space on your mobile pages, because every pixel counts—much more than on than a regular website. Try and simplify your pages as much as possible, and really think whether each module or option you are showing is needed or could be shrunk in size.

You should also avoid using overly elaborate visual elements, because these often take up too much space—cleaner and functional mobile web page design is the goal here.

In particular, you should not use promo or banner ads on your mobile pages, because they can take up a huge percentage of the first visible area that a visitor sees, increasing the chances of them not seeing what they want and leaving prematurely.

To help you discover what elements are needed and what are influencing conversions the most, you can also use inclusion/exclusion and real estate tests on your mobile pages.

Put a Link to the Full Site on Each of Your Mobile Pages

One of the simplest but most important things you need to add to the bottom of your mobile web pages is a link to see the regular full website. This is important to offer just in case your mobile version is a scaled-back version and doesn't solve some of your visitors' needs, or they simply want to see the regular full version instead. This is very frustrating for the visitor if they can't do this and is a cause of many unnecessary premature page exits on mobile websites.

Make Your Fields and Buttons Bigger So That Visitors Can Click Them Easier

Research has found that visitors make twice as many mistakes when using buttons and forms on mobile devices than on regular websites. This is because it's much harder to interact with website elements like forms and buttons precisely without using a mouse.

As a result, it's very important to make buttons, form fields and other interactive elements much larger so that visitors can click on and interact with them much easier. This is particularly important to do for form fields that are found on login and register and purchase related pages. This is often known as making your website elements "fat finger" friendly.

Check Your Checkout and Other Key Conversion Flow Pages in a Mobile Browser

If you aren't optimizing your critical conversion flow mobile pages that lead to conversions, then all the great work optimizing the rest of your mobile website will be wasted. This is because visitors will not put up with poorly designed checkouts, registration or signup processes that aren't very usable on mobile smart phones, and will often leave your mobile website to find one that makes it easier for them to use.

In particular on these conversion flow pages, you should make sure your fonts are easily readable and your buttons are easy to see and click.

So go ahead and check how easy it is to use your conversion flow pages, and always get feedback from your visitors using tools discussed in Chapter 4. Overall, to increase your conversion rates you need to make it as easy as possible for your visitors to check out or step through your other key conversion flow pages.

Test Your Mobile Pages to Optimize and Increase Conversion Rates

One last important point to convey is that you shouldn't just build a mobile website, forget about it and move back to testing your regular website. You need to continue to test your mobile website to improve how it engages and converts. You can use many of the test ideas in this book for your mobile pages, particularly regarding buttons, headlines and forms, because they will often have a big impact on your mobile website conversion rates—just make sure they look good and are usable on smaller screens!

Friday: Consider Making an App Version of Your Website

Apps have become wildly popular with the explosion in the use of smart mobile phones like the iPhone and Android phones and have become an excellent way of delivering content in a mobilized, miniaturized fashion. Many savvy marketers have begun to take advantage of this trend by creating app versions of their websites so they can be downloaded on these smart phones or tablets. Yes, doing this will definitely add to the "cool" factor of your website, but rather than just automatically thinking you should do this for your website, there are several things to consider.

First, specific types of websites will benefit more from this. If you have a particularly unique or feature rich website, then these are great candidates for creating an app version of your website. This is because you can take advantage of greater coding and design functionality in apps that are harder to pull off in traditional mobile browsers (for example, because they get downloaded first rather than constantly loaded each time, they can be more bandwidth-intensive). However, there are some drawbacks to this. App versions of websites can be harder to update and control after the visitor has downloaded them, so it's hard to test and push changes live to all of your app website version users easily. They can also be deleted very easily. In other words, don't rely on this option instead of a creating a mobile version.

And last, don't force your visitors to download the app version of your website when they are on your mobile version, as this will frustrate your visitors and cause them to bounce. Ask them once initially, and then only occasionally in the future, not every time.

Keep Them Coming Back—Optimize for Repeat Visits

8

Repeat visitors are often the most engaged type of website visitor and will often convert much higher than first-time visitors. This week you will focus on this to help increase your website conversion rates. You will learn best practices and test ideas that will get more of your website visitors to come back, including how to test and optimize specific web pages and email campaigns to encourage repeat visits.

Chapter Contents

Week 24: Focus on and Generate More Repeat Visits

This week you are going to learn more about the importance of getting visitors to come back to your website. These visitors who are returning to your website are known in web analytics tools as *repeat visits* (or repeat visitors) and can have a great impact on increasing engagement and conversion levels on your website.

Monday: Learn the Importance and Benefits of Repeat Visits

Today you will learn about the importance and benefits of increasing the number of repeat visits on your website.

The major reason is that visitors who come back to your website are usually more interested and engaged in using it than first-time visitors. This is because they have already visited your website, are more likely to know more about it, and often know more about the benefits of using it. Even more important, because they are more engaged, repeat visitors are much more likely to convert for your website goals than first-visitors to your website are.

Therefore, generating a higher number of repeat visits often increases the overall engagement and conversion rates of your website.

Focusing on repeat visitors also has another major benefit; it is usually much cheaper and easier to attract these than trying to attract new visitors. Instead of having to always rely on running extensive and costly online marketing campaigns to attract new visitors, your repeat visitors will come back to your website at little or no cost (unless they use paid search ads to get back to your website).

This is one of the key reasons that more money should be spent initially on optimizing websites before spending considerable budget on driving new visitors to it—it will make your marketing campaigns much more cost effective, because more repeat visitors will come back for free from these as a result of a more optimized website.

A great way to increase the chances of your visitors coming back to your website is to increase the opportunities to capture their email address. This email address often gives you permission to stay in touch with and market to them via email campaigns, and encourage them to return to your website.

Another good way of increasing visits is by creating and promoting content on your website that increases the chances of visitors coming back to use it. If you make them register or sign up to access this content, you will often also get the benefit of using their email address to market to them.

It's also important that you use your web analytics tool to understand which traffic sources your repeat visitors come from most and least, and what content on your website influences them to return. Once you have analyzed this, you can focus on and improve these traffic sources and content so that they increase the number of repeat visits from your visitors.

For the rest of this week, you will learn in more detail about how to get visitors to come back to your website and increase the chance of them engaging and converting.

Tuesday: Check Your Repeat Visits and Analyze for What Causes Them to Come Back

Today you will check your current levels of repeat visits, set a target, and then analyze what is currently causing them to come back most often. This will help you understand how your website is currently performing and creates a benchmark for to review in the future to monitor your efforts to optimize this repeat visit rate. You should also set a target for this too.

The first thing you need to do is check and benchmark your repeat visit rate and then set a target for it. In Chapter 2 you should have already done this, so if you haven't, you need to log in to your web analytics tool and see what your repeat visit rate for the last 30 days is, and then set a realistic target; a 20 percent improvement in this is not unrealistic.

Next, it's important to understand what elements of your website or sources of traffic are causing your visitors to come back. This means you can focus on frequently returning sources to emphasize them further, and understand and optimize sources that aren't currently returning as often that really should be. To do this you need to set up a high return rate visitor segment in your analytics tool, which should be defined as at least five visits per unique visitor per month. To help you do this, refer back to Chapter 2 where you set up other visitor segments.

Setting this visitor segment up allows you to track these frequently returning visitors to help you understand and analyze what they are doing that is causing them to come back, such as their traffic sources or content they visit.

After you have collected a few weeks' data for this high return rate visitor segment, you can start to analyze patterns to help understand what is causing visitors to come back most often. Here are two things to look at that will help you analyze this better:

Top Traffic Sources for High Return Rate Visitors Run a top traffic sources report for your high return rate visitor segment. Once you have analyzed and understand the sources that are high on this report, you should focus and capitalize on increasing those further. You might also notice that some of your traffic sources aren't showing as high as you might have expected on this report, such as from newsletters or other websites, and you should focus on optimizing those sources of traffic better.

Top Pages or Sections That High Return Rate Visitors Are Looking At Run a top pages and sections report for your high return rate visitor segment. This provides great insight into what is engaging your repeat visitors the most, and will give you an idea of what you possibly need to focus on creating more of and increase your repeat visits. This may also reveal major pages or sections on your website that are not often being visited again very often, so you can try and fix and optimize them. This is particular important to examine for your pages that are associated with your conversion goals.

Wednesday: Obtain More Visitor Email Addresses to Market to and Encourage Repeat Visits

One of the best ways to get a visitor to come back to your website is to obtain their email address and send updates and newsletters to them. Because of this, you should increase your efforts to capture as many email addresses as possible. Today you will learn some best practices to help you do this.

However, first it's important to mention that you should always get your visitors to opt-in to receive your emails, and don't buy and import third-party email lists, as emailing un-opted in visitors like this will often come across as spam and get you in legal trouble.

Create a Newsletter and Prominently Promote It on Your Website

One of the easiest ways to obtain more email addresses is to get visitors to sign up for a newsletter on your website that offers value to them. To capitalize on this, try to create a weekly or monthly newsletter that contains latest related industry, product, and news content about your website. This newsletter keeps your website on your visitor's mind and is a great way to get visitors to come back to your website. You should also promote signup to this newsletter across modules on your website and explain the benefits of doing so, which is a subject that will be covered in more detail in Week 25.

Allow Visitors to Sign Up for an Account or Member Profile

Many websites give visitors the option to create an account or a member profile. This usually provides some benefit to the visitor, such as saving their details or enabling them to communicate with other visitors on the website. The benefit of doing this is that when visitors sign up for these, they have to provide their email address. And if they opt-in to receive emails from you, you can send them emails to encourage them to come back.

Therefore, if you don't already offer the ability to create either of these on your website, you should consider offering it as a way to increase the number of email addresses you receive. Then don't forget to promote on your website that you can now register for an account or member profile, and the benefits of doing so.

Offer Visitors Something for Free in Exchange for Email Address

As discussed in Chapter 5 in the theory of reciprocity, giving your visitors something of value for free will increase the chances of them feeling obligated to buy from your website or use it.

When you test offering them something for free on your website, you should make them fill in their name and email address in order to receive it. You could entice them by offering free coupons, a free trial, a free ebook, or a product/industry whitepaper. Not only do you get their email address in order to send the free item to them, but you increase the chances of them engaging/purchasing with you in the future to reciprocate.

This free content is a great traffic driver to your website too, and if you promote this free item well enough on your website (and create marketing campaigns around it), it will greatly increase your traffic levels and the number of email addresses that you get.

However, don't forget to clearly state that you won't spam them when they give their email address to you (which is a subject you will learn about next). You should also only email them about things relating to what they signed up for and not just add them to a general mailing list; otherwise, they will consider this as spam.

Always Reassure the Visitor When Asking for Email Address

Back in Chapter 5 you learned about visitors' common security and privacy concerns when giving their personal information to websites. This is very prevalent when visitors are asked to submit their email address, as many people think they are going to get spammed. If you don't allay these fears and anxieties, you will greatly reduce your ability to generate email addresses to send email marketing campaigns to.

To help address this, next to any form asking the visitor for their email address, you should clearly state your security and privacy policy (with a link to your page that explains this in more detail). In particular, you should state that you won't spam them, sell, or rent their email address. Zappos.com does a very good job of using this messaging, as you can see in Figure 8.1.

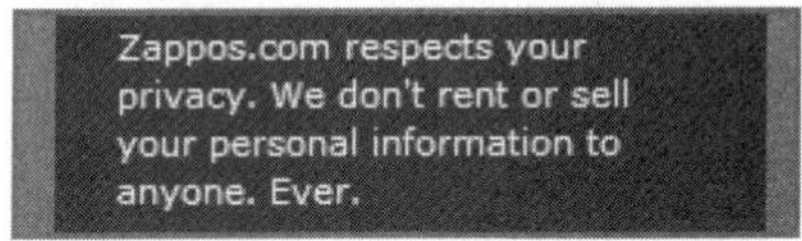

Figure 8.1 Example of email address reassurance messaging

Set Up Auto-Responder and Follow-Up Emails

A great way to increase the chances of visitors coming back to your website is to make better use of the email addresses that you receive. One of the best things you can do is to set up and make use of auto-responder and follow-up emails. This will be discussed more in Week 26.

Next, you will learn that another great way to get email addresses is to create content that not only requires visitors to give their email address to register for it, but also brings visitors back to use it.

Thursday: Create Content That Encourages Visitors to Come Back More Often

To encourage your visitors to come back more often, you should also create content on your website that engages them. Today you will learn some ways to create this engaging content that is designed to bring them back to use it.

Start a Related Online Community

A great way of producing engaging content to bring your visitors back is to create a community section on your website. This allows your visitors to communicate and engage with other members on your website, usually in the form of participating in forums and discussions. This online community should be free of charge, and members should get their own customizable profile and be able to contribute their own content, including discussions, photos, and videos. To help run this, you would need to find a community administrator who is willing to take on this task. You would also need to try and attract a critical mass of users; otherwise, it might not flourish.

There are several inexpensive community platforms that you can use to build and easily customize an online community for your website; Ning (`www.ning.com`) is a particularly good option to evaluate.

Start Creating a Related Blog

Another way to engage your visitors with great content is to create a related blog with engaging original content and prominently show options for visitors to sign up for your blog updates via RSS feeds or email.

If you produce great content for this, it will increase the chance of visitors signing up to receive it. To help you do this, you can use guest authors to write for your blog, including those in related industries. A great source of content can be the contents of your newsletters, which is particularly good if you don't have much time to create additional content for your blog.

To encourage visits to your website from the feed reader, you should use just a snippet of the full blog article when you are creating your RSS feeds, and include a link for them to read the full article. If you don't do this, visitors will simply read your content in their RSS feed reader (like Google Reader) and won't actually visit your website that much (unless you can provide them good reasons in your articles to use other features on your website—then you could let them read the whole article in their feed reader).

A good tool to help you manage and customize your RSS feeds is Feedburner.com (`http://feedburner.google.com`).

Regularly Create Original Content

The better your website content, and the more often you produce new content, the more likely that your visitors will come back to it naturally. This content can also form the backbone of your newsletter campaigns, too. Creating content in a series works particularly well, and you should give your visitors the option to sign up to read these through RSS feeds like those just mentioned.

Creating regular new fresh content is also great to help improve your search rankings because they give rankings boosts to websites that do this.

Friday: Retarget Your Repeat Visitors via Contextual Banner Ads on Other Sites

Today you will learn about an advanced way to bring visitors back to your website that will usually result in much higher engagement and conversion levels from them.

Online advertising technologies have advanced so much recently that you can now use highly relevant banner ads to bring visitors back to your website. This is done by targeting and showing them more relevant ads relating to content they had previously seen on your website. This is known as ad remarketing or retargeting and helps keep your website top-of-mind for when your visitor is finally ready to come back to your website. If and when they click on these ads and come back, they are usually much more likely to convert on your website than normal visitors.

For example, a visitor browses cameras on your website; then the next day they visit one of their favorite other websites and quickly notice banner ads for your website advertising the cameras they had seen on your website. They may notice your prices are cheaper than those on the other sites they have since browsed, click on your banner ad and purchase the camera they wanted on your website. For a visual representation of this, see Figure 8.2.

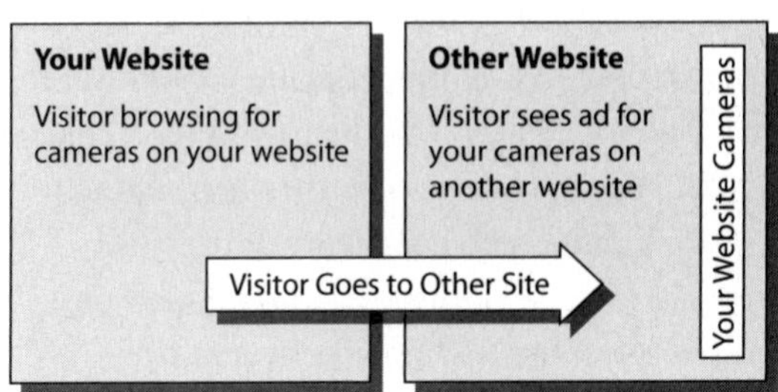

Figure 8.2 Visual representation of ad retargeting

This can be used for many things, not just for advertising products. For example, you could retarget your visitors with ads that explain the benefits of your service, or target them with coupon codes.

You can take your ad remarketing to an even higher level by applying tests in your banners ads to find best performing click through rates, and you can even use advanced targeting to reach particular types of visitor segments who have been on your website.

However, be careful what definitions you use to trigger this future ad remarketing when visitors are on your website. Don't just trigger it for something they see a few times on your website; you need to make sure they really are interested in it before you retarget them. If you don't do this, you will risk wasting these remarketing ads on your visitors, possibly frustrating them if the ads don't really appeal to what they wanted on your website.

To learn more about setting up this ad retargeting, there are a number of options for you to evaluate, including tools within Adobe Test&Target and Google Doubleclick. (`www.google.com/doubleclick`). There are also ad networks that are set up specifically for you to do this, such as AdRetargeting (`www.adretargeting.com`) and AdRoll (`www.adroll.com`).

Even though this is often more expensive than traditional banner advertising, it can often yield much higher visitor return visit and conversion rates. Therefore, if you have the budget to test this, you should definitely consider using this method to bring visitors back to your website.

Week 25: Optimize Your Registration or Sign-Up Pages to Get More Repeat Visits

To increase the number of email addresses you receive from visitors and therefore improve your chances of repeat visits, when visitors sign up or register on your website you need to optimize the related pages for these conversion flows. There are many things you can to do optimize these, and today you will learn some best practices and test ideas for doing this.

Monday: Check the Performance of Your Registration or Sign-Up Pages

First, you need to understand how your registration or sign-up pages are currently performing for conversion rates and other engagement metrics. This helps you set a benchmark that you can later revisit to see how well your optimization efforts have fared for these pages and the resulting many extra visitors that come back from doing this.

To do this, you need to check the completion rate of these page flows and the drop off rates between the pages. As discussed when optimizing checkout conversion flows, you can do this by running a funnel report in your web analytics tool. For example, in Google Analytics you simply pull the Funnel Visualization Report for your registration or sign up flow pages and check for the overall conversion rate of this and the pages that show the highest drop off rate (this first requires you to set up a goal for this conversion flow with all relevant pages within it). This is great for understanding which pages of your flow are problematic and need most optimization attention.

In your web analytics tool, you should also check the exit rate for the first page of your registration or sign-up page, so you can see how engaging it is or how much friction it is causing for your visitors. If the exit rate for this page is higher than 50 percent, you should definitely test and optimize it using best practices found later this week.

Now let's examine some best practices and test ideas for these types of pages that will increase conversions and result in more email addresses for you to send email campaigns to.

Tuesday: Focus on the Benefits of Signing Up or Registering

One of the most important things that your sign-up or registration process needs to convey is the benefits of doing so to your visitors. Today you will learn how to do a better job of this to increase the amount of visitors that complete the process.

A common mistake that many website designers and marketers make is to simply place links to register across their websites and expect visitors to naturally know the reasons why they are being asked to register or sign up or the benefits of doing so. This is because these people are usually far too close to the website and don't put themselves in the shoes of a potential visitor whom they are trying to persuade to register or sign up.

Therefore, you should never presume they know these reasons and benefits, and go ahead and put yourself in your visitors' shoes to see if your website makes the reasons why a visitor would want or need to register or sign up obvious.

The best way to make sure they at least see these benefits is to prominently display these before they arrive on your registration and sign-up pages—for example, on your home page or top entry pages. You should also test using bullet points to convey these benefits, as you learned about in Chapter 6.

It's also particularly beneficial to explain whether it is free to sign up or register, and you should also state how long it takes to complete the process (for example, that it takes less than one minute). This is because visitors are more likely to be persuaded to join or sign up if it is free, and they also like to know how much effort is likely going to be needed from them before they invest time in trying to do so.

If you test all of these best practices you will more than likely get a good boost in the completion rates for your signups and registrations.

Next, it's critical that you then repeat these benefit bullet points on the registration or sign-up pages. An ideal place to repeat these benefits on registration pages is at the very top, or in a sidebar next to the form fields. As you can see in Figure 8.3, Yottaa.com does a great job of showing the benefits of signing up with them (as well as emphasizing that doing so is free).

You should also avoid making use of pop-up windows or light boxes as registration or sign-up pages. While it can often look "cool" on your website to do this, it can often have negative connotations for conversion rates. This is because they often restrict the space to successfully convey benefits and some are hard for the visitor to figure out how to close when not needed or navigate through (often causing them to leave in frustration).

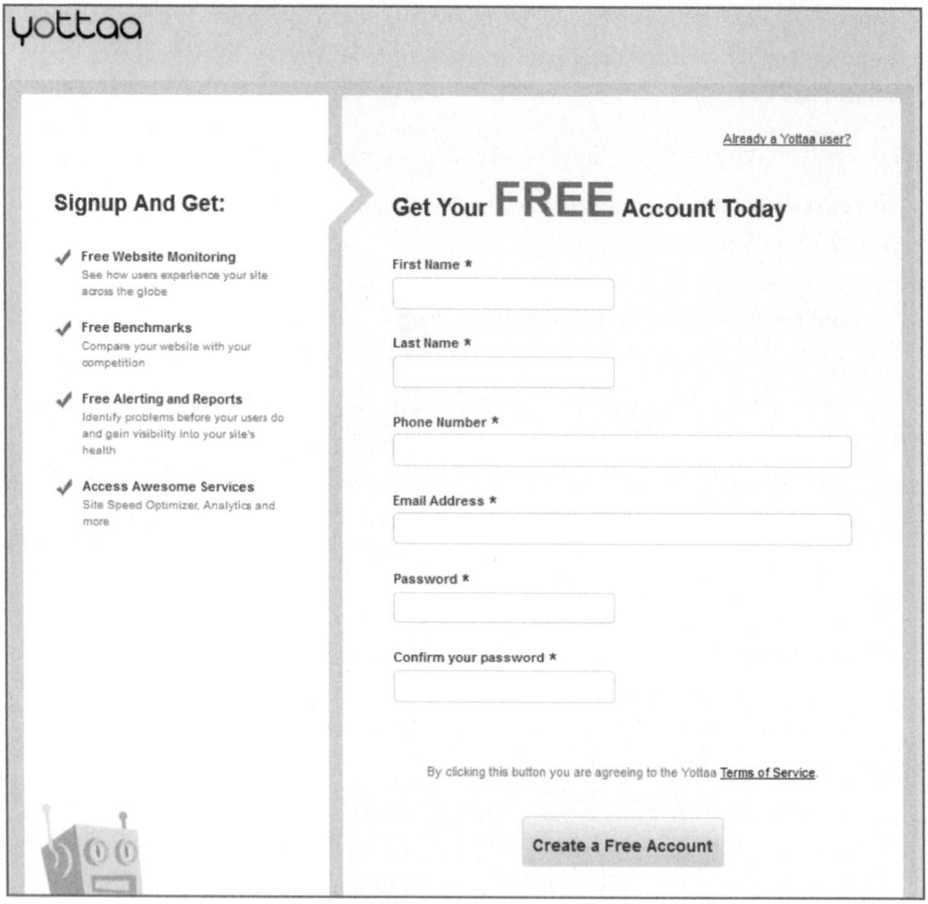

Figure 8.3 Example of showing benefits on a sign-up page

Wednesday: Optimize Your Sign-Up and Registration Forms and Pages

Next, you will learn about other major ways to optimize these sign-up and registration pages. In particular, one of the most critical things to optimize on your registration and sign-up pages is the forms on them that ask your visitors for information. This is because in order for your visitors to successfully register or sign up, they need to complete your form quickly and easily without encountering any frustrations that may cause them to abandon the process.

Remove Unnecessary Fields in Your Forms

One of the simplest and quickest ways to increase completion rates of your forms is to remove fields that aren't really necessary or mandatory.

Just because any extra nonessential information may be valuable to you or your sales team doesn't mean you should ask for it, or even worse, make it mandatory—remember that website visitors are still very wary of giving away their personal information, particularly with the rise of personal identity theft.

Common examples of fields that can have a negative impact on form completion rates and should be considered for removal are date of birth, phone number, and income bracket. To help you find potential fields to remove, go ahead and run inclusion/exclusion tests on your current set of form fields to see which ones negatively impact form completion rates the most.

Asking for More Information during Signup

As a rule of thumb, the more fields you have on a form that you use to ask for more information, the lower the completion rate will be for it. However, some websites that sell high-priced services or products have found that adding more fields to help target the prospect better will actually increase the quality of the leads being submitted, and even though they get fewer leads, they increase the number of sales generated (in other words, fewer leads but higher quality).

State Which Fields Are Mandatory on Your Forms

To help improve your form usability and completion rates, you should place a bolded asterisk next to your form fields that are mandatory, with an explanation of this at the top of the form. This is because it's frustrating for a visitor to not know which fields are mandatory, which often causes incomplete form error messages.

Ideally you shouldn't even have fields that are not mandatory anyway, and you should ask yourself why you even need the field if it's not, and test removing them.

Improve Your Form Completion Error Validation

One of the biggest causes of premature abandonment of a registration or sign-up page is due to poor handling of error messages that appear after a visitor does something wrong when submitting the form. Instead of just refreshing the page with a vague or technical sounding error message at the top of the page, you should employ best practices like highlighting the field in red that contains the error, with red text next to it that explains how to remedy the error. This is known as *contextual error validation* (displaying an error message where the error is). For a good example of this error message handling, see Figure 8.4.

Email	incorrect@email	Email taken or invalid. If you have an account sign in
Password		
Display Name		

Figure 8.4 Good example of form error validation

Another best practice is to use inline validation. This is where each field is validated while your visitors progress through your form, and means they don't have to wait until they submit the whole form to fix any issues found and risk confusing them. For example, you should validate email addresses for the correct format and also check username availability as soon as the visitor clicks out of that corresponding field and onto the next one.

Also, reducing the likelihood of error messages for fields that are left blank is another reason to indicate which fields are mandatory, as just discussed.

So go ahead and review how your forms handle error messages to see how they fare, and then test making these improvements to help increase form completion rates.

Optimize the Number of Steps in Your Registration or Sign-Up Process

Now you know some best practices to optimize the fields in your forms, it's important to optimize the actual steps and process of signing up or registering, and the pages associated with them.

First, if you have numerous pages in your sign-up or registration flow, you should consider testing condensing these to fewer pages. Often having fewer steps to register or sign up can seem less daunting to the visitor and can help increase the chances of them completing the process. Ideally you shouldn't require them to have to go through more than three pages to sign up or register for something, as this will decrease the chance of them completing it.

However, on the flip side, you shouldn't cram all your fields into just one page if you have more than 10 fields, as visitors can be overwhelmed by this and abandon your page, therefore you should test splitting these longer forms up into two pages. Sometimes having a very short first step page will make the visitor think that the sign-up is very easy, and increase the chances of signing. The main point is to test varying the number of page steps to find a flow that increases signup completions the most.

Just as you learned about optimizing a good checkout page flow, you should also make use of a progress bar at the top of the pages and show step numbers. This helps indicate to the visitor how many steps are ahead and where they currently are in the flow.

Thursday: Optimize Your Newsletter Sign-Up Forms

As discussed in Week 24, a great way to encourage people to come back is to create a newsletter and get them to sign up for it. To be able to do this effectively, it's also important to optimize the way that visitors sign up for your newsletters. To help you do this, today you will learn some best practices for optimizing these to increase your newsletter opt-in rates.

Don't Make It Mandatory for Visitors to Fully Register to Receive Your Newsletter

To increase the chances of your visitors signing up for your newsletter, you should require as little information as possible from them to sign up. Other than a form for their email address, the only other thing you might want to include is a field for their name and check boxes to signify which newsletters they want to sign up for (if you have multiple). You can always ask them for more registration information after they have finished signing up for the newsletter.

In a nutshell, don't make them have to sign up for a full account to sign up for your newsletter because this may deter them from doing it.

Test Using Newsletter Sign-Up Modules across Your Website

You should make it as easy and quick as possible for people to sign up whenever they want to; don't make them have to click to a newsletter info page first to be able to sign up.

The best way to do this is by using a newsletter sign-up module that has an email input box and submit button. The best place to have these is in the sidebars or footer of your website because this will also promote your newsletter much better across your website, and will give it more exposure. These modules should also contain links to learn more about the newsletter, a few words about the benefit, and links to your newsletter samples and email privacy policy.

As a good example of a newsletter sign-up module that follows these best practices, Figure 8.5 shows how Zappos.com does it in their footer.

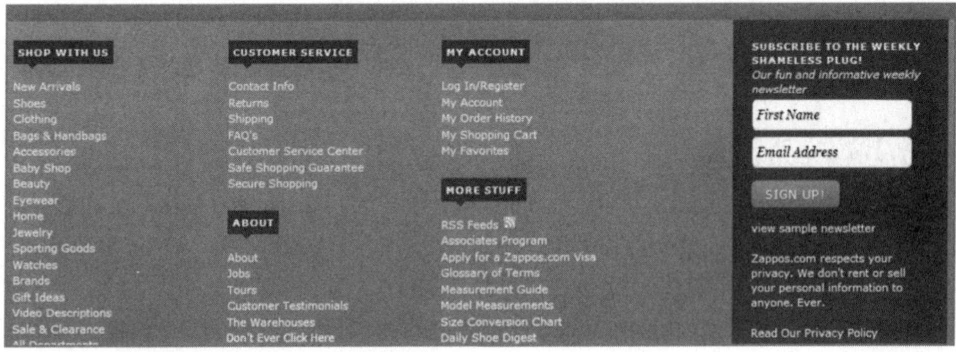

Figure 8.5 Good example of a newsletter sign-up module

Restate Your Email Privacy Policy to Help Relieve Visitors' Email Sign-Up Anxieties

As you learned about earlier in this chapter, to reduce visitor email sign-up anxieties and increase email sign-ups you need to reassure your visitors that their email address will be safe.

One of the best places to restate this is right near your email sign-up buttons. This reassurance messaging should explain that the visitor's email address won't be sold, rented, or used for spam purposes. TravelZoo.com does a great job of trying to relieve this anxiety, as you can see in Figure 8.6.

Join Travelzoo® to get access to the best deals and e-mail alerts:
E-mail: Where do you live? USA ZIP Code: Sign Up ›
Our Promise: The facts | No tricks | No hidden extras | No spam

Figure 8.6 Example of privacy reassurance near sign-up box

You should also provide a link near your sign-up button to your privacy policy page so they can learn more details about it.

Use a Newsletter Details Page to Show Images of It and Benefits

Don't presume that visitors will know the benefit of signing up to your newsletter. To increase the chances of them signing up, you should create and allow them to visit a newsletter details page. This should explain the benefits of signing up (for example to get the latest news or coupons), ideally shown in bullet point format, and also examples of the newsletter, either in the form of links for past newsletters or screenshots.

Friday: Test Other Ways to Increase Completion Rates on Your Registration or Sign-Up Pages

Today you will learn about several other best practices to help increase the completion rates of your registration/sign-up forms, ultimately helping to get your website more repeat visits and better conversion rates.

Test Your Calls-to-Action and Headlines

First, you need to test the wording and style of your calls-to-action (CTAs) and headlines on your sign-up and registration pages. For example, you should test emphasizing words like "free to join" or "takes less than two minutes to join" if any of those are the case. As you will remember from Chapter 6 where you learned much more about this, these headlines and CTAs have a very strong influence on your conversion rates, so you should test and iterate on them for these pages.

Optimize Your Captcha Boxes

Visitor validation tools have now been added to many website sign-up and registration pages. These get visitors to read something and then type in what they see or the answer in order to prove they are human; they are often referred to as CAPTCHA or ReCaptcha boxes. While these benefit the owners of the website by limiting the number of robots and spam coming through, unfortunately they often really frustrate the users of them. A very common complaint from users of these is that the verification words are too hard to read and therefore takes many attempts to complete the form. In really bad cases, visitors will often give up on it, causing them to abandon a sign-up or registration page entirely.

As a result of this issue, you should always check how hard your codes are to read and fix if they are usually too hard and always offer the ability for the visitor to change the phrase or word if they can't understand it. To prove this point, Figure 8.7 shows an example of a very hard CAPTCHA code to read.

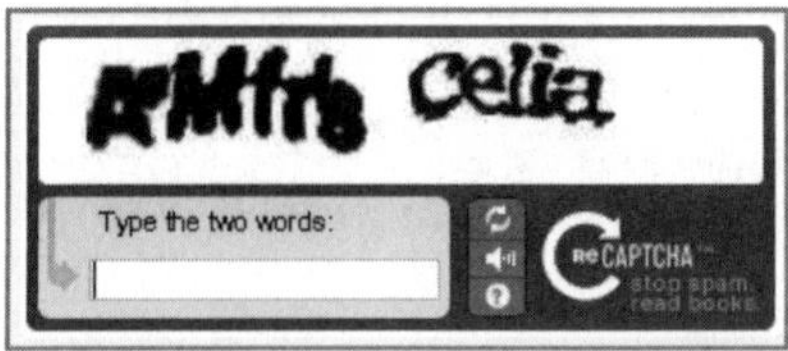

Figure 8.7 Example of hard-to-read ReCaptcha words

As an alternative form of human validation to test, you could ask simple math questions or use the service provided by SolveMedia (`www.solvemedia.com`).

Offer Third-Party Website Registration Functionality

A newer best practice to increase registration and sign-up rates is to skip the need for your visitors to fill in your registration pages altogether, instead allowing the visitor to register with their login credentials from another popular website like Facebook, Yahoo, or AOL.

This functionality allows visitors to instantly register with your website without the need to give their details to your website. Using third party login credentials like this also makes it much easier for your visitor to remember their username and password when they come back to your website, and visitors may often feel safer knowing their login and registration information is not being stored on your website.

Therefore, you should test showing functionality for this prominently on your registration and sign-up related pages and see how much it increases your registration or sign-up completion rates. Figure 8.8 shows a good example of third-party sign-up options to the right of the 1iota.com sign-up page.

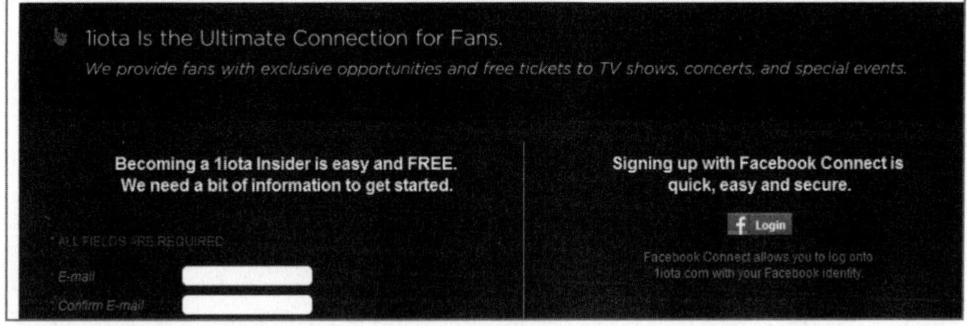

Figure 8.8 Example of offering third-party website registration functionality

Test Your Order, Registration or Sign-Up Confirmation Pages

As mentioned in the shopping cart optimization week (Week 21), online marketers often pay little attention to their website order confirmation pages, which is unfortunate because they are prime candidates for engaging your visitors further to get them to come back and convert for other goals. Your registration, sign-up, and newsletter opt-in confirmation pages are also prime candidates to optimize for these same reasons.

Here are several things you should test adding on your confirmation page, no matter what the confirmation is for:

- Test upselling other related information or products.
- Test adding quick-start steps section so that visitors know what to do next.
- Test adding most popular or most useful links section.
- Test allowing visitors to create a full account (if they haven't already).
- Test allowing visitors to change their newsletter subscription offers.

Next you will learn how to optimize the emails you send to your visitors in attempts to get them to come back and convert.

Week 26: Optimize Your Email Marketing Efforts to Get More Repeat Visits

As you learned about over the last two weeks, once you have got your visitors' email address you can send them email campaigns if they have opted-in. This often results in a much higher chance of generating repeat visits from them and converting them in a future visit for your other conversion goals.

It's important build on this by improving and optimizing your email marketing efforts they receive because doing this will increase the chances of them coming back to your website and engaging and converting. And realize that influencing and converting them doesn't actually end on your website—it should continue in your emails that you send to them.

Regardless of how well you think your email marketing efforts are performing, even if they have very high open rates or click through rates, there are many best practices to help improve them even further. Therefore, for the rest of this week you will learn best practices and test ideas to optimize many types of email marketing campaigns, including your confirmation emails and follow-up emails.

To improve your chances of success with this, it's also important to know that ideally you should have someone within your company dedicated to email testing and optimization efforts.

Before you move on though, you need to take a quick snapshot of your current email marketing performance levels, so that you can measure how effective your improvement efforts have been. To do this, you need to log in into the tool that you use to send your emails, and work out averages for the following key metrics:

- Open rate (percentage of recipients who open an email)
- Click-through rate (percentage of recipients who click a link in the email)
- Click-to-open rate (percentage of openers who click a link in the email)

Monday: Learn Best Practices and Test Ideas for All Email Marketing Methods

Today, you will learn about some best practices and test ideas that apply to any of your methods of email marketing.

Optimize What Your Emails Look Like with Images Turned Off

It's important to realize that many email readers have images turned off as a default setting, which can have a major impact on your emails. If your visitors do have them turned off in their email readers, this results in them not seeing your images, and instead only seeing a small red X and a blank image.

This is particularly problematic if you have images in your emails that consist of or contain calls-to-action, or if the whole email is image based.

There are several ways to help remedy this issue. First you should always make sure you place alt tags on any of your images, as these word tags will show instead. Next you should also make use of additional text links in your emails for your calls-to-action to increase the chances of them being seen.

To fix this you can also try using CSS to create your buttons instead of using images, or you can try combining background images with regular text to achieve the same look of an image, which is good because this will also still show the button text if they have images turned off.

Optimize What Your Emails Look Like on Mobile Phones

A significant amount of internet users are now reading their mail on smart mobile phones like iPhones and Android phones. According to a recent study by the Relevancy Group, as many as 39 percent of consumers currently access one or more of their personal email accounts on a mobile device. Therefore, you need to check what your emails look like on the leading mobile devices and their much smaller screens to identify and fix any issues you see.

Offer Alternatives If Readers Want to Unsubscribe from Emails

If visitors click on the unsubscribe link in your emails, rather than simply letting them unsubscribe on your website, you should suggest other similar newsletters or alerts that they may be interested in. Or you could suggest that they can change how often they receive emails that they get, so they get them less often. Bloomingdales.com has a great example of this on their unsubscribe page, as you can see in Figure 8.9.

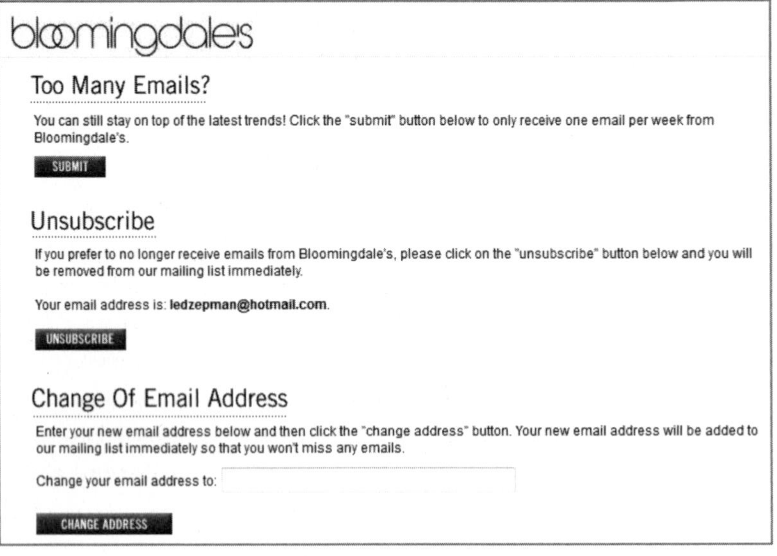

Figure 8.9 Example of offering alternatives to un-subscribers

Check and Improve Your Email Delivery and Bounce Rates

While it's important that you optimize the contents of your emails, you also need to increase the chances of your visitors even receiving your emails in the first place. Various things can cause an email to not get delivered (like spam) or bounce (such as emails that get returned to the sender because the email address no longer exists).

One of the main things you need to ensure is that your emails don't get considered as spam by email account providers. Any good email marketing provider should offer options to spam check emails, so you should use this option to ensure higher delivery rate every time you are sending a major email campaign.

Another good way to increase the chances of your email being delivered is to include a link at the top of your emails that asks the visitor to add your online businesses' send email address to their address book to ensure future delivery of your emails.

You should also ensure that your email service provider is doing their most to ensure very high delivery rates and low bounce rates, as this can vary in quality depending on cost of service.

Get Subscribers to Opt-In to Your Emails

Lastly, it's important to reiterate that you need to get your visitors to opt-in to receive your marketing emails before you do so, otherwise they will be considered spam. This opt-in involves them checking a box on one of your sign-up or registration forms saying they agree to receive emails (for example future updates, news or offers), and then send them an automated email asking them to confirm their opt-in request. If you send emails to addresses that haven't been opted in, this will increase the chance of your getting spam complaints from the recipients, getting your emails blacklisted, and possibly getting your online business in legal trouble.

Tuesday: Run Email A/B Tests to Find the Most Engaging Emails

Just as it's very important for you to run many tests to optimize your website, you also need to run many tests in your emails to optimize them. This will ensure that your emails meet the needs of your readers better, and increase the chances of them being engaged by your emails and returning to your website, hopefully to convert for your goals.

Therefore, today you will learn some great test ideas for optimizing your emails. First though, let's review some ways of testing in your emails.

If you are using an advanced email marketing tool, it should include some ability to do email A/B testing. This enables you to send completely different versions of emails to your visitors to see which ones convert better.

If you don't have an email marketing tool that offers testing capabilities (or has poor capabilities) you should consider upgrading to one that offers this, such as MailChimp (`www.mailchimp.com`), dotMailer (`www.dotmailer.com`), or Lyris (`www.lyris.com`).

As another option for you to consider, some advanced testing tools like Adobe Test&Target allow you to test images in your emails (only images because text can't be switched out in emails very easily using testing tools).

Test Your Email Subject Lines

Testing your subject lines is the first thing you should be doing because it's the easiest and most important thing to optimize your emails and increase open and response rates. If you don't optimize them and your subscribers don't even open your email, then it doesn't matter how much time or effort that you put into optimizing the content of your emails because they won't even be seen.

Go ahead and start doing some testing of your subject lines to see if you can improve your open rates. Here are some best practices for testing subject lines:

- Put your most important point at the start of it, in case it gets cut off.
- Keep it relatively short.
- Use personalization.
- Spark their interest.

Don't just optimize one set of email subject lines either. You should ideally test the subject line before you send any large email campaign to increase response rates because each campaign is likely to have different goals and need different approaches to increase open rate. To find more ideas for testing subject lines, refer back to Chapter 6 for best practices on writing headlines, as these also work well here.

Use Name Personalization in Subject Line and Email Content

Personalizing emails can really help increase open rates and click-through rates. This is because studies have shown that people love hearing and seeing their name and are more likely to be engaged when it's used effectively. Using personalization also makes your email readers think that the person sending the email already knows you, which usually builds trust and the likelihood of them opening or responding to the email.

Most email marketing tools allow you to personalize your email by inserting the recipient's first name or full name in the subject line or email body. To understand the likely great impact on your open rates, go ahead and create a few tests that insert the recipient's name into the subject line and the greeting (for example, "Hi Rich, Have you seen…").

Segment and Target Your Emails to Make Them More Relevant

As you have learned throughout this book, targeting content that is more relevant to different visitor groups is a great way to increase conversions. You can do the same for your email marketing efforts to increase the chances of them engaging and clicking through to your website. This can be done in most advanced email marketing tools.

In other words, don't just send all of your email subscribers the same emails; you need to target particular visitor groups better. For example, you should segment your visitors who haven't opened any email from you or visited your site in several months and send them an email encouraging them to come back. You could also try sending follow up emails to users if they don't open the initial email within a set time period. As another good idea, you could also segment and target your email recipients by city or state to make regional offers.

Shorten Your Emails

It's important to design your emails to be shorter to increase the chances of someone reading and engaging with them. Recent studies from MarketingExperiments.com have shown that halving the number of words on emails increased click-through rates by 16 percent. The best way to do this is reduce long blocks of text and use bullet points instead, using the best practices you learned about in Chapter 6.

In addition to this, your email text should provide teasers to entice the reader to come back to your website to see more (with usage of "read more" links). Don't just cut and paste chunks of content from your website, with no call to action to read more on your website.

Test Including Useful Links at the Top of Your Emails

To help highlight key articles or important links in your emails, you should test adding a useful links menu area at the top of your emails. This should include links for your main calls-to-action and articles or features in your emails, or links for the major categories on your website. It should also include useful links for changing subscription options (including unsubscribe), deliverability tips, and a way to view the email in a web browser.

This lets your email readers know the most important links in your email and ensures that your best content is shown in the email preview pane, which is often not very tall.

This is also important to do for your emails that contain a considerable amount of different content, like your newsletters. Figure 8.10 shows a good example of this in Family.com's newsletter.

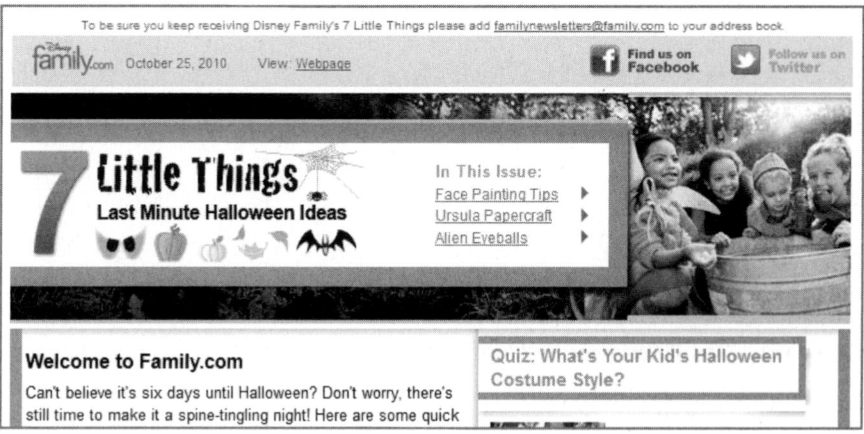

Figure 8.10 Example of useful header links in an email

Test Different Headlines and Calls-to-Action

Last, and very important, remember to test your headlines and calls-to-actions because these usually have the greatest influence on whether your visitor engages with your email and clicks through to your website. Use the best practices discussed in Chapter 6 to optimize these.

Wednesday: Create and Optimize Your Confirmation Emails

Another important way to help increase email engagement and the chances of visitors coming back to your website is to use great confirmation emails. Done right, this email can set great future expectations, but if done poorly or not all, it can frustrate and alienate a potential repeat visitor. To help you with this, today you will learn some best practices that you should adopt and test in your confirmation emails.

Optimize Your Product Order Confirmation Emails

If the visitor has just ordered something from your website, not only do you need a good order confirmation page (as discussed previously), but you also need to send them an order confirmation email immediately.

This should contain full details of their order, costs, expected delivery date (or download links if the product is web based), and customer support details. If you are shipping their order, ideally you should also include a link so that the customer can actually track their shipment.

To encourage repeat purchases from them, you should include any relevant coupons or discounts in this that apply to future purchases. You could also consider testing adding upsell items, or items related to what they just purchased. Just make sure you keep it relevant and not overly sales-like.

Optimize Your Registration Confirmation and Welcome Emails

If the visitor has just registered or signed up on your website, rather than just sending them a basic email registration confirmation to say thanks, you should do much more with this.

Instead, you should turn this into a welcome email that also contains recommended next steps for the visitor to take, and top content they would likely be interested in. This will increase the chances of the visitor understanding what they should do next and how to make best use of your website, resulting in them coming back to your website more often.

Thursday: Create and Optimize Your Follow-Up Emails

If you are selling products or services that require more significant efforts to get your website visitors to buy them, you should consider using a carefully selected series of follow-up auto-sent emails to try and convert them over a longer period of time. For example, if you are offering a free trial of something, you can use these follow-up emails to gradually educate them on reasons they should purchase the full service—no need to rely on hard-selling them in your regular marketing campaigns.

A well-created series of follow-up emails can actually make your readers think you are personally sending emails to them and having a one-to-one conversation with them, often increasing their level of engagement and chances of them returning to your website and converting in the future.

These are different from regular newsletter emails, retail news email updates, and marketing emails, because these follow-up emails have the express goal of trying to get the visitor to purchase over a series of carefully created auto emails.

To help you create, manage, and automate the sending of these, you need to use specialist email marketing tools like Aweber (`www.aweber.com`) or Constant Contact (www.constantcontact.com). Some other more generic email marketing tools offer some limited automated follow-up email functionality too.

To increase the likelihood of recipients of these coming back to your website and eventually converting, today you will learn what to put in these follow up emails and how to make best use of them. This should be used in conjunction with the other email best practices covered earlier this week. And don't forget to make sure they opt-in to receive these emails first before you send them!

Plan a Good Series of Follow-Up Emails and Vary Their Contents

The first thing you should do is create a long term plan for your follow-up emails that is designed to engage and get your readers to come back to your website and convert them over a period of months. Don't just send many follow-up emails over the first week and then stop, because not only will this increase the chance of spam complaints, it will limit your chances of longer term success.

For the first few of your follow-up emails you should provide as much value to your readers as possible and avoid selling or promoting anything, or you will risk them unsubscribing or accusing you of spam (even though they have opted-in). Only once the visitor has built up trust with your emails can you do this.

For example in the first follow-up email you could ask for feedback, then the next week focus on "best of" or helpful articles, and then in a future week focus on a specific product or service benefit. Varying the type of emails you send will keep them engaged longer and increase the chances of them eventually converting.

Make Your Emails Seem Like They Are a One-to-One Communication

A great way to increase the effectiveness of your follow-up emails is to make them seem more personal and not just mass-emails. This is best done by personalizing the email with the reader's name in the subject line and welcome message. (You could even test placing a signature at the end of the footer with your name on it.) Readers are often more likely to click links in personal sounding emails like these than ones that seem like mass generic emails that sound like they are being sent to hundreds of people at once.

Use Different Follow-Up Emails for Prospects and Customers

If you eventually manage to convert your reader over time through these follow-up emails, you should take them off this initial follow-up list and move them to a customer follow-up list instead. By doing this you can send them support and "how-to" emails to help them make better use of the product or service they just purchased. If you don't do this, you will frustrate your visitors by trying to get them to purchase something they have already purchased, and they will unsubscribe (and possibly complain of spam).

Friday: Try Using Advanced Email Optimization Techniques

Today you will learn about some other advanced email optimization techniques to increase the chances of your visitors coming back and converting.

Test Using Shopping Cart Recovery Auto-Emails

Sending shopping cart recovery emails can work very well for enticing shopping cart abandoners back to your website to complete their conversion. In fact in a recent survey by eConsultancy, 84 percent of companies who sent emails targeting cart abandoners saw an increase in conversions. Yet the same report stated that relatively few online marketers actually use this tactic, so using it represents a great way of gaining competitive advantage, too.

In their most basic form, these auto-triggered emails can just be a subtle reminder to your visitors that they still have items left in their shopping cart. This is something that Amazon.com makes use of that you may have encountered before.

You should test making more advanced use of these though. Many online marketers have had great results by using wording in them to communicate urgency—for example, that prices may go up soon or items may not remain in stock for much longer. You could also try and influence them to complete their purchase by offering discounts relating to purchasing it.

Figure 8.11 shows a good example of a shopping cart recovery email being sent from Alaska Airlines.

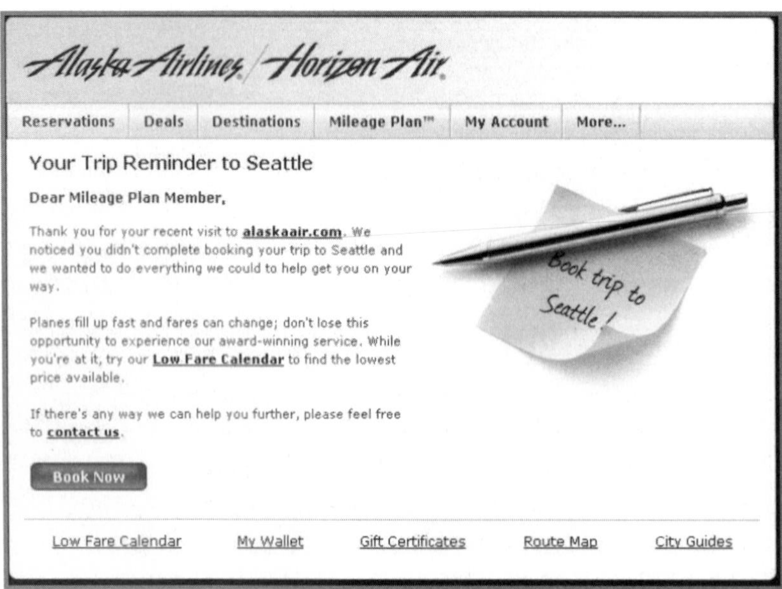

Figure 8.11 Example of a shopping cart abandonment email

It is best to send these emails shortly after visitors abandon your shopping cart because this is the most critical time to get them back to your website before they forget completely (strike while the iron is still hot).

To help you create these advanced emails, there are companies that specialize in offering these advanced email marketing services such as SeeWhy (www.seewhy.com) and RedEye (www.redeye.com), which also offer other trigger-based email services.

You can also set these up by linking your email marketing platform to your web analytics tool, and synching up data for when a visitor triggers a certain event (abandoning shopping cart) to then push this event alert to the email tool, which looks up the email address of the visitor (if they have been there before and registered) and sends the shopping cart recovery email to them. You will need to work with a web analytics consultant to implement this on your web analytics tool and email marketing system though because this not an easy process.

Send Reminder Emails for Inactive Registered Users

Don't just rely on your visitors coming back to your website naturally, because they will often forget about you after a while. In order to get these inactive visitors to come back to your website, you need to try pulling them back using email reminders.

This is best done by setting up functionality that enables you to send auto-timed emails to registered users based on periods of account or login inactivity. For example if a visitor hasn't logged in for 60 days, or hasn't posted in your community for 90 days, this could trigger an auto-email reminder to them.

In those emails you should mention some of the benefits of your website, which they may have forgotten about, and new features. To convey these reminder messages in your emails, you need to say something like, "Hi there, we noticed that you haven't logged in for over 60 days and wanted to check in to remind you of X." You could also try enticing them back by offering special coupons.

Send Emails to Purchasers for Reviews of Recent Purchases

Sending emails to recent purchasers asking them for a review is not only a great way to get more reviews for building social proof of your website, but it is also a great way of engaging and getting them to come back to your website. These auto-emails should be trigger-based and sent about a few weeks after a visitor makes a purchase and not sent immediately (this gives them time to receive it and make initial use out of it).

If you are lacking reviews on your website, to encourage more you could offer some kind of incentive for them to give one, like a discount on a future purchase.

9 Review and Learn From Your Results, and Keep Testing and Optimizing

In this last chapter, you will review and learn from your website optimization efforts over the last few months. You will also learn how to take action to get the most out of your optimization and testing efforts in the future. Remember that website optimization isn't just a one-off project—it should form a continual critical part of your online business strategy.

Chapter Contents

Week 27: Review and Learn from Your Optimization Efforts So Far

In this last and very important week, you need to review and learn from your website optimization results so far and see just how far you have come with your efforts. In particular, you need to review your test results and their impact on your success metrics and website conversion rate, and then review how your internal organizational optimization efforts have been faring.

Monday: Revisit Your Success Metrics and Targets

Before you tackle the rest of this week, you need to have been using the best practices and test ideas described in this book for at least two or three months. This is important because it takes some time for all your efforts to begin to work together to impact your success metrics and conversion rates.

The first thing you need to do is review Chapter 2 for the key success metrics for your type of website and check the targets you set for each of them. Then you need to log in to your web analytics tool and pull the last seven days of data from it to see how they compare to your target. If you have improved your web analytics weekly reports to include all these success metrics, it will make it much easier for you to check these (and great job for adding those!)

Hopefully after two or three months of testing and optimizing your website, you should have seen some percentage point lifts for many of your success metrics and overall website conversion rate. If you have double-digit percentage lifts, then you have been doing a fantastic job. For any success metrics that still seem to be low and not improving, you need to devote more time in the next few months gaining more insight into these and testing some different ideas on problematic pages.

Specifically, you need to make sure your conversion rates are improving for your home page and key conversion flow pages (whether this is your checkout flow or a conversion flow more unique to your website). And don't forget to check to see how your efforts have fared to improve your traffic source first steps of these conversion flows, too.

Another significant indicator of your optimization success so far is to revisit and check your repeat visit rate. A well-optimized website is likely to have your visitors coming back far more often than before. So go ahead and log in to your analytics tool to review your new repeat visit percentage for the last seven days; it should be higher than it was when you first checked in Chapter 2. If it's not much higher, revisit Chapter 8 and consider trying some of the other ideas that you may not have tried yet, such as setting up a related online community, blog, or newsletter. While these may seem hard to create and run, the benefits can quickly add up.

It's also very important that you don't stop testing just because you may have seen some good lifts in your success metrics and conversion rates. As you learned about in Chapter 4's testing best practices, you really need to be learning and iterating from your tests to achieve even higher conversion rates and success metric lifts. If you have beaten any of your targets (or are close to beating them) you should now set some new ones to try and beat over the next three months. Then you need to continually check these success metrics and conversion rates on a quarterly basis, and set more targets for them each time.

Tuesday: Review Your Use Case Completion Rates and Resurvey Your Visitors

Next you need to revisit the use cases you created for your website in Chapter 4 to see if these are any easier to complete. These use cases are the most common important things that visitors need to easily achieve on your website. Ideally, your website optimization efforts have not only improved your success metrics and conversion rates, but also made it easier for your visitors to complete these major use cases.

And bear in mind that sometimes you may have inadvertently pushed a winning test that actually makes it harder for visitors to complete a use case, or you may have launched some new content or functionality that makes it harder, too.

Therefore, you should revisit the use cases that you created in Chapter 4, and try doing each one on your website, regrading the ease of completion. Some of them should have higher completion grades—at the very least they need to be just as easy to complete as before. You also need to use the website feedback tools like Loop11 or UserTesting that were discussed in Chapter 5 and see if your website visitors can complete your use cases well enough (hopefully even easier). This puts your use cases to the ultimate test.

If you find use cases that are still no easier (or worse) to complete by you or your visitors, you need to devote extra time over the next few weeks to try and optimize related pages for the use cases that are problematic and improve the visitor journey through completing it.

Next, you need to continue to involve your visitors' all-important opinions and feedback and rerun the visitor website surveys that you set up in Chapter 5. It is important to hear their latest voice on things you may have changed or launched through your optimization efforts, and when you are setting up the survey questions you should ask questions about those topics. You should also try gaining visitor feedback by asking questions on your web-chat tool if you have added one of those on your website.

Remember that ideally you should get visitor feedback before launching any major change to your website, because a negative response from them can have major negative impact on your conversion rates.

Wednesday: Rerun the Website Optimization Checklist

While reviewing your optimization efforts over the last two or three months, you may be excelling in some areas, but not in others, and it's important that you pinpoint these areas needed for improvement. For example, you may be doing a great job of testing your shopping cart and home page, but you may not be doing much targeted testing or gaining very much insight from your visitors.

To make sure you are doing as much as you can to optimize your website, you need to revisit the website optimization checklist found in Chapter 3. Go ahead and answer each question in Table 9.1, which is a blank copy of the same checklist. To really make sure you have a well-rounded website optimization program you need to make sure you are ticking as many of these yes checkboxes as possible—and be as honest as you can too!

Table 9.1 Website optimization checklist

	Question	Yes	No
1	Does your company currently run more than one test per month?		
2	Does your company use a website testing tool better than Google Website Optimizer?		
3	Does your company have more than two members of staff dedicated to testing?		
4	Do you have a website optimization executive sponsor to help you gain budget and buy-in from key stakeholders?		
5	Does it take your company less than two weeks to get a test prioritized?		
6	Does it take your company less than two weeks to implement a test?		
7	Does your company act on test results and do follow up tests to improve (iteration tests)?		
8	Does your company use your web analytics tool to generate insights for testing?		
9	Does your company make use of any visual analysis tools to gain visitor insight, particularly for ideas for testing?		
10	Does your company use usability and feedback tools to gain visitor insight, particularly for task rate completion analysis?		
11	Has your company created key use cases for your website?		
12	Does your website make use of multiple social proof elements like reviews and testimonials?		
13	Does your company use targeting for your testing to improve your visitor experience and conversion rates?		
14	Does your company have a test plan and strategy for at least the next 6 months?		
15	Has your company tried testing your key conversion flows like checkout pages?		
16	Has your company tested your key entry pages?		
17	Has your company tested your call-to-action buttons?		
18	Has your company tested your headlines and other text?		
19	Has your company tested your email marketing campaigns?		
20	Has your company set up and tested a mobile version of your website?		

After you have gone through the questions in this checklist, go back and look at how you originally scored back in this checklist found in Chapter 3. You should have added at least five yes checkmarks; if not, then you need to spend more time focusing on these efforts with some help from other team members (or website optimization consultants). You should also note down anything on this checklist that you still haven't done yet, and pay particular attention to trying those in the next few months.

Thursday: Review What You've Learned from Your Test Results to Create Better Future Tests

Today, you need to review two very important other things. First, you need to review your test results for learnings to help you create better future tests. Second, you need to review how your internal efforts and processes have been working to set up and run these tests and identify areas of improvement that are still needed.

To get started, go ahead and spend some time reviewing all the tests that you have run, and find the ones that have the highest impact on success metrics and revenue. You should be able to detect some patterns or trends with your best performing tests; maybe particular visitor segments are always performing better or particular modules across your pages are highly influential on conversion.

Don't just ignore your bad test results though; you should also look at the ones that had a negative impact. Then you need to try and understand why that might be the case, and to look for any common patterns or issues. For example, certain people may be continually contributing bad test ideas, or you may find you are often using poor choices for multivariate tests.

Performing this review is critical because you need to continually iterate from your test results to create ones with even better results in the future.

While you are reviewing your test results for common findings from best and worst results, you also need document your key findings. This is because you need to create a presentation to review with your testing key stakeholders. Reviewing this with them will help inform them of your progress and will help you build a testing culture and an optimization organization (your recent efforts to build this will be reviewed next).

Also, if your testing has really paid off and you are getting amazing ROI, this is a great time to ask for increases in testing budget by presenting some of your best test results to your senior management. Gaining increases in the budget might mean you can start using another visitor feedback tool, hire another testing team member, or invest in a better testing tool, all of which are going to be very helpful on your path toward an effective long-term website optimization program.

Friday: Review and Improve Your Internal Testing Process Performance

As you learned in Chapter 3, one of the most critical things to realize is that you need much more than just a testing tool; you need an organization that is set up to deliver a high number of high-impact tests—an optimization organization.

Hopefully, you have identified and begun to address some of your problematic internal barriers and HiPPOs that were covered in Chapter 3 and begun to crack some of the biggest issues embedded within your organization that may have prevented you from testing effectively and efficiently.

Therefore, next you need to take some time to review how your efforts have progressed toward growing this optimization organization. Go ahead and create a report on what has been working well and what still needs improving. You will present this, along with your test results findings, in a quarterly review meeting that you will be planning. Use this list of optimization organization elements to review in particular:

Building Internal Relationships First you need to review how your efforts have been progressing in terms of building relationships with other key departments. For example, is it easier and quicker to work with your IT department than before you started reading this book? And is your design and brand team any easier to work with than before?

Working with Project Management Next you need to understand if you are you still having troubles with project management to prioritize and launch your tests. At the very least you should have identified issues and begun to formulate a plan with them to improve how your website tests and resulting winner launches get prioritized—ideally in a scrum or agile environment.

Obtaining an Executive Sponsor You should have also managed to pinpoint and start leveraging an executive sponsor by now because having one is critical to help you obtain testing and budget resources and test prioritization at the executive level.

Expanding the Testing Team Have you managed to expand your team at all yet? At the very least you should have the budget approved and be writing the job specification for new testing members and have one in place within two or three months. You should consider outsourcing this new role initially if you are having issues with finding or obtaining budget for this person; there are many great optimization companies or agencies that can help fill this for you.

Starting Weekly and Quarterly Testing Reviews Hopefully, you have already started running weekly website optimization review meetings to go over your optimization efforts and to plan new tests. You should have planned your first quarterly review meeting too, as one of the key things you need to do next is to set up an initial one of these meeting to go over your testing and internal process findings that are being reviewed in this week.

You should also have started sending regular testing email updates because not only do these help keep everyone in the loop regarding your testing efforts, but they are also key to helping build a testing culture. You should also have already started running or preparing testing training sessions for your team members because these can be a very cost effective way of improving testing skill sets of your team.

After you have done this review of your internal optimization process, the next step is to go ahead and schedule a first quarterly testing and optimization review meeting with all of your key stakeholders. Here you will review the report that you have been creating this week that summarizes your learnings from test results and how your testing process has been working and what needs improving. This review will be vital to fuel your website optimization and testing efforts over the next quarter to keep up momentum and should help you come up with a list of new things to test and process improvements to work on.

Also, it's important to keep your eye on the progress that your company is making toward becoming a full-fledged website optimization organization. The best way to understand this is by printing out and studying the website optimization lifecycle that was discussed in Chapter 3 and continually drive your online business toward the last step of it, the optimization organization. And remember to consider outsourcing and partnering some of your testing efforts so you can learn and gain more expertise that is necessary for this type of organization.

Keep Optimizing and Testing: Your Website Is Never Perfect!

Just because you have read and implemented some of the best practices and test ideas in this book doesn't mean your work is done or nearly over. This is because website optimization is a continual process—a journey, not a destination. Ideally, testing should form the bedrock of your online strategy, and nothing should be launched without testing and optimizing it first.

Finally, you also need to realize that your website is never perfect; you shouldn't think of it as completely finished. You are likely to be (and should be) continually adding new features, functionality, and content that will need optimizing and testing to better engage and convert your visitors.

Because of this, I suggest you pick up and review this book every six months and apply the best practices and test ideas on anything that has changed on your website (and remember, parts of your website may often change without you even knowing it—many companies build or change different parts of websites in silos). Rereading this book will also serve as a good refresher and reminder of the best practices in the four necessary disciplines of website optimization: web analytics, website usability, online marketing, and website testing. In fact you should go ahead right now and put this time in your calendar to help remind you to review this book again in the future.

You should also always be on the lookout for new things to improve and test on your website. One of the best ways to do this is by keeping up to date with the latest website optimization techniques, case studies, and tools. To help you keep informed with this you should subscribe to the many optimization blogs that are listed here: `http://bit.ly/optimization-blogs`

Another way to come up with test ideas in the future is by using competitive intelligence that you learned about in Chapter 4. Therefore, you should run quarterly checks on your competitors' websites and industry-leading websites to see what new things they are doing to come up with some new test ideas (and go ahead and schedule this time in your calendar too).

And last, don't give up if you have a few bad test results, either. Indeed, it can often take several iterations of your tests to find some that really hit home in terms of conversion and success metric lift. If you really are struggling to make any progress toward optimizing your website after reading this book, you should find a good website optimization consultant or agency to help you.

See you in another six months when you review this book again, hopefully with an even more optimized website!

A

Website Optimization and Testing Tools

Tool Name	Type of Tool	Cost of Tool	Level of Tool Functionality	Chapter Where Tool Is Described
Google Analytics	Analytics—Regular	Free	Basic	Chapter 2
KISSMetrics	Analytics—Regular	Budget	Intermediate	Chapter 2
Clicky	Analytics—Regular	Budget	Intermediate	Chapter 2
Adobe SiteCatalyst	Analytics—Regular	Expensive	Advanced	Chapter 2
CoreMetrics	Analytics—Regular	Expensive	Advanced	Chapter 2
Webtrends	Analytics—Regular	Expensive	Advanced	Chapter 2
Google Website Optimizer	Testing	Free	Basic	Chapter 2
Optimizely	Testing	Budget	Basic	Chapter 2
Visual Website Optimizer	Testing & Targeting	Mid-range	Intermediate	Chapter 2
Unbounce	Testing	Budget	Basic	Chapter 2
Adobe Test&Target	Testing & Targeting	Expensive	Advanced	Chapter 2
Autonomy Optimost	Testing & Targeting	Expensive	Advanced	Chapter 2
SiteSpect	Testing & Targeting	Expensive	Advanced	Chapter 2
Monetate	Testing & Targeting	Expensive	Advanced	Chapter 2
MockFlow	Wireframing	Budget	Intermediate	Chapter 3
BTBuckets	Targeting	Free	Basic	Chapter 3
Cognitive Match	Targeting	Budget	Intermediate	Chapter 3
Quantcast	Competitive Intelligence	Free	Basic	Chapter 4
Compete	Competitive Intelligence	Free	Basic	Chapter 4
Crazy Egg	Analytics—Visual	Budget	Basic	Chapter 4
GazeHawk	Eye Tracking	Mid-range	Intermediate	Chapter 4
Attention Wizard	Eye Tracking	Budget	Basic	Chapter 4
ClickTale	Analytics—Recording	Mid-range	Intermediate	Chapter 4
Userfly	Analytics—Recording	Budget	Basic	Chapter 4
TeaLeaf	Analytics—Recording	Expensive	Advanced	Chapter 4
4Q	Survey	Free/Budget	Basic	Chapter 4
SurveyMonkey	Survey	Free/Budget	Intermediate	Chapter 4
OpinionLab	Survey	Expensive	Advanced	Chapter 4
Adobe Survey	Survey	Expensive	Advanced	Chapter 4
ForeseeResults	Survey	Expensive	Advanced	Chapter 4
KISSInsights	Survey	Free/Budget	Basic	Chapter 4
Get Satisfaction	Feedback & Ratings	Budget	Intermediate	Chapter 4
UserVoice	Feedback & Ratings	Mid-range	Intermediate	Chapter 4

Tool Name	Type of Tool	Cost of Tool	Level of Tool Functionality	Chapter Where Tool Is Described
Kampyle	Feedback & Ratings	Expensive	Intermediate	Chapter 4
UserTesting.com	Usability & Task Completion	Mid-range	Intermediate	Chapter 4
Loop11	Task Completion	Budget	Basic	Chapter 4
Usabilla	Usability & Task Completion	Mid-range	Intermediate	Chapter 4
User Zoom	Feedback—Multiple Types	Expensive	Advanced	Chapter 4
Concept Feedback	Expert/Visitor Feedback	Free/Budget	Intermediate	Chapter 4
BoldChat	Web Chat	Budget	Intermediate	Chapter 4
SnapEngage	Web Chat	Budget	Intermediate	Chapter 4
LivePerson	Web Chat	Expensive	Advanced	Chapter 4
Google Browser Size	Layout Check	Free	Basic	Chapter 5
CrossBrowserTesting	Browser/Resolution Check	Budget	Intermediate	Chapter 5
Adobe Browser Lab	Browser/Resolution Check	Free	Basic	Chapter 5
BrowserShots	Browser/Resolution Check	Free	Basic	Chapter 5
Google Page Speed	Page Load Time Check	Free	Basic	Chapter 5
OctaGate Site Timer	Page Load Time Check	Free	Basic	Chapter 5
Yahoo YSlow	Page Load Time Check	Free	Basic	Chapter 5
Adobe Tag Manager	Tag Management	Budget	Basic	Chapter 5
WinSoftMagic	Video Compression	Budget	Basic	Chapter 5
Akamai	Delivery Optimization	Expensive	Advanced	Chapter 5
Google Site Search	Internal Search	Free	Basic	Chapter 5
FusionBot	Internal Search	Budget	Intermediate	Chapter 5
Adobe Search & Promote	Internal Search	Expensive	Advanced	Chapter 5
SafeSite Certified	Trust & Security Seals	Budget	Basic	Chapter 6
Mongoose Metrics	Call Tracking Analytics	Mid-range	Advanced	Chapter 6
PowerReviews	Reviews & Ratings	Budget	Intermediate	Chapter 6
BazaarVoice	Reviews & Ratings	Budget	Intermediate	Chapter 6
Adobe Scene7	Image/Banner Optimization	Expensive	Advanced	Chapter 6
Oculu	Video Analytics	Mid-range	Intermediate	Chapter 6

Tool Name	Type of Tool	Cost of Tool	Level of Tool Functionality	Chapter Where Tool Is Described
SitePal	Visitor Greeter	Budget	Intermediate	Chapter 6
CodeBaby	Visitor Greeter	Budget	Intermediate	Chapter 6
Tweople	Visitor Greeter	Budget	Intermediate	Chapter 6
Fivesecondtest	First Impression Check	Budget	Basic	Chapter 7
Runa	Discount Optimization	Budget	Intermediate	Chapter 7
CustomCart	Highly Flexible Shopping Cart	Mid-range	Advanced	Chapter 7
Adobe Recommendations	Product Recommendations	Expensive	Advanced	Chapter 7
mobiReady	Mobile Site Analysis	Free	Basic	Chapter 7
MoFuse	Mobile Site Creation	Budget	Intermediate	Chapter 7
Mobify	Mobile Site Creation	Budget	Intermediate	Chapter 7
AdRetargeting	Ad Retargeting	Mid-range	Advanced	Chapter 7
AdRoll	Ad Retargeting	Mid-range	Advanced	Chapter 7
MailChimp	Email Marketing Testing	Mid-range	Intermediate	Chapter 8
AWeber	Email Follow-Up	Budget	Intermediate	Chapter 8
Constant Contact	Email Follow-Up	Budget	Intermediate	Chapter 8
SeeWhy	Email Remarketing and Checkout Recovery	Mid-range	Advanced	Chapter 8
RedEye	Email Remarketing and Checkout Recovery	Mid-range	Advanced	Chapter 8

B Test Idea Tracker

Page/Element to Test	Test Hypothesis and Insight	Difficulty of Testing (1–10, with 1 as the lowest)	Likely Test Lift Value (1–10, with 1 as the lowest)

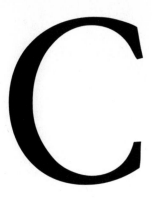

C Test Results Tracker

Test Date	Page/ Element Tested	Test Details	Success Metric Used and % Change	Lessons Learned

Index

Note to the Reader: Throughout this index **boldfaced** page numbers indicate primary discussions of a topic. *Italicized* page numbers indicate illustrations.

Numbers and Symbols

A

B

C

D

E

F

G

H

I

J

K

L

M

P

Q

R

S

T

U

V

W

Y

Z